M000169154

In Search of
Decency

Copyright © 2013 Michael Heyn

The moral right of the author has been asserted.

Apart from any fair dealing for the purposes of research or private study,
or criticism or review, as permitted under the Copyright, Designs and Patents
Act 1988, this publication may only be reproduced, stored or transmitted, in
any form or by any means, with the prior permission in writing of the
publishers, or in the case of reprographic reproduction in accordance with
the terms of licences issued by the Copyright Licensing Agency. Enquiries
concerning reproduction outside those terms should be sent to the publishers.

Matador
9 Priory Business Park
Kibworth Beauchamp
Leicestershire LE8 0RX, UK
Tel: (+44) 116 279 2299
Fax: (+44) 116 279 2277
Email: books@troubador.co.uk
Web: www.troubador.co.uk/matador

ISBN 978 1783060 610

British Library Cataloguing in Publication Data.
A catalogue record for this book is available from the British Library.

Typeset in 11pt Aldine401 BT Roman by Troubador Publishing Ltd, Leicester, UK

Matador is an imprint of Troubador Publishing Ltd

Dedication of My Book

To My Father and Mother Who Set For Me an Early Compass
Leo Luitpold Heyn
Mary Kay Roan

To My Loving Partner Equally Dedicated to Our Journey Together
Suvira Chaturvedi

To My Daughters Who Hold Within Them What I Value Most
Tanya, Natasha and Kavita

To the *Peace Corps* and the *United Nations*
For the Opportunities and Inspirations They Instilled In Me to Serve Their
Ideals

To the *Poor and the Rich* across the Globe
Who Have Shown Me What is Possible

Front Cover: the author and members of the Manzanares, Peru, Chicken Farm Cooperative (1964)

I acknowledge with deep appreciation all those who have in one way or another contributed to the review of this book

The views expressed in this memoir are entirely my own

Table of Contents

Prologue to the Journey

Lying flat on the ambassador's floor in Liberia, bullets shattered my understanding of life, compelling me to rethink the meaning of what I had seen over and over again, so many people suppressed across all cultures in which I had lived. People dominated by a few driven by greed and power, power enforced by those bullets now overhead that required answers from me, answers I did not have, bullets that demanded courage to search in the chaos for decency.

Learning from the poor by living among them, joining the front lines of the United Nations, witnessing through fifty years the worst and the best people can do to each other, I struggled to understand the roots and contradictions of so much inhumanity in the face of the promise of change I saw and questioned everywhere: why Peruvian villagers distrusted each other, yet Don Jose guided me to bring them together; why I despaired as a Nepali child died before we reached a remote clinic, yet people overthrew their kingdom; why a poor man of Malawi saw through the hypocrisy of my efforts to end his poverty, yet witnessed the end of tyranny I had done my best to facilitate however imperfectly; why the America in which I grew up and worked remained an unbending light of hope despite injustice toward its underclass and support of dictatorships; why indeed war in Liberia jolted my soul yet led to Africa's first woman president under whom I had worked. Experiences that steeled my resolve to find the answers.

This is the story of my journey through life. It is the story of my experiences and what I have learned living and working across many lands and among many people. It is a journey through fifteen countries including my American origins and my concern for its future. It is the story about understanding the seeming complexities and yet the ultimate simplicity of our common human relations within and across these cultures. A story of what we have in common in how we treat each other. It is a story about what divides us between rich and poor, powerful and powerless. It is a search for decency, where and how it exists, to know how it can bridge our divides. It is a call to recognize the unfailing spirit and capability of all human beings to overcome these divisions based on the good will of people to come together, to achieve the common good.

It is also a call for a bold way forward relevant as much to Yemen as to America. It is a way some may believe impossible, to address our human failings based as I have seen on a determination of people reaching across assumed insurmountable barriers to support each other. It is a message of confidence in results that can be achieved by purposefully crossing over our divides and empowering each other. It is a call for a partnership of rich and poor to do this, no matter how antithetical this may seem. It is a call for reform of democracy to share the power. It is a belief, that in the practice of these new relationships and the decency on which they are based we can transform our way of life.

Chapter 1
Liberia

A Look over the Edge
1990

Return to Liberia with military escort

Skeletal remains on the UN compound

Overcoming obstacles to reach Liberian refugees in Guinea

In Prince Johnson's Camp, President Doe's arch enemy

1

Under Fire

Bullets overhead pierced the air from all directions. The incessant clap of distant shots compelled our attention and gravely unsettled us. Our primal sense of danger rose deep from within.

We ran across the US Embassy grounds on Mamba Point in the capital Monrovia. We climbed the stairs to the ambassador's quarters. Some dozen embassy staff milled around in a controlled state of anxiety. Someone shouted us to the floor. We lay and eventually sat there for what seemed hours. It was not clear what else we should expect and the sounds of conflict grew louder. There was more going on than gun shot. As far as we could tell nothing had hit the embassy, but the explosion of mortars soon began to intensify. With each passing hour, the eerie tapping of machine guns closed in. It was 9 September 1990 and the fighting went on through the night. We returned to our sleeping quarters during an unexpected lull in combat. At dawn all was quiet.

I had not slept. But the sudden peace was a great relief. Later in the morning, as we gathered again in the ambassador's quarters, more distant sounds of fighting re-emerged. These continued throughout the day and into the second night. During the day, I managed to send cabled messages to the UN in New York. They were terse, vivid accounts of our predicament, to the effect that: *unexpected developments on the ground have resulted in renewed and chaotic fighting between the army and forces of both Charles Taylor and Prince Johnson. We are holed up in the US Embassy and uncertain of further developments.* Not surprisingly, I later learned these messages caused particular concern at UN headquarters for our safety. Liberia was unpredictable and very dangerous.

On the third morning we approached noon without a sound of hostility. Terry Lewis, our UN team field emergency operations officer, had accompanied me to Monrovia. I shared with him a hope that we had seen the worst. His response that 'there's always worse than the worst' broke my tentative ease. By late afternoon we heard the hum of a US naval helicopter. We understood they were coming to take out those on a priority list. It was not certain whether we were on that list. Hurrying to our rooms to collect our belongings, we made straight for the landing pad. Some fifty to sixty souls had already gathered there including a few embassy staff but mostly former government officials and other sundry Liberian influentials who had taken refuge in the embassy. Each desperately sought safety in neighboring Sierra Leone. They knew the helicopter could have them there in less than an hour and a half. Embassy staff in charge informed us that only twenty-five could embark on this first flight out. They began reading off the names. Elated and relieved that we were on the list, we felt a certain guilt in boarding and glancing at the grim faces of those left behind.

Helmets and ear mufflers muted the enormous engines as we ascended and hugged the coast northward. I settled on a wooden bench staring at those perched across the aisle. Several Liberians sat immobile and emaciated. I recognised one of them. At first glance I was not sure given his skeletal frame. I leaned over to Terry seeking a nod of some kind. He had already seen my quandary. Lifting my ear muffler, he shouted: 'one of the ministers!' As I later learned, the minister had barely survived the atrocities of the war. Hidden in his family compound, he survived while many others did not. He found his way to the US Embassy, was recognized and taken in. He was one of the few fortunate officials in the high government ranks to make it out of Liberia. Others remained trapped to suffer the worst that humans can do to one another.

At the time, I was a bit more than half way through my UN career. I had just realised my long-held ambition to be a UNDP Resident Representative and UN Resident Coordinator. The position carried development management and some diplomatic responsibilities, and in some countries was equivalent to an ambassador. But the work was mostly focused on "development". UNDP was (much to my liking) a decentralised organization. We had considerable scope to negotiate with governments and were responsible for a program of development and an annual allotment of funds.

I was appointed to the position with the endorsement of the then Administrator of UNDP, William Draper III, a US entrepreneur who made his original mark as a pioneering "venture capitalist" in the nascent Silicon Valley of the 1960s. I also owed considerable thanks for my promotion to other UNDP colleagues and friends, particularly to those in the Africa Bureau, all of whom apparently spoke well of me to William Draper. Yet it was the spontaneous rapport that I sensed I had established with William Draper that also seemed to make a difference. We were both Californians, and I had attended Stanford in Palo Alto, only minutes away from his business base in Atherton. In many ways, he reminded me of my father, a self-made business entrepreneur. Both were no-nonsense realists who believed that the risk taking environment and hard nose attention to bottom line results in the private sector were very relevant and greatly needed in addressing social and human development challenges.

I had not anticipated a posting to Liberia. It came as a result of an unexpected opening in the position. My nationality must have helped given the historical ties of Liberia to the US. I understood of course that West Africa was a world apart from the cultures and mores of East and Southern Africa which I knew much better. But even then I was not prepared for how different Liberia was from the rest of the continent.

Liberia had been colonised by freed slaves shipped back to Africa by the American Colonization Society (ACS) sometime in the early 1820s. The solution for ridding America of its most awkward historical inheritance (especially since its own constitution had not done so) was first proposed by none other than Thomas Jefferson. It was later institutionalized by white politicians and religions leaders who founded the ACS. They identified an area of West Africa that lay just below the left shoulder of the continent that juts furthest out into the Atlantic. It was an area originally populated by Africans from its eastern border (current day Cote d'Ivoire) and from the north (Mali and Guinea) during the twelfth to sixteenth centuries. Ironically, these and some existing indigenous tribes (particularly the *Kru*) began to supply slaves to Europeans who sailed down the western coast in search of them. Named the "Grain Coast" by the Portuguese traders, the area was unsettled by Europeans except for some few trading posts set up by the British in the seventeenth century. So outside colonization came only with the arrival of the American former slaves in the early 19th century.

Liberia's first black governor and subsequent president, Joseph Roberts, declared Liberia an independent republic in 1847. There was just one thing its new constitution left out (not surprising in light of the American model and prejudices on which it was based): it denied voting rights to a significant proportion of the population, namely the local people living there long before the "Americo-Liberians" showed up. The former American slaves were of mixed blood, lighter in colour, and bore airs of superiority given their exposure to Euro-American culture, English language and adherence to Protestant Christianity. A sort of instant suppression of the masses followed. It left a lot of unsavory cultural practices, animosities and eventual clashes in its wake. Efforts to "civilize" the local people were resisted by them in favour of retaining cultural traditions and religious beliefs. Their many uprisings against the new elite were all firmly and harshly crushed sometimes with American help. I had read up on some of this history in preparation for my initial "familiarization" visit in late 1989, but I was unsure how that past reality shaped present day Liberia. I was even less aware of how it would impact me.

Abduction

In taking this assignment to an unknown culture, and as I looked back on my decision to do so, I was struck by how self-centered and insensitive I was to my family in taking the job. It was not because of the difficulty of the posting or the living conditions which I believed we could all adjust to. My most reprehensible behavior was my failure to inform and consult my children about the move. I sprang the news on my three daughters quite late. It was in June 1989 at the graduation of my eldest daughter, Tanya, from UCLA. I was thinking more about surprising them with "my success" rather than how they would receive it. They were happy for me and tried to show it, but I sensed even then some doubts on their part of what I was doing.

My youngest, Kavita, was particularly more apprehensive than I recognized at the time. She was very happy in Kenya where we lived just before moving to Liberia. She attended the international school with many friends from many lands, but news of our impending move was particularly ill-timed for her. It came not long after a traumatic event in her life.

Only ten at the time, Kavita was abducted. She was returning home in the family car of her friend Bindya whose mother was driving and suddenly swerved off the road. Rather she was forced off. Three young Kenyans jumped out of a battered vehicle and pointed guns. The mother felt compelled to open the locked door. Kavita sat frozen in the back seat. One of the abductors entered and pressed a knife to her throat. They ordered the mother to drive out of town.

Bindya was Indian by origin and her mother spoke Swahili. As she drove, she talked to the abductors continuously. She begged them to take the car, her watch and jewelry, 'just let us out of the vehicle.' They refused. Before long they were well outside Nairobi. It was high on a plateau of farmland that rises and levels off before dropping into the Rift Valley. Then, without explanation, the abductors stopped the vehicle. In an isolated area they pushed the mother and two girls out. The three were instinctively relieved to assume it was the new car the abductors were after and not themselves.

Finding themselves in the midst of a small plantation, their apprehension that the abductors might return soon overcame their sense of relief. Rows of coffee bushes covered the hills. They ran in a frantic state up a side dirt road. They found quick shelter and hid in the bushes for more than an hour. Slowly they emerged like baby foxes from a den, the mother led them gradually and observantly down the road. On seeing a small farm house, they knocked. An old Kenyan woman opened the door and let them in. Bindya's mother shared with her in Swahili the traumatic experience they had just undergone. By good fortune, the farm house had a phone. Bindya's mother called her husband who rushed to the scene and brought them back to their Nairobi home. We first learned of what happened when they called us from there.

Controlling our worst fears, we rushed to pick Kavita up. She did not appear badly shaken. We were greatly relieved, but we knew it could not be that simple. Back in our home we gave her as much comfort and consoling as we knew how. Looking back, we wished we had spoken to her more often following the incident to let her bring out more of her suppressed feelings. Although our lives gradually returned to normal, as time passed Kavita began to show signs of a growing anxiety. She insisted to know exactly where we were going each time we left the house. She clearly needed greater certainty than before about the events of her daily life. She needed to know the details of any plans we might have for the future. Yet she remained a brave and confident kid. We continued our best to put it behind us. It was only as we arrived in Liberia some three months later that we saw more pronounced changes.

Invasion

I made an initial visit to Liberia without the family before we moved there. I was both shocked and fascinated. I had already lived under many difficult circumstances and was quite prepared for hardship. But there was something about the look of Monrovia. The capital was surreal. For me it was an imagined blend of an American Old South black neighborhood and a West African village. Unexpectedly shabby and run down, low lying neighborhoods skirted stagnant watery lagoons lapping up against dilapidated bungalows on the brink of collapse into the murky liquid. Other areas were more upscale, but never modern. In many ways, I liked the atmosphere. It was unpretentious and welcoming. The people open, talkative and friendly.

Before I arrived in Liberia, I had already made acquaintance with a government official named Amelia. She was a deputy minister of the ministry of finance and planning. We met in late 1989 attending a development meeting in Amsterdam. I liked her instantly. Very informal and possessing that odd but appealing American twang. When I met her again in Monrovia she introduced me to some of her colleagues. I had a feeling of being home. The halls and offices of government were modest and run down. But there was always an air of friendliness.

Then came my introduction to the Liberian handshake. Nowhere else in the world does a handshake come as close to an act of pure sensuality. It's not the shake, it's the slow aftermath. You both pull away ever so gradually across each other's palms and then snap the fingertips at the climax of the gesture. The rhythm is what counts. That took me some time. Perfecting it is like a period of initiation. You sense that everyone is watching and waiting to see if you can master it. I practiced it a lot on casual acquaintances whom I would meet in the markets. Only gradually did I dare to try it on my government counterparts. After a couple of months, I mastered it. I learned that once you got it right, you have that first sense of real acceptance. It bridged a lot of gaps.

A couple of months after my initial visit, my spouse Suvira and Kavita and I arrived together in January 1990. Filled with excitement as the UN vehicle picked us from the airport flying the flag, we began our new life. Wide-eyed as the white car streaked and bumped through the dark silent night, we arrived at "Hotel Africa" on the outskirts of Monrovia.

A massive, heavy-curtained suite with overstuffed furniture added to the drama. Waking in the morning, our daughter drew open the thick curtains as we looked out on a desolate beach. Fishermen prepared to launch scruffy, multi-colored fishing canoes out to sea. A rough sea and a strong sun. We requested transfer to the bungalow we had reserved on the hotel compound. Pleasant and furnished in simple toned-down colors, it was home until we could find more permanent housing.

I had a habit of listening to the BBC every morning. Almost by chance that morning a report came over the air of an armed group crossing the border into Liberia from neighboring Cote d'Ivoire. It was a rebel group, we later learned, bent on overthrowing the Liberian President, Sergeant Samuel Doe. Doe was indigenous. He had 10 years earlier (1980) overthrown the ruling Americo-Liberia elite. In the process, he murdered all the Americo-Liberian ministers. Tying them to poles on the beach, he had each of them shot—following which he personally disemboweled the then President William Tolbert. For the next decade, Sergeant Doe ruled as the proverbial dictator with an iron fist.

I learned that Doe and his new ruling elite were Krahns. It was a tribe deeply feared and despised by most other interior tribes, particularly the Gio and the Mano. Slowly I acquired some understanding of the complex ethnic roots of the conflict unfolding. To complicate it further, I learned that the oppressed tribes were inspired and organized to rebel against Doe not by one of their own leaders, but of all things by an Americo-Liberian named Charles Taylor. Taylor lived in America for many years (initially as a student at Bentley College in Massachusetts). He later worked in Doe's government. Subsequently charged with fraud and embezzlement of government monies, he returned to America, ended up jailed on extradition proceedings, escaped (with assistance of the CIA as later confirmed), and eventually returned again to West Africa.

The invasion was an immensely confusing drama. I actually took little notice at the time as I began my work routine. The first morning the driver came and drove me to the office. Located at the other end of town, I had to pass through Bushrod Island (not actually an island) and its long strip of open roadside markets. They were part of the famous chain of West Africa markets that ran from Mauritania, Senegal, Guinea, Sierra Leone, Ghana, Nigeria and Cameroon, with Liberia squeezed in the middle. By far the predominant vendors were women, always dressed in arrays of colors and wrappings that conveyed a festive mood. They sold everything imaginable.

I later learned of the "Mama Benz", ladies who transported their goods, including chickens and small pigs, on commercial flights up and down this West African Coast. They made a lucrative business. Some of them could indeed afford to buy a Mercedes Benz. While some Liberian women participated, they were fewer in number due to their poverty and a need to concentrate on their own local trade.

The UNDP office was a two-storied modern bloc building. My office was toward the back. Though a bit small, it had an ample window on one side looking toward the adjoining building through some palms. The dark wood furniture and dusty curtains that needed a good shake conveyed an air of soberness. The air conditioner was strong. I definitely needed that. The office staff, like most professional Liberians, was well dressed and exceedingly polite. In the short time we worked together, I acquired much respect and affection for them.

Determined to be an effective UNDP Resident Representative with fresh ideas and a commitment to visible results, I began moving about the government halls, meeting ministers and their staff. Liberia's major problem was its economy, devastated by many years of bad management, overspending and corruption. It was a prime candidate for "structural adjustment", the favorite panacea of the World Bank in those days. It was also complicated by an odd dual-currency system. You could use both Liberian and US dollars, traded officially at about 5 to 1, but on the black market the difference was triple or more. It was hard to figure out the real value of things. In this atmosphere, I proposed UNDP technical support for a structural adjustment loan. More importantly, I offered, sure of myself as I was, to negotiate World Bank willingness in the face of a very negative impression of Liberia's readiness for such a loan. Little did I realize then how unrealistic these proposals were.

In the meantime, further occasional news items on BBC alerted us of a steady movement of "rebels" advancing across Nimba County in the north toward the capital Monrovia on the western coast. They called themselves the National Patriotic Front of Liberia (NPFL). They reputedly had support from neighboring Cote d'Ivoire. But as unexpected as this trouble was, no one imagined then it could not be contained. President Doe immediately dispatched the AFL (Armed Forces of Liberia) to suppress the trouble. Their tactics were vicious. They shot rebels on the spot often following prolonged torture. They attacked unarmed civilians and burned their villages to the ground.

I continued my rounds of government meetings. My real aim was to get some focus, discussion and interest on 'decentralized participatory development' in the outlying counties. That was UN jargon for a simple idea of involving the village people in deciding their needs and in implementing small development activities with the help of local government—setting up a health clinic, or a small school or growing a cash crop. A bit to my surprise several ministers, especially the ministers of interior and agriculture, expressed genuine interest. They agreed that not enough had been done in the past to reach out and involve people in any meaningful way in development.

We took these discussions to the point of some early planning. I scheduled field trips to see realities in the rural areas. The initial visit was to the town of Buchanan in Grand Bassa County where I met with local civic officials. I had no time to get into the countryside. Shortly afterwards, however, I visited Harper in Maryland County down the western coast to the far south. My visit drew an enthusiastic response from the local authorities. We traveled extensively to the back villages. We got there by four-wheel vehicle over rutted dirt roads. It gave me the feeling of a far-removed land and people. There was not the desperation that I had so often seen in my earlier work in India or Ethiopia, but there was this sense of being totally cut off and in poverty. Everything was based on survival agriculture. There was little trade, yet people there had very clear ideas, they wanted to earn money, they wanted better education for their kids, they were ready to do whatever it took.

I came away encouraged. We decided to put together a program to support community peoples' efforts as defined by them. We needed a project to do this. Probably some kind of skill training leading to income earning, a loan program to finance small scale production, and some follow up technical support. It would take time to design it properly.

In the meantime, I grew more concerned about the mounting tensions in the country. I began to wonder (only to myself) whether my ambitions for Liberia were out of touch with reality. I also began to question whether this planning was fair in terms of the expectations it was raising among so many poor people.

On returning to Monrovia, we met much more dramatic news from the north. There had been further fighting between the rebels and the army. The rebels were taking the upper hand. My daughter began to overhear the evening news on local TV, and rumors began to spread in the school. She became increasingly anxious and despondent. It was not out of any specific fear. It was a general uncertainty of what was happening around her. She began to rebel in her behavior and threatened to leave home. She went so far, while I was in Maryland County, to pack a bag for her departure. Suvira became extremely upset, not certain what to make of the sudden change in disposition.

We arranged for Kavita to ride horses from a stable in the hotel compound. We even considered buying one for her. She enjoyed riding immensely. We thought her troubled feelings would dissipate. We also thought we should fly her cocker spaniel from Nairobi to join us. This was a great success. But we could see that she remained uneasy and unsettled. And of course, the news continued to worsen.

At work, I had to shift my focus. The situation got much more serious. I consulted UN colleagues in New York and Geneva. More and more people from the countryside began to flow into the city. We understood we had to organize for food and shelter to avoid chaos.

UN emergency offices in Geneva sent us an "old hand" named Bryan Larner (who became a dear friend) to assess the situation. The assignment of Terry Lewis followed. An experienced ex-British Army officer who specialized in emergency relief, he had worked in many emergency environments especially in countries of the former Soviet Union. He was both enthusiastic and calm. That impression was later confirmed when we were together pinned down in the US Embassy. He displayed full confidence in what he was doing. I benefited greatly from his continuous practical advice and know how in managing relief for displaced people. It was not an easy task. It required early contact and confidence building with the traumatized people. Following up with timely delivery of basic supplies and assistance to maintain their trust, Terry always carried out the job with detailed preparations, planning and good logistics.

Terry also recruited a small team of young UN volunteers. He found them among a wide array of internationals working in schools and churches in Liberia. Highly motivated, they worked as a close knit team and began immediately to organize relief to nearby locations on the outskirts of Monrovia.

Evacuation and Siege

I became increasingly concerned about the UN families still residing in Monrovia, not least my own. I recommended to UN headquarters that UN dependents be evacuated. We managed to get them all out, including Suvira and Kavita, on the last commercial flight to leave the country. I remained behind with the core dozen or so of "essential" UN international staff. I felt an enormous sense of responsibility. I also felt confident that I could do the job, whatever it took. I knew it would be much more difficult and wearing with Suvira no longer at my side.

In the meantime, rebels moved closer to the capital. About this time, the NPFL split. The splinter group (made up largely of men from the Gio tribe) named itself the Independent National Patriotic Front of Liberia (INPFL). They were led by the infamous Prince (Yeomi) Johnson who soon became Sergeant Doe's worst nightmare. Prince Johnson was from Nimba County and had joined Charles Taylor during the original insurgency across that county. Due to an internal power struggle with Taylor, he broke away in June 1990. Johnson managed to take control of much of the area around Monrovia, especially the northern part beyond the Free Port, before Charles Taylor's forces arrived. During this period, he swore to take Sergeant Doe dead or alive. That threat played heavily on Doe as he remained isolated for months in his presidential palace in the center of Monrovia.

With the increasing chaos, even more of the rural poor flooded into Monrovia. We began to prepare for the worst. We established what we hoped would be a safe haven and food distribution point in Monrovia's main football stadium.

Liberia was one of the earliest of a series of civil wars around the globe which the UN later confronted with increasing frequency over the 1990s. We had to find our way as we went forward. We soon sensed that the residents of Monrovia were beginning to panic. They felt neither a trust in their government and the Krahn ethnic group that dominated it, nor the rebel forces of Charles Taylor moving toward the capital. Our work was complicated by low stocks of food in the West African region and by an insecure port. Nevertheless, we managed to deliver a few hundred tons to a couple of towns north of Monrovia. We were completing our preparations for the main distributions in Monrovia. By this time, thousands of displaced streamed continuously into the city. We rushed through night and day to prepare rudimentary living arrangements for those rapidly filling the stadium.

Attack

During one of these busy days, half a dozen Liberian local leaders who had just fled the interior of the country came to see me in my office. They sought a safe place for their people and UN protection. I explained that we could not provide refuge. But I also let them know we were in the process of setting up food distribution in the stadium. This did not satisfy them. The next morning they returned, this time with dozens of followers. They refused to leave our compound, though I insisted they must. I informed New York, but the situation rapidly turned more serious as several hundred gathered and stayed on the compound over the next couple of days and nights.

I came to work early the third morning and immediately sensed a heightened problem as a small delegation waited my arrival outside the gates. I was shocked at their news. That army soldiers had invaded the compound. They shot and killed our guard. They took away into the night some forty to fifty men, women and children.

Doe's army became his personal tool to strike fear into the people. He used them indiscriminately to hunt down and imprison and sometimes kill his enemies. The army soldiers grew increasingly edgy and untrustworthy as the rebel forces drew closer. They roamed the neighborhoods of Monrovia in their jeeps, shooting their rifles, demanding valuables from the local population. They beat those who did not comply. Even before Suvira's evacuation, we would travel by UN vehicle at night to official government receptions. We felt very uneasy passing as we had to through increasing numbers of roadblocks. Drunken army guards blatantly harassed, delayed, and even verbally threatened us with future consequences in spite of our diplomatic flag.

Doe had far more severe ways of intimidating his enemies. Although I never saw what was rumored to be his prime means of eliminating them, other diplomats claimed to have seen the prized leopards he kept in the lower reaches of his presidential palace. He allegedly fed these beasts not infrequently with those enemies. Diplomatic lunches that Suvira and I attended at the presidential compound were always noted for furtive glances and knowing nods of the diplomats as we ascended the same stairway that also led to those lower quarters.

As the rebellion spread, Doe and his army henchmen grew increasingly paranoid. They suspected anyone coming in from the countryside as siding with the rebels. Their brutal attack of the innocents on our compound astonished and repulsed us. But in retrospect it was perhaps not entirely surprising given their state of mind.

Immediately upon learning about the attack, I alerted UN Headquarters. I then called the diplomatic community to our office to bear witness to what had happened. Reports soon came back that many of those who had been taken away the night before were killed on a nearby beach.

In calling New York, I spoke with the UN Assistant Secretary General for security coordination who at that time was Kofi Annan the future UN Secretary General. I explained the litany of what had transpired. Some hours later, we were informed that an evacuation of all UN personnel had been ordered. The *New York Times* reported the incident in its May 31, 1990 edition as follows:

Liberian Soldiers Reportedly Attack U.N. Center
By KENNETH B. NOBLE, Special to The *New York Times*
Published: Thursday, May 31, 1990

Liberian Government soldiers were reported today to have entered a United Nations compound here and abducted about 40 refugees who had taken shelter there in the face of a continuing advance by rebels toward this nervous capital.

Witnesses said that eight soldiers, some of them wearing masks, entered the compound of the United Nations Development Program early this morning and shot to death a civilian security guard. They then rounded up the refugees, stripped them of their clothes and took them away to a deserted site on the outskirts of the city.

According to several refugees who managed to escape from the abductors, the others were later shot and killed by the soldiers. This afternoon, four unidentified bodies were found near the place where the incident was said to have occurred.

In all, about 400 refugees had been sleeping at the United Nations compound, most of them people who came from Nimba County in the north where the rebels are said to have drawn the bulk of their support among members of the region's Gio and Mano tribes.

The encampment of refugees grew in the last two weeks. Last Friday, about 200 of the Gio and Mano tribes people came to the United States Embassy seeking safety and shelter. They were told by officials that there was liitle that could be done for them and they were directed to the United Nations and the International Red Cross.

Speaking of the attackers today, Michael Heyn, the United Nations representative in Monrovia, described the group that stormed the compound: "From the reports we have, they were army soldiers, dressed in army uniforms, driving army trucks," he said. "The guards tried to prevent them from coming in, they shot one and bayoneted another, and they began shooting indiscriminately. We were told they grabbed people with children in their arms and threw them on the trucks." More than 300 people remained at the compound after the assault.

Mr. Heyn added that he was "completely astounded and unbelieving" that such an incident could happen and said that it was a serious infringement of international law.

Because of the incident, the United Nations Secretary General announced in New York today that it had ordered the immediate evacuation of all personnel from Liberia. The move is expected to complicate relief efforts because the United Nations remains one of the main agencies providing food, and organizing medical help for the tens of thousands of displaced people who have fled northeastern Liberia since the fighting began five months ago.

Late this afternoon, President Samuel K. Doe went to the compound to talk to diplomats. As he entered the gates, he was confronted by an angry crowd.

"I want you to know that those people who would do this kind of thing, they are doing it on their own," the President said, "and I'm going to deal with them drastically."

The brief speech was met with scattered hissing, and some of the young men in the crowd taunted the soldiers who were with the President. "Don't believe him! Don't believe him!" one of the refugees shouted.

The warfare started when about 250 guerrillas invaded half a dozen hamlets in the northeast region. The Liberian Government sent troops and provincial policemen to oust them.

Since then the rebels, led by Charles Taylor, a former Cabinet member under Mr. Doe, have increased their force by several thousand and have pushed the army virtually out of of Nimba County, Liberia's primary agricultural, mining and logging region. The rebels now sey they have beseiged Buchanan, the port east of Monrovia.

Protest by U.N.

UNITED NATIONS, May 30 (Reuters) (Special to *The New York Times*) – The United Nations has protested to Liberia over the attack by masked troops early today in Monrovia. Eleven foreign staff members still in Monrovia are being evacuated to Dakar, Senegal, a spokesman said.

Left Behind

We were actually about fifteen internationals at that time, and going out by land convoy did not appear safe. With incredible efficiency and determination, our UN colleagues in New York arranged what again turned out to be the last flight out, this time on a chartered Russian aircraft. As reported, the day of our departure, President Doe came to our UN compound to disclaim any involvement in the attack. Those Liberians still remaining on the compound openly scorned his words. Doe had no choice but to return cowed and unvindicated to his palace.

The evacuation was controversial. Although no colleague ever confided in me on the matter, I heard an occasional remark that leaving Liberia was not a good precedent. I myself had some second thoughts about the decision after it was announced. It meant that we had to leave our national UN colleagues behind. They had already expressed to me their concern about not being eligible for evacuation. UN rules in fact established differences between the international and national staff on matters of evacuation. Nationals were entitled to be taken to safe havens within the country, but not to another country unless there were extreme threats to an individual person. Except possibly for one or two, the majority did not qualify under these criteria. As we began our evacuation of internationals, the national staff remained dignified, encouraging us to return soon and assuring that they would care for their own safety. But it was far from clear where that safety could be found. I did sense a definite uneasiness, possibly a hint of abandonment as we departed, though never a word was spoken.

Equally disconcerting, the UN would no longer be active in providing relief supplies (and moral encouragement) to the many thousands of internally displaced. They continued to congregate in chaotic ways within Monrovia as well as in a few towns northeast of the capital. Our departure undoubtedly struck fear in those who already received our assistance, though the numbers were relatively small.

In subsequent crises in other countries, the UN began to take a stronger stand in keeping UN personnel in the country even in the face of considerable danger. There was a continuing debate within the UN about what was the right course and balance in these cases where no option was available that would not risk harm. Liberia was at the beginning of a long line of such crises, and the decision was made on the experience up to that point. In fact, as with other emergency cases up to that time, UN security rules were very cautious and required withdrawal of all UN personnel under circumstances precisely of the kind we faced. I took little consolation later from the fact that criticism of the UN withdrawal was matched by an equally sharp criticism of the US Government's refusal to send in troops. Their reversal of that policy some thirteen years later (2003) when they landed nearly 400 marines on Liberian shores thereby preventing further bloodshed was a demonstration of their "learning curve" over that period.

I recalled the considerable gratitude expressed by the UN staff and volunteers whom we evacuated at the time, most all of whom felt they were under extreme danger. And in later years, I noted the growing controversy and the views of some within the UN about unnecessary risks that were taken in exposing UN personnel to insecure environments. Such was the case in Iraq and in the continuing and unabated violence in Somalia. Nevertheless, at the time and for some time after, I continued to have mixed feelings about the decision to evacuate. I have noted long since those days that UN emergency culture has evolved considerably. On the one hand it focused on ensuring increased security precautions and protection for its staff. On the other, keeping essential UN staff in place except under the most extreme and dangerous circumstances became more the norm.

I do vividly recall the interview I gave to the *BBC* at the time. *BBC* radio was and remains highly esteemed across the developing world, no more than in Africa where honest and truthful reporting by national media and governments is rare. I was amazed at the speed by which the *BBC* learned of what happened at our UN compound. Within a few hours of the event, my office phone rang and *BBC* London was on the line. They asked me to describe what had happened. It was precisely at the moment when I was most highly agitated about what I considered a flagrant atrocity. I was determined to share that story with the world. I described it in sharp detail and with obvious emotion. I tried to contain myself, but my animated and high pitched voice dominated subsequent *BBC* replays of the interview. My remarks as best I recall them were something along the following lines:

'There just occurred one of the most shocking and flagrant violations of human rights. I have been speaking to several hundred Liberians who are still gathered on our UN office compound completely traumatized by events of last night. Late into the night, two army vehicles pulled up and smashed open our gates. The armed men, dressed in army uniforms, wore masks to disguise their identity. They shot and killed our night watchman. They brutally forced about fifty people, including women and children, into their trucks and drove off into the night.

Some fifteen minutes ago I learned from those who went in search for these innocent victims that they were shot in cold blood on a nearby beach. This was not an isolated incident, though it is certainly the worst so far. The army troops have been threatening and harassing thousands of people flooding into Monrovia in desperate fear for their lives. Some thought they could get UN protection by staying on our property. They refused to leave. They told me they would not do so because they did not trust anyone in the government or the army as they were sure they would come after them. Unfortunately those who committed these terrible acts were uninhibited about doing so on UN soil. This is the current state of Liberia, a situation of complete chaos and lawlessness. The tragedy is that the Liberian people are now not only the victims but clearly the targets.'

My purpose in revealing these brutal facts in a completely undiplomatic manner was to make it clear who was most likely behind these heinous acts, namely Samuel Doe and his army henchmen. I wanted to give a clear sense of the likely premeditated nature of the events. My purpose was to expose Doe not only as a long-time dictator, but as a villain of the worst possible kind who was able and willing to kill his own people to maintain his power.

The *BBC* coverage was worldwide and many of my colleagues in Europe and New York later confirmed they had heard it in its entirety. The message was crystal clear and continued to be broadcast on *BBC Africa* for many days after.

New Responsibilities

Our evacuation plane landed in Dakar. Most UN staff disembarked and remained there for some months. Terry and I immediately departed for Rome. I spent a couple of days debriefing colleagues at the World Food Programme (WFP) Headquarters. They had skillfully managed to bring limited amounts of food into Monrovia. I wanted to let them know how exceedingly grateful we were. I then proceeded to Geneva and reported the situation to a UN meeting of the international donor community. Again, I described the events in great detail. There was all around disbelief and outrage. Some of the ambassadors and other representatives present expressed real indignation over the apparent inability or unwillingness of the Liberian leadership to protect its people in their very own capital. As for the UN's role, there was genuine gratitude and praise for the work the UN emergency office in Geneva was doing before the attack, and not least for the work of our team on the ground. I was naturally proud and felt that our actions had been understood and valued.

Then I was off to New York to attend a series of working sessions in the UN Secretariat where the Liberia situation was discussed in great detail to determine the best role and course of action for the UN in the aftermath of the evacuation. But no conclusions were reached.

At the same time I took the opportunity to consult with one of the most respected Liberians living in the United States. Ellen Johnson Sirleaf had long provided a strong voice for democratic reform and human rights in her country. She was then living in Washington. D.C. and active in lobbying the US Congress on behalf of Liberian causes. She brought me up to date on a range of political complexities in both Liberia and Washington. It was helpful to my further understanding of what had proven to be an as yet intractable and growing crisis. Just by chance, Ellen became my boss a year later when she assumed the post of Director of the UNDP Africa Regional Bureau in New York. I had by that time left Liberia, but I found her especially encouraging and supportive in my next assignment to Malawi. More importantly, of course, Ellen became the President of Liberia in 2005, the first woman African head of state.

In any event, and under the circumstances, we did not make much headway on what the UN should do next in Liberia. I was encouraged to take a break. I went back to Portland, Oregon where Suvira and Kavita had been welcomed into the home of her sister and husband, Drs. Mahendra and Sarojini Budden. Their steadfast kindness and generosity sustained us through this and future crises of our careers.

My visit was a much needed relief. Yet the tensions I felt and lived with over so many months never really abated. Conscious of the urgent unfinished business we had left behind with increasing numbers of Liberians continuing to seek refuge in neighboring countries, I decided to call Jim Bishop at the US State Department in Washington. Jim had been the US ambassador in Liberia and we developed a close working relationship before I evacuated and he was reassigned to Washington. We spoke of the current situation, and to my surprise he seemed very keen for an immediate return of the UN to the country. I did not respond in any specific way and we left the matter pending.

Not long after, I received a call from UN headquarters asking me to return to New York for further discussions regarding the role of the UN. I left the next day. A meeting had been set for an exchange on the issues with a delegation of the US State Department headed by an African-experienced diplomat, Princeton Lyman. It was well known, and depicted in the American press at the time, that the US was positioning some four naval warships of the US Sixth Fleet carrying some 2000 US Marines off the coast of Liberia. As mentioned, the US government was in a deep quandary whether or not it should land those Marines in an attempt to stabilize the country. Clearly the special historical ties of Liberia to the United States gave reason in the minds of some Americans for this sort of intervention. There were just as many, probably more, opposed to any such overt action as unjustified in the absence of clear current US interests. Much criticism ensued in the international press. They pointed to the fact that no other major power had any such special relations with Liberia. In their view, the US was unconscionably reluctant in the absence of any material interests such as oil. Those interests were much clearer in the case of Iraq, and were purported as the main underlying justification for the First Gulf War which ensued around the same period.

Again, no firm conclusions were reached in our dialogue. But it was clear to all that the most urgent matter was dealing with the flood of refugees streaming out of Liberia to neighboring countries. A UN decision was quickly reached to establish a new base of operations for our UN team to address this emergency. I soon found myself on a plane to Conakry, Guinea.

Conakry was a lovely city. Its charm in my mind radiated out of a few of my personal preferences. For one, the abundance of trees and tropical greenery covered it in swaths of cooling shade. But mostly the vestiges of its French past appealed to me. Not so much any presence of the French people (whom I have a special affinity for from my days as a student in Tours) since not many remained behind in this former colony. It was more the unique blend of the African and French ambience, including the exquisite cuisine that one found in the many small restaurants (*lapin au moutard avec pommes frit* was a favorite of mine, especially compared to the best of the chickens in white sauce I had grown accustomed to in Monrovia). I celebrated a memorable fiftieth birthday in one such restaurant surrounded by our team and other good friends from UN agencies.

Our task was clear. We needed to identify and assist the steady flow of Liberian refugees who continued to cross their own borders into Sierra Leon, Cote d'Ivoire and Guinea. Our modest team consisted of myself, now with a new proud title of UN Special Coordinator for Emergency Relief Operations in Liberia (reporting to the Office of the UN Secretary General rather than the UNDP), Terry, our field operations officer, and a half dozen UN Volunteers. We traveled constantly between the three countries to assess the refugee situation and determine and prepare for what could be done.

Refugees

Our visits to the interior of Guinea were particularly poignant. Tens of thousands of Liberians had come across from Liberia's Lofa county. It was the rainy season and the roads were nearly impassable. It took us a day and a half by road from Conakry to reach an interior rainforest area where many Liberians clung to life. Once in the area, we soon found we had to ford streams that had become roaring rivers. At the first of these, we emerged from our vehicles to have a closer look. Local villagers and young boys emerged out of nowhere and quickly surrounded us. They clearly sensed our predicament. With some broken French and English on both sides, we managed to communicate. We learned that unless we crossed at this point, we would have to detour back another half day to cross at another location hopefully less flooded. We could not afford to lose that time. So, literally, we plunged ahead.

Not completely certain how deep the river was, we used lots of hand gestures with the locals to figure out we could get through if we kept our windows rolled up. I wasn't completely convinced this would work. No one said anything about the motor which surely would be submerged. But as a matter of blind faith in the local wisdom, we decided to try.

The village men and youngsters jumped into the river ahead of us. They formed a sort of corridor through which we were meant to pass. I had a feeling this was not the first time they had done this. Those who ventured out into mid stream were barely able to hold their heads above the rushing waters. Meantime, we piled back into our two vehicles, and started up the motors. We moved slowly forward, down the embankment and into the brown 'murky' swirling water. Our drivers knew that once in the water they could not hesitate or stop for anything. I became concerned for some of the youngsters who in their enthusiasm were swimming in the middle of our path. Down and down we went into the turbulence, biting the solid rocks on the river bed to keep us going. At the midpoint, the lead car in which I was riding suddenly stopped. Stuck in a soft muddy spot, the wheels began to spin, churning up water like a small washing machine. The vehicle began to float a foot or two downstream. I looked back at my teammates in disbelief. None of us said a word.

Within a flash, we were surrounded by all the villagers who had entered the water. By this time I also noticed that the water was rising nearly half way up our side windows. I also assumed our motor must have been fully submerged. The taller men gained some leverage on the river bottom and began pushing us forward. The young boys could not touch the bottom. They swam alongside shouting and waving encouragement in a manner that easily crossed language barriers. Our 4-wheel drive began to get some traction. The underwater manpower gave us the momentum we needed. The vehicle lurched forward with new vigor. We soon crawled up the opposite embankment.

The second vehicle waited behind. The villagers signaled that it should move further upstream. It also then plunged bravely into the watery torrent. This time the villagers found the right spot for a smooth crossing. The vehicle traversed in short order. I was amazed. Here we were in the middle of Guinea. No one knew us. There were no modern facilities (except our own vehicles) in sight. People reacted without a thought for their own safety. They clearly had considerable concern for ours. I could never forget their generosity and their humanity in extending us their help without condition. The free spirited and joyful manner in which they demonstrated a genuine brotherhood for us in our time of need, was simply astonishing. Faced with such a stark and inexplicable contrast to the gratuitous cruelty I witnessed in Liberia, I felt profoundly impressed. From my gut, I concluded rather grandly but with conviction at that moment that such simple unconditional kindness and caring was the only basis on which we might ever hope to overcome our human adversities. I still believe that.

We soon saw that most refugees congregated in the main interior regional towns. We met with the local Guinean leaders there. They had been extraordinarily kind and generous to the Liberians. Again, I took particular note. We tried to give whatever moral support possible. Bringing in food over the existing road conditions was impossible in that season. We promised to return as soon as the roads dried, to distribute food and medicines and plastic tarps for their shelter. It was not a very satisfactory response. But at least we understood the extent of the needs we would later have to meet.

Other reconnaissance trips also took us by road from Conakry south to Freetown, the capital of Sierra Leone. It was always an adventure. Some of the high level Liberian Government officials had taken refuge there, along with many other refugees. Talking with these government bureaucrats was a sad affair. Most had fled Liberia in great haste, leaving spouses and children behind. Preoccupied to find a safe way back to their families, they constantly pressed us to take them to Monrovia with UN protection.

One of the saddest moments for me was when I met up again with Amelia from the ministry of finance and planning. She managed to escape Liberia, but she had to leave her husband and children behind. Emotionally drained not knowing where they were or their fate, she pleaded for my help, counting on our friendship to break through the expected UN rules and regulations. But it was impossible for me to act. She and other government officials like her continued to linger and wait.

Sierra Leone was an extremely poor country. In some respects it was worse off than Liberia. Nevertheless, it exuded a certain nonchalance in the streets about events in neighboring Liberia. We enjoyed the relaxed air of the place.

We always ate excellent Lebanese cuisine. We also drove deep into the interior of the country to make contact with the Liberian refugees. Except for the diamonds that were occasionally mined (to a far lesser extent than that which later financed Sierra Leone's own civil war that followed), we saw nothing but stark poverty. The same raw poverty we knew from Liberia but even harsher in the eastern regions of Sierra Leone. The area was bone dry. The local people had little to nothing to eat for many months of the year.

Sierra Leone was in fact a carbon copy of Liberia, defined mainly by enormous disparities between rich and poor. We thought at the time that such flagrant inequalities would become the same match that had ignited the conflagration in Liberia. That it would soon set fire to Sierra Leon. We were not wrong.

Returning to Conakry from Freetown was something I learned to dread. The trip in both directions was over washboard roads truly unique in the size of their ruts and the fierce degree of vibration they created in any vehicle and human body that traversed them. My body seemed to be particularly vulnerable. By the time I completed each return trip—to this day I do not know how to explain it—I had huge blisters full of water under each eye. It took several days for these to drain. The lines carved on my face remain there today. They are a constant reminder of those unforgettable days.

Sudden Return

We continued our rounds between the three countries for another month. On one of those trips to northern Cote d'Ivoire along the border with Liberia, I first learned of what was to become my imminent return to Liberia. Cote d'Ivoire was basically untouched by this human drama. A good infrastructure of roads and communications were in place along the main routes. While inspecting some refugee camps, I decided that same evening to make a call to UN headquarters to report my initial findings. I barely started my reporting when I learned that the US government, in particular the US embassy in Monrovia, had reported a significant break in the fighting around Monrovia and signs of a return to peace. The message was clear. I should return to Liberia immediately. This took me by surprise. Monrovia was still very unstable and dangerous in many respects. Yet I understood the case for a renewed UN presence. Restarting emergency assistance to desperate Liberians who continued to suffer far outweighed any possible risks. I prepared to return immediately.

My return was unforgettable. I had been advised to get there without delay and by whatever means. I drove all night from northern Cote d'Ivoire back to the capital, Abidjan. I arrived in the UN office very early that morning to seek assistance with a flight to Freetown. I learned it was a public holiday in Cote d'Ivoire. Nothing would be open. There were no commercial flights to Freetown. On further inquiry, I learned that I could charter a flight. But I had to charter the entire 737 for myself, including a full complement of hostesses and crew. I figured I had no choice, the arrangements were made. Flying solo in such a plane was strange in the extreme. Not sure exactly how to attend to just one passenger, the five stewardesses just did what they normally did. I benefited from unlimited offers of champagne and food though I was in the mood for none. The gracious crew and I ended up chatting about how we all hoped the problems of Liberia would not spread. Everyone stood on the stairway platform to bid me farewell. I felt special in a very odd way.

The real drama began as soon as I descended the stairs and touched the tarmac in Freetown. The US government was arranging my transport to Liberia. I was not prepared for what that meant and what followed next. Four US Marines in flight outfits and helmets approached rapidly by jeep across the tarmac. They soon surrounded me in great haste. Fitting myself into a helmet and flak jacket, I felt this must be fiction. They scurried, nearly lifted me, across to the nearest hangar. Within less than a minute, a giant helicopter whirled toward us. Before I knew it, I was on board and well out to sea. Some minutes (and 20 nautical miles) later I saw through the portals what appeared to be a US naval ship. We landed. The American crew seemed to have no clue who I was or what I was doing there. A simple 'how's it go'in?' greeted me most of the way to the lower deck.

I soon felt at home and I dined in the officer's mess onboard. We discussed a gamut of American insignificancies from baseball standings, to our home towns. It put me at ease. I bunked down that night with the regular crew. Everyone was friendly and reassuring. I was certain they had no idea of this nor how much I appreciated it.

In the early morning after some navy eggs, I stood on the upper deck. I had grown up in a navy town, and had been on board navy ships far larger than this ship. At that time I had even been shown around a full-scale aircraft carrier by my friend's dad who happened to be the commanding admiral. But nothing prepared me for this ride. The seas were in a robust mood. Everyone took it quite in stride. But I was internally exhilarated. Was I really doing all of this, on a US navy ship somewhere in the Atlantic, rolling over each wave not knowing what to expect next? The sun was brilliant, the temperature warm and only a group of seagulls broke the rugged silence of that turbulent sea. About noon, I received the news I should prepare to return to the helicopter for another forty minute flight, this time to Monrovia.

The helicopter floated low and smoothly over the open sea toward the capital. On the horizon I could see the coast of Liberia. It appeared to be that same tropical haven where only a few weeks earlier I accompanied my daughter to one of the safe beaches for riding her "boogey board" in the surf. As we swirled down for a final landing on the US Embassy compound, I saw the US ambassador waiting for us to alight. Peter de Vos and I had never met previously as he assumed his ambassadorship while I was back in the US. He greeted me warmly. I had an immediate sense he was genuine and wanted to be a close colleague and friend in a time of considerable challenge and stress for both of us.

Peter immediately informed me that while the situation had improved, there had been some shelling of the port the day before. I recalled instantly that it was at that port that my meeting was to take place the next morning with General Arnold Quianoo, the head of the West African ECOMOG (Economic Community Monitoring Group) joint military intervention force in Liberia. The force had been set up by ECOWAS (the Economic Community of West African States) in August 1990, consisting of 4,000 mostly Nigerian troops.

The ambassador assured me that he expected this "temporary flare-up" to subside shortly. I would certainly be able to keep my appointment the next day. I wasn't about to question his advice and wisdom, whatever my internal trepidations.

He and I spent a couple of hours chatting about what had happened since my evacuation. I found it very informative and helpful. At one point he offered an opinion I had not anticipated. He told me he would have done exactly as I had done in evacuating the UN when I did. He thought that at that time security had become extremely precarious and that the UN had no security apparatus as did the US Embassy to ensure basic protection. I was certainly not expecting such a justification for these UN decisions. I was not sure how to interpret them. In the end, I felt he was thinking I had some guilt about whatever had been my role in all of this and wanted to express his understanding and support. I surmised his purpose was to make our work ahead that much closer and hopefully effective. I appreciated the intent of his words.

Accommodated in one of the embassy compound bungalows overlooking the harbor, I began to unpack my bag. At the same time I took a look outside the window that faced a small beach lower down a steep cliff, held up by a small forest of gnarled trees. I noticed some movement in the trees. I soon realized it was a Liberian woman scavenging for anything she could find to eat. As she drew closer, I saw her tattered soiled blouse and sarong. She stooped incessantly to pick up small objects. Upon closer inspection, I realized these were small seed pods fallen from the trees. She also pulled up occasional weed-like vegetation. She stuffed these items into the front fold of her sarong. I immediately concluded these were final desperate acts to feed her children. Clearly Liberia had become a land of desperation in the very short time since I had left.

Facing Fear

I rested that afternoon. As I did so from a well positioned sofa looking out through the large bay window of the bungalow directly at the far distant port, I began to notice small military boats heading out to sea. I got up for a closer look. Soon water exploded near each vessel. I suddenly realized they were under attack. From what little I knew, I assumed it was probably Prince Johnson forces shelling and hoping to sink government military boats.

Up to then, I had always thought I was someone who did not frighten easily. I prided myself in always managing to convey calm under stress (I had long ago liked to think I had adopted Hemingway's ultimate mantra of "grace under pressure" as my own). But as I sat there alone, I sensed the real possibility of my own mortality. Rational or not, I felt the deepest fear. The situation was clearly serious. There was a war going on down there, no matter how limited or brief. Yet I knew that if I were to question plans at this stage, I would be putting the reputation of the UN (not to mention my own) at grave risk. I did not sleep a minute that night.

The next morning I walked slowly to the ambassador's office. It was with a sense of fatality I did everything to conceal. I asked to see him. After a bit of chatting to convey my calm, I posed the question and received the immediate answer. Sure, the meeting at the port scheduled for eleven am was still on. There was nothing to worry about. As expected, all fighting had ceased overnight. There was no expectation further hostilities would ensue now that the government vessels had fled.

I sat in stony silence and took it all in. I began to brace myself for what appeared to be my inevitable trip to the port. I hung around the office area waiting for the ride down. Around ten am there was a sudden rush and scurry at the embassy gate. A small contingent of embassy staff had been out of the compound on an errand earlier that morning and had returned. They rushed up to the ambassador's office. I was still sitting there. The news was shocking. After holing up for months in his "palace" compound out of fear of the rebels, Samuel Doe had decided to make a visit to the ECOMOG commander at the port. Not only that. He was doing so standing up in the back of his open limousine waving to people in the street who could not believe their eyes. Nothing else was known for the moment. Probably my meeting with the ECOMOG commander should be postponed in light of this unexpected development. That sounded good to me. So we waited.

Pound of Flesh

Samuel Doe had many enemies. None was fiercer than Prince Johnson. His reputation for atrocity in his own camp north of Monrovia was renowned. He hated Doe. He was obsessed to capture him. So when he received word of Doe's movement, he moved as quickly and powerfully as a bolt of lightning. He mustered 200 of his armed men and headed for the port. Doe had taken precautions of his own, though his guard numbered only about sixty, they were well armed. But when Doe arrived at the ECOMOG compound his guards agreed to relinquish their arms before entering. Doe proceeded to the second floor office of the ECOMOG commander for discussions. Soon afterward, Johnson and his men arrived. Johnson refused to have his guards disarmed.

There followed an acrimonious exchange and standoff in the car park in front of the offices. Doe and the ECOMOG commander must have witnessed all of this from their vantage point. Suddenly someone on Johnson's side opened fire and all hell broke loose. Most of Doe's guards were killed on the spot. In a matter of seconds, Prince Johnson ran up the stairs to the commander's office. He grabbed Doe and shot him in the legs to prevent any chance of escape. He tied him up and drove him to his camp. There Doe pleaded for his life. His cries and emotional outburst were in sharp contrast to what I had previously seen as a smug (though bland) personality. He was not a very tall man, maybe 5' 6", and as he knelt before Johnson with his shirt torn off he pleaded for mercy. He seemed miniscule. Certainly not the profile of a dictator.

Laid out on the floor, the process of Doe's amputation began. First his ears were cut off, then his fingers. His eye was gouged out. Ultimately, he was castrated. While this was going on, Johnson sat calmly at his desk drinking a Budweiser beer. He kept pressuring Doe for his bank account number. Doe bled profusely and lost consciousness and death quickly followed. The excruciating details of that ordeal were captured on video. It was shown all over Africa for many months thereafter (some segments were even replayed on *BBC*).

What followed I have already described at the beginning of this chapter— an explosive outbreak of fighting all over Monrovia, followed by our eventual evacuation to Freetown. A couple of days later, I was safely back in Conakry.

Return to Chaos

I spent the next few weeks preparing for a donor fund-raising in aid of the plight of the refugees. We were organizing to hold this in The Gambia. As it happened, The Gambia was also the venue of peace talks arranged by West African governments. The talks had taken a positive turn. We were encouraged.

I began to wrestle with a difficult decision. Was it time to return to Liberia? Answering that became one of the most excruciating decisions of my life. I knew there was urgent need for emergency relief. I also knew that Liberian peace could never be trusted. The danger was as grave as was the urgent need for our help. The US government reacted to the growing danger by finally sending a small naval force and helicopters to evacuate foreign nationals and diplomats. I was concerned for the safety of our team should we now return, even though most of them were anxious to get back into action. I also knew that important work needed to be done outside of Liberia to help one third of the population who were now refugees. Not least I kept thinking of my own mortality and especially what my death would mean to my family. It was selfish but very real. I spent several nights in my small Conakry apartment agonizing over this decision, alternately falling into despondency and trying to pull myself back up.

In the end, I again thought about the reputation of the UN but mostly concluded that a return was the right thing to do for the people of Liberia. It was just a few weeks since our last frantic departure. We estimated nearly half a million Liberians had been displaced within Liberia, and possibly 150,000 had been killed (the UN announced these figures which some later criticized as an overestimation—though it was almost impossible to know the true situation). Faced with these staggering realities, I dispatched a cable to New York proposing our immediate return to Monrovia. It was approved.

The situation and role of the UN in Liberia had to entirely transform. Our small imagined world of development activity had vanished. The primary interest and role of the UN now by necessity of events had to shift to one of helping people in dire need. The UN had to focus on building an environment in which peace and stability could take hold.

As a first step, Terry and I decided to make a reconnaissance visit back to Monrovia to assess conditions on the ground before bringing in our full team. The US embassy offered to facilitate our work. Again they provided accommodation, this time in housing of former US staff now evacuated. Our enjoyment of these quality arrangements never materialized as the still non-functioning electricity left us in oven-baked bedrooms for several sleepless nights.

Besides our quick work to gain a rough idea of food, medical and housing needs, we took some time to revisit neighborhoods and areas of the city familiar to us. I also took the opportunity to visit the newly constructed house fronting the beach that I was planning our family to move into just before the war broke out. We approached the house, near the UNDP office just off the main road. Startled and grateful for the untouched like-new condition in which it stood before us, I hopped out of our Land Cruiser with a sense of good fortune. I stepped up to the front door and opened it. What was not apparent from the outside was brutally evident within. While the outer walls of the structure remained firm and standing, the entire roof had been blown away by what must have been a direct mortar hit. The inner walls were shattered. The cement debris lay in all directions. My sizeable rental advance to the landlord to help him finish off the construction of our new home was obviously a huge mistake (nevertheless I learned my case set a new precedent within the UN—I eventually became the first ever to be reimbursed for financial loss resulting from war).

Later we wandered along the beach in front of the house. There were a number of young boys sitting on rocks staring aimlessly out to sea. Their plight was hard to define. We felt their hopelessness with real sorrow for what they had lost. Theirs was a dark future.

As we returned along the beach to our cars, I commented on the occasionally soft and squishy sand beneath our feet. I wondered why. As we neared the end of this section of beach we saw the reason. First was the protruding hand. Not far beyond, a black face and open eyes glared out from beneath the white expanse. We learned on our return to the embassy that scores of people had been executed and barely buried under those sands.

Around the time of our return, a new Interim Government of National Unity (IGNU) had been set up by consensus of West African governments. When we expressed an interest to visit our UNDP office and compound in the Monrovia's southern suburb of Sinkor, these interim Government authorities advised we should not do this on our own. The area was still not safe from wandering combatants. The government sent us armed military personnel carriers which drove us to our compound.

Again it was a shocking revelation. Skeletons lay strewn and discarded around our compound, possibly including those who had sought further refuge there on our departure. Bearing a disturbing witness to these remains, Terry and I paused to contemplate in silence what might have occurred in our absence. The office had been totally gutted. Our torn files covered the floors. Broken walls and windows, smashed furniture and equipment, everything in ruins. Before seeing all of this we thought we could re-establish our office operations. It was clear we could not.

Nevertheless, Terry's and my assessment mission concluded that in spite of serious continuing security concerns, the overall situation should not prevent the restart of emergency operations. Clearly there was urgent need for UN assistance. I recommended the earliest possible return of our full team. We headed back to Conakry to prepare for this.

We prepared in stages. Our team moved from Conakry to Sierra Leone where we set up a support camp on a beach area just south of Freetown. We knew that communications with the outside world would be better managed by a small team operating from there than in Monrovia. It was a rather idyllic spot, with the Pacific Ocean running stark deep blue just off shore. The waves rolled gently with enormous girth for at least a mile before crashing on the shore in front of our camp. The few days we were there, we found every possible excuse to swim out half a mile and float on those giant rolls. Exhilarated by their powerful gentle movement, we ignored any thoughts of what might lurk below.

Terry spent every evening briefing our team of volunteers on the planned relief operations. There was a lot of excitement. We were finally "going in." Again, we traveled via US Navy helicopters, this time hugging the coast south straight to Monrovia rather than out to sea.

Immediately on our return, we decided to further investigate the conditions we had left behind. For me, this meant a trip out to the Hotel Africa where Suvira and I had left all our personal belongings. My immediate concern was for Kidogo, the cocker spaniel we had flown over from Nairobi. I had entrusted the dog with a French couple living in another bungalow at the hotel. They were determined not to evacuate even during the fighting that ensued after Samuel Doe's killing. They eventually and reluctantly did evacuate. Kidogo was left on his own.

When I arrived at the hotel compound, everything was deserted except for a half dozen hotel guards paid to keep an eye on hotel property. Seeing our bungalow completely ransacked did not surprise me but I felt shocked nevertheless. We were naively sure at the time of Suvira's evacuation that we would eventually return and find our possessions intact. Suvira had left most of her clothing behind, especially her lovely silk saris and Indian jewelry. But except for a few stray items I gathered up, everything else had been looted. I asked the guards about Kavita's dog. They began to shake their heads. 'Very brave dog' they each repeated. As it turned out, Kidogo (meaning "little one" in Swahili) managed to survive some six weeks. The guards would watch him scavenge the little garbage that the hotel disposed. He undoubtedly joined the larger dogs to hunt for any edibles, including presumably monkeys, lizards, and whatever else frequented the property. I was devastated to learn that Kidogo had died only three days earlier. My grief was equally for Kavita who loved that spirited puppy. I never told her the real story of his struggle and lonely demise.

I asked about my vehicle. It was not standing under the canopy of the bungalow where I had left it. The guards took me to the back of the main hotel near the kitchen area. There it was. Though very pressed to understand why it was not taken by Prince Johnson or any other bandits roaming the area, I felt fate had obviously worked in my favor. It took us a while to recharge the battery, but once done, it started up immediately. I was much relieved.

I began to drive the car out of the hotel gates and down the road toward Bushrod Island and Monrovia. Before I had gone a quarter of a mile, I saw someone walking toward me in the distance along the road. He was Liberian. There was something about him that made me believe I knew him. As I drove

31

closer, I pressured myself to recall who he was. As I came within fifty feet I began to slow down to say hello. It was only then that I realized my folly and possible danger—the young man was wearing my favorite Hawaiian shirt (parrots and all!). In an instant I recognized he was most likely one of the looters of our bungalow. Any effort to convince him to return my garment was unlikely to receive a warm welcome. A semi-automatic weapon slung over his shoulder reinforced that conclusion. The rapid acceleration of my Corolla must have caught him by surprise. He stopped abruptly and stared in my direction. I did not give the slightest hint of my prior intentions to converse. I fixed my eyes dead ahead and sped down the open road.

We spent our first days setting up our operations in Monrovia. This included installation of our portable satellite dish for telephone communication back to camp in Freetown. The British embassy offered us their compound for an office and residence since most of their staff had evacuated. We moved in immediately. We also reconnoitered the emergency needs of the thousands of internally displaced people living on Bushrod Island. We calculated the needs for emergency supplies in order to launch a worldwide UN appeal for financial support.

Our return was welcomed by all, none more than the new "Interim President" of Liberia, Dr. Amos Sawyer. He was an academic by background and a man of obvious fairness and goodwill in my mind. One day soon after our return, one of our UN volunteers came running into our compound to inform me there was a military vehicle outside our gates. An officer wanted to see me. I gave a double glance to my other colleagues. I headed for the gate. Opening it, I learned to my amazement that the military vehicle was a tank. The officer approached and explained that the Interim President had sent him to ask me to meet with him straight away. By this time, fighting had started up again in Monrovia. It was mostly street and sniper fighting. The downtown area was not safe—we were in a more secure location just over the hill from the city center not far from the US Embassy. None of the embassies' staff were roaming the downtown streets unless there were clear and urgent needs to do so. I shared these thoughts with the officer who assured me that my personal safety would be guaranteed (hence the tank!). In fact, behind the tank was a large black Mercedes limousine. I was informed it had been Samuel Doe's, and that it was heavily armored. I was invited to sit in the limousine. The chauffeur would take me to the President's residence in an old hotel downtown. I gave another much longer glance to my colleagues. I entered the limousine.

You may think you could imagine that ten minute trip I took to meet with the President. You never will. It was entirely unworldly. Just sitting there in that big black vehicle behind the tank was incredible enough. What I witnessed as we came over the hill was unbelievable. In each street and lane we passed there were small bands of young men. They crouched and stood in every imaginable position. Almost all of them had painted their faces with white powder. They were naked from the waist up, or even the waist down except for some scant underwear. They wore what seemed an unlimited range of headgear, always fanciful and colorful. And they wore bras. Not everyone, but quite a lot of them. They wore other female attire of various kinds. They wore sashes around their waists. I could not figure out what it all meant though I had heard of these warring rituals. I later had confirmation that the most prized trinkets were the rotting remains of body parts of their slain enemies. Many apparently thought that such attire would ward off bodily harm; that bullets could not penetrate them. The eeriest feeling I had as I rode along in silent observation was when some of them stopped to look at me. They paused just for a moment, looking over their shoulder to see what or who it was. I had no idea what they thought. I later surmised they were somewhat familiar with the movements back and forth of the black limousine. They just as quickly got back to their fighting.

I rushed rather quickly up the stairs of the hotel led by a couple of presidential aides. On the top floor, I walked down what seemed to be an interminably long, dark corridor. As I entered the room the blinding light of the outside dazed me. The sound of gun and mortar fire was overwhelming. It was a micro world of war in full explosion. It was as though I was perched there to make a documentary of conflict. It took a few seconds before realizing the President had already extended his hand. I reached for it with considerable embarrassment.

He had entered the country only a few days before. We sat and I sensed he was nervous. I felt it was not so much about the sounds of war. He seemed very preoccupied. I later realized it was about what he wanted to share with me. His main message was about the critical importance of the UN presence and role. He was deeply concerned there should be no further evacuation in spite of the fighting. He assured me all would be done to protect UN personnel. I told him that we had no intention of leaving. I explained we were then preparing for distribution of food on Bushrod Island. I could see both his determination and sense of doubt. As the conversation went into a second hour, I began to share with him the importance of his presence among the Liberian people. I shared my conviction that only he could give them renewed encouragement and hope for the immediate future. I suggested that he may wish to join me the next morning on our daily visit to the Island area. Somewhat to my surprise he agreed enthusiastically.

The next day we drove together in his car. Word spread ahead that he was coming. People filled the street as we advanced. I suggested we get out and walk the rest of the way on foot. He did so and I followed behind. The reaction was electrifying and people were jubilant. At last, someone they could trust. Someone who would look after them. Accompanying us that day was a high-level official of UNDP in New York whom I knew, Ahmad Tajan Kabbah. He had come to assess our security situation. He was very taken by this gesture of coming together with the people. Little could he know then or even imagine that he would one day face similar circumstances as the newly-elected President of Sierra Leone.

Many weeks were spent going about Bushrod Island to update ourselves on the peoples' predicaments and needs, and to bring in supplies. The images of these weeks were indelibly printed on my mind. I recalled one day when a dilapidated medical aid ship arrived unexpectedly in Monrovia's port from Accra, Ghana. We went on board. It was already filled to capacity with desperately poor people from Bushrod Island seeking medical care. All were in a terrible condition. A small boy, maybe five or six, stood in an open area of the ship among other orphans. His body was so emaciated his posterior could no longer be distinguished except for his open anus that appeared now to be at the lower end of his back. Other Liberians of all ages lay about the rusted decks under silver-foiled "blankets", all with deep dark sunken eyes empty of hope.

On another occasion, we paid a visit to Prince Johnson's camp, the first since our return to Monrovia. I never ceased to be amazed at the organized display of pillage within the camp. All the vehicles, refrigerators, air conditioners, motorbikes, furniture and whatever else that had been looted from homes and offices in Monrovia were set out in neat rows grouped by their respective categories. It looked like a giant open warehouse where goods were about to be auctioned. Most of those items were meant for resale, but without a market most rotted away.

On one such visit, to my utter surprise, one of my former UN staff stepped out of the crowd of camp followers. These were people who for an unlimited number of reasons became caught up in the terrified environment, most joining the camp as a way of survival. When my female colleague stepped hesitatingly forward to greet me, I had no idea who she was. She whispered her name in a voice full of both fear and joy at seeing me. I simply could not believe it was her. She was a secretary in our office, always well dressed and mannered, quiet but confident. She now wore tattered clothing. She had lost a lot of weight. I asked her how she had come here, but she avoided the question. I also inquired if she planned to return to her home. She replied that she was safer where she was. She faded back into the crowd. I could see she preferred that I move on.

You would never meet Prince Johnson after 12 noon. That was when he would start to drink and become violent. It was well believed that he would personally kill at least one person a day, for whatever offenses he considered serious, real or imagined. One morning we arrived about 9:00 am and were escorted into his office for discussions about keeping open supply routes for aid to displaced people north of his camp. As we sat and talked over these matters, one of his assistants entered the room. He leaned over and whispered audibly so I could still hear, 'we found her and are holding her for you.' To this Prince Johnson replied, 'rape her, and then I will come'. On those orders, the man left the room. I felt horrified. I also felt helpless. Prince Johnson sat in his homemade realm of evil, beyond anyone's moral or legal enforcement. These atrocities were commonplace at that time. They would become much worse as the war went on. The young women of Liberia were frequently slaughtered in the most unthinkable and unbearable ways. The followers in Johnson's camp were far too terrified to confront these acts. As an outsider I would bring the matter to the attention of our team and other aid workers, but we all knew full well that it was beyond justice until the anarchy ended.

On another occasion, one of our best UN volunteers, Sean Devereux, recognized a young boy in the camp. He belonged to the Catholic school on the outskirts of Monrovia where Sean had taught before joining us. He embraced the boy and spoke animatedly with him. He did this in front of Prince Johnson. Johnson showed no reaction. As we were about to leave the camp, Sean went back to Johnson's office without my knowledge and asked his permission to take the boy back to Monrovia. Johnson gave no clear answer. Sean stayed behind, again without our knowing it, and he only began to return to our UN compound in the early evening. As he rode out of the camp, he could see another vehicle following behind. Further down the road the vehicle overtook him and forced him off the road. Prince Johnson's henchmen took Sean back to the camp and put him in their improvised prison cell where he spent the night. We did not realize any of this until late that night when we were gathered for some socializing with our friend Tajan Kabbah. It suddenly dawned on us that Sean was missing. We knew there was nothing we could do until the next morning.

Just as we prepared to head out early to search for Sean, he entered our compound. He confided his foolishness to us. We were upset and it was a lesson for all of us. Sean was one of our most dedicated volunteers. He acted entirely out of good will. He was dedicated to the UN and later joined volunteers in Somalia. He tragically lost his life there, shot by an insurgent.

The routine of most days was spent organizing and getting food out of storage areas and transported to desperate people. The food would come by ship to the port of Monrovia. It had to be unloaded by crude and broken crane equipment. It was then stored in large warehouses along the wharf of the port. On one occasion, we managed to overview the unloading of some 100 tons of rice, hand carried by local crews paid by day to stack it in the warehouse. The next morning we headed to the port with several empty trucks to load the rice for distribution. We were not prepared for what we saw on arrival—a full scale invasion of the warehouse by desperately poor boys and men. Many carried shovels, iron bars, and other tools to open and extract the rice and to ward off anyone who got in their way. ECOMOG had stationed a few soldiers near the warehouses but they were easily overwhelmed by so many hungry souls. We managed to get a message through to the ECOMOG headquarters nearby. They soon sent reinforcements, but not until nearly a third of our supplies had been looted. It was another wake up call for all of us to expect desperate acts. From then on we became much more security conscious to avoid or minimize loss and damage.

Final Degradation

One of the worst experiences I had was on a visit to the Liberian border from the Sierra Leon side where we had traveled periodically to coordinate with our base camp. We decided to travel down from Freetown to the border area to get a better sense from people crossing over from Liberia each day of conditions on the Liberia side, in what was widely referred to as "no man's land". What we learned was beyond our belief. Liberia has long had a very dark side. The practice of sorcery, known in Liberia as *Juju*, is long standing and has commonly included human sacrifice. The rituals carried over into the civil conflict. There were many rumors of combatants, especially the leaders, eating their enemies.

Those rumors were usually shared in the quiet moments at night as humanitarian workers sat about reflecting on the extremes of what they had heard was occurring around them. But hearing similar tales from the actual victims of violence was a far more compelling and repulsive experience. It sickened each of us to the core.

Less than a mile back from the border on the Liberian side, a camp had been set up by the rebel forces. The purpose of the camp was to screen all of those wishing to cross over into Sierra Leon. The real purpose was to confiscate their goods so that they crossed without a worldly possession. But we then began to hear of more horrendous activities. Most of the people crossing were women with small children. Each woman was raped in the camp, not once but several times over several days, before permission to cross was granted. If any family came with a male head of household, the price was so outside any realm of civility that we at first refused to believe it. But after hearing the same stories from many who crossed over, it became clear the stories were true.

The rebels would gather the family in any location on the road or in the forest near the camp. They would have the family sit in a circle. The man would be tied up in the middle. One of the rebels would decapitate him. Other rebels would then force the family members including the smallest children to dance and sing as the act was completed and the head placed on a long pole.

The nightmare of Liberia drifted beyond its outer limits for me in those stories. It was a look over the edge.

Chapter 2
Quest for Answers

Each person has inside a basic decency and goodness. If he listens to it and acts on it, he is giving a great deal of what it is the world needs most. It is not complicated but it takes courage. It takes courage for a person to listen to his own goodness and act on it.

Pablo Casals

First of Many

Regrettably these events and incidents in Liberia are all too common place in the world of the 21st century in which I write this account. But my days in Liberia (1990) seem very long ago in the context of modern civil wars in which the UN and the international community attempted to play a role. What I experienced came before the genocide of Rwanda, the utter and unending chaos of Somalia, the ethnic cleansing of Bosnia and Kosovo, the extremes of the Taliban, the fanatical suicides in Iraq, and the mass rapes of the Congo. These later civil conflicts heightened our expectations and bitter acceptance of the worst in human behavior. There was less anticipation of such atrocities in Liberia. Even though they were committed on a lesser scale than those that followed, for me the blatancy and intensity of these acts was traumatic.

Before Liberia the UN was less confronted by most civil inhumanity. The Biafra and the Congo civil wars of the 1960s, the civil atrocities of Central American insurgencies/counter-insurgencies of the 70s and 80s, all resulted in similar inhumane behavior committed in the name of revolution or blatant suppression. But the UN was not as intensely on the front lines of humanitarian relief and development in those conflicts as it is today. Of course food supplies and medical help were organized as during the Congo Wars of the 1960s. But they remained peripheral to the main UN military intervention compared to the scale of humanitarian operations in later conflicts. These more significant humanitarian roles exposed the UN to civilian atrocities as never before. The heinous acts of Liberia were therefore far more shocking simply because more or less for the first time *we were there.* We were far less conditioned to deal with them. Liberia was a watershed.

Liberia was also a turning point in my life. Never could I have thought it possible to find myself in the midst of live combat. Bullets overhead is something you do not forget easily. It compels a rethinking of who you are, where you are, how you got there, and where you think you are going. It brings a new reality to your life. It brings immediacy to the importance of understanding your motives and your goals. It pierces your ego and creates doubts about your carefully constructed life. Your understanding of life.

In my case, it brought about a lot of fundamental questioning. What was I doing working in "development"? Indeed, what was development? Was what I did, or thought I was doing, making any real difference in peoples' lives? Was I going to the core of the problems, the root causes of peoples' poverty and the injustices—indeed all too frequently the atrocities—they endured? Should I be trying harder to do so? How?

What I saw in Liberia was surely humanity coming unhinged. But was it an isolated aberration or a common feature of our human condition? It forced me to question why it occurred and what caused it. I began to conclude the obvious. Inhumanity was created by humanity over long periods of time. It cut across all cultures. Peoples' desperations did not exist by chance. They were created. They were the result of human actions or inactions. Whether they were intentional or unintentional, the effect was the same. I began to see more clearly what I previously barely understood. Human indecency, injustice, poverty and suffering were phenomena of human values gone bad. They were the result of basic human weaknesses. Very basic—greed, power and pride. They were the result of the way some people in all societies practice and benefit from the misfortune of others. They were self-serving and rewarding to those who figured out how to make them work in their favor, or thought they did. They offered easy reasons for understanding why the so-called weak, backward and lazy in society could not and should not participate or benefit equally.

Liberia had become a model of such demented values. A powerful elite ruled over others to their own benefit. It was as simple as that. Whatever trappings of modernity existed, they could not conceal this underlying and fundamental deceit. There was no equality of opportunity. There was no empowering of people to play a part in society's common decisions. There were no equal rights, and there was no caring. Of course there were decent and caring Liberians among the elite. I knew many of them. But their values did not permeate the elite culture. It consisted of rampant discrimination. There was an enormous gap between the wealthy and the poor. Eventually, the elite were replaced, all in the name of the people. But this was a further betrayal of the people. The corrupt values of the elite carried over into the new regime, at the expense of the people. It only served to spread the disease. Led by the infamous Sergeant Samuel Doe, the new rulers were even more vicious, greedy and repressive. Society was sick, but no one ever bothered to diagnose let alone attempt to cure it.

My revelation was in beginning to see through all of this. It would never have happened, at least not so soon, unless I had confronted these realities face to face and very personally. And that certainly happened to me in Liberia.

Yet Liberia was not the only basis on which I reflected on these matters. I have been privileged to witness and engage in the life of people across many countries. I have compared these experiences, some fortunately more positive than others, and have searched for commonalities. I have asked myself whether what I have understood about the root of these problems is true. And if so, whether and how the lessons I have learned can lead to change, or at least serve as a basis for how to avoid the problems. I have also asked whether the more positive experiences I have encountered can help us find a better way to live our lives together. I have tried to raise and address these questions on the basis of my own personal experience and study. I share what I have learned from all of this in the hope that it will join with and build on the experiences of others. That it will lead us to the positive change we want to envisage.

Learning from America

Again, these deep concerns and queries are not limited to any one country, they have relevance to all. Since the country and culture in which I was born had the earliest imprints on my own values and how I have perceived those of others, let me begin a further line of inquiry by reflecting on America. In so doing, I will try to comment on the tremendous merits, failings and potentials of America as I have personally understood and experienced them both from within the society and as an outside observer looking in.

Living outside my homeland for most of the past fifty years has given me a heightened appreciation of its most positive attributes and a deeper understanding of its failures. America's founding embodied and exemplified the very highest in human aspiration. America committed itself from its inception to a course of freedom and equality for all. This included basic freedoms of expression, assembly, worship, and not least, the "pursuit of happiness". Growing up in America, I found these ideals to be real. I felt free. I never imagined or experienced constraints to what I hoped to be and wanted to do. I perceived and accepted others as my equal. Without thought, I assumed and experienced that they looked at me in the same way. I benefited from a simplicity of lifestyle that ran through most of America following World War II. Comfortable was not privileged, and the pursuit of more never seemed as important as the fulfillment of the present.

Early I learned values common among my family and community. The importance of treating others respectfully and decently. I learned to expect the same in kind. I found America full of almost unlimited opportunity. And I was continuously inspired to pursue it to the fullest.

And yet this set of American ideals and my experience of them were tempered over time by a growing realization that they did not apply to all and that in certain respects they did not fully apply to me. The virtues and inspirations of America were in fact practiced in the reality of American life with a parallel set of values that were far less ideal. America was human. Whatever its achievements in promoting human decency, it was also subject to hypocrisy and failings. America's acceptance of slavery from the very birth of the nation was but one example. Its annihilation of millions of indigenous peoples, through conflict and disease, its frequent invasion of its Latin neighbors, its foreign policy responsibility for the death of millions of Vietnamese, all are extreme examples of its many failings to live up to its ideals.

America continued to debase its ideals of human decency in a multitude of ways. Too much of America began to exhibit a culture of greed and selfishness. The deepening of its materialism, the overriding compulsion of its elite to accumulate wealth at the expense of others, its seeming determination to sweep the poor under the national rug and to talk only about the "middle class"—all of this blinded it to the core values of equal opportunity on which it was founded. Profit became the driving force. The ultimate irony of this transformation was the loss of freedom that accompanied it. America fell under the unperceived "control" of the subtle and powerful forces of capitalism that pressured it into a ceaseless process of wanting more, buying more, and indebting itself more. It was an unending cycle of never having enough.

The process was manipulated through a highly sophisticated media. It continued to artificially generate "need" and "want" and a perceived sense of gratification that insulted our intelligence. At the same time, and for similar purposes, the same media dulled our sensitivities to violence which we no longer recognized. The result was a growing sense of alienation and isolation, not only of those left behind, but even for those who benefited most. It resulted in less compassion and empathy for the plight and suffering of others. Over time it devalued family, friendship, neighborliness, and caring. It created barriers between the haves and the have nots, not only among those within America but toward those outside it. It dulled our interest and knowledge of the world and peoples around us. It created an enormous divide between us, and between America and other cultures.

Despite these failings, America remains an inspiration. It often practices generosity and compassion for the less advantaged (though not enough for the truly poor). In spite of its weaknesses, America continues to symbolize and stand for rights and justice for all human beings. America's ideals continue to live in the hearts of its people and those of other nations. America is an experiment in human decency still in progress. It often falls short of its intentions and goals, but never allows the dreams on which it was established to die. America is an imperfect human creation, but continues to hold the hope of much of the world. America remains the model of both the transformation and the alienation that continues to take place. In this context, the question is whether America is prepared to recommit itself to the highest human values of its founding fathers and to its long held traditions and moral codes that value decent human existence above all else (however imperfectly they were embedded in the US Constitution). If so, the profound query and hope is whether it can begin to play a pivotal role in creating a new way of human relations aimed at bettering life for all.

Common Voyage

And beyond America, what about those other nations and cultures, specifically the fourteen others in which I have lived over these many years? Are they any different or better or worse? Have they not all fallen short as institutions for human good? Have they not all been controlled, in one way or another, by elites who practice greed and live well at the expense of others? Are there not many of them who espouse the same ideals and at the same time treat their own people with neglect, disdain and even cruelty? Some of these countries that I came to know so well have indeed evolved into extremes of human abuse and suppression. But are any of them devoid of people and leaders who long (and in some cases fight) for the same high human ideals of decency? My experience is that there are not. I have found that all countries and cultures are a mix of good and evil in how they promote and practice a common decency for and among human beings.

And what do I derive from these observations? I have found that all human beings seek the same basic elements of a decent life. They all wish to be treated with respect, and fairly, justly, and equally in terms of opportunities to realize and enjoy that life. They have all shown, in small ways or large, their capability, readiness and eagerness to seize these opportunities if given a chance. I have found a strong commitment to these goals in all societies in which I have lived, whether openly by the institutions governing, or by individual leaders, groups or citizens, including the poor. And in those countries where these ideals are truly suppressed, I have never known them to be extinguished—living on as they do in the hearts and minds of many.

In short, I have concluded that global humanity is on a common voyage. We are all in search of the same decent life. Some of our governing human institutions have gone further or more successfully in realizing that life for the majority of people. None have reached their goals. All have failed in some important ways or others, but their quest continues.

The fundamental question is do these values prevail sufficiently as a moral imperative to keep us on the path of steady progress toward the decency at the core of life that we seek for everyone. I have found that the obstacles on this path are many. That the difficulty of the voyage is similar and still discouraging within and across all countries and societies. The obstacles are the same familiar ones: selfish motives and arrogance, hunger for power, and persistent greed. I have seen the barriers purposefully constructed for these reasons. I have noted that they take different forms and degrees of intensity. But they are all intended to keep people down, apart and in their place.

From my life experience, I am ever hopeful that we as a global community have an opportunity to change these conditions. I firmly believe we have a common stake in doing so, and doing so together. The critical question is how we would go about doing this. I have devoted much of my personal journey in searching for the answers. I now hope that by sharing these experiences with you we may reach clearer conclusions on which to act. The details of what I have experienced and learned are very different from one country to the next. Yet I am convinced there are certain common themes, principles, and practices which cut across all of these disparate human struggles that hold the essence of the answers for us.

Underpinnings

So before we retrace my journey together, let me share with you from the outset what appear to me to be the most basic underpinnings of any improved human relations and conditions that we may hope to achieve. I share these not as any particular formula for success, but as simple life elements that run through human nature and have the power to bring us together in a common endeavor to improve our world. I want to share these elements with you in broad brush at this early stage. I hope as I recount my journey that they may be helpful reminders, perhaps indicators, of what we are looking for and what we need to put in place to build a better human experience based on common human moral values. I hope they will help us figure out the practical side of realizing our ideals and our dreams. The simple precepts and practices I have in mind are:

OUR COMMONALITY—*that human hopes, joys and sufferings, and the desire for a better life are shared by all of us*

MORAL CONSENSUS—*that all societies and cultures share a basic set of human values for decency toward one another that are essential to building our common humanity*

HUMILITY—*to own up to our failures to achieve our ideals, and yet to persist in pursuing them as central to who we are*

RESPECT—*for the equal and innate capacity of all, especially the latent power of the poor, to contribute to these common aspirations for the common good, and the willingness of the rich to set aside any arrogance by which some may live to share their power for these same ends*

TRUST—*for one another to bind together in our common quest, earned through what we do rather than what we say*

OPEN COMMUNICATION—*to bridge the yawning gap between people by facilitating an exchange of ideas about what works best for changing human relations and conditions and how we should pursue these*

EQUAL RESPONSIBILITIES AND ROLES—*to ensure the change takes place in everyones best interests and on the broadest plane*

ACTION—*to organize ourselves to actually do what we have decided needs to be done*

COMMITMENT—*to guarantee throughout all realms of our society that the changes we initiate are sustained*

Underlying these principles and practices is a strong and optimistic belief in the power of individuals to overcome their adversities on the one hand, and on the other in the possibility for people of all societies to truly commit to common values centered on the well being of all. It appears to me that it is in this chemistry of a simultaneous commitment to change by individuals and by the broader society that the lasting possibilities for change exist.

I hope that in sharing my journey, we will gain a much better understanding of the pervasive impediments to treating each other decently, but also the enormous and unfailing spirit to overcome them. I hope it will stimulate our further search for answers, reconfirm our moral bearings, and lead us to new and practical commitments that will change our lives for the better.

So let me begin this journey with you, and let me start where for me it all began.

Chapter 3

Growing Up in America

1940 – 1964

My Grandfather
Michael Heyn

My Grandmother
Therasia Heyn

My Father
Leo Luitpold Heyn

My Mother
Mary Kay Roan

My Sister Mary Therasia Heyn and I at the edge
of our forest across from the Summit Hotel

Beginnings

Knowing oneself is not a simple matter, so I have discovered. Figuring out what one believes, and why, and understanding whether the way one behaves and acts is good or bad, constructive or destructive, purposeful or meaningless, is an enormous and all too often un-attempted task of life. And even if the challenge is taken up, it can easily lead to confusion and despair as one's road in life is so full of conflicting forces and mixed unclear results. As one explores life's past, and is fortunate enough as I have been to live in highly varied human and cultural settings, one may have some advantage in understanding universally shared human values that throw light on and enrich one's own beliefs. If so, it has certainly been my blessing.

But I am convinced this does not alleviate the primary challenge to first understand the roots of how I came to believe and value what I did. I believe this can only be achieved by first probing how I grew up and what impact it had on me. I am equally convinced that sharing this with you in quite some detail is the only way I can enable myself and you to understand the foundations of who I am and why I hold the views and vision I do today. In doing so I need to confide that I found this self-exploratory journey into my past both joyful and poignantly painful. In writing about it I have also come to understand that I had to travel this past with great humility to avoid the pretensions of insight beyond what my experiences warranted. And yet, if I have any hopes of contributing some meaningful insights, however limited, into the nature of human relations and the potential for building a better world based on justice and human decency such as what I am proposing hereafter, then it seems important to probe what inspired me from my earliest years to pursue these ideals.

My search began with one of my first recollections: wandering alone in a forest at the age of three. It was 1943. I remember vividly the sense of power the trees had for me. They were not thick and tall, but thin and numerous, and they seemed to go forever on into an increasing darkness. I remember touching the rough craggy bark and feeling a sense of wonderment entirely different from what I had not known when touching my mother and father. It was an early moment of awe, and I had explored and discovered it myself.

Some two years later, that same forest took on an ominous demeanor. A criminal had escaped from the local prison. A huge army of guards and police overran my secret world with their howling dogs. My parents informed me that the man had killed someone. He was very dangerous. We must stay indoors until he was caught. For two days I experienced my first sense of fear. Then word came that he had been caught. My wooded world at the edge of our home returned, but with my greater sense that it could shelter both good and evil.

Our home was across the road from my father's resort hotel in the mountains of western Pennsylvania near Uniontown, some fifty miles from Pittsburgh. It was a magical place to start life. Isolated but exciting. I think it imbued in me a sense of adventure and exploration from those earliest years of my life. Our house was more like a cabin, well finished, all in wood, furnished with a rustic touch. It was warm and cozy and wonderful at Christmas. A black and white spotted hunting dog ran about at will. A maid cleaned and cooked. I suppose she was part of the hotel staff. A special perk my dad allowed himself living as we did so near the hotel. He used to dress up in suit and tie each morning. He strolled down our long driveway and across the highway over to the hotel. He managed it for more than twenty-five years beginning in 1918. He always put me on his lap for a brief chat before he left, sharing some words about the day ahead that I should enjoy. I felt very good that he cared about me. I was proud of him.

Foundations

My father had immigrated to the US from Germany a few years before 1918 though I do not know the exact date. He was in his late twenties. He was from a family of eleven children. I do not remember all the stories he told me of his youth. The overwhelming sense I had was that of a difficult early life. His father was a harsh disciplinarian even for those days at the turn of nineteenth century Germany. Corporal punishment was by no means uncommon. My father suffered quite a lot from his father's hand or so his stories seemed to imply. It was for that reason I assume he left home at the tender age of thirteen to strike out on his own.

His father, Michael Heyn, was an inn and tavern keeper in the small Bavarian village of Urspringen. I still have 1880s photos (actually a postcard) of that inn (and it still exists). It stood square, solid and strong with a steep sloped roof, along the mud road of the village. Many years later, I visited the village (in 1960). I met for the first time my uncle Cornel, aunt, and the cousins who still lived there. The houses of my family were quite respectable, pleasant and even modern on their interior. My aunt and uncle were very kind, generous and full of life. I found most Germans that way. They took me on excursions into the countryside. We visited the nearby enchanting city of Wurzburg where eighteenth century palaces recalled days of German music masterpieces and splendor. Each day we returned to their home for an afternoon tea. It was a major feast of cold meats, cheese, salad and dark bread. A wonderful treat. It made the dinner which soon followed quite a physical challenge. I had come on this visit with a female student friend. We met crossing the Atlantic by ship together on the way to our respective overseas campuses, hers in Florence, Italy, and mine in Tours, France. I thought of her at the time as a new found love in spite of the fact we hardly knew each other and our relationship remained platonic. She was vivacious, and my relatives liked her. We had some pleasant evenings with other family members who dropped by, including my uncle's daughter, my cousin, who had tragically lost her husband due to some electrical fault in the refrigerator he was repairing. She was still heartbroken. One evening she began to cry. I tried to console her with a long embrace and small words of sympathy. My relatives greatly appreciated that gesture.

This serene and happy visit was a stark contrast to the years of turmoil and immense hardship my German family suffered during and after World War II. Rebuilding their lives was an enormous and difficult undertaking. They shared stories of these times and how they survived. It gave me a better understanding of how adversity can be a stern and wise teacher of the importance of life's values.

My father's early hard life must have given him some of this insight. He had no more than an eighth grade education. Yet he was very perceptive, curious, intelligent, aware, determined and ambitious. Not surprisingly, he thought his best chances of surviving and hopefully succeeding was by working in hotels, about which he at least knew something. He started at the bottom by washing dishes in the hotels of southern Italy and later in Switzerland. His ambition and innate brightness enabled him to move progressively to more responsible and better paying positions. Eventually he assumed management of small and ever larger hotels throughout Europe, including London (where he worked at the Ritz). At one point he held prominent positions in the Semiramis and Sheppards Hotels of Cairo, Egypt (the latter famously burned to the ground in the 1952 student riots that drove the British out of Suez). All of this while still in his twenties.

My father shared with me his adventures and exploits in the Middle East through vivid stories that excited my imagination. He had a great fascination and appreciation of other cultures. He acquired his knowledge of these less through books than through people. He was outgoing and gregarious and loved being with people who were smart and interesting. People who had done something with their lives mostly in business. He sought out the unusual and unique, including people who fit that description. He showed me photos of himself and Charlie Chaplin riding camels near the Pyramids outside Cairo. I had little idea what the Pyramids were. But I was enthralled by his tales of mixing with Hollywood stars in the deserts of a far off land. He was also very talented with languages. He spoke five: German, English, French, Italian and Spanish, as well as some Arabic. It was a necessity of his work. It was a mystery to me in later life that he did not impart or even encourage me to speak these languages. I think it was part of his commitment to see me grow up as an unbridled American without European trappings.

One of his brothers, Roman, had already traveled to the United States and had married a well-to-do American, my aunt Gertrude Hotchkiss, whose family owned Pitney Bowes which to this day continues to manufacture mail and office machines. At a certain point, he invited my father to immigrate to the US. I am not sure I ever knew the ways in which my father began his life in America. What I am sure of is that he acquired a lasting gratitude, admiration, respect and love for America. He saw it as the land of freedom and unlimited opportunity because that is what it gave him. To him it was not just words but his actual life experience. His brother had done well in the family business of his wife, and he extended a helping hand to my father. As a result, my father eventually became the owner and manager of that resort hotel in the mountains of western Pennsylvania where I was born.

Top of the Mountain

The Summit Hotel was splendid, certainly to my young mind. It gained fame as a refuge of enjoyment that attracted clients from New York and other States throughout the country as its reputation spread. Part of that reputation was grounded in its history and its famous clientele. The hotel was located at the top of Route 40. Authorized by Thomas Jefferson as the first National Road between east and west, the hotel was constructed along it in 1906. It became one of the nation's most coveted inns for relaxation and splendid views from its "great porch", perched as it was at 2300 feet above the surrounding mountain ranges and valleys. It attracted the rich and famous which included Henry Ford, Thomas Edison, J.P. Morgan, and visits by Presidents Harding and Truman hosted by my father. With over one hundred spacious rooms, it also catered to a regular flow of weekend vacationers from the business community of Pittsburg.

It had a wonderful lobby. Warm sofas and beautiful oriental carpets lay all across the dark wooden floors. My father loved animals. He let his 6 dachshunds roam freely about the hotel. He even tethered a rather well-behaved monkey to a large tree-like pole to greet the guests. He had a great sense of slapstick humor that went down very well with the American guests of that era. He was often referred to as the "colorful German" whose hospitality, engaging humor and intimate attention to his guests made the hotel nationally famous.

And his kitchen was renowned. 'You can tell good cuisine by the soup they serve', my father would always say. He was a stickler for detail. The tables would always display fresh flowers, often roses. My early life was shaped, at least it seems so in retrospect, around the tables of the hotel dining room where we ate quite often. It was a marvelously open space, with huge windows looking out on the surrounding woods. The tables were covered with white dining cloths. Each wooden chair had a white cover backing and a soft cushion in floral design. For whatever reason, my father hung oriental paper lamps throughout the room. While that seemed incongruous in some ways, it created a magnificent atmosphere especially at night as each cast a soft glow and created a warm and luxurious atmosphere. My life-long love and enjoyment of hotels and restaurants undoubtedly was rooted in this experience.

And the bar! It was down the stairs from the lobby. It was a nightclub really. He had turned it into a elegant fantasy world. Naming it the "Baron Munchhausen Room", after a famous Bavarian noble goof-around who exaggerated everything under the sun, my father brought in acts from far and wide. Many of them were comedians. Al Jolson came. He was famous for transforming himself into the look of an old Negro singing songs of the South. A rather shocking spectacle by today's standards but quite normal in that day. The acts were broadcast on radio which is what all Americans were glued to. Later Jolson made some disparaging remarks over the radio about the hotel in an interview in 1936. My father was livid and sued Jolson (*Summit Hotel v. National Broadcasting Company*). Jolson called my father, apologized and tried to make amends, telling him that 'I'll talk so much and so nicely about the

Summit, people will think I own it'. My Dad was not impressed, figuring the damage had already been done. He firmly informed Jolson, 'When you get done paying me, you'll think you own it, yourself.'

Many years later while I was studying law I learned more about what my father had told me. His suit became a landmark case. Unfortunately he lost the case. Initially, *NBC* was ordered to pay damages, but in 1939 the Pennsylvania State Supreme Court reversed that decision. It was one of the earliest cases dealing with defamation on the airwaves. It was a seminal case because it set the precedent that the liable party is not necessarily the individual who makes the remarks but the station which sends it out over the air. My father (or his unimaginative lawyer?) had neglected to sue the radio station. Not a mistake too many others made afterwards. Naming multiple parties in a suit became the standard procedure.

Outside, the hotel had all the charm and class of a mountain forest retreat. The pool was Olympic size, surrounded by numerous wooden cabanas for dressing and lots of chaise lounges. The high diving board was the greatest challenge of my young life. At the age of five, I somehow whipped up the courage to go off it, at least feet first. My Dad had arranged for a large contingent of hotel staff (maids, waiters, chefs, stable hands, and so forth) to be present. As I broke the water, the round of applause and cheers was of Olympic proportions—a nice ego boost at five.

My mother was Irish American. She was very proud of it. She had come to my father's hotel to sing Irish songs for which she was well known. My mother had struggled equally in her early years. She was born in Columbus, Ohio, and her family was not well to do. She had set out at a young age to make her own living. This took her to New York where she followed a career of professional singing in clubs throughout the city.

My parent's decision to marry was, on hindsight, not a particularly wise one. Their personalities were diametrically opposed. My father was confident and outgoing; my mother lacked confidence and was basically very shy. She was very artistic and creative, which did not communicate much to my father's sense of the more practical and well ordered. For these and other reasons, not least my mother's growing alcohol addiction, the marriage was an unhappy one, which became increasingly apparent as my young life unfolded. The brunt of the discord fell much more on my sister, Mary, who was two years my senior. But I also could not escape the tension of the relationship.

My parents did share a concern about our upbringing cut off as we were from other children and without playmates. That was soon remedied by a regular visit to the home a few miles down the mountain of one of the hotel staff. He worked in the hotel boiler room and he and his wife had a couple of youngsters our age. Most of our time was spent in their backyard, playing in dirt and sand. The highlight in my memory was when their father and mine came up with the idea of hanging each of us from the clotheslines. They figured out a way to lie each of us in a folded sheet held to the wire by a series of clothespins (and whatever other devices they came up with). The rig up was such that they could sail us off from one end of the clothesline to the other at a good clip. On one occasion they showed off this stunt to our mothers. Their reaction was torn between the absolute delight of the spectacle and the imminent threat we might launch into free flight somewhere along the way. I remember being conscious even then how grateful my dad and mom were we had someone else to play with. They expressed their gratitude to our neighbors profusely. They treated them with respect and friendship without any thought of the boss/worker relationship back at the hotel.

At Christmas, my world was completely absorbed in the reality of Santa Claus. My father dressed up as Santa, full beard and all. He placed gifts around the tree as my mom, sister and I peeked unnoticed from behind the hall doorway. The next morning on one of those Christmases, my greatest joy was finding a train already moving around the tracks over lakes and bridges, with cows in the pasture and sheep in the corn. Those were among the very few times I recall my parents shared a common joy. A marked contrast to the animosities that mostly prevailed and worsened as my tender life went forward. The strain of my parent's relationship often resulted in prolonged periods of silence between them. It often lasted for days. Even weeks.

It was probably during one of these periods that my sister fell victim to their refusal to communicate. My sister had started the first grade. She had to be driven each day six miles down the mountain to Uniontown where the Catholic school was located. She was always picked up that same afternoon at 3:00 pm by one of the hotel staff. One day she was dropped off as usual. The driver returned to the hotel. My mother and father forgot it was a religious holiday. Possibly they were too absorbed with their own problems to remember. My sister discovered that all the doors to the school were locked. No one was around to tell her what to do. Sitting outside the school for some time, she decided on what appeared to be the only realistic course. She started walking back up the mountain. She walked almost half the distance along a parallel path.

The driver headed down the mountain to pick her up at the usual time and was totally shocked to see her hiking up the other side of the road. I can only imagine what a fright this gave to my parents. Unfortunately it did not seem to bring them closer together in spite of the trauma they had caused and the mutual guilt they felt. Fortunately, my sister took it all quite in stride. It later became a well worn family tale.

Heading West

When I was six we moved West after the end of the war. My father had sold the hotel. Our destination was California. As we moved westward, my father was increasingly enthralled with the beauty of nature that continued to unfold. His enthusiasm reached a high pitch as we entered Colorado. He decided we should stay and enjoy it for a year before moving on to the Coast. We rented an old Victorian house in a lovely tree lined neighborhood. My sister and I were enrolled in a local Catholic school. It was my first recollection of interacting with schoolmates, some of whom I did not find very friendly. They honed my early diplomatic skills not to confront and not to give in. Thinking back, the quality of the education was not so good, or I just didn't take to it so well. The nuns were big on rote learning and my early reading and writing skills were stifled (and as a result, I am a slow reader to this day).

I remember a particularly embarrassing childhood experience in that school. Whenever we needed to go to the bathroom, we would raise our hand to show it. One day I needed to go quite badly. I gave the required signal. Whether the nun just didn't pay attention, or whether I was a bit shy in displaying my need, the end result was that I was not given the permission. The only way out was to pee in my pants. I did just that. I didn't say a word. No one seemed to notice. Eventually as school was letting out the nun noticed the puddle on the floor. She whisked me up and over to the steam heater on which I sat until my parents collected me. It was my dad who came. When told what happened, he became very agitated, blaming the nun for allowing this to happen. My concern was my growing predicament as my classmates still milled about outside the room trying to figure out what was going on. My shame was considerable. It was not relieved by my father's continued chastisement of my teacher. He was not very patient or tolerant of what he considered poor management, whether in the hotel or the classroom.

Colorado (Colorado Springs to be precise) was an exciting new land for my dad. He was fascinated and enamored with American culture and history of the West. The cowboy culture of Colorado was much to his liking. He wanted me to be a part of that culture. In those days it was common to find a small corral of stuffed horses and bulls along the road, and maybe a mock ranch house. The proprietors rented out for a small charge a cowboy outfit with hat, boots, stirrups, a vest and even leather chaps. Once geared up, I was hoisted up on one of those animals. They were always in some violent bucking or bronking position. The log pole holding up the brute was always concealed as some kind of fence pole. Photos were taken at my Dad's insistence. Fortunately that was just the proof I needed. As we continued our journey to California and I began my new life, I had no hesitation in impressing my friends with tales of my ranching background.

My dad was a very energetic and ambitious businessman by nature. Although he kept referring to his well earned "retirement" after so many years of hard work in often lonely surroundings, he could not help but look forward to something to invest in and manage. Not far from Colorado Springs lay the famous "Garden of the Gods." It was an expanse of giant red rock outcroppings in a sage brush setting. It clearly deserved to be conserved and protected for its unique beauty. Mostly it was. But sections were privately owned and even for sale. My father decided to buy up some acres and build houses for resale. Looking back, I am not sure I would admire his decision to disfigure such pristine nature. But he was excited to be back in business. He seemed to have forgotten the enormous headaches that come with such commercial adventures. I did not notice any stress at the time. Later when we were well established in California, he suddenly drove back to Colorado to deal with his investment. I have ever since assumed he ended up selling it at a loss as these individual houses were not easily marketed. At the time, however, the project must have given him a much needed outlet from the strains of his marriage and some standing in the local business community.

He made several business acquaintances and loved to joke around every time they got together. I recall one such friend and each time they met one of them would say 'Cement mixer, putty, putty'. Both would roar into uncontrolled laughter. For my part, I was totally perplexed. Much later I learned it was a song made famous during the early 1940s by a jazz piano playing virtuoso named Slim Gaillard with ridiculous almost incomprehensible lyrics that sent everyone into stitches. My dad and his friend had clearly made it into a brand of their close relationship, a kind of inside joke based on some investment fiasco or more likely some off color connotation. It was healthy for him to have those friendships. From my perspective, I was proud to see my dad so active. I was always impressed when he pulled out his maps of the subdivision he owned and cast a proud eye across his property so contrary to his normally self-effacing manner.

While still in Colorado, the tension between my mom and dad continued to grow. Neither my sister nor I seemed to understand what it was about and failed to recognize it as a symptom of a highly dysfunctional family. We felt an inexplicable uncertainty in our lives.

California Dysfunction

Eventually the year ended and we moved on to California. The American pride that my dad wished to implant in me sank deeper as we awed our way across New Mexico and Arizona.

My dad knew where in California he wanted to live. We headed straight for it. His dream was to live in La Jolla. In those days it was truly the jewel of Californian ocean side communities. As luck would have it—and my mom's quiet stubbornness would insist—this would not be possible that year since the Catholic school was filled to capacity. Probably at considerable pain to my dad, we moved further down the San Diego shoreline to Coronado. That was a charming town, less pretentious than La Jolla. It had an island atmosphere surrounded as it was by beaches and bays. There my sister and I entered Sacred Heart Elementary School.

My sister was vulnerable. She had already been deeply affected by my parent's marital turmoil. Neither of us had any idea of that at the time. We took up temporary residence in a Spanish colonial apartment complex just a block from the school. My parents decided to organize a birthday party for her. She was new to the school and was still trying to make friends. It was clear in hindsight how marred her confidence and self esteem were. This must have been picked up by her peers who apparently sensed her weaknesses. My parents decorated the apartment with an array of crate paper and balloons. They made lots of sandwiches, cake and the mandatory Cool Aid. The party was to start at noon with several games planned before the feasting began. By 12:30, we were wondering why everyone was late. By 1:00 my parents were desperate. Not one of the dozen girls invited showed up. My parents probably did not know any of the other parents and were clearly at a loss of what to do. After some time, my sister began to cry. We all felt terrible. I got out my marble set and we played for a while. But nothing could wash away the hurt she felt. And that I felt for her. Possibly it was an unfortunate case of miscommunications. But I always thought it had something to do with my parent's troubles and their inability to communicate just enough to plan their children's celebrations.

Even after we moved and settled into a modest house which my parents rented for the year, our family chaos did not subside. It grew angrier each time. My dad apparently began to see the pain and fear of it all on our faces One day my sister and I got back from school. On entering the house we found party regalia and a lot of gifts strewn around a festooned living room and across the mantel piece. Any reason for celebration was not obvious. On asking my Dad what was the occasion, he simply said he wanted us to know how much he loved us. At the ages of seven and nine, we were not too interested to probe further. We lost no time tearing open those unexpected gifts least they somehow disappear.

In spite of the inner family strains, our first year in Coronado was formative. The town was completely flat and totally navigable by any kid with a bike. In no time, I was all over the place. I was pretty friendly I guess. I made a lot of friends easily, at school and around our house. Those were the days when a family kept a running account with the local grocer. I would pop in any time to our chosen family market (called "Day & Night"). I picked up some candy bars or another comic. It was also a time when the "Good Humor" ice cream truck passed through the neighborhood every day. The familiar ding-a-ling tune drew us instantly into the street to get a Popsicle or Fudge Bar. It was a period of low needs and expectations. For a child, it was a time of having all you wanted. There was just no sense of needing more.

My sister and I finished the school year. With a spirit of starting a new life, my mom and dad moved us to La Jolla. It was one of the few times I recall feeling the joy of family togetherness. My dad found us a wonderful house at 1555 Virginia Way (sadly, torn down many years later). It was dark brown and shingled. Enormous, or so it seemed to me. It set on spacious grounds with two huge regal palms guarding the entrance. It had a large wonderfully cozy old fashion living room with big stuffed chairs, sofas, and recessed cushioned benches at each bay window. The windows overlooked the Pacific. A stately dining table and matching chairs became the hub of dinner parties my parents hosted with an increasing circle of friends.

I have never forgotten the New Years Day party of 1950. My dad loved American football. Nothing was more important than the annual Rose Parade in Pasadena and the Rose Bowl. It pitted the Pacific Conference Champions against those of the Mid-Western Big Ten. He and my Mom invited a bevy of friends over for baked ham and mouth watering trimmings. Hard drinks were much in style compared to today's wine culture. There was no shortage of supply and all the cheer that went with it. And there was the betting tradition. Everyone was expected to contribute to a common pot of cash. The trick was to pick the game's final point spread as close as possible to the final score. The game was especially important that year. It was between my Mom's home team, Ohio State, and the undefeated University of California Golden Bears. It was a terrific contest. Ohio State won (17-14) in the last two minutes. Everyone congratulated my mom. She beamed radiantly. Something I had seldom seen before.

It was also at this time that my dad bought one of his dreams, a brand new Cadillac convertible. It was white, with white wall tires, a black convertible roof, and dark red upholstery. It smelled like the real leather it was. It had all the accessories of the era's luxury vehicles. It cost my dad $5,000. A lot of money in 1950. It was a really big joy to him. He literally spent hours outside the garage behind our house, waxing the car and caring for the leather. Our house perched on the rim of a canyon full of Eucalyptus trees. I still vividly picture my dad stooping over his car canopied by those delicate trees in the evening light.

My mom had her dream as well. The garage was actually the ground floor of what was otherwise a standalone guest house in the back garden. It was marvelously isolated. A perfect dwelling in which to practice her music and singing. She used to spend hours of her own practicing her scales and a retinue of songs. Under her influence, even I sat there for hours "composing music" with the simple talents I presumed to have.

My dad began for the first time to play his guitar. It was a talent from his days in Europe and Egypt that I never knew he had. My sister and I sat entranced on the front porch under the two regal palms. His repertoire was limited, but I remember every one of them like it were yesterday. They were a mix of American (*Streets of Laredo*) and Latin (*When They Begin the Begin*) music. His (and my) favorite was *Solemente Una Vez* (translated as *You Belong to My Heart)*. It would be years later that I took up the guitar (in San Francisco) and learned to play each of those songs with my daughters as captive audience.

Those early days in La Jolla were indeed an unusual time of unexpected joy for all of us. But it was soon mixed with a return of bitterness. The splendid social life my parents enjoyed after so many years of turmoil began to slide back into my mother's alcohol addiction and angry confrontations of the years preceding. It is hard to imagine from my present vantage point that only my mom was to blame for this acrimony. My dad's strong willed and dominating personality, possibly devoid of any understanding or sympathy for my mom's addiction, must surely have aggravated every such occasion. All of this was muffled and incoherent to me as it filtered up from the floor below and disturbed my restless sleep in the late of night. I felt afraid and sad. I am sure my sister did too. We never really spoke about it. Eventually my Mom moved out of their bedroom and into mine. I shifted to my Dad's side. He had placed my single bed in a corner of their master bedroom.

Breaking Apart

My parents separated when I was ten. I was crushed. My father had organized for all of us to take a holiday to Yellowstone Park. We were to leave the next day. I came into the small den off the bedroom where he worked every day on his typewriter to answer an array of correspondence. When I entered his "office", he informed me he had just opened a letter from an attorney of my mom informing that separation papers had been filed at the court. My father was in a state of shock. He always dominated the relationship. He suddenly felt vulnerable and devastated. His immediate concern was about us. What would a separation mean? How would we live together? It was the beginning of a long period of pain for my father. My mother was adamant. His attempts to seek the intervention of the church were fruitless even though my mother was a devout Catholic.

Within a few weeks, the separation took on a brutal reality. My father moved out of the house. We stayed on in our wonderful home but only for a few more weeks. My mother moved us down the coast to Pacific Beach where we took up residence in a modest apartment on the second floor. I started school and attended for a year.

It was a time of mixed feelings. Whatever was happening in my family life, I had an equally important life of my own as a kid growing up in America. I made friends right away. I was always active. Those were the days of vacant lot baseball (most blocks had a vacant lot, and baseball was the king of sports for all of us). I returned home from school about 4:00 pm each day and after

60

grabbing a half sandwich I headed across the street to that lot. Others were already there or soon showed up. We played until it was nearly dark. I always came home exhausted and hungry. After a warm meal and a little study I was soon in bed.

My father moved to an apartment nearby overlooking the sea. We used to walk across and visit him. We spent most weekends there. He took us on fishing trips on those weekends. Sometimes he dropped us off for the day on the bridges that spanned the inlets of the newly developed Mission Bay. My sister and I remained there unaccompanied by anyone. Oblivious to the bridge traffic that flowed incessantly in the background, we felt entirely safe. More precisely we never had a notion we might not be safe. We caught flounder and halibut. On occasions we caught gar fish, those prehistoric looking ones with the sharp teeth. We loved it.

My dad later bought a small trailer on the banks of Lake Wolford in the mountains behind Escondido. We rose at 4:30 or 5:00 on Saturday mornings, much to my mother's disapproval. It took us two hours to reach the lake to get in the early morning fishing. We sat in the small motor boat for hours catching crappie, bluegill and occasional bass for which we trolled. Lunch on the boat was always same. Dark German bread, usually pumpernickel, and meat sandwiches. Usually pretty dried out by the time we opened them. Certainly not the soft-white fare my mother had accustomed us to. But we weren't bothered. The thrill of fishing had become addictive.

Family life would break these innocent days and push me into a premature adulthood. My mom was quite unstable and she used to go into a rage (despite her basically introverted nature) without much reason, though undoubtedly the strains of the separation she insisted on had played on her. One night this happened and the shouting between us was very loud. We soon had the police called by the neighbors knocking at our door. Among other things we often fought over whether we could go over to visit my dad. My mom sometimes refused to let us go. When the police asked what the fighting was about, I told them. One of the cops asked what I would do if he refused to let us go. I said I would keep on fighting until I could. He didn't like the answer. He told me to stay put.

My father turned to religion, a growing belief that God and particularly Jesus would come to his rescue. Never really practicing Catholicism, he began to seek out and turn to other religions. He settled on Unitarianism. That seemed to suit him well, given its much more ecumenical philosophy. But his religious practice was more personal rather than institutional. He shared with us his faith that God would look after us and keep us close together. He often expressed his beliefs in moments when he viewed exceptional natural beauty. This regularly happened when we watched glorious sunsets over the Pacific from his large apartment window. It all instilled in me, unaware though I was until later life, a very personal religion. A spirituality based not on church conventions and demands, but rather on simple, straight direct communication with God totally unfettered by rituals or guilt.

My dad once again found diversion and relief in the business world, this time among the business circles of San Diego. One of his favorite activities was to go downtown to the Merrill Lynch brokerage house. He sat and watched the big board for hours on end. He often became animated with his friends on the likely reasons for any turn in the market and the probable end result of the day. He also joined the San Diego Club. Again, it consisted mostly of business people. He took my sister and me there every once in a while for lunch. It had an impressive atmosphere with a sedate dark wood paneled dining room. We usually had a roast or turkey dinner with lots of gravy and potatoes. I really enjoyed that. He always had us dress up. He wore a suit and tie fitting to the elegant dress of those days. It was a splendid way to spend time together. It gave me a feeling that my dad had a lot of class, which he did.

Island Refuge

It was about this time that my mother moved us back to Coronado. Coronado became my home for the next most formative ten years of my young life. It was the place where I found stability for the first time. It was the place where the best of American life took hold of me.

As we knew from our first time living there, Coronado was like being secluded on a wonderful island. In those days, you could only go over to San Diego by ferry, or else take the 22 mile ride around the "Strand" that formed the Bay. It was a world unto itself, but in many ways represented a microcosm of middle America. Coronado was famous for two things. It was home to one of the largest naval bases in the US. The North Island Naval Station took up half the island's land space. A busy place of work for all the many naval personnel residing in Coronado. Coronado's other claim to fame was the Hotel

Del Coronado. Built in the late 1800s, "The Del" with its Victorian grace facing the beach and ocean, became and remained the Mecca of Hollywood celebrities.

And Coronado was the home of World War II veterans. Not just the officer class. It was home in equal numbers to ranks of sailors and petty officers. Others of modest means also lived in Coronado during the war and many stayed. Housing was not that expensive. Many found affordable housing in what became known as "The Housing Project." Built by the navy during the war, it consisted of "Quonset Huts" and double story pre-fabricated buildings. We had moved to Coronado in 1952 and by that time the "Housing Project" was filled with people from modest economic and mixed ethnic backgrounds. They were mostly poor white people, but also Mexicans and Blacks—still referred to as Negros. It was from this mix of Americans that I found my deepest friendships.

On our arrival in Coronado, my mother moved us into a very humble house that she could afford. It was single storied, painted gray, with a peaked roof and a small front porch. There was hardly any yard, front or back. The finish inside was basic plaster board with wood framed doorways. The floor was partly wooden and mostly linoleum. The kitchen was Spartan. The fridge had a round vented motor on top.

My dad immediately followed us back to Coronado. He rented a small guest cottage behind a house across the street from us. My mom was not pleased. Again we went back and forth. We carried the tension both directions.

But my mom was happy to be back. She had established a lot of friends in Coronado during our first stay there. They were all Catholic. She met them of course mostly through church and school events. They were very kind and loyal to her. She clearly needed and cherished that. That was mainly why we returned.

My sister and I plunged back into school. Sacred Heart Elementary School was in the physical center of Coronado so it was easy for us to ride our bikes there. The style of the nuns was caring but no-nonsense. The education was focused on the basics. You were expected to know your stuff.

I joined the "Safety Patrol". This was like a small police force responsible for getting everyone safely across the street before and after school. We wore red sashes and V-shaped military-type hats and held out "Stop" signs on a synchronized signal. The captain gave that signal with a shinny whistle. After some time I worked my way up to captain. I was thrilled to be in charge. My dad was very proud. He used to show up at the start of school each day, every day. He was great at making quick friends. That's how he met and took an immediate liking to Pop Malar. Pop was an old-time police officer, probably in his late sixties. Everyone knew Pop. He was great with kids, perhaps not least because he was about their same size. Wherever there was a kids' event, there was Pop—Saturday movies and so on. One of his official jobs was to supervise the Safety Patrol at Sacred Heart. My dad and he hit it off. Most probably as a result, Pop took a shine to me—which may have had something to do with my surprisingly rapid rise to captain's rank! My dad's constant showing up in the mornings and afternoons proved somewhat an embarrassment over time. But overall I felt good and proud to have him there to see me perform.

My mom had by now moved us to another house. My dad was supporting her and us, but the amount agreed by the lawyers was apparently quite modest even for those days. She would never have been able to afford a move up in our housing but for the kindness of the couple from whom she rented the house. They rented it to her for $110 per month. They never raised that rent over the next twenty years. That quiet kindness made a deep and lasting impression on me. I never knew the background leading up to this, but I suspect that my Mom's Catholic network had a lot to do with it. The house at 817 Margarita Avenue was modest but very nice and in a choice neighborhood. It was low lying, Spanish ranch style, with stucco walls and a red tile roof. It didn't look very big from the street, but it took up most of the property behind. The house wrapped around a brick courtyard full of geraniums, cacti and ice plant. You could get to my room by going around the back and entering off the patio. That proved very handy over time.

For the first time since our parents separated, my sister and I began to feel "at home". I continued to bike to school, nothing was very far in Coronado. While still in the 6th grade, marbles absorbed my entire pastime, in school and out. We played in the dirt, in the park across from the school and any dirt lot after school.

Soon sports became the center of my life. All the friends I played sports with were the most important part of my life. I was now in the seventh grade, and "flag football" became my passion. I loved physical activity and the thrill of competition. Sacred Heart was part of a Catholic school league. We played a different team each Saturday. Probably best was that I was part of a team and well liked—though I didn't really think or concern myself about that. It gave me a solid feeling of security and confidence—though again I didn't think of it that way then. But looking back, I needed it.

Actually my dad was the one who worked up my passion for sports. He wasn't much of an athlete himself—though he was a fanatic about keeping in shape and taking his daily walks. But he loved spectator sports. He listened on radio and later television to every kind of sporting event. He especially liked American football in those still early days of the NFL. We watched the weekly game together every Sunday. He also frequently drove over to the Hotel Del Coronado to watch a tennis match or a swimming competition. He was passionate about baseball, especially the genuine American heroes he felt many of them to be.

This all seemed quite incongruous with his overall demeanor. He was very European in his manner and lifestyle. My dad always dressed up for the day. Slacks, a dress shirt and tie, a good quality sports coat, and often a Fedora brimmed hat. Even his walks along the Coronado beach front each evening were done in those same clothes minus the sports coat and hat. He never snacked. He paid close attention to his diet though he loved good food and the company of friends. But when it came to sports, he was totally American. He always spoke very highly of America for the many opportunities it opened to all people, and none more than for the sports players who rose from all walks of life to become American icons. He continued to remind me how fortunate I should always consider myself to be an American.

I joined the Boy Scouts, based on a lot of prodding from my dad. That was a good thing. It involved loads of outdoor activity. I came to enjoy that as much as the sports. And there was the competition and fun of earning "merit" badges. You could choose from what seemed an unlimited list of interests, and many of them fascinated me. I went after each of those badges with great determination. I was just plain curious and excited by each of the topics. I loved working through the many steps required to get one. It was a very rewarding feeling for me. I collected a lot of those badges, which I proudly wore on my green sash. I kept rising in rank and I liked that too. My dad was real proud of course. Unfortunately he did not see me later become an Eagle Scout, but I knew how much prouder he would have been.

By now I was in the seventh grade. About that time, my father started to see another woman. She was from Germany, but had been in the States for quite some time. Her name was Elizabeth Hoffman. I thought it was good for my dad. But I also had mixed feelings since having a dad with a blonde girlfriend half his age was not very common. He also seemed uncertain about whether it was the right thing for him to do. That changed over time as they became very close, fell in love, and began living together (she staying over at his apartment though not all the time).

I was so absorbed in my school and friends and in scouting that I didn't make too much of it all. Not until I traveled with my Scout Troop to the "World Jamboree" that was held in Irving, California, in 1952. We prepared a lot for that. We needed a theme for our campsite. We chose a rope ladder barrier to our camp. With the help of the Navy Seals who had a base in Coronado, we rigged up some very high telephone poles and suspended between them a checkerboard mesh of heavy rope. You had to climb to the top and over to enter our compound. It was a big hit. Scouts from all over the world—my first exposure to a global community—climbed that rope ladder with real zeal. By the time they got over it they felt very privileged to meet us on the other side.

One day, one of my scout friends told me that my dad had come to see me and was waiting outside. He also offered that my dad had a good looking blonde with him. I was immediately and deeply embarrassed. I came outside the camp and greeted them both but did not invite them in. They sensed my unease, I could tell, and soon left. That must have hurt my dad a lot. I felt guilty then, and still do. But that was how I reacted. Again, in those days, parents did not have young girlfriends or boyfriends (at least not the ones I knew) even if they were divorced or separated. Certainly they didn't bring them to your Jamboree Camp. I realized, not then but later, how very hurt and shamed I felt to have "divorced" parents.

One summer my dad could not take us anywhere since as I mentioned he had to return to Colorado to sell his property. That was a stressful time for him. One of the very few times I can remember he was angry and rude to me. Elizabeth was taking care of us in his apartment back in Coronado (which was not an easy chore for her I am certain). I kept writing postcards to my Dad asking him to send me some small gifts from Colorado that I could trade with scouts at the World Jamboree. He got very agitated. He sent me some Indian pottery, but told me he was very busy and could not spend his time on these matters. I was hurt, but the pottery turned out to be the best luck for me. For whatever reason, Scouts from other countries were not keen to trade anything for those small clay pots and objects. So I started giving them away as gifts. That seemed to take Scouts from all countries by surprise. They expressed a deep gratitude each in his own unique cultural way. Some even returned to visit me again. It was my first lesson in the power of giving without expectation.

Early Manhood

On April 2, 1954 of my eighth grade year, I was home after school and saw Elizabeth parked outside our house in my dad's car. I looked through the window curtains for some time. She didn't come in; she never would have since as far as I knew she and my mom had never met. So I went out to see her. As soon as I got in the front seat she began to cry uncontrollably. She collected her composure after some time. She then told me. My father died that morning. My father had had a heart attack some weeks prior. I had gone to see him at Scripps hospital in La Jolla where they were now living. I was shocked by his appearance and bearing. Lying in the hospital bed, he looked completely washed out. He tried to have a normal conversation with me. Told me to take care of those pimples on my face. To keep up my scouting. I sensed he was making a special effort to comfort me but that he was very sad. I was shaken but somehow never thought of it as something fatal. I figured he would recover soon and life would go on. But he didn't, and I just couldn't believe it now. I went back into the house and lay on the sofa. I lay there for several hours. When my mom came back, I told her what had happened. I continued to lie there. I knew how much I loved my dad, but only then did I begin to comprehend how much he meant to me.

In spite of the turmoil of our family life, he never faltered in his total love for my sister and me. I began to recall so many moments that made him so special to me. How in ordinary ways he set an example for all my life. While our family chaos would have a continuing impact on me and my confidence, it was largely counteracted by his fierce love and what he inspired in me. It was the respect he instilled in me, for the values he demonstrated through his actions more than his words.

I knew even then that he had implanted in me a great sense of justice and kindness and decency, though I later reflected on how often I fell short to live up to those ideals. His compassion for a couple of my friends from very poor homes made a deep impression on me. With one friend in particular, he took special interest and time to provide counsel in weekly talks. He even provided a small allowance to encourage him.

My dad also had a special feeling for the plight of young women who were in trouble. It must have had to do with something he experienced in his past. He became a patron and small benefactor for the "Sunshine Home for Girls", at least I think that was the name, somewhere in Los Angeles. They were young girls who had become pregnant and were often disowned by their families. He thought that a great injustice. He was especially sensitive to the treatment of children, perhaps as a result of his own difficult upbringing. He never raised a hand to me or my sister. Whenever he saw another father or mother discipline a child in public, physically or verbally, he would go up to them and say that was neither right nor needed. Long before the civil rights movement a decade later, he frequently spoke of the injustice suffered by the Negro people. He told me many anecdotes of their innate kindness, intelligence and musical genius. Some of it would be considered patronizing today, but he meant it genuinely and such thoughts were certainly out of the mainstream beliefs of that time.

He also was compassionate with his German family. He extended a helping hand to them when they were in greatest need. At the end of World War II, the German people were desperate. He sent them a regular supply of money and food. Later, he invited his brother Cornel to send over his son for education in America. He mentored and cared for his nephew (my cousin), Udo Heyn, like his own son. He insisted that he work his way up in America. He enrolled him in San Diego State College, but also got him a job at the local gas station. We often passed by that gas station to see my cousin dispense gas and hand out free abalone shells to the customers. My dad got a big kick out of that. He saw his nephew getting a real American education.

We would often hang around that gas station talking to the owner and other attendants and listening to professional fights on the radio. Those were the days of Joe Lewis and later Rocky Marciano. One of my dad's favorite was Light Heavyweight World Champion, Archie Moore who made San Diego his home. Even to this day he holds the world record for the most career knockouts (over 130). My dad sat there in his convertible Cadillac with the radio at full blast surrounded by all the gas pump attendants. He cheered and cringed with every blow of the fight. He got everyone pumped up with this passion. They felt very much at ease with him. He always had a way of making people feel equal and respected and they always reciprocated with respect for him. It was a great lesson for me and for my cousin, neither of us having seen such spontaneous and natural respect and friendliness shown by a businessman for working people.

My dad did what he did in life because it was the right thing to do. Not because he was obligated by social mores, laws or even religion, but because it was decent. My dad was my hero, then and now. I only began to barely understand why as I lay there on the sofa thinking in my own way what I respected most about the life he led and the values he practiced.

That day was a signal turning point in my life. I almost instantly felt the import of it. I knew that I would from then onward have to assume much more responsibility for my life. I also began to have a new understanding of my mother. I felt I could not rely on her to manage my life as a traditional mom would be expected to do. Yet I also knew that I had been blessed with a mother who had created and exemplified for me a set of values that remained equally important throughout my life.

My mother was as compassionate as my dad. But in a completely different way. She was very perceptive of other people, picking up instantly on anything that went amiss of her values. She had become quite withdrawn and was on a continuous emotional roller coaster. It was tough for me and my sister. But we dealt with it by just getting on with our lives. She was hurting a lot over those years. But she never gave up on a core of beliefs that defined her life. For her, everyone deserved and had a right to be treated with respect. She was deeply offended if not treated that way herself, or if she saw others treated badly. It made no difference your economic or social standing; everyone was equal in her eyes. Everyone had positive human qualities and should be appreciated for such. She couldn't stand boastful people. She simply felt that one should be oneself and let it speak for itself. There was no need to embellish on it.

Her humor about people who thought too much of themselves was very earthy. She occasionally referred to someone who particularly disgusted her as a "piss ant". It was not particularly meant unkindly, more as a way of helping them in her mind get back to the place where they must have come from. And she was funny, very funny when she was on an upswing. It all tied around showing how people made fools of themselves when they tried to be who they were not. She had a strong inner pride about herself, though she had a difficult time confronting the offensive and ridiculous. Very possibly she felt it was not worthy doing so. People would reap what they sowed she believed. In the meantime, just be true to yourself and get on with it.

She had an abiding belief in the power of prayer. She was as Catholic as they came. Her rosary her constant companion. Her faith was in things sorting themselves out if we trusted in God and did the best we could. 'Take things in stride, they'll work themselves out', she constantly reminded me. She was far better read than my father. She was addicted to biographies and history, an addiction I later inherited. She was a Democrat (quite a contrast to my staunch

Republican father who more than once embarrassed me in the Coronado Village Theater shouting out over the movie newsreel about that jackass Truman). She was a working member of the Democratic Party. She was passionate about the rights and needs of everyday people and in her good times she would help get out the vote. She was an early addict of television. She never watched the frivolous, mostly the news, the special features and in those days good drama. She felt very close to the President of the United States, especially the Democratic ones. She adored Kennedy—a Catholic President was a dream come true, a prayer answered. She genuinely believed, or fervently hoped, that I would one day become president. That was the highest achievement for any man and she thought I had the qualities for it. I hoped she was right because my youngest aspirations hid the same ambition. So clearly something had rubbed off.

My mom was proud of my achievements, in school and out, but mostly because she expected it. She never pressed me in my studies. In fact, she practiced more of a benign neglect. She imparted in me a sense of self worth and high expectation. At the same time, she embedded in me the understanding that none of us should feel too important about ourselves.

I knew from that day as I lay on the sofa that I would not be able to rely on my mom to mentor my school work or show me to the next steps in my young life. Yet I also knew that whatever the origins or source of her torment and occasional odd behavior, she had instilled in me a basic sense of decency and a concern and respect for others. I somehow knew even then that whatever I did, it was my mom's and dad's basic beliefs and values that would steer me.

Early Motivations

I entered Coronado High School as a freshman in September 1954. Coronado High had a diverse student body, not so much ethnically though there was a good percentage of Mexicans and hand full of Blacks. It was more in terms of economic levels. Of course, many in my class were from navy families. A few had Admiral fathers. But there was also a mix of kids from business and professional families, and a somewhat lesser but still significant percentage from poor economic backgrounds. None of us gave the slightest thought to any of those social or economic divides. We made friends freely and on the basis of whom appealed to our inclination for fun and for sports. It was an entirely equalitarian environment, though we didn't even realize (or think about) it at the time.

Coronado High School had a good academic reputation. Looking back, I think the quality of teachers and teaching was quite uneven. Fortunately, there were just enough outstanding teachers that if you applied yourself you would come out with a good education and preparation for college. Probably what really made the school stand out was the openness and close interaction between students and teachers. Quite a few of the teachers took a great personal interest in their students. They tended to give special time and attention to those with whom they felt a special affinity or thought had unusual needs or potentials.

In my case, it was my Latin teacher, Luis Martinez, and especially my math teacher, Ben Cooper, who took a real liking to me and went out of their way to give me counsel and guidance and a certain parenting which they must have felt I was missing. Luis Martinez had a wonderful sense of humor and liked to tease all of us in his class with small observations and comments that were basically insignificant but touched us beyond his expected teaching role. He kept an eye on me outside his class to see how I was handling my studies and what my aspirations were.

But Ben was special to me far beyond these academic endeavors. He seemed to like what he thought was my inquisitive and enthusiastic spirit and my sincerity and determination to accomplish what I set out to do, or so he told me. When he recommended me for college he put forth my capacities as 'the most impressive overachiever I have ever known.' Ben thought I had tremendous potential and he thought I would do well. My understanding of what he was saying, in between the lines of whatever we were discussing, filled me with a sense of confidence and ambition I may not have had so fully otherwise.

When it was time to apply for college, my mind and applications were focused only on Catholic universities. Luis Martinez was Catholic. He was my designated career counselor. He was very pleased with my choices (Marquette, Loyola, Notre Dame, etc.). Ben thought I was shooting way too low. He insisted that I apply to Stanford. Stanford was the highest goal of every one of the good students in our school. There was plenty of competition among us, not to think about competition from all across California and the rest of the US. But Ben knew I had what it would take to do well there. He was sure I would be accepted. My SAT exam results were strong but likely not Stanford caliber. On reflection I attributed that to my family environment which was devoid of reading and learning ambitions (just ambition). But I went along with Ben's counsel and applied to Stanford. I am quite certain that my rejection was a far more crushing blow to Ben than it was to me. It didn't do my ego much good mind you, but I saw it much more of a long shot than did he. In the end, I was accepted by Notre Dame and was happy with that opportunity, mostly because of its iconic Irish football team and Catholic reputation that were so important to me at the time.

My main ambition at Coronado High was to play on the football and basketball teams. Over time these became immensely important in how they centered my life at that time and built my confidence. In my freshman year, I tried out for the "B" football team. On the third day of practice, I rammed as hard as I was able up against the blocking practice machine. I hit an iron bar and dislocated my shoulder. That pretty much put me out of action for most of the season. An unexpected and disheartening piece of luck compared to my dreams of early stardom.

The next year, I came back with even greater determination. Fortunately, the big stars had already moved on to the varsity team. I found myself more competitive with the new line up. The coach was my geometry teacher. He was totally fixated on football. We literally spent the entire geometry hour every Friday of the season going over diagrams of plays for the upcoming night game (as I said, the quality of teaching was varied). To this day I cannot figure out how the girls in our class endured this manly battlefield strategizing. Somehow this coach thought I had good athletic skills. He tried me out at quarterback, liked what he saw, and I played the full season at that position. I was ecstatic. In fact, my quarterback skills were not that good, and I knew it. I had a friend, Phil Torrey, who moved away from Coronado the summer before. I knew from practicing with him what real throwing talent was all about. His passes could thread the eye of a rubber tire from thirty yards eight out of ten times. But what I lacked in such high quality skill I at least partly made up for in sheer enthusiasm and determination. I had a good "roll out" pass, and used it as often as I could. I made good play decisions in the huddle, and more than once carried the ball over the goal line myself. It was a good year for me.

My junior year was a tremendous let down. As I moved up to the varsity team, I found there my good friends with the real star power. I tried out at quarterback. I clearly did not have what it took. I spent the entire season on the bench.

But my senior year was magic. My opportunity to play and play well was made possible through an unconnected event at the end of my junior year when I was elected student body president of the high school. My success in achieving that office was unexpected. I was fairly popular in school, but I was not seen as a standout leader. In fact, I joined a select group of friends who distinguished themselves by their purple jackets with white leather sleeves and their ducktail hair styles which I also adopted. These were truly the 50s. They accepted me only after I agreed to hop scotch down the entire school hallway at lunch hour. We used to hang out together for beach parties. We would take in an occasional movie in order to shoot U nails at the screen with miniature sling shots. When I decided to run for president, most classmates and teachers were surprised. What made the difference was my speech at assembly on election day. It was not so much the content of what I said—'striving together will be the backbone of our success'(!)—but how I said it. It was probably the first time I realized my innate talent for making a moving speech based on my sense of timing and my passion for what I had to say. The student body seemed electrified. I won by a fair margin.

So, as my senior year began, the varsity coaches saw an opportunity to use me not so much for my football talents, but for the leadership they hoped I could provide to the team. Knowing my shortcoming to play in the backfield, they decided to try me out on the line, at "Center" position no less. At that time, I was about five foot ten and weighed only about 155 pounds. Not exactly your common notion of a center lineman. I practiced hour after hour to hike the ball well, and I got very good at it, including the more difficult snap (without looking back) for the extra point.

But playing center was not what made me stand out. Fortunately in those days, the common practice was for the offensive team to stay on the field and continue to play defense. The coaches decided to put me in the "linebacker" position on defense. That's where I really got to shine. The linebackers' job was mainly to prevent the runners on the opposite team from moving the ball forward to gain yardage for a first down. Linebackers stood in a crouched position just behind the defensive front line. From that position our tackling ability depended on our quick assessment of where the runner was heading or likely to head. The idea was to meet him on that path, preferably behind his own line of scrimmage. It was a matter of striking a crushing blow to stop the runner in his tracks. Whether and how I would do that with my unimpressive 155 pound mass was not quite clear. But in fact the mass was not the critical factor for bringing down these brutes. It was more the quickness of getting in the right position to surprise them or at least confuse their running plans. I greatly enjoyed that challenge. And of course I still applied the maximum of my every pound to bring them down.

Due to the great running skills of my close friend, Hal Tobin (the same impressive back fielder who was my teammate and close friend at Sacred Heart) we came within one game of the league championship. Unfortunately we lost. But for me that disappointment was at least partly overcome when the California All State Team (small schools) was announced. Both Hal and I ended up on it, he on the first team and I on the second team. Never in my wildest dreams would I have expected that. It meant a lot to me. The honor was especially humbling and gratifying in my knowledge of my own athletic limitations. I am sure Ben was mumbling something about overachiever.

In between all of this I started dating Sheila sometime in my junior year. She lived just two blocks from my house. I used to see her walking to school. She was a dark brunette with blue eyes and a cute smile. She was two classes behind me. I learned then that I could not take my relationships with girls lightly. I suppose it was a need I had to compensate for the instability of my home life. But it was also because I just didn't like the idea of taking such matters frivolously. After a couple of months, I asked Sheila to "go steady". I gave her a large black stone metal ring to wear around her neck. That was the way it was done. I was not going to have anything less.

During my high school years, my mom's mental health became even more unstable and unpredictable. It wasn't just a matter of her occasional bouts of overdrinking. Those came in cycles as her moods swung between one extreme and another. What was more disturbing was her increasingly schizophrenic behavior. She would go into a state of unreality believing she was someone else, combined with a clear paranoia that different people were out to humiliate her. Sometimes she would demonstrate her fears and frustrations in absurd ways, or would seek attention from those who tried to ostracize her. One time she purposefully fainted at the communion rail during a morning mass. I did my best to ignore these antics for what they were. Still I felt helpless in the face of what I did not really understand.

A perennial grief that my mother harbored was the absence of a romantic life. She felt this very strongly. One time she went out for the evening with a younger man in navy uniform whom I did not know. It was her right to do so of course, but I just didn't feel good about it. On their noisy return at 2:00 am that woke me up, and in spite of his rather intimidating size, I chased him out of the house and half way down the block. Sometime later, the monsignor of our church told me I had done the right and courageous thing. How he ever knew that happened is still beyond me. I later suspected it was my mother herself who told him in the confessional.

Sometime later, my mom met Maurice Hubert. They started to see each other. He was a naval officer stationed at North Island Naval Base. She brought him to our home on several occasions. He came from a French background somewhere in Louisiana. He was quite handsome, fit though not very tall. He was well mannered and polite. He carried a certain air of confidence. My mother was obviously proud of him. As time went on she clearly fell in love with him. I did not know much about their relationship. But I noted that after some six months he no longer came to visit. Apparently he had been reassigned to a naval base in another state.

My mother's mood and condition inevitably swung low again as she openly pined for him. I learned a lot about her on those occasions. Whatever the origins of my mother's afflictions, I knew in my heart they were not of her own making, that she was an exceptionally loving and caring person toward me and toward others, with the regrettable exception of my father. She was exceedingly passionate when it came to love, and equally so in its loss. She was obsessed for a very long time about losing Maurice. She continuously played recordings, and sometimes sang the songs made famous by *The Ink Spots,* a group renowned across America from the 1930s through the 1950s. Her favorites were *If I Didn't Care, I'll Never Smile Again,* and *Till We Meet Again.* The depth of her feeling and sorrow penetrated my heart each time she often sang the refrains:

> *I'll never smile again*
> *Until I smile at you*
> *I'll never laugh again*
> *What good would it do*
>
> *For tears would fill my eyes*
> *My heart would realize*
> *That our romance is through*
>
> *I'll never love again*
> *I'm so in love with you*
> *I'll never thrill again*
> *To somebody new*

Within my heart
I know I will never start
To smile again
Until I smile at you

When she was drinking, she would begin to shout his name very loudly, over and over. On one of those occasions, I was back in my bedroom waiting for my friends to come by for a night out together. I imagined a dreadful and embarrassing scene when they would arrive. I decided to avoid that by leaving the house. I slipped over the hedge of our neighbor's lawn and lay there on the ground in the dark. I waited for my friends to show up. They did. On approaching the front door they hesitated outside, probably having heard my mother inside. Then they knocked on the door. My mom answered, undoubtedly in a befuddled state, said something, and they turned and left. They strolled back to their car talking quietly among themselves. It was one of several indications I began to have that people in Coronado, including some of my friends, knew of my mom's travails and odd behavior. They probably knew a lot more than I did.

After some time (it was in my senior year), my mom's condition became impossible. She not only acted strangely, but often could not sleep. She grew huge water-filled bags under her eyes. Somehow, her brother John, who lived in Chillicothe, Ohio, learned of what was going on. He flew out with his wife to see what they could do. They decided there was no remedy possible within our family. My mom needed to be "committed" to a mental health hospital. This was a blow to me. It was also somewhat of a relief. The hospital staff came to take her, not without some resistance. That left me on my own.

To their immense credit and my everlasting appreciation, my sister and her new husband moved into my home and stayed with me for my senior year. My sister had a lot of problems of her own, undoubtedly due to the breakup of our parents. She sought whatever emotional support she could find among her friends and particularly her boyfriends. She had gone to the girls Catholic High School in San Diego for her freshman year. But then she convinced my mom she should transfer to Coronado High School. There she began to hang out with young girls who most likely also had family problems. That led to going out with boys who were in the same predicament. Those young fellows, and I knew most of them even though they were two years ahead of me, had developed a tough exterior—clearly a defense mechanism to the void and turmoil in their family life—and prided themselves in drinking and fighting on the weekends. My sister was welcomed into their fold. She began to go out with one in particular. His mother was very strong and unrelenting in defending her three boys. His Mexican father was quite aloof (though I found him exceedingly mild mannered and kind). One day my mother informed me that my sister, then 19, informed her she was getting married. My mom was never able to provide firm guidance to my sister. When this happened, she simply acquiesced to what God would work out. My sister and her boyfriend did marry. And that is what passed.

I never mentioned or shared any of my personal life with my friends. Nor with any of my teachers, not even to Ben. My coping strategy (as I would call it in hindsight) was just to get on with my life as though everything was normal. And I must say that the rather unusual situation and arrangement did not seem to bother me very much. At least I thought not. I just showed up for school each day, studied a lot each evening to get good grades, played sports, ran for president of the student body, and applied for college.

I continued to lead a reasonably normal teenage life. Summers were always a special time in Coronado. We hung out at the beach most every day. Surf boards were not yet common in those days, but body surfing had a long and respectable tradition. Catching the occasional eight or ten foot wave that thrust your body forward at the top just before it broke and sent you crashing onto the water or sometimes to the bottom required practice and skill and not a little courage. We also played a lot of beach volleyball, not least to boost our image as beach boys among the goggling (or so we thought) females (who did not play much volleyball themselves in those days).

While occupying myself with all of this I would keep an occasional eye out for white tents down the beach in the direction of the famous Hotel Del Coronado. Those tents were usually a sign that a Hollywood film crew had come down to film a segment of some upcoming movie. It often meant the possibility of some day labor to earn a few extra bucks. One day at the end of my senior year, those tents appeared. I spotted them before anyone else in our group and made a mad dash down the beach. I came upon one of the film crew who looked like he might be in charge. Asking him whether there was any work for the day, he told me I could grab a shovel and shift sand over to dunes nearby. I got right to work.

It was around 10:00 am and there was not much movie making going on. After about half an hour shoveling, I noticed from the corner of my eye someone had opened the tent door near where I was working and emerged onto the white sand. I looked up and at first wasn't sure what I was seeing was what it was. But after a few seconds my brain confirmed what my senses had already told me. It was Marilyn Monroe. She was dressed in a white beach robe. She and I were the only ones around at that moment. We made eye contact. I just couldn't figure out whether or what I should say. Fortunately for me, she took the lead: 'Hi, what's your name?' My impressive but unelaborated reply was 'Mike'. 'They've got you working already do they Mike?' 'Yeah, just for the day', I again replied. 'Well, you be sure to take good care of us Mike'. Again, trying not to embarrass myself, I kept it sweet and short with 'I will'. Through the rest of the day, Marilyn would return to her tent where I was still working. She would every time offer a 'Great job Mike' or something similar. Always in that soft voice of hers with an equally soft smile.

I returned the next day but the filming on the beach was already done. I learned overnight that it was the production of *Some Like It Hot* with Tony Curtis and Jack Lemmon. I caught a glimpse of both of them later that day rushing along the walkway in front of the hotel, but Marilyn was nowhere to be seen. The significance of my tryst with her struck me only years later. I still recall it often.

I also took on summer jobs. The summer between my junior and senior year I decided to find some short-term employment to earn some pocket money. I had to travel out to the eastern suburbs of San Diego early each morning. There was an old housing subdivision built before the war and the houses had run down and were mostly abandoned. A contractor was hired by the local municipality to tear down the houses. Instead, he cleverly figured out how to get rid of them while making a few extra dollars in the process. I and a few other teenagers were put to work in a way I never expected. Our job was to saw each house in half with a handsaw. Without much further thought, each of us was assigned a house and soon found ourselves atop and sawing down the middle of the triangle-shaped roof, then down one side of the house, and on our backs under the house to saw through the floors before heading back up the other side to complete a clean cut of the house into two parts. We helped to maneuver these half houses with assistance of cranes onto flatbed trucks which each day took the harvest down the 26 mile stretch to Tijuana where they were sold at local prices to those who could not afford much else. It was an eye opener for me into a world of survival on both sides of the border I had no idea existed.

At our graduation on completion of my senior year, I was awarded the Jik

Wong trophy. That was for the most outstanding student of the graduating class. I cherished that honor as one of the most valued of my life, even to this day.

I owe my friends and the people of Coronado more than they will ever realize. It is the place that taught and enabled me to grow up with a genuine sense of respect and caring for each other. It provided me an opportunity to seek and appreciate the value of every individual. Not for any status they may had, but for the way they treated me with kindness and respect, and how I wanted to reciprocate in kind. It gave me another incredibly solid and worthy foundation for my life.

Early Challenges

It was time to move on. My first real plunge into the outer world. We met on the station platform for the first time, five of us with parents in tow bidding us farewell. It was still more common in 1958 to take the train rather than fly. We set out on our three day journey with an excitement you would expect of proud new freshmen of Notre Dame. None of us thought twice about sitting up all night catching a wink of sleep as we could, playing cards all day, and sharing our own reasons for having chosen the special place to which we were heading.

Our initial arrival on the Notre Dame campus was awe inspiring. The massive golden dome first set the adrenaline flowing. But also the expanse of lawns and lanes, the old stone and the new brick buildings, the forest of trees everywhere starting to turn their colors as one looked across the campus in any direction. We met our new roommates, mine from Saginaw, Michigan, and we emptied our trunks and slid them under the bed.

Notre Dame was (is) special. I only came to appreciate its quality after I left. Looking back, it provided probably the best academic education I ever had. The professors (all men, as was the college) were highly intelligent, sensitive and dedicated to their students. And they were inspiring teachers. The diminutive but passionate professor of western civilization provided me an opening to a human history I never realized existed, at least not in the impressive dimensions, profound richness, and great suffering that he revealed to me. My English professor was from Montana. He taught me how thoughts and feelings were best conveyed and understood when kept as simple as a cloudless sky. My number theory professor was of German origin. He seemed to appreciate my passion for the subject though I was only above mediocre in the class. My

French professor was a father of the holy cross order which had founded and continues to run the university. His own French origins brought the subject to life. I forever struggled to master it. My military history course (for inexplicable reasons, I had suddenly decided to join the ROTC to become an officer, assuming I suppose I would otherwise be drafted on graduation) was taught by a captain of the US Army. While I grew to dislike the rigid military uniform we had to don for field marching once a week, I also grew to admire his discipline and commitment to his profession. My logic professor exemplified for me the highest standards of a philosopher and a pure intellectual. His reasoning inspired me forever after to find the firmest base and clearest path for any case I wanted to make.

My problem was that my overachiever nature was catching up with me. I took nineteen credits each Semester (compared to the average/expected fifteen), and that turned out to be a heavy (near impossible) load for me. My slow reading meant that it took me twice, even thrice the time to get through the assigned reading as my peers. So I had to spend every waking hour reading and taking notes. I used to do that standing in the lineup for breakfast, lunch and dinner. I spent very little time in leisure. I took in two "Fighting Irish" football games (probably the main initial reason I had chosen Notre Dame), but later found them too time consuming. I never went off campus into South Bend to take in a movie or enjoy a dinner out. I literally wore myself down. At one point I had to spend the weekend in bed resting and recuperating while my college buddies went off to Chicago. On top of this incessant slogging, I had to put up with the winter blizzards of Indiana. That was something my California make up was ill-prepared to endure. All in all, it was not a pleasant time. I was not happy.

But I did get what I wanted—good grades. I ended up the year number three in a freshman class of over 1,500. Toward the middle of the second Semester, I was invited to interview for the General Honors Program. It was a stream of less structured educational experience and learning that the brightest in the college were offered starting their second year. The panel interviewed me for an hour. They asked a wide range of questions on many subjects. I did reasonably well (though nothing very outstanding). But when it came to describing my favorite books and analyzing the author's intentions, I failed miserably. I was probably not incapable of such analysis, but up to that time I had almost no exposure to any serious literature (and therefore a surprisingly short list of books to cite). I had even less basis on which to share my thoughts about their authors. So I was not selected. Nevertheless, the panel offered me (over the summer) enrollment in the special program without need of further interview, presumably based on my end of year grades (which they must have found surprising given my unconvincing interview). I was seriously considering joining the program when my education took a sudden turn.

Sometime after my Christmas break at Notre Dame, when I went home (this time flying) to Coronado, I began to wonder if I really wanted to continue my college years in this superlative but unappealing (at least for me) university environment. I blamed my negative thoughts on myself rather than Notre Dame. I had brought on most of my own misery by my compulsive behavior. But still, I had the feeling (even if based only on the number of times I fell on the ice going to class) this just wasn't for me. I continued to plunge ahead in my second semester and didn't take seriously any idea of a transfer. I don't even remember what inspired me to apply for such a transfer, but I did it rather spontaneously and without much conviction that it would happen. My lack of commitment was further confirmed by the fact that I applied to only one place.

I returned to Coronado for the summer vacation, and was so happy and relieved to be home among my friends and the days at the beach. I took up a summer job as a teller at the Bank of America. My first experience with work in a professional setting. The bank manager, Mr. Vega, was from Spain (quite unusual for Coronado). He was a very conscientious and committed manager. I learned a lot from my short time working under him. Not so much about being a teller, but just from observing how he managed the bank operations and especially his friendly attitude, mixed with firm business demands from his staff. That impressed me quite a lot, and influenced how I tried to do the same in later years.

The bank closed at 3:00 pm, and we went home by 4:00 pm, still plenty of time to enjoy the rest of the day (and night) with friends. One day I rushed home to put on my swim suit and found a letter my mom had placed on the desk in my bedroom. I instantly recognized who it was from. Although I had almost forgotten that I had applied, I opened it with considerable anxiety. Quite unexpected and remarkably, it confirmed that I had been accepted as a transfer student to start my sophomore year at Stanford University. I was overjoyed.

I saw Stanford as an incredible opportunity to be part of one of the most outstanding universities in America, if not the world. I also liked the idea of remaining in California where I felt very much at home. I relished the return to a moderate climate. So Stanford it was.

I took a range of the required and selective courses, including biology and accounting, but my main interest was in the social sciences. I decided early on to major in political science. I was inspired by my experience as student body president at Coronado High to hold public office. Mostly I was moved by the image and campaigning of John F. Kennedy who was then just starting to run for president. Kennedy came to Stanford and gave a speech to the student body in the main auditorium, Memorial Hall. It was his presence that struck me more than anything. He had a way of electrifying a crowd even before he began to speak. Much of that was the growing mythology the media had created about him. But more was the compelling stature he projected along with an open friendly manner. Probably humor was his greatest strength; letting the enormous intelligence he possessed shine through in a very human and captivating way. So political science it would be.

I also had the honor to meet President Charles De Gaulle. He had come to inaugurate the new Stanford medical school. I and a few others were rather randomly selected to represent a cross section of the student body. I felt exceedingly privileged to shake hands with the president at the ceremony.

Whether that was what inspired me or not, I one day soon after decided to apply for the new overseas study program Stanford was just then establishing. I was rushing to a class when a brochure announcing the new program caught my eye on a bulletin board. The campuses offered were three: Stuttgart, Germany; Florence, Italy; and Tours, France. I thought this could be an exciting way to spend my junior year. The application deadline was that very day. I filled out the form in a hurry, had no problem (thanks to General De Gaulle!) in quickly choosing Tours as my preferred campus, and slipped the application under the door of the designated office. Some weeks later I received notice that I had been selected. I was very honored.

I had never been outside the United States except for those regular excursions to Tijuana, so going to France was something special. It seemed even more so by the fact that our maiden group was traveling there by sea. We met in New York, literally at the dockside (on the West Side of Manhattan), and boarded a Holland Lines student cruise ship. It was a wonderful voyage of ten days during which I got to know all three campus groups. As I already mentioned, I met a girl (who had chosen the Florence campus) who would later accompany me to my relatives in Bavaria, Germany.

Within a few of weeks of our arrival at Tours in October 1960, John F. Kennedy was elected the thirty-ninth president of the United States. The night he won, most of us gathered in the foyer of our small campus residence to celebrate. We soon learned that another group of students, French medical students from the nearby University of Poitiers, was marching through the town toward our building. We were not certain what it was all about. They entered our building as if it were their own. They made it clear they were there to celebrate Kennedy's (and just as likely in their minds, America's) victory. Kennedy had ignited a flame among many young people around the globe. This was a spontaneous manifestation of that. It was genuine. I felt a sudden sense of bonding with these future doctors. I was surprised they could feel and share so much unsolicited passion. And passion it was as the night dancing wore on. Soon the clothes came off in some kind of primal demonstration of brotherhood. I barely spoke a full sentence of French in those initial days in Tours, but the sheer physical and emotional exchange we shared enabled me to communicate, as intimately as I ever had before, my beliefs and hopes for the future of America and the world. It was an awakening moment for me. I learned for the first time the power that emerges in sharing a common human spirit across language and cultural differences that requires nothing more than a determined deep genuine desire to express it.

Our courses at the Tours campus were tailored to the setting. They extended my horizons markedly. We studied French literature, from Proust's *Remembrance of Things Past* to Stendhal's *The Red and The Black*. It provided me marvelous new insights into the philosophy of French authors. We studied European and French civilization and history. And of course French itself. I was hard pressed to keep up with my classmates. It was not a matter of any lack of comprehension or analytical skill, it was purely and simply a matter of the massive volume of reading that was expected. That was my nemesis throughout my college life. It really hurt my opportunities to make good friends. In this case, sadly I sacrificed special opportunities to get to know the local French people better.

On one occasion, I joined with six others from our group to spend a day with a count and countess and their daughter. They lived in a lovely, stately, rather romantic French villa further down the valley overlooking the Loire. The lunch was superb, all five courses. Needless to say the wine was exceptional. Everything done with such grace and style. As it turned out, the daughter who was our age apparently took a liking to me. There followed many weeks thereafter when she, and her father, tried every manner possible to arrange for me to meet with her. But I was so immersed in my reading that I never took up the offers. I felt ashamed about this introvert (not to mention rude) behavior for many years after.

The year abroad was not really a year, more like six months (two quarters). It went by quickly. I was soon heading home via a stopover in the Ireland that my mother never knew, but that I assured her was just as she imagined.

Returning to Stanford, my senior year was intense as I was determined to get top grades to ease my entrance into graduate school. I took some tough political science courses, including political theory and international law. I excelled in them. I also relished a few elective subjects, particularly music history and art history. They not only enriched my liberal education, but instilled in me a lifelong appreciation and passion for both.

I graduated *cum laude* (with honor) from Stanford. While I was naturally proud of that, it was a mixed feeling. I felt my academic achievements came at a rather high price to my social relationships and a broad college experience.

Early Marriage

Nevertheless, I was happy to have done well. I was completely preoccupied with my upcoming marriage to Sheila in mid June of 1962. That proved to be an experience I would not look back on with joy. It had nothing to do with my relationship with Sheila which had in fact improved with the sense of emotional security I felt the union would bring. What upset the entire marriage ceremony was the behavior of my mother. She was very displeased. More accurately she was dead opposed to the marriage. She thought I should wait to meet other young women. I resented this. Her mood turned very sour and withdrawn. Nevertheless, she helped with the wedding preparations, and attended the pre-wedding dinner at the Hotel Del Coronado (in which my closest fraternity brothers joined). But at the end of the dinner, she began to speak disparagingly of the marriage. I cut her off with some quick words of thanks to those who had attended.

The next morning, we all showed up at the church at the designated hour, except for my mom. The ceremony hung in suspension for more than an hour waiting for her. She never arrived. We went ahead. We had a lovely reception at the Naval Officer's Club on North Island, hosted by Sheila's parents. The whole incident was emotionally humiliating and draining for me despite my best efforts pretending to ignore it. It took me the first few days of the honeymoon to return to normal. Not without a visit to a hospital in Miami to be diagnosed with anxiety-related stomach pains. But my new independent life had begun. I felt good about that.

Finding My Path

Still at Stanford before our marriage, in my senior year, my early ambitions to become a politician were maturing as I took more and more political science and related history courses. I was especially impressed with the profiles of historic American politicians. This of course included F.D.R and what he accomplished in the face of great economic depression and eventually war-time adversity. But outstanding of all for me was the political life and values of Abraham Lincoln.

I read about Lincoln's humble beginnings, his political maturing, and his constant and consistent adherence to fundamental beliefs. I took an entire course on his life, professional and personal, and continued to read volumes about him. I was most inspired by his example of balancing pragmatism and principle in order to achieve what was right for the country. I was inspired by his courage. He never gave up in the midst of the darkest days of the civil war. He took unpopular positions in his early political years on issues that put his future political career severely at risk. This included his opposition to the 1846—48 Mexican American War (which caused immense suffering to American Indians and poor Mexicans residing in the disputed territory), and his strong criticism of President Polk for his pro-war policies. This was at a time when most politicians and the public at large strongly favored American expansionism. The fact that he sacrificed his seat in Congress partially as a result of this stand, created for me the model for a political career based on a selfless concern and struggle for what was right. Equally impressive was his reemergence from political retirement to fight a dominating politician of his era (Stephen Douglas), specifically against the spread of slavery to the Nebraska territories. It was in my mind a supreme example of the ideal of courage and the power of a commitment to simple decency that politicians (alas, all too infrequently) can bring to bear for fundamental social change.

It was with these examples in mind that I determined myself (however sincere or naïve I may have been at the time) to be a politician. I decided to start down that road by going to law school. I studied diligently for the graduate records and the law school exams. I came out with good marks. I applied to Stanford, UC Berkeley, and Hastings law schools. I hoped my advantage would be at Stanford. It was the only school where I sought to be interviewed. I made my case with the Dean. I told him it was my interest to serve people in ways that would bring long term benefits to their lives. I was not interested in serving corporate interests to produce material goods for peoples' short term gratifications. He apparently appreciated those thoughts and the attitude and values they reflected. He told me so, and within a few weeks I received my acceptance letter.

As it turned out, the law was neither what I thought it to be (a sure fire tool to realize justice and right) nor what I thought I wanted to spend my life doing (a great deal of detailed research and an unending game of wordsmanship to outmaneuver the opposition, too often regardless of what was the just thing to do). Nevertheless I did gain a more realistic understanding and immense respect for the law, especially its knack to find compromise solutions to difficult human failings and mistakes. I definitely benefited for the rest of my life from the disciplined deductive reasoning that the study (and practice) of law demands. I understood the merit of the "case system" of study. But I also found it immensely tedious (again, given my shortcomings in absorbing large quantities of material quickly) and therefore frustrating. I enjoyed the mock trial work. I think that if I had gone on with the law, I would have been best as a trial lawyer. But I reminded myself that my end goal was not to become a preeminent lawyer. Rather it was to become a politician committed to the public good. I also knew that would not happen quickly or easily (if at all), and that I would have to spend a lot of time practicing what I might not enjoy in order to get there.

So it was toward the end of my first year of law studies that I began some serious soul-searching. I pushed myself to think through what I wanted in life. There was in me this strong drive to do something for others, something that would make a difference in their lives. A deep sense of injustice if something was not done. I was not sure at the time where this drive came from. I did feel that my Catholicism must have contributed to some of these thoughts. I reflected again on how I had benefited and was greatly influenced (unconsciously at the time) by the values of both my parents. Not as much in what they did with their lives, but in what underpinned their character and integrity. I even wondered if the emotional challenges of my early life had inspired in me an empathy for others far more challenged than myself, that I may not have otherwise had. But I realized even then that I should not fall into too much certainty or self-righteousness about my motivations and goals. I simply needed to figure out what for me was the most practical way of realizing them. I needed to find a way that most stirred my passions and determination. I concluded that I was most unlikely to find this in the practice of the law.

During the summer following that year of law studies, Sheila and I had decided to travel around Europe on a shoestring. It was Sheila's first trip abroad and I enjoyed showing her all the places I had come to cherish. But it was a temporary distraction for me. It could not take my mind off a burning preoccupation with my future. It was in Rome that I received my grades by postcards, clearly less sterling than what I had become accustomed to expect of myself. It was a further wake up to what I was sensing and sharpened my mind on the shift I had been contemplating.

Returning to Palo Alto, I went into a serious search for what would be my best path ahead. My first instinct was that, in spite of my inclination to set out in a new direction, I should not give up on the law. I thought to discuss it over with the Dean who had been so instrumental to my admission. But it was at that point that I knew I had to be completely honest with myself. I would never be happy as a practicing attorney. My real interest had transformed much more directly to an ambition to help disadvantaged people live better.

I decided to explore the possibility of becoming an anthropologist. Stanford had an excellent anthropology department. I met with some of the staff to learn about their approach and program. As I did, I began to realize that my interest was not so much the study of human behavior in varied cultural contexts, as important as that was to my interests. It was rather in understanding people's real life social, economic and political difficulties and how these could be overcome. I wanted some sort of inter-disciplinary and practical view of peoples' real life challenges. And I felt a particular inclination to know this about people living in other countries and cultural settings.

It was during this search that I began to recall my father's rapture with Latin America. He had traveled and written a short book about his sojourn in Mexico with my mother before the start of World War II. But his interest went well beyond Mexico. He had a tremendous fascination with South America, particularly the high Andean countries of Bolivia, Ecuador and Peru. He was enthralled by their rich history and civilization. I became inspired by those same interests. I began to take them on as my own. Stanford had a well known center of Latin American learning, the Institute of Hispanic American and Luzo-

Brazilian Studies. It offered a multi-disciplinary curriculum that spread across courses in Latin American history, economic development, and current social and political affairs. It enabled its students to undertake studies in a wide range of departments in each of these subject areas. It seemed to offer precisely what I was looking for. I applied and was accepted into the masters program.

I felt at home and excited in this new environment. I relished the history of Latin American societies and their pre-colonial civilizations. The human drama of the constant struggle for freedom and prosperity in these countries attracted me. I was captivated by the overriding greed for power and wealth that stifled and suppressed those aspirations even to the current day. I studied under world renowned Latin American historians and economists. I studied issues relevant to the practical daily life struggles of poor people including their lack of food, water, health and education. I contributed to a monthly publication of the school's journal of current Latin American political analysis. This honed my keen interest and skills for in-depth exploration and understanding of human conditions at both the level of political society and the daily grind for survival.

My lifelong interest and passion for "development" of poor people was ignited in this study of the Latin American experience. I barely scratched the surface of what I wanted and needed to know, but I was certain I had found my calling. I soon began to realize I had to know how people persisted to overcome the enormous odds against them. I felt I had to live among them to know their difficulties and their hopes and to learn whether there was a way their lives could improve.

Ever since hearing John Kennedy speak at Stanford, I was inspired by his empathy for people around the world who had much less opportunity than we did in America. It was with enormous admiration and excitement that I heard his call for a new young America to get involved in these struggles of people abroad. Even his choice of words in naming his proposal the Peace Corps seemed unusually insightful of a core purpose. His vision enormously inspired me and thousands of other young college graduates motivated by his call to duty.

As I contemplated this possibility, I received a call from my sister informing me that she and her husband were at wits end in dealing with my mother who was then living with them. Her strange behavior was becoming a strain on their marriage. Without much consideration for the practical implications, I offered to have my mother come to live nearby me and Sheila in Palo Alto. My sister was very relieved. My mother arrived a week later. I found her a new and lovely apartment near ours. I helped her move in and I visited with her every week. But I soon found that she made no effort to establish social contacts or develop any interests. This concerned me and I spoke with her about it. It was to no avail. I decided there was not much more I could do. In any case the pressure of my studies kept my mind at some distance from the problem in the hope that it would somehow resolve itself over time. Backing off and focusing instead on my own immediate life was my way of dealing with the deep personal frustration I felt with unchangeable behavior in my family. It was a personal detachment that I saw as necessary to prevent emotional depletion and deep anxiety. I am far from certain it was the decent thing to do.

My interest in the Peace Corps intensified. The first poster calling for volunteers to join the Peace Corps appeared on campus earlier that year. I instinctively felt this was what I wanted to do.

Sheila and I applied as a married couple. After some screening process (including a rather absurd and humorous knock on the door of our neighbors by FBI agents to find out about our activities and political viewpoints), we were accepted. Sheila graduated from San Jose State College with high marks. I fulfilled my course work and thesis for the masters and completed the program with outstanding grades that I thought reflected more my passion for the subject than anything else. The final degree also required a satisfactory fluency in the Spanish language. While I did not join the Peace Corps for this reason, it was certainly a fortuitous coincident that my commitment to working in a developing country would be the answer to the language proficiency I needed.

In filling out the application form, we indicated a specific interest to go to Peru. It was with considerable surprise that the acceptance letter and enclosed brochures informed us we were going to Peru.

From that point onward, my life transformed, beyond my American upbringing and privileged opportunities, into a new and ever-changing world that challenged, questioned, and inspired me relentlessly.

Chapter 4
Peru

A Village Education
1964 – 1966

Early morning call to
community work

Building the Manzanares
Cooperative Chicken Farm

Celebrating traditional folkloric music and dance at Manzanares' Annual Festival

Everything about the Peace Corps was exciting for those who ventured forth. Never did I imagine why and how it would change my life so profoundly.

Preparations

We learned we would undergo orientation and training at Cornell University in Ithaca, New York. Sheila and I arrived on campus in mid June of 1964. We took up residence in Bebe Hall. We soon found that our fellow volunteers shared many of our ideals. It was a time well spent. Beyond an introduction to the history and anthropology of Peruvian civilization, for which Cornell was famous, we immersed ourselves in an intensive introduction to spoken Spanish. Our Spanish teacher was Spanish. He was impressive in his elegant European manners, quiet reserve, sophistication and knowledge of Latin American culture. His younger assistant was a good looking Cuban whose family had escaped the country and was strongly opposed to Castro's rule. My sympathetic notions of Castro's revolutionary struggle to free his people from dictatorial oppression were clearly not shared by him. It was the first of many encounters I would have with intense Latin American political viewpoints.

Our stay at Cornell had its absurd side. Mostly the psychological testing. Formally known as the Minnesota Multiphasic Personality Inventory (MMPI), the test attempted to probe one's inner psyche through a series of progressively ridiculous questions on what was assumed to be deeply held desires. The ultimate query was to know whether you ever had a wish to have, or had actually had, sex with your mother (or your father as the case may be). Looking back, it is amazing to me that neither I nor any of the volunteers protested any of this. I think we were just too embarrassed to bring it out. We did joke among ourselves about it. Clearly any of us who had slept with our mothers were not going to admit it! We concluded it was the work of some loony set of academic psychologist, pressured by an equally whacky group of government bureaucrats. We supposed their "gotcha" tactics were aimed at catching anyone of us enough off guard to expose our incapacity to cope under stress. Or whatever!

We had some great fun organizing evening skits depicting our versions of what it was like to live in a Peruvian village. My own role was as a local Peruvian journalist covering by live radio broadcast what I enthusiastically announced was an "on the pot" report of the arrival of the first Peace Corps volunteer in the village (I learned later that journalists hardly ever visited villages, and that few villagers had radios).

We were soon flying off to Puerto Rico. It was another well intentioned experiment by a Peace Corps struggling to find itself. A "survival course" in a rainforest no less. The notion presumably was that Peace Corps volunteers had to have nerves of steel (and an ability to leap tall buildings!).

We flew from New York City to San Juan. The next morning we were off in a small plane to the island of Vieques. It was beautiful and strange. The US military leased much of it as a test firing range. Another area was home to an immense US government satellite dish probing outer space. The rest was nothing but beaches and rainforests, and that's where we headed. The Peace Corps had established a remote survival training camp. Our task was to demonstrate our mental and physical abilities to handle anything we might later encounter in Peru.

Rising the first morning early, before heading to breakfast, we had our initial test. The morning light revealed several bamboo outhouses. Our instructor identified the ranking of each in an ascending order of prestige: the "three holer", the "four holer", the "five holer", and the most coveted of all, the almighty "six holer". Upon entering one of these, I found two of my friends already perched there. We were soon joined by two more, and with myself already seated, we seemed to take some pride in having a "full house". We completed our morning rituals in silence, I not entirely sure whether the others shared my disgust, but none of us admitting to anything abnormal to the start of our day.

We soon learned there was a lot more testing to come. There were no set end goals, only a chance to show our "cool under fire". We all felt a certain keen competition to excel and demonstrate our skills whatever the challenge.

Vieques Island had one of the highest hydro electric dams in the Caribbean. We found ourselves walking along the top of the dam, ropes and belts in hand. Our assignment was to "belay" off the dam to the bottom. First of all, none of us knew what that meant. This was all well before the era of the "bungee jump" or the rock climbing culture of today. We assumed it had something to do with using ropes to find our way to the bottom. And that was pretty much it. A crash course at the top got us quickly up to speed on enough (we were assured) simple techniques to complete the task. One by one we lined up to make the fatal jump backwards. It sounded easy enough. But when we got into that 45 degree lean over the edge with nothing but 600 feet of thin air between us and the trickle of water below, it was a soul searching moment. The trick was not just to drop down. Rather it was a matter of jumping out behind you as far as possible, remembering 'to keep those knees bent before you come slamming back into the dam'. OK, again sounded reasonable (if you were good at ignoring fear and probable pain). And that first swing out into space indeed proved very effective in shutting down your breathing and accelerating your heart beat. Bent knees definitely helped. Then shoving out hard again, loosening the rope and lowering yourself, coming back to the concrete some yards below, it was soon starting to feel familiar. It must have taken about ten to fifteen minutes to reach the bottom, but it sure felt a lot longer. There was a clear sense of exhilaration and accomplishment as we all managed to reach our goal. It seemed that we shared an un-murmured "bring it on" as we thought about whatever they planned to throw at us next.

And we were soon facing the next. The camp had a twenty-five meter swimming pool. We learned it was not for our leisure hours. It was uniformly ten feet deep. We were asked to go through a series of endurance tests in the water. The first one required dog paddling in place for several minutes, up to twenty or thirty for those who could do it. Soon after, the instructors pulled out black rubber objects that turned out to be large slices of car tires. Several of these were thrown into the pool sinking quickly to the bottom. Our feet were then tied together with nylon cord. As we lowered ourselves into the water, we were told to swim to the bottom and retrieve a piece of tire. Except for one or two, most of us did not find that very difficult. Then we had the cord removed from our feet and switched to our hands. We went down to the bottom again, this time feet first with a heavy upward movement of the arms and palm-opened hands. We grasped the tire pieces with our feet and brought them to the surface. Most managed to do that one as well. What came next was a bit unexpected. Both our hands and our feet were bound. We were again asked to retrieve the tire pieces whichever way we could. The only possible way was with our teeth. This proved a little testier. It was not only a matter of forcing our bodies headfirst to the bottom with strong dolphin kicks, but also a matter of wrapping our teeth around the edge of the tire. We usually had to first nudge the tire onto its side with a butt of our foreheads. We then went after the exposed edge of the rubber with our teeth, trying not to gag once we had it firmly in our grasp. Bringing it up to the surface was the easy part, mainly as we were so desperately motivated to return to oxygen.

About half of our troop was able to complete this feat. One of my good friends was not. We had done the task in groups of eight, all of us moving to the bottom at the same time. Our three instructors stood at the edge of the pool watching the events unfold. Each time, the water was stirred up and visibility below the surface became difficult. Each instructor focused on only one or two of us at a time. Clearly they were unable to watch all of us all the time. My friend was not comfortable with this particular test, not least because of his mediocre swimming skills and hidden fear of water. So at one point, as I was resurfacing with a mouth full of tire, I instantly recognized utter panic. My friend had somehow managed to position himself head up and vertical at the bottom of the pool, with no tire to show for it. He was flailing but unable to move upward to the surface. His movements became increasingly desperate. His face horribly contorted. Within the few seconds that I viewed all of this, I felt he was giving up. I saw his motions slow. His body began to relax in a seeming acceptance of his fate. I sensed it was a matter of life. In my own state of panic I burst through the surface, spat out the tire and yelled to the top of my lungs—'man down!'. At first the instructors seemed not to grasp what I was uttering. Another precious few seconds went by. Finally their eyes darted across the pool bottom and connected with the pending catastrophe. All three dove at once to the rescue and brought his semi-unconscious body to the surface. Immediate respiratory resuscitation applied, my friend coughed up a couple of cups of water. Traumatized, but out of danger. Our instructors sheepishly assured us this was the first such incident. The entire episode was the talk of the camp that evening. We agreed we needed to keep an eye out for each other.

The water tests were not over. Those of us who had passed all the tests up to that point again had our feet and hands tied. We were asked to swim the entire length of the pool like that—under water. After a quick furtive glance at one another, we undertook the feat, one by one. I was the last to attempt it. To my surprise, and with rather unabashed and shameful pride, I found myself the only one to complete the task. In all honesty, I began to like this stuff. I figured it must have been rooted in my love of sport and drive to win. The other volunteers noticed the change in my confidence though they did not say so. They congratulated me on my achievements and welcomed the emerging leadership I was starting to assert. It was a good feeling.

We then moved on to the final challenge. In a rain forest, the moisture of night gathers on the underside of the forest canopy and falls like rain the next morning. Our new task was to survive in that forest on our own for a night. This did not seem such a daunting task. But we were doing it in the pre-outward bound and survival TV environment. We had little notion of what to expect. Our group had mixed reactions. We were all up to challenges, that's why we joined the Peace Corps, but some who were comfortable with one physical challenge were much less so with another. Most of us saw it as nothing more than a scouting overnight. I was among those. I held little trepidation for what was to come.

We were allowed to take a few items with us: a tarp, some cord, a flash light, a knife, and a compass. A few of us snuck in a small paperback book to break the monotony of what we were sure would be a long, boring night. We all marched together for a couple of hours, entering deeper and deeper into the tropical foliage. Led into new and ever more confusing directions, at certain points our instructors dropped us off, one by one. As the light began to wane, we each alone set up our 'camp' for the night. We searched for any edible food (we had been instructed what to look for), pitched our sleeping arrangements, and set about getting a good night's rest. In the morning we were expected to find our way back to the main camp. Tricky, but not something we couldn't handle, what with compass and all.

I felt pretty cool and collected about the whole thing. I had camped in forests (admittedly drier than this one) many times (though never entirely on my own). So, what's the big deal? After nearly an hour, I came across a small clearing in the forest. I spread the tarp out on the ground, and began searching around for a snack. That was not as easy as I expected. All the edible items we had learned about didn't have any recognizable relatives in this forest. Not even a mushroom or a forest berry. I gave up after some time, confident in my ability to forego a meal for one night.

I gathered some leaves under my tarp, bunched them into a low pile, covered them with the thin nylon jacket I had brought along, and prided myself in my pillow for the night. Darkness fell and I pulled out my flashlight. After a few minutes of doing nothing, I remembered the paperback and started to read (a racy detective novel I recall). I felt very self-assured. I thought about the return trip in the morning and how I would make good use of the compass, my instincts, and get back to camp first!

As I was about to finish a chapter and turn off the flashlight, I thought I saw a slight movement from the corner of my eye. I waited a few instants. Noticing nothing further, I proceeded to finish my chapter. Again the motion. This time a bit more pronounced. It was somewhere in my peripheral vision on the ground and it seemed to be advancing in my direction. Slowly I turned my head toward the motion. At first my vision was unfocused and blurred. Gradually as clarity returned I saw what my inner senses told me all along. On a pile of forest debris stood a gigantic spider. It was no exaggeration. It was big by any standard. I did not like spiders and I had never seen one this big. It was larger than a tarantula, though it was sleek and streamlined rather than hairy. What defined it most were its legs. They were at least six inches long though a good foot long seemed no exaggeration to my then current state of mind. More impressive was their shape and consistency. Each leg looked like a wooden branch, and had three or four segments, each hinged to the next by some sort of joint pin. The movement was mechanical and smooth. And definitely the movement was in my direction.

Without taking my frozen eyes off the monster, I began to slowly turn and position my body to face its advance. Almost without knowing, I leapt to my feet. The spider stopped in its tracks. For a few seconds we stared eye to eye. Then without warning it sprang. Crawling was clearly not its motion of choice under such circumstances. To my uttermost relief, the spring was in the opposite direction, into the nearest foliage. With two more springs it was absorbed by the pitch blackness beyond the gaze of my light. I stood there for a full two minutes or more doing nothing but watching intently for any follow up sign of its presence. Nothing appeared.

I have never had the slightest fear of snakes. In fact, while at Stanford, I kept a pet snake in my room and fed it a white mouse every week. I managed to convince the biology lab assistant to smuggle those out for me. But spiders were a different matter. As far as I can figure, it all goes back to my childhood in Pennsylvania. Those times when I went on my own into the forest behind our house. I remember uncovering logs and rocks. Almost always some kind of crawling creature would emerge, usually at a rather rapid pace and always in my direction. Those things scared me from that time onward. I remember standing alone outside the porch doorway of that same house surrounded by a swarm of bees. They were relentless in circling me for their own purposes in spite of the yells that my mother obviously could not hear. I also remember the time a cockroach crawled unnoticed onto my sock feet. Its presence paralyzed my whole body until my Dad came rushing in response to my screams from the next room. Insects have never been my thing.

So there I was, the hero (in my own mind) of the great outdoors (jungle or not), not having any idea what I could or should do next. One thing I was certain about, I was not going to sleep on the same level as that creature, knowing it still lurked somewhere out there. After a few minutes of contemplation, I came to the conclusion that the only salvation was to get myself up off the ground. I had my tarp and a large spool of cord. I determined myself to fashion a hammock. It took me more than an hour to weave the cord. When it was ready, I used a slip knot to fasten it to each of the four corners of the tarp. I then fastened the other end of the cords to each of two trees spread about 6 feet apart. I lifted myself carefully into the suspended tarp. I marveled at my success. I lay there staring at the stars. It must have been thirty minutes later in a half doze that I heard the snap of the cord. I braced myself for the hard landing that followed. I got up quickly, knowing I was defeated. There was no way I was going to start weaving again. There simply was no guarantee it would prove any stronger than the last time. I certainly was not going to return to the ground level position. I also knew I could not find safety among the tree tops. These trees were very slim and tall. Their branches stretched out thirty or forty feet above the ground. There was no way I could get up there.

I spent the rest of the night standing. I leaned up against one of the thicker trees to lessen the burden of the night as best I could. As dawn broke, and the nearby foliage began to resume a less eerie appearance, I wasted no time in packing my few items. I headed off. In fact, I had no idea where I was. I kept glancing at my compass to make sure I was moving in a generally southern direction (where I recalled our camp was located). But everything continued to look the same. I walked what seemed like several hours but was probably not more twenty minutes. Out of nowhere one of the instructors appeared, accompanied by two of my companions he had already picked up from another nearby location. We continued to rustle up the others along the route. I later understood we had been dropped off in a circular pattern so that none of us could have been far from the others.

Out of an initial 120 volunteers who entered the program at Cornell, and after our experiences in outdoor endurance in Puerto Rico, just less than one hundred remained standing in late August 1964. Those who did not make it were mostly self-eliminating; apparently having decided this kind of adventure was not for them. Those of us who remained were no less the wear, but neither were we any clearer what we had done to qualify ourselves to live in a Peruvian village.

Without a pause, we were off on a flight to Peru.

First Impressions

Lima was massive, amazingly sophisticated and European. It breached our North American stereotypes. We had another few days of local orientation, but our time was spent mostly with eyes and mouths wide open to all we were taking in. "Pisco Sours" sipped in the splendor of the Hotel Bolivar lobby got us off to a good start.

Other introductions were closer to the reality we were entering. We met volunteers already in the country who took us to their work sites in outlying slums. It was a powerful introduction. These slums were enormous. They made lasting impressions of rutted dirt pathways, overflowing sewers, children in rags, and one-room shacks housing ten or more until the next fire vaporized them and the struggle would begin again. The smell was heavy. Some kind of sulfuric acid appeared to be spewing from a nearby factory. Volunteers worked in schools teaching English, others organized cleanup campaigns, and a few worked in a local health clinic. Admirable, but it was difficult to see what mark they could hope to make in such a sea of poverty.

About twelve of our own volunteer group, Sheila and me included, were soon off by train to Huancayo some 130 miles directly east of Lima at over 11,000 feet in the altiplano (high mountains) of central Peru. Its Montaro Valley would be our home for the next two years. The train ride was another good introduction for us, this time to the incredible diversity of Peruvian topography and lifestyles. We first passed through semi-desert agricultural lands where rich landlords owned huge tracts that produced crops for city markets. We soon ascended rapidly into the Andes. The aridity and bare slopes of the mountains were stunning. Not a single tree to be seen. As we went higher, life became more desolate. We reached the mining town of Cerro de Pasco. Desolation here took on tones of gray mining machinery and heaps of extracted materials. Bleak was a better description. Miners and their families moved about barefoot and steeped in poverty. The only sign of modernity was a cluster of well-groomed housing high on the hillside overlooking the mines. The foreign mangers resided there. We would one day return to spend a day with a couple and their small child. When we did, six months later, we found the home comfortable and even pleasant, but the manager seemed overly anxious to impress us with his position and status. His wife and the young daughter were noticeably subdued. I sensed they were both unhappy. I wondered how poverty and wealth and power seemed to mix so easily in that environment and create unhappiness on both sides. I thought for a long time how sad that was. I wondered whether my work would ever have any relevance and chance of answering such enigmas at least on the poverty side.

We arrived in Huancayo late in the afternoon. To our surprise we lodged in the Hotel Tourismo. A handsome colonial hotel, it provided considerable unexpected luxury. We refreshed ourselves in the well appointed dining room. But before finishing the meal a pounding and splitting headache began to throb in my head. Relaxing in the hotel lounge and later my room did not reduce my agony. It was altitude sickness. Though considered a mild form, the headache exceeded all stories I had heard and lasted throughout the night. As dawn broke, the headache suddenly slipped away. I never experienced it again.

The Peace Corps regional coordinator for our region was known as Tex. He was a tall and unassuming fellow. He knew a lot about our area and was quite clear why the Peace Corps was there. Over breakfast he shared with us his simple vision of what we should be doing—getting people to do things for themselves that would make a better life for them. It would not be our technical or professional skills (assuming we had any) that would benefit the people. It would be our ability to organize people around their own ideas of what needed to be done. It should be a process of their own making, something that bore results they valued. It was in effect the concept of "community development". That was what the Peace Corps was all about in those early days. Years later the Peace Corps would evolve more toward technical skill building. We all thought that was a mistake. Our role as community facilitators was precisely what was needed most. Peoples' innate and traditional capacities would provide most of the rest.

With those thoughts in our head, we all jumped into a couple of 4-wheel vehicles that Tex had waiting for us. Soon we were on very muddied and difficult roads that headed out of Huancayo and stretched along the flat and pastoral expanse of the valley. Our first stop was an hour out. We exited our vehicles and walked to the top of a hill. We could see the entire northern end of the valley. Tex began to explain what was where. We easily spotted every small town and village he described to us. We were the first Peace Corps volunteers in the Montaro Valley and would have to create our own way of working. Tex had done a lot of leg work already, visiting and meeting with the local leaders. He began singling out for each of us the town or village where we would be assigned. Seeing our new homes in the distance filled us with excitement.

Our good friends, Bill and Teddy Evenson, would be going to the small town of Sicaya. It was on the main road down the valley. Tex turned to us and pointed out a more distant community, a village called Manzanares. We would live among its 300 families for the next two years.

The Village

After dropping off the Evensons, Tex doubled back and took us over ever-worsening roads for another hour to reach the village plaza. The night before, I had shared with Tex in a private aside that we wanted to work in a place of real need in a remote location. I was genuinely motivated (undoubtedly demonstrating some bravado as well) to spend my volunteer days closest to what I imagined was the main reason we were there—to work with very poor people who had no other opportunity to improve their lives. Tex apparently settled on this village as something that would be challenging enough, leaving even more remote areas to our single volunteer colleagues. As time went on and our inner resources were tested, I appreciated his judgment on this.

We were greeted by a small village committee headed by the village mayor. We then marched together to a smaller side plaza with lovely pine trees. In front stood a double storied mud building. It was the town hall. The village leaders decided that a corner section on the second floor would provide a good home for us. It wasn't yet ready though, so we took up temporary residence in a small room on the ground floor. We assembled the wood framed beds we purchased in Huancayo and had a good first night's sleep.

We woke to the sounds of shouted slogans. We dressed quickly and went outside. A parade of about fifty people was entering the pine-lined park in front of us. They carried banners in Spanish which didn't make sense to us. They seemed to be protesting something. It suddenly entered our heads that maybe that something was us.

Sheila and I looked nervously at each other, not quite sure what to do. I decided that we had to say something. So I made my first extemporaneous speech in broken Spanish. I thought it best to thank them for welcoming us (just in case there was the slightest chance that is what they were there to do). I expressed how much we looked forward to living with them. But somewhere in the middle of my speech I noticed the youngsters chuckling while the elders looked perplexed. I tried to ignore it all while I finished up my speech. But I knew something was wrong. It was only weeks later that I learned the folly of my ways. Apparently in my anxiety to assure the gathering of our friendship, I had told them I was especially happy to be there with my new husband! The difference between *esposo* (husband) and *esposa* (wife) had obviously not yet made a sufficient impression on me. Anyway, the village amusement at my expense was probably a good start.

The procession that confronted us that day was neither a protest nor a greeting. It had nothing to do with us (most villagers had no idea yet who we were). It was rather a show of support for a local teacher who had been fired from the school. It was clearly a self-centered and comical introduction to the community that we had created in our own imaginations. Fortunately, jumping to incorrect conclusions such as this one, tended to diminish over time as our Spanish skills picked up.

Learning Spanish was of course crucial to our life and aspirations in Manzanares. We knew we had to bring those skills up to working level in the quickest time possible. We soon discovered that the children were the best instructors. Those kids (mostly from four to twelve years old) were fascinated by our presence. They were constantly gathering at our door from early morning to watch and talk with us. We ended up talking with them throughout the day as we went about our business. The big advantage was that they either ignored our mistakes (making us much less self-conscious) or more often corrected those mistakes in an unintentional and completely natural tutorial give and take. Our Spanish fluency improved markedly as a result. We never reached professional proficiency, but we sure knew how to communicate with villagers.

Sheila turned her early rapport with the kids into her work for the next two years. All families in the village rose early, usually around 5:00 am. The women rose even earlier to light the fires and prepare the morning meal. The older children took care of the younger ones and got them dressed and groomed quickly. Breakfast consisted of boiled corn porridge. Once downed, the older children headed off to school. Any child under three years was wrapped onto their mother's back for the long walk to the fields. Those between four and five years would walk alongside their mothers. Once there, the mother would release the youngest. They would play in the dirt as best they could under the watchful eyes of the next older up.

Sheila observed all of this in our early days in the village. She talked with the mothers who responded enthusiastically to the idea of a child care and pre-school program. Everyone was very happy with this and more and more left their small children behind in Sheila's care. Sheila developed a regular routine. She rotated the kids' activities through the morning between play, games and simple learning of alphabet and numbers. There were also a few snacks which the parents helped to contribute. It was an instant success and gained Sheila a lot of respect and standing in the village.

I wasn't so sure what I wanted to do. While pondering that, Sheila and I got busy working with the head master of the local secondary school. Surprisingly for such a remote community, Manzanares had its own high school, but no primary school. Dr. Victor Justo was the enthusiastic principal. He heard about our arrival and took initiative to invite us to their small campus on the outskirts of the village. Manzanares was a village of *mestijo* people, a mixed breed of indigenous peoples who had intermarried with Spanish descendants. Physically they were more akin to their indigenous side including their diminutive size (men were seldom over five feet tall). The teachers were also *mestijos*, but clearly a little higher on the Spanish blood line and more physically robust. They would come every school day by bus from Huancayo. Dr. Justo (who was responsible for two other schools in the valley) would join once or twice a week. The instruction was basic, and as in most countries of Latin America, the main learning technique was rote memory. There was very little opportunity for either creative expression (except in the very colorful dances during school festivals) or practical vocation.

Dr. Justo and I discussed these inadequacies of the school curriculum. He pointed out that many youth had dropped out of school due mostly to pressing family economic needs. We came to a preliminary conclusion that skill training was a critical need in the village, especially for the young adults. People from *Manzanares* did not migrate to towns or cities but remained at home to help and eventually take over the small (no more than one hectare) family farms. We consulted the village leaders, and they were positive to the idea of a night school. The first challenge was to find skilled teachers in such a remote location. Fortunately, some of the teachers in the high school had some sort of trade or domestic skill. They were "motivated" by Dr. Justo to volunteer their time. They did it with genuine dedication.

The community leaders identified community tradesmen willing (no one was paid) to share their time and skills. We used the school classrooms for the new courses. The schedule was set at 7:00 to 9:00 pm every Wednesday. We organized six courses: carpentry, animal husbandry, horticulture, cooking, sewing, and family life. The village instructors proved to be very talented and professional in imparting skills. They all became my closest friends.

The night school sparked a tremendous response from the community. All age groups attended. Young kids from the next village over who could not get that kind of practical training in their regular classes joined. A few older villagers who wanted to pick up a useful at-home occupation to bring in a little extra income were among the most active.

The "Family Life" class was put together at the request of the village men. Dr. Justo decided to teach it himself. But he was unsure what the men wanted him to teach. For the first couple of classes he just rambled on about family responsibilities and the importance of educating the young. When he noticed the men were not showing much interest, he asked them what they would like to learn. Without hesitation the response came: Sex! The men were very keen to know what sex was all about other than for making babies. They were especially curious about sex practices. They wanted to know what was right and what was wrong.

Dr. Justo was a devout Catholic. His answers were meant to be helpful, but they tended to perpetuate the notion of sex solely as a means of procreation. The men were not satisfied. They became bolder and pushed him to reveal some of his own sexual experiences. They wanted to know about masturbation. Was that ok? Dr. Justo bravely shared his frequent urges and tests of will power. He confided this was often brought on by the feel of the soft white sheet rubbing across his body in the middle of the night. The men took it all in wide-eyed.

I am not sure what they gained from all of this. I can image it served to break down certain traditional taboos, for better or worse. I did notice it created a new relationship between Dr. Justo and the village men. They seemed more open and trusting and relaxed, though they always showed respect for the class difference that could not be eliminated.

I wondered about the women's side of these issues. How much were they hearing from their husbands? What would they have liked to hear about on their own? Unfortunately the cultural setting at that time made it impossible to discuss the matter. I was to learn later that the men continued to talk quite a lot among themselves about the subject. I found out first hand (more on that later) what a great source of jokes it became during village drinking bouts. In fact, I considered this "loosening up" of male inhibitions (or was I just not understanding how loose they already were?) an important contribution of our night school. In any event, we had a lot of good fun over those two years elaborating on the topic, mostly with drinks in hand.

At the end of the school year, we held a graduation ceremony. Dr. Justo pressed me to order graduation diplomas designed with overlapping flags of Peru and the United States. It also depicted a man and woman in traditional hat and dress and an array of animals and crafts that the students had produced. The diplomas were a big hit. I was later told they hung on the walls of many village homes for years after.

The night school taught me a lot. It demonstrated the deep thirst of poor people for education and skills that could help them in their daily lives. It laid bare the simple powerful force of community people coming together around a common activity that would benefit them all. It demonstrated the long held capacities of poor people. Capacities mastered and passed down through generations and capacities to share those skills with others. It was a deep insight for me into their core potential and commitment to improve their lot if given a chance. It was in "giving them a chance" that the core decency and spirit of helping others revealed itself among all of those involved. It was my earliest understanding that while decency was fundamental and the "door opener" to positive human relations, to be fully meaningful it needed to be matched by practical opportunities to turn it into a benefit to people.

Manzanares was an on-going education for me is so many other ways. I felt an immediate warmth and empathy for the people. I developed a profound admiration for their self-respect. Their determination to get on with their lives whatever the odds if the barest of opportunities arose. Above all, I enjoyed and admired their sense of humor. As I later moved on to other countries, I found such humor a common, cross-cultural and global characteristic of poor people. Undoubtedly it was and remains an essential means of declaring independence and flaunting tremendous odds in the face of unrelenting adversity and injustice.

Sindero Luminoso

Manzanares was poor though not as desperately poor as in other regions of Peru. The Montaro Valley was fertile. Although land holdings were small, people owned their land. It was rarely flooded. People did have to worry about winter frost that could kill their potato or corn crops. But that never seemed to impose a total loss of the harvest. People lived in sparsely furnished mud brick homes that were often bitterly cold at night. But they usually had enough potatoes and corn to eat. The children seemed generally healthy though I suspected high infant mortality that was accepted as their fate.

But although absolute destitution was not to be seen, it was clear that people were poor. While hunger and famine were never evident, it was equally true that the lot of the people had not changed for the better in living memory. The extremes of poverty were greater in neighboring central regions of Peru such as Ayacucho, Huancavelic, Apurimac, and of course in the southern region of Cuzco. We visited these areas during our stay and saw a greater desperation there.

Yet Junin region in which Manzanares and the Huancayo Province were located had sufficient, sometimes significant, poverty to create ample frustration among the people. Eventually it made it possible for a Maoist movement, known as the Shining Path (*Sindero Luminoso*), to bring ideology and violent tactics to this area. None of this was at all evident during my time there. I gave no thought to the matter. In fact, my impression at the time, just starting as I was to travel my own long learning curve and influenced by the Peruvian government propaganda and its campaign of community development (*Dessarrollo de la Communidad*), was one of optimism and expectation of better times. As I followed events twenty and thirty years later, when the leader of the Shining Path, Abimael Guzman, organized a reign of terror that eventually killed 70,000 people across Peru (most of them in the central provinces), I found it hard to believe it was the same peaceful rural countryside I had known. It became the battleground between police and military and the rebel forces throughout this region. What I realized those many years later was that while many of the rural people I had come to befriend in Manzanares did not in fact support this Maoist insurgency, their poverty had created the conditions for it to flourish and to entangle them in the chaos that ensued. I also learned even later that this movement would have a strong influence far beyond the Montaro Valley when the rural-based terrorist tactics of the Shining Path became a model for a similar movement in another country in which we would later live and work—Nepal. In both cases, it was the oppression of poor people by ruling elites that made these movements possible, indeed inevitable.

At Home

But while the seeds of these events had been sown long before we arrived in

Manzanares, they had not flowered during our time there. They would not do so for another 15 years. Our experience was one of living day to day with the people to find some small ways to improve their lives. And during our first few months in Manzanares, we were equally preoccupied with getting settled into our own home.

The rooms on the second floor we were promised kept getting delayed. I decided to take matters into my own hands. I hired a young mason, the nephew of Don Victor who owned the only *tienda* (shop) in town. He was good at his work. Within a week we had the right side of the second floor nicely plastered. The area was divided into two rooms. The first was the entry room where we placed our wood framed and woven straw sofa and chairs. I built a few simple shelves for the 200 books and novels the Peace Corps had provided us. Here we greeted and entertained anyone who would visit. A doorless opening with a hanging curtain led into a second room which was much larger. This was our combined bedroom and kitchen. We had purchased wool blankets in the Huancayo market and stacked three on each of the side by side twin beds. That made for a heavy sleep, but proved essential in the coldest of nights. Otherwise, we used a kerosene heater to warm the room before we turned it off to sleep. It heated the room surprisingly well. The problem was twofold: the kerosene gave off a strong pungent smell that was sometimes intolerable; the second was the difficulty to replenish it. Kerosene was in short supply, cost a lot and was difficult to transport by bus. But we managed. Our cooking was done over a two-burner wicker kerosene stove that also gave off a bad smell. But we really surprised ourselves on the dishes we prepared. We used a portable metal box oven that we placed over the two burners. We baked bread, prepared casseroles, and occasionally even roasted meats. We cooked a lot of red beans and rice. Toward the end of our first year, I started to get serious boils on my legs. I couldn't figure out what was causing it. I was concerned about my own treatment to lance and drain them of puss. I later learned it was due to a nutritional deficiency and I took some additional vitamins which eventually cleared it up.

The biggest challenge of the first three months was our toilet. I knew what had to be done: just dig a ten foot deep hole in the ground, and enclose the sitting area with a wood and corrugated sheet frame. A lot of work, but pretty straightforward. I started on it within two days of our arrival. I began digging with a small shovel I had borrowed from Don Victor. I got a good start and was down two feet within the first two days. But then I ran into trouble. The stones

I encountered were not large. They were small, about an inch in diameter, but they were clustered and massed into a solid pack like a cement foundation. It was like drilling through pavement with your hands. My slow progress was excruciating.

The problem was not the wait. The problem was more immediate. How were we going to go to the bathroom each day? Village life is seldom private, but privacy for basic human functions seemed particularly basic and non-negotiable to us. I mentioned the problem to Don Victor who was sympathetic. He offered use of his latrine in the meantime. This was in the courtyard inside his *tienda*. It was in a corner, very dark, dingy and not well kept. It would mean walking six or seven minutes in the dark of night to get to it. Sheila and I decided this was not an option. There was only one solution. Tin cans. We would squat over one every morning, taking turns to use our bedroom for this purpose. We would carry and dispose of the solid waste in a small shallow hole near the corner wall of our compound—there was no other choice. As for daily urinating, we again used the tin cans. In this case we disposed of it out the window at the back of the town hall onto the sun drenched areas below. Evaporation in the high and dry *altiplano* was a fairly rapid process. Nevertheless, we did manage to burn a large hole in the grass which remained as a reminder for the rest of our time in Manzanares. How much the villagers knew of our stress was never clear. We were grateful for their discretion if they did.

My Friends

The town hall had a custodian, Don Pedro. He lived in a small room on the ground floor below us. We knew from his tattered clothes and meager rations he was very poor. But a gentler and kinder human being you would be hard pressed to find. Don Pedro always greeted us with a warm smile each morning. He inquired about our health, and how we were doing in our work with the rest of the community. At one point, I had fallen ill with serious diarrhea while still working on the latrine. I often struggled with diarrhea throughout my stay in Manzanares. I lost some 40 pounds over the two years. I was too weak to go outside. Don Pedro brought me a simple broth he had made and comforted me with stories of his life before Manzanares. He had grown up in another part of the valley and his parents were extremely poor. He had gone up to grade five in school, but he had to quit to help out his parents. His parents had no land of their own. As a young adult he worked as a day laborer to make ends meet. A friend had informed him of the custodial job in Manzanares. While it paid him very little, it was steady and he had a room for himself. He was not married but had a grand niece on his sister's side who was about eight and use to visit him. He was very proud of her, and would bring her to our room every time she came.

Don Pedro was very conscientious about his responsibilities as custodian. One time the Evensons walked across the hills to visit us unexpectedly. We were in a mood for some fun, perhaps to release some sense of isolation which we occasionally felt. We started jumping off the balcony of the second floor. We were not destroying anything in the process, but Don Pedro came out of his room. He did not wear his usual smile, and while he was not rude or aggressive in any way, he told me in simple straight terms that this was not respectful in the town hall. I and my friend should stop. He conveyed a sense of righteous anger without offending us. I felt instantly chastised and humbled as I knew his sense of propriety had been crossed. He was correct in feeling so. I had betrayed the basic sense of decorum of the village as well as his own sensibilities. I remained deeply embarrassed for some time afterwards. Don Pedro never mentioned the incident again. He never wavered in his friendship and respect (at least I felt so) for me. It was another lesson in my journey of learning. A lesson about the simple but important codes of respecting cultural norms. And a lesson in an immense kindness that crosses cultures to sustain friendship despite transgressions. It was all taught to me by a very poor dignified and decent man.

I had begun to make close acquaintance with a few of the village men. I initially met them as they would come to Don Victor's *tienda* for supplies or just to meet and talk during the early evening hours. Don Jose lived in the house adjacent to the *tienda*. He was a splendid man. A bit rotund, but strong and firm. Like most men in the village (and in Peru) he wore a mustache, and it seemed to highlight a broad smile he would always have ready for me. He wore the same light brown brimmed hat down close to his eyes. In my mind he could easily have been a central character in a Latin novel about a steady head of family who remained unphased and uncorrupted by the adversities surrounding him. He had four small children. He was extremely proud of them and they clearly loved him very much. Without showing it, I also fell in love with those kids, as rambunctious and full of life as they were. Don Jose always had an upbeat notion of what was possible. I saw him as a natural leader for getting something done in the village.

Another acquaintance was Don Alfredo. I met him at the school where he was the carpentry instructor for our night classes. Don Alfredo was exceedingly skillful at his trade. One day I came back on the bus from Huancayo with several poles of 2" x 4" lumber and a few sheets of ply board, all for the purpose of making a tall cabinet with shelves and cupboards for our kitchen. I was about to start the carpentry work with my inadequate knowledge of what was required when I ran into Don Alfredo. I shared with him what I was up to. He immediately offered to give me a hand and we agreed to meet at my house the next afternoon. Don Alfredo asked to see a drawing of what I wanted to build. He found my rough sketch sufficient. When I explained how I planned to go about cutting and joining the wood, he listened quietly and began to make some suggestions. With each suggestion, he showed me how it would be done. Pretty soon he had me doing some credible village carpentry, giving me his assistance over the next 3 days. In the end, we built a handsome cabinet which I painted a light green to match the other furnishings in our home. What impressed me most was how Don Alfredo did all of this with severely arthritic hands. Each hand was gnarled by huge bulges at every joint. He would sometimes reveal a small sign of pain as he planed a board or sawed a timber. The quality of his work suffered nothing from this disability. He never complained. He just kept the problem to himself.

Don Ricardo was another villager who lived further up the hill from all of us. He was an extraordinarily handsome man with angular and symmetric features profiling his face. He walked very tall and with natural dignity. He was better off than most in the village, clearly a result of a well organized and disciplined life. He did his share of family farming, but he had some other business outside the village. I never found out what it was. I suspect most others in the village never did either. He was a prime candidate, as far as I was concerned, for membership in any enterprise we might later undertake. But I always found him skeptical of communal work and reluctant to join. Still, we seemed to grow in our admiration for each other (certainly me for him). Not least was my fascination and respect for the way he raised his sons. They were twins. I guessed they were somewhere between thirteen and fifteen years old. What was so remarkable was how much they looked like him and carried his dignified bearing as they strolled down the village road behind him. They were extremely polite, clearly proud of their heritage. They displayed a quiet confidence about any purpose they seemed to be pursuing. I began to see in them the enormous latent talent of so many villagers that I would observe throughout my life. I thought this true especially of the young who were so full of energy and capable to do whatever they wished if given an opportunity.

The Project

I was going through a lot of self-reflection. I tried to imagine what might make a good project I could help to organize in the village. I really had no clue what was realistic nor whether the villagers were genuinely interested. Nevertheless, I decided it was time to plunge ahead. I called together a group of about a dozen acquaintances, simply to discuss whether and what we might want to do together. We met in Don Victor's courtyard one evening. I shared with them what I had been seeing in the village. They did a lot of hard work in their fields, but the harvests were small, and not much was left over to sell in the market. I asked them if there was anything we could do through some sort of cooperative effort to earn money. They told me of their own ideas, and even a few prior attempts to do something like that within their families. But they also pointed out the difficulties to start up any small business without some loan to finance it. Loans were available from village middle men, but they charged a lot for it, and no one could afford that. Also, there were difficulties getting products to market as these were located quite some distance from Manzanares.

As we talked we began to consider what might be possible if we worked together on it. Several ideas emerged, including some joint farming of a cash crop. But we agreed there was no land for doing this. We started to focus on animals. Could we raise any for sale and make some money. We had a couple more night meetings to explore things further. We soon settled on the idea of raising chickens, not for eggs, but to sell for others to manage. We knew there was a good market for young chickens if raised safely through the most dangerous period. That was the first 30 days when they normally died from the cold or disease in high numbers. We agreed that's what we should do—not that it was a risk free venture. We convinced ourselves we could mange.

I came away from these meetings elated. In my first attempt to get some kind of community development started, something was beginning to gel. It was now a matter of getting everybody to put up some money to buy the chicks and to commit time to raise them. I suggested before our last meeting broke up that we meet again in a week to set out how we would work together.

I arrived early at our agreed meeting place, this time Don Jose's house. Don

Jose was his usual optimistic self. As we waited for the others, he began to share where we should get the chicks and how we would incubate them. The time passed. After nearly an hour Don Afredo and Don Victor joined us. The four of us continued to mull over how we should proceed. I grew anxious wondering what happened to the rest of our group. When I broached the subject, Don Jose became very animated. Evidently he had been quietly brooding as well, and he vented his anger. 'You can't trust anybody in this village when it comes to money, and they won't trust you,' he continued, and 'No one wants to put up the money first, until they are sure it won't be stolen or they won't be cheated in some way.' That is why 'you can never work with others outside your family to get anything done'. Everyone would tell you they were ready to join in, but as I could see for myself, they really were not. My spirits dropped dramatically. Having discussed the project in some detail and knowing the risks, why did they say they would do something and then not do it? But Don Jose kept insisting 'that's how people are in our village and you better know that now rather than later when it's too late.' We agreed to make contact with the missing members of our group the next day and to keep in touch about any future meeting. We disbanded about 10:00 pm. I returned to my residence feeling completely defeated.

The next evening I returned to Don Jose's house. I asked him what we should do. He had revived his normal good spirits and expressed willingness to go with me to the homes of each of the members. We began to make the rounds the next day. We heard a common litany, just what Don Jose had told me. Everybody had too little money and could not afford to trust it to others. Don Jose then tried to motivate them with a different line. We were doing this with "Senor Mike", it's different and we should put our past experiences behind us. No one seemed convinced (and I was the last to want them to agree on that basis). But they began to soften a bit when we told them it would not cost each member very much. We had worked out some details and found that we could get help for free from the government. I had met with the agricultural extension officer for the area some two weeks prior to our meeting. He offered to try to get us some materials at no cost. I said that I would re-approach him and see what he could do. Everyone thought this was a reasonable idea.

The next morning three of us took the bus to Huancayo to talk to the extension officer. He was out in the field, but was expected back by noon. We waited. He arrived about 1:00 pm. We explained our situation. We were enthusiastic about the prospects for raising baby chicks, but we lacked equipment and had very little money. He responded generously. It would be no problem for him to loan the necessary brooding equipment to us (a small kerosene stove and a large conical tin cover, enough for 500 chicks). He also would arrange to purchase day old chicks from the government hatchery at a lower price. We were delighted. We agreed that unless he heard from us again he should proceed with all of this and deliver the chicks a week later. We returned to Manzanares with the good news. We gathered our group spontaneously that very evening. All agreed to put up the modest sum required under these arrangements. Don Victor would take in everyone's contribution to keep in his safe at the *tienda*.

Don Alfredo had a small room he used to store his harvest. He offered to let us use it for brooding the chicks. The extension agent assured us the kerosene stove would keep the brood warm and safe each night. But we were not going to take any chances. We came up with a backup plan. We would set up a night watch, each of us signing up to 'sleep with the chicks' once every ten days. It was a good thing we did. The extension agent brought the brooding equipment two days before he delivered the day old chicks. We made everything ready for them. When the chicks arrived, we took turns each night on the sawdust floor suspended between half-sleep and high alert. The first night went by smoothly. The next night was more problematic. Don Pedro was on watch and had to relight the stove three times. As we went through the next twenty-eight days, we found the stove was reliable 90% of the time but could not be relied on entirely. We were glad and proud of our decision to set up the watch.

We had bought a total of 200 chicks (our agreed contributions would not allow us to purchase the full 500 the extension officer had offered). Because of our own due diligence, we lost only eight chicks during the month. That was considerably less than the usual 15% attrition the extension officer had predicted. We packaged the chicks in ten cardboard boxes and carried these to the early morning bus waiting in the next village. It was a bumpy two hour ride to the market town. We had brought some posters, a kind of advertising strategy (my idea!) that we would apply once we reached our destination. One of our group members was a local artist. He drew colorful images and short sharp messages about the technically advanced, high quality chickens of the Manzanares Cooperative. The signs collected an instant crowd. The response was in fact remarkable. The quick glance of experienced farmers who inspected our chickens was enough to confirm the healthy state of our brood. We sold out the entire batch in less than an hour.

The ride back to Manzanares was memorable. We sang the entire way despite the puzzled looks of other passengers. Our morale was higher than ever. We sat up much of the night talking about our success. I felt very proud, including the role I had played to facilitate our coming together for this purpose. But I felt that the real message was not about the importance of organizing people, as evident as that was. The real triumph was in poor people seizing opportunities if given a chance. The latent power of the poor to better their own situation was just below the surface. However temporary and tenuous that achievement might be, it was possible. It was truly a landmark day for me in all my time in Manzanares. I did not try to anticipate what lay ahead, but delighted in that moment of sheer accomplishment.

La Vaca

Just about this same time, Manzanares celebrated its annual festival. Each and every village in the valley proudly held one on their chosen day. The Manzanares festival lasted two days. The first day involved the planting of a strong, tall tree in the center of the main plaza. In the late afternoon, the local orchestra entered and played while circling the tree. Each band member dressed in traditional black pantaloon pants and vests. Everything was bordered with multi-colored sashes. A soft wool rainbow hat scooped down to cover each ear. The instruments were traditional and modern. Most prominent was a large harp held up at the waist while in full recital. Several wind instruments, mostly French horns (or something to that effect), and percussion devices, kept up a steady beat. Most important were the hand flutes. These gave the distinctive sound and character of centuries of Andean culture. The music was raw and heavy, sweet and uplifting. It seemed to convey the passion and tribulation of a people who knew a millennium of oppression yet celebrated a pride in who they were. The women danced to it in colorful long skirts, white blouses and black vests under white brimmed black banned hats. The men sported more somber shades of brown and black. They danced as though in a trance, stomping out the rhythms with their feet. Sheila and I joined the frenzy and found the motions and emotions easy to follow. Bobbing up and down, eyes half closed, we felt honored to be there and closer than ever to the people we had come to serve. We began to get a feeling that we may be far more served by them.

The heart of the festival was its second day. Early morning the men of the village began bringing in log poles to fence off the main plaza. In the afternoon, orchestras returned, several this time. The celebration was in full swing when the first bull entered the plaza. It charged quickly, looking for an exit. A young man jumped into the ring and confronted the animal. He barely managed to dodge the horns as the bull continued its frantic search. Then the poles at one corner of the plaza opened and the bull rushed out. A second bull entered. This time an older man entered the ring. He seemed much less steady and sure of himself. The crowd suddenly exclaimed, *'viva el borracho*—long live the town drunk! This time the bull appeared more enraged and determined. He headed straight for the old man. The impact drew an immediate and horrible gasp from the crowd. Almost before he hit the ground, one could see the long gash in the old man's left ear. Blood stained the small arena for the first time. He lay completely still. Several young men jumped in to distract the bull. The boys lifted the old man. He had regained consciousness and was waving feebly with obvious pride to his adoring fans.

Sheila and I had been watching all of this from one side of the plaza. We mixed in with others straining to get the best view. After the first bull exited, I leaned over to Sheila and asked whether I should give it a try. She looked at me in disbelief and assumed I was joking. After I then saw the fate of the old man, I had serious doubts about my impulsiveness. Still, something triggered in my brain. This was my moment. And it would never return. Without a word beyond 'hold this' as I shoved my small camera into Sheila's hand, I leaped over the log barrier on our side and found myself running to the center of the ring. Rather comically, the next bull had not even appeared. Nevertheless, the crowd was stunned and their silence pierced the atmosphere. Just then the gate opened and the bull rushed in. The crowd went wild. A roar of "Senor Mike" filled the air. I had entered the ring with my jacket in hand. I began waving it at the beast assuming that's what I should do. The bull just stood there. He was not as large this time. But the horns seemed even longer (as least they did to me). He started to move around the plaza ignoring my gestures. Suddenly he recognized my presence and turned in my direction. He charged at full speed. I met the animal in the blur of a moment. I felt its body but not its horns. My adrenaline was in full supply. I sensed real danger as I turned to find where he had gone. Suddenly the crowd again began to chant, *'Senor Mike', 'Senor Mike', 'Senor Mike'!* Young boys were in the ring with me. They had already led the bull in a different direction.

The next thing I knew I was lifted on the shoulders of a score of men. The chanting continued as I was taken on a full circle around the ring. My main thoughts were, how did I manage to cheat those horns, and what a great feeling this is! Once outside the arena, I received innumerable *'abrazos'* from every man in sight. The bull fight continued. I was too absorbed in my own "heroism" to remember any of it.

That evening and all through the night, *coca* (the traditional coca leaf that numbs the body) and *aquardiente* (the traditional spirits distilled from potatoes) were passed around endlessly. The talk was mostly of *'Senor Mike'* and what he had done. What a day and night to remember!

Some weeks later, my boss, Tex, paid a surprise visit to Manzanares. I was glad to see him, and immediately asked the village leaders to come to the town hall to greet him. Some days before, I had seen Tex on our weekly visit to Huancayo. I gave him the usual brief report of what was happening in the village. Of course, I mentioned (actually it was the main feature of my account) that I had tried my hand at bull fighting. He was surprised. I could see he was duly impressed (my main intention) as I shared all the details of the bull's charge. Anyway, when the village leaders gathered to meet him (he was well liked by them), Tex expressed his appreciation for the work we were all doing in our chicken cooperative. He then mentioned that I had shared the story of the bull fight. He said he hoped that might go down in the annals of Manzanares's history! As he recounted what he knew, I noticed some of the men glancing at each other. Finally the mayor spoke up in reply, confirming how much they liked "Senor Mike" and how much they appreciated his courage. The men nodded in agreement, each with a broad smile on his face. There was one detail however he thought we should know. Tex asked what it was. Then the bombshell. The mayor explained that by village tradition, a *vaca* was sent into the ring between the main *toros* of the festival. Senor Mike had run into the ring when *la vaca* was scheduled to enter. Senor Mike had fought a cow, not a bull! To the villagers, it was known as a "cowfight", not a "bullfight". Tex looked at me dumb founded. He waited for an explanation. I had none to offer. It was the first time I had heard this. My red face set the men into a round of friendly but unbridled laughter at my expense. Tex added his own little dagger. Taking off his jacket he demonstrated the finesse by which he assumed I must have avoided the cow's horns. I realized my doom (and loss of my hard won reputation) had been sealed, not as a *torero* but as a *vaquero*. I had no choice but to join the laughter. Only later did I realize and appreciate what I had gained.

That the men of the village had expressed their respect and friendship by feeling utterly comfortable in enjoying my humiliation.

Struggling to Begin

Some couple of weeks after the festival season, our small cooperative group met again to plan what we would do next. There was a lot of democratic discourse on how we should proceed. Through some form of genuine consensus building we concluded that constructing and operating a "chicken farm" would be our best next step. But we soon faced the realities of that joint decision. Where was the land for such a farm? Whose land? Purchasing land was expensive, and was not likely available. We settled on "borrowing" some land from Don Guillermo. He was a member in good standing. We did not (want to) question what might be his future intentions about our continued use of his land. After all, what was the alternative!

Then there was the question of whether we should bring others into our cooperative. Generally there was still quite a lot of skepticism and reluctance among the villagers about what we were doing. We reached out to a few others to join, a few more did, and we had some twenty members.

But the most difficult issue, again, was how much cash we would have to put up to build the farm. This was our biggest headache. Although we did not have to pay for the land, the cost of constructing a chicken farm, this time for both meat and eggs, would not be small. Add to this the cost of buying month-old chickens. We figured we needed at least 500, preferably 1,000 chickens to make the business profitable. We needed to purchase are own brooding equipment this time, not to mention cement for the floors of the chicken co-op. It would all together cost a hefty sum. It represented a fund outlay that none of the villagers had previously risked. But without that capital we would get nowhere.

Several months followed, frustrating months for me as I was a natural eager-beaver to get things done. The uncertainty and delay went against my inner grain. The other co-op members were clearly more relaxed about it. They knew in their own local wisdom that either we would find a way or we wouldn't. No amount of pushing would make a difference. Nevertheless, I continued to pressure for the cash. A few loyal members spearheaded our efforts to convince the others. Time lay heavy as it moved slowly with little results.

Routines

Sheila and my life took on a routine. There was daily water to be collected for our cooking and our bathing. I would go every other day to Don Victor's well to collect it in a large metal milk container. It was quite heavy and took me about half an hour to complete what became a bothersome task. I would sometimes get lazy (and selfish), and Sheila would do the chore. Lugging that container was far more difficult for her. I felt ashamed each time she did it. We boiled our drinking water on top of our stove in a huge dark blue and white spotted porcelain tea kettle. At our altitude, it took almost half an hour to bring it to boil, and we had to keep it boiling for another thirty minutes to rid of all microbes. That used up a lot of kerosene. We had to replenish it by regular hauls from Don Victor's *tienda*. Every evening we would light our kerosene primus lamps. We had two, one for each room. They gave off quite a lot of heat, but in the colder season we also lite up our kerosene heaters to keep warm until bedtime. We were up every morning about 6:00 am, washing up. We never had a bath in Manzanares (which probably exacerbated my boil problems). We fixed breakfast around 6:30 am, usually some oatmeal or boiled eggs. Then out we would head around the village. I making visits to our co-op members or hopping over to the secondary school, and Sheila running her pre-school class.

Every Saturday morning we walked half an hour to the next village at the end of the bus line. We would try to catch the 8:00 am bus. By the time we got there at 7:45 am, it was already packed. Villagers loaded on all their goods and wares for selling in the market. That always meant we were sitting next to either a bunch of chickens wrapped in a woman's shawl around her back, or some pig or goat which moved in small circles in whatever tiny aisle space was left. If the bus was completely full, I had no choice but to climb up on the roof where young boys took their seats by choice. The initial thrill of holding on in that elevated position for one and a half hours over deeply rutted roads to Huancayo wore off quickly each time we repeated the journey.

Saturday was market day in Huancayo, and villagers came in from all over the valley, even from some of the more remote mountainous locations. The market stretched under white-tarped stalls for a good two miles down the main street of town. It was colorful. Villagers sold not only their fruits and vegetables, but all their hats, sweaters and crafts. Numerous tourists came up from Lima by the train. They would arrive late morning, shop in the market, spend the night at the Hotel Tourismo, and return Sunday on the noon train back to Lima.

Our main purpose was not to attend the market, rather it was to meet all our Peace Corps colleagues who came in for the one-night weekend stay. Everyone felt a great need for that weekly companionship. Living in the villages was what we were there to do. But no matter how idealistic we felt about our work, we did feel a certain isolation, both physical as well as cultural. Speaking the whole week in Spanish was something we were all rather proud of, but it was always relieving and relaxing to return to free-flowing chatter in our native language.

All volunteers knew the routine of the weekend. We always met up at 10:00 am for breakfast at the same spot, the Restaurante Olimpico. It was a very special place for us. When you entered you looked across a large wide open room with old shiny wood floors and wood tables and chairs. On one side was an open kitchen. All the cooking that took place there before our eyes was done over wood burning stoves. The immediate impression was one of red and yellow flames, heat, and the searing sound of large iron skillets readying the meals above the din of an always crowded and hungry clientele. That clientele consisted of Huancayo's better off (though not rich) residents and inevitably one corner of the room filled with Peace Corps volunteers. The restaurant served great French Fries with two fried eggs which is what we all inevitably ordered.

After breakfast, we each headed out to check in to our favorite local hotel for the night. These hotels were pretty much the same—dark and grimy. The one that Sheila and I settled on had small rooms each with one small window that was sealed in by iron bars giving an impression of the local jail. The floors were smeared with a fresh coat of kerosene applied to make them clean. They reeked from the fumes all through the night. The rooms were cheap, and that's why we kept going back.

Peace Corps volunteers were paid $200 a month in those days, which was actually quite a good sum and more than we needed for our living. But we all wanted to save as much as we could for our travels around Peru. We put up with our hotel standards for that reason.

After the hotel check in, we would usually run around town doing various errands, mostly to buy some provisions to take back to the village, for ourselves or for others. By mid day we were ready to meet up again, and we all returned to the Restaurante Olimpico for lunch. We always had the same great lunch: a large white bean dish the restaurant was famous for, accompanied by rice (or those French fries), and either a small piece of beefsteak or some pan fried chicken. It seemed we were always famished, and everything went down well and fast.

Saturday nights were for fun. We would get together at one of the apartments or small houses of fellow volunteers who were living in Huancayo, or else at Tex's house. There was always plenty to eat with either some common cooking going on or some sort of pot luck collection. And inevitably we had plenty of drinks, either local brews or imported ones that someone had brought up from Lima. There was plenty of music and dance, and a lot of laughter and fun making about our village life. It was a terrific spirit of comradeship, and it really helped each of us keep a positive frame of mind and spirit throughout the two years.

Sheila and I were determined to see as much of Peru as we could while we were there.

Usually accompanied by other volunteers, we were off every chance we had for a few days or a full week. These trips took us to places like Machu Picchu, the ancient center of the Inca empire near Cuzco. That was 1964 when few tourists were visiting the site. We felt we had it almost to ourselves. It was an extraordinary place. It was a marvel to see firsthand the engineering miracles this civilization had performed in constructing their mountain city with massive finely honed stones. We had learned that one particular mountain you could see in the distance from the ancient civic center was accessible by foot an hour's walk from where we were. We decided to go there. Reaching the base, we saw a smaller trail ascending and winding its way up the mountain. We thought it would be marvelous to reach its peak. We began the ascent and found the view more spectacular with each step forward. We also found the trail gradually narrowing. The drop off from its edges was increasingly vertical. My outdoor feats (and reputation) from Puerto Rico had followed me. My companions looked to me to lead the way. This I did for more than half the way up that ribbon trial, until I reached a certain point where it measured no more than a foot in width. At this moment, I experienced a feeling I had never felt before. One of deep fright and near panic. I faced the wall of the mountain rather than peering down the sheer cliff to the jungled gorge below.

My companions saw my sudden change of mood and composure. We all stood there for more than a minute in absolute silence. I then confided that there was no way I could continue. To my surprise, most of them did not share my fright and expressed a determination to carry on to the top. We first had to backtrack to a wider part of the trail so that those behind me (and Sheila who decided to go back with me) could pass around. This they did, and Sheila and I began our descent. We reached our starting point at the base after an hour of careful and measured footing around each bend and decline. Our friends in the meantime continued their climb, reached the top, and returned within a couple of hours. I felt deeply embarrassed. Yet I had no doubt I made the right decision. Everyone was gracious about it. They kept reminding me of my glory days outdoing everyone in my underwater world back in Vieques (I wasn't sure if they saw me as an old soldier who had lost his nerve, or as a one-sport champion, but I wasn't at this stage in a mood to question their complements). It was to be one of many brush ups with fear that I would experience in life, and my judgment and resolve to overcome or find my way around them.

Another trip took Sheila and me to the *selva* of Peru. This is at the edge of the immense Amazonian basin that spreads for thousands of miles through and past Peru into Brazil and a final outlet into the Atlantic of the South American coast.

We traveled by bus from Huancayo to Tingo Maria, the first major town entering the steamy region. Tingo Maria was typical of towns bordering the selva. Streets full of shops of all kinds, low lying cement constructions. What was magnificent was the setting. Bright green peaked hills surrounded the town, thick with jungle overgrowth. The town itself rested along the shores of a powerful muddy river rushing toward the Amazon.

Our first destination was Pucallpa the town that first embraces the Amazon. We spent two nights in a modest hotel, and the days motoring out into the Amazon and along its banks. But the true adventure was flying from there to Iquitos, much further into the Amazon basin and inhabited by the tribal peoples who have resided there for time immemorial. The flight was like nothing we had ever experienced before. A small Falkner aircraft took us and some eight other passengers across a vast and unrelenting green tropical expanse. Our minds wandered wildly as we imagined what would ever happen if our plane went down in that unknown region. We knew that tribal people in fact inhabited these tracts, but we could see no signs of any life beneath the thick vine entangled canopy.

Our arrival in Iquitos was like entering a Rudyard Kipling novel transplanted and set in a new and far more mysterious land than the India of which he wrote. It was not the living accommodation we found waiting for us that caused our excitement, although that was mysteriously splendid in its own right. Owned and managed by a French couple, it was built right along the Amazon, made entirely of bamboo. Each room had a small marvelous porch reaching over the water where the soft evening glow mixed with aviary sounds emanating from deep in the distance. What amazed and excited our souls was the boat trip the next morning further down the Amazon. We stopped at one village after another to meet the local people and see their way of life. Simplicity defined their open rattan and bamboo huts high on stilts, unobstructed in what would have in our minds required neat divisions between cooking, sleeping and relaxing areas. Life was a smooth and even flow for these people, spending their days weaving their simple utensils and geometrically designed clothing, and sharpening their hunting arrows. Children and adults and the old mingled, conversed, and played together without any seeming recognition of distinctions or status. These people were poor by our standards, in some cases extremely so, but they bore a definite dignity that inspired wonder.

It raised in my mind more questions about my work in Manzanares and about my life ambitions. It brought to the surface a word of caution about what I was assuming to do. Peoples' poverty was always an indignity based on a core indecency of those in power, of that I was becoming certain. But I also was coming to understand that beneath such poverty lay a richness of human spirit and capacity. I began to ask myself whether and how it was possible to help people out of their oppression and poverty, and what role and potentials those same people must assume to change their own lives fundamentally. I knew that I had no clear answer to these questions. I felt I would be limited in finding the answers by the biases of my own cultural moorings. But I had ever so slight a premonition that these matters were not as simple as they seemed. That I should not presume to know too much, and that I still had a lot to learn.

Continuing the Struggle

Sometime in the last six months of our sojourn in Manzanares, I and my fellow *cooperativos* came to a decision that we must move ahead in the most practical way possible. This meant, firstly, that we must build our chicken farm using traditional practices of the village rather than contracting a builder and laborers to do it for us. It also meant that we had to trim our goals and begin with a smaller farm and fewer chickens. With these guideposts in place, we came up with a much more modest budget that would require a far less costly contribution from each member. We set ourselves to work immediately on this basis.

Manzanares, like all other villages in the valley, had a long tradition of communal house raising. Practiced for centuries, it was the reason that everyone in the village had their own home. Sometime shortly before dawn, our co-op members gathered in the chill of the morning under thick woolen shawls each holding some local instrument in hand. Led by Don Jose, we began our procession through the village, beating the drums and playing the flutes that signaled our intentions and conveyed our invitation to join a day of communal work. By mid-morning several villagers had joined, usually with some shovel or tool in hand. The practices of this tradition were well known and anticipated. For their readiness to contribute a day's work (or in our case, several days work), the villagers would expect two rewards. The first was already in preparation by the women of the village who had begun preparing a hearty stew-like lunch at the construction site of the would be farm. The second expectation, indeed obligation, was an ample supply of beer and *aquardiente* that would be opened only at the end of the day's work.

Our chicken farm would of course be made of adobe brick which required a simple mix of water, dirt and straw. The straw was brought by the members, and the dirt would come from the foundation site of the farm. That left only the water. And oh yes, where was the water this morning? Normally it was streaming down the small irrigation canal at that hour. But not this morning— of all mornings! I learned of this in total disbelief and with considerable irritation. How could we have failed ourselves in such a ludicrously simple way? I led a charge of a hand full up the mountainside behind the village. I began to lose my vaunted reputation for calm and politeness as I muttered and scolded whoever was listening about how this should never have happened. After some forty-five minutes, we reached a point about half way up the mountain where the irrigation warden had diverted the water as he always did on that day of the week. With shovels in hand and anger spurring me on, we opened up again the flow of water in the direction of Manzanares. We then headed back down the mountain ahead of the flow to clear the debris and ensure the water's rapid arrival at our village.

Meantime the group that accompanied me continued to keep their silence, mimicking my actions to clear the canal, but voicing no commitment as to what we should expect. What I soon learned is that the water did not flow as fast as I had assumed. Its course down the mountainside usually spanned an entire night to reach Manzanares. I realized at that moment that my actions had not saved the day. I was defeated. My return to the construction site empty handed would,

I was certain, mark the end of our communal initiative and probably our cooperative ambitions.

As we rounded the final bend to enter the village, I suddenly realized that the village was out in full force and had already prepared many mud bricks with loads of water to spare. Before I could even think of how this happened, I saw the simplicity of the solution that had taken place during my absence. Half a dozen donkeys rotated in front of Don Victor's *tienda* each carrying two empty vegetable oil cans across their backs. Filled to the brim with water from Don Victor's's well (this was the same source of water I had been using every other day for my drinking water) the canisters carried and emptied at the farm a continuous flow of running water as plentiful and reliable as the stream before it ran dry. The villagers welcomed me back, each bearing the same knowing smile. I would sooner or later learn their ways (and their wisdom). At that point I joined in the work already in progress as all of us mashed and sloshed the earth, water and straw with our bare feet.

This cooperation continued for another four days. Each evening we finished our labor and sat together along the long rising wall of the emerging farm. The women served up stew piping hot with large laddels into metal dishes and joined us for a feast. On alternate days, they prepared a *pachamanca* of roasted *cuyo* (guinea pigs) and potatoes wrapped in leaves placed over hot stones then covered with earth deep beneath the ground.

It was during these nighttime celebrations of our progress that we drank with free abandon the *aquardiente* and beer that followed the meal. We gathered closer together as the night air set in and our conversation grew more animated and full of fun. One such night the village men (the women had by that time returned to their houses) brought back up the taboo subject of the night school—sex. They began to share their understanding of what was right and wrong. That created a considerable amount of hilarity. At a certain point, one of the men turned to me saying that he had a question he had been meaning to ask me for a long time. How was it with white men he wondered, were they the same as them. I wasn't sure what he meant and I asked him to be more specific. He then shared his main curiosity. Do white men have the same size penises as theirs? I was somewhat taken aback by his blunt inquiry even though the question was not out of line with our conversation. I fell silent for a moment, pondering my answer. Then at his further prodding, I responded that no, white men's penises were not the same size as theirs, they were much larger. Everyone fell completely silent, apparently not surprised by my answer, but maybe disappointed in finding out that it was true. Then after a few more moments, the same fellow raised his voice ever so softly, almost in resignation, to pose one more question—how much larger? Again, I was silent for another moment until I had found a clear answer—'*como un caballo!*' (just like a horse!) I replied. The men hung fully suspended for a millisecond before breaking into a huge roar and round of laughter at my absurdity that could only mean that we were all equal (more or less).

In another couple of days our farm was up. With sturdy eucalyptus beams cut to hold the shining corrugated roof, we spread a final layer of mud across the adobe brick to give it all a new and finished look.

Within another couple of months we purchased 500 one-day old chicks (we could not afford our original plans for 1,000 chicks, nor could we afford month old chickens—we had to settle for raising them from day one as we had done before). They were New Hampshire Red chickens bred for egg production. We had partitioned off one room of our building as a brooding area, and after one month, moved the young chickens into the larger open range room with outlets to an outdoor courtyard area. The chickens soon produced plenty of eggs. Our hopes soared that our cooperative would soon become a respectable business enterprise.

From the Heart

It was about this time that our two-year stay in Manzanares was ending. The final month in the village was very strange, an inexplicable experience for me. I became unexpectedly anxious about leaving. On the one hand, I was ready to move on in my life. The isolation of the village was beginning to wear on me. On the other hand, I had made a strong bond with the village people, especially of course with the members of our cooperative. I had doubts even then whether my time in the village had made any difference to the lives of these people. I had doubts whether the way I had gone about my work was the right way. Whether it was based too much on my own drive and determination to get something accomplished (for my own recognition and glory?). I wondered whether I could and should have found ways to get the people to take more initiative and more responsibility. Instead they relied perhaps too much on me to always follow up every detail to make sure things got done.

And yet I also wondered whether they were guided in their interactions with me by a larger wisdom. I wondered whether I was being honest and fair with the people in Manzanares. Surely they knew I was a passing visitor in their lives. I would soon be moving on. They were the ones who would have to live with the consequences of whatever we started. Looking back some years later, I felt amazed to think how much the people were willing to do at my urging without any particularly reassuring reasons to believe it would work.

I began to understand this willingness as a measure of their deep-seated desire to hope their lives could improve. I also contemplated whether and what my presence had done to help them trust each other a bit more. And if so, would it last after I had gone. I certainly wondered whether the pre-school, the night school and the chicken cooperative would continue because they really were important and beneficial; or whether they would fade and be forgotten soon after our departure. I wondered whether their cooperation was more out of a sense of respect for us, or perhaps their unwritten and unspoken code of village values: that having made a commitment to welcome us to their village, they had an obligation to help fulfill our purpose as we seemed to understand it. At the least, I hoped they had seen unexpected possibilities to which they genuinely wanted to commit themselves.

I wondered also whether there was something less tangible that was going on in those two years. Something that grew out of our unforced and voluntary relationships day after day. Something that had no visible results but that had meaning to them and to us.

It was this that most affected my feelings in that last month of our stay. I felt a very deep closeness and attachment to the village. I felt a tremendous admiration for their courage and their endurance and their survival and especially their humor against all the odds. I felt very strongly about the injustice that kept them where they were, with little or no opportunity to improve their lives and those of their children.

One night in the last week of our stay, I woke up in the middle of the night and found myself shaking. I also knew from the sweat that chilled my body that I had just had a terrible dream. It was not something clear and specific but more a sense of helplessness that lingered on after I awoke. My shaking was uncontrollable. I had never experienced that before. It grew steadily worse and more violent. Sheila woke and saw my condition. She had no idea what to do. There was no chance whatever of getting to a doctor or a hospital, cut off as we were. I continued to shake for nearly an hour before it gradually began to subside. Eventually I lay still. We fell back to sleep. The next day we did not speak of what had happened. We seemed to share a sense of some kind of shame. As though we knew what it was and that it best be buried and put behind us. It did not repeat itself ever again over the rest of my life.

That same day the community and the teachers of the school held a farewell ceremony for Sheila and me at the school. There was a large turnout from the community. The words of gratitude were humbling. When it was my turn to speak, I could hardly bring the words to my lips. I expressed profound thanks for the experiences they had given us. I said I would remember and cherish these forever, and for the friendships we had made. I began to cry without a sound or an expression. Tears streamed down my face as I stood in silence. I was embarrassed and sad. Above all I was proud, immensely proud for what these two years had meant to us and to them in all those intangible (and unknowable?) ways.

As the years passed, I lost track of what happened to 'our projects' and to our friends in Manzanares. I became totally self absorbed in the events and excitement of my unfolding life, giving only the most occasional thought to those unusual and miraculous days. As time went on, I began to gradually understand the profound influence those days had on me. I began to probe more deeply what the experience had taught me. I began to realize that whatever may be the answers to the poverty of so many, and whatever may be my minute role in finding those answers, they were likely to emanate as much from the heart as from the mind.

While I did not fully comprehend what I was trying to understand, I began to be more certain that those two years in a Peruvian village had laid a foundation for the rest of my life. A foundation that nurtured all my aspirations and guided all my motives over my entire career from that time onward. A foundation that created within me a moral code and commitment that gave purpose and meaning to my entire life.

Chapter 5
London

Days of Study and Reflection

Back to School

At the beginning of the second year of our stay in Manzanares, I began to reflect on my future and what I wanted to make of it. I had come to appreciate the potential importance of the work I was trying to do (however imperfectly). It was not just my work in Manzanares, but how that kind of work might play out across the rest of my life. I began feeling more and more justified in my decision to build my life around the goals of human development (however vague or pretentious that sounded). I knew for certain that I wanted to continue down this road.

It was in those reflections that I began to ponder the value of further studies in development. I had been exposed to some of the concepts and cases in my masters program at Stanford. I learned a great deal more through my practical experiences in Peru. But I felt there were too many gaps in my formal knowledge. These needed to be filled.

I applied to several graduate schools in the US. These included Princeton's Woodrow Wilson School of International Studies and the John Hopkins School of Advanced International Studies (SAIS). But what intrigued me most was the program at the London School of Economics. It was really not just the program that attracted me (I applied and was accepted to the masters program in the department of international relations). Rather, there were two other very different reasons. The first was that John F. Kennedy had done his graduate studies at LSE. He remained my current day hero in spite of his tragic assassination shortly before I entered the Peace Corps. I felt I would be following his legacy. The second reason was that I felt London and LSE in particular would be a much more globalizing experience compared to a return to a US university.

I spent many Manzanares nights by the light of the primus lantern studying for the GRE examination. My scores were quite respectable. I accepted with jubilation my entrance into LSE even before the other universities had informed me. I was exhilarated with the thought that I could build on my first hand knowledge of what it meant to be poor. I was determined to make certain that a further investigation at LSE into development and poverty would enable me to better understand the causes and hopefully some of the solutions.

Latin Learnings

Before restarting my studies, I was determined to learn all that I could from the life in Latin America beyond Peru. So, at the end of our Peace Corps assignment, Sheila and I made our way home to California by a circuitous route around Latin America. We began in Ecuador (actually traveling there just before departing Peru) where after a visit to the ancient capital of Quito we traveled by train to the port city of Guayaquil. The engineer invited us to sit in the engine room. We were stunned when the engineer refused to stop or even slow down at a certain point on the desolate mountain track as a small open inspector car came into view some 1,000 meters down the tracks. Two peasant railroad workers pumped a seesaw device that edged their tiny car slowly forward. Glancing back at the sound of our on-rushing train, they suddenly realized they were in its direct path. Our engineer refused to slow down. The two railroad workers leapt off the cart just before our locomotive smashed into it with full force. We watched in total disbelief. It spun high into the air of the nearby jungle and disappeared into the thick underbrush. Though we strained to see what happened, the fate of the two workmen remained unclear and forever unknown.

At the train's termination some distance from the port of Guayaquil we boarded a boat for the final leg of the journey. Guayaquil matched its image as a rough and ready place. When I stepped off the boat, I soon found myself surrounded by thugs reaching for my wallet. Foolishly I resisted, was punched soundly and saved only by an unloading bus whose stop I happened to be occupying. Besides the chip off my front tooth, it was nothing but an adventure that I would later enjoy embellishing.

We than began our circuit of Latin American countries with a first stop in Chile. Besides enjoying the splendors of the capital, Santiago, and the coastal resort of Vina del Mar, we soon realized that our initial impressions of Chile were much too positive. The realities underlying our superficial exposure to the country revealed long standing social economic tensions and divides. Chile had been dominated since its inception by landed elites. Despite frequent shifts in political power between conservatives and reformers, the fundamental grip and control by the elite was never in doubt. During our visit, a period of optimism imbued the country with the presidency of reform-minded Eduardo Frei. He introduced many social and agrarian reforms but these remained tenuous due to the opposition from both those who felt he had gone too far and those who felt he had not done enough. The country later transitioned through a much more radical period of "Marxist" reforms under Salvador Allende. He nationalized mining and industry and supported significant land reform for poor farmers against the interests of the landed elite and even the United States. A right wing coup headed by the Army Commander, Augusto Pinochet, supported by the US (CIA), resulted in seventeen years of tight-gripped authoritarian rule that witnessed horrendous human rights violations side by side with free market reforms. As I looked back over this history (long after our visit), Chile seemed a classic example of a deep socio-economic divide that continued to rupture the fabric of its society. Only in the 1990s and 2000s did it seem to turn toward a positive model of democracy based on a willingness of a coalition of parties (known as the *Concertation Coalition*) to seriously address the conditions that kept it divided and in turmoil for so long. It seemed to me to provide an interesting and still too rare example of what may be possible when political leaders and people join to address the disparities that have defined and disrupted their relationship for so long.

Flying high over the Andes, we next landed in Buenos Aires. The broad Parisian boulevards and European way of life completely rattled and delighted our still innocent American assumptions of this ever surprising continent. We ate *charisco* style steaks grilled on open charcoals. We even attempted the tango in a blessedly dark and obscure salon popular with locals who knew what they were doing. All of this we enjoyed within our profound state of ignorance about the long tumultuous history of Argentina. A history that swung between oppressive military dictatorships and strong leftist movements of workers and students. These swings eventually brought Juan Peron to power over a decade (mid 1940s to mid 1950s), followed by right wing military coups. Then an eventual return to power of Peron and his wife, followed in the mid 70s by the darkest period known as the "Dirty War" in which allegedly some 30,000 "disappeared" lost their lives at the hands of the military dictators. It was a history and a country that personified for me an enormous gap between rich and poor, and all of the bitter injustices and atrocities that such a gap most often breeds.

In Rio de Janeiro, Brazil, we experienced the stark contrasts between the high life of Copacabana and Ipanema beaches and the innumerable "favelas" or slums that covered most hillsides of the metropolis. These were filled with the poor and less fortunate. They suffered the daily threats and humiliations of crime, police corruption and high unemployment. They were the "other Rio" that lived on the lowest rung of a divided nation in which a rural–urban divide was even more pronounced especially among those living in the northeast region of the country.

We moved on to Caracas, Venezuela, Panama City, and Teculcicalpa, Honduras. In all of these, people lived sharply divided between rich and poor. In the case of Teculcicalpa which I revisited some few years later on a UN mission, even the quaint red tiled roofs and quiet streets of the city had transformed into an overcrowded and congested urban center reflecting the deep poverty that had migrated to it.

As we traveled across these lands, our eyes constantly searched these broader contexts of each country to understand the rapidly changing environment. And what we found in all cases was this same pronounced and growing divide between the very rich and the very poor. We witnessed the same deep poverty and hopelessness that we had seen years before in Haiti and more recently on the outskirts of Lima. We soon concluded this was the real Latin America. While the vast majority of the urban poor had come with high expectations of a better life, most fell into an even worse existence than the village life they had left behind.

We also found that many of the rich and the middle class held an open disdain for these rural and urban poor—a disdain that widened the gap between them. I remember flashing back at the time to our journey to Guayaquil. I recalled with sadness the train engineer who refused to release his foot on the automatic break. I remained astonished by his seeming total indifference for the peasants he left stranded, possibly hurt or dead alongside the tracks. This was the Latin America that had known revolutions fought to remove despots and poverty. But it was also the Latin America in which the economic progress of a few continued to create a cold divide between themselves and those left behind.

Back Home

We were soon home in Coronado. We expected to enjoy our family and friends and to share all that we had experienced. It proved not so easy. Readjusting to that home world I knew so well became unexpectedly difficult. I felt out of place. I tried to pull out of this state by holding a reunion of old friends at my sister's home. I prepared a slide show of our Peace Corps adventure. It conveyed vivid scenes of the villagers at work and in various festive moods. There was little response, and I sensed a certain disconnect and uneasiness among my friends about what I had shared. One friend questioned whether these people were really poor. They seemed well fed and having fun. I tried to explain in vain that children's red cheeks did not indicate prosperity. They were signs of the harsh cold and strong sun of their winter environment and, in some cases, their malnutrition. But an overall skepticism seemed to prevail.

I later realized how unrealistic it was of me to expect a full understanding of what I had experienced. And probably I was not sufficiently sensitive and skilled in explaining the cultural and economic differences. Most likely it was more an inner tension on my side that I felt between these worlds and the seeming impossibility (or at least my own incapability) to reconcile and bridge that divide.

To London and LSE

Soon we were off again. We landed in London in September 1966. It was an exciting time for Sheila and me. We had a few weeks to roam this wonderful city and hunt for our apartment before classes at LSE began. We settled on an apartment in South Kensington which was a convenient hop by tube to the school.

Classes commenced in early October. I attended the first gathering of the master candidates for the department of international relations. The department head greeted us warmly. He encouraged us to be active in our quest for knowledge. He went so far as to say that he never found the American students (of whom there were several besides myself) wanting in their readiness to voice their opinions. He hoped other students would do the same (to which I wondered how much confidence we American students should really feel in doing so in the context of a sophisticated, cosmopolitan and learned LSE setting, given our more generally parochial backgrounds). The professor continued with a brief description of the international relations program. He stressed subject matter and issues of current international debate and concerns for resolving international conflict.

As these initial days unfolded, I began to have serious doubts about how relevant and useful this program would be to my purpose for being there. I knew of course even before applying to LSE about the content of the curriculum. But I had not focused sufficiently on the details. I simply assumed this program would relate the subjects to the context of the so-called developing world. What soon became clear to me as the first course lectures began was that I was in the wrong program. Theories and practices of international relations were not why I wanted to pursue further graduate studies. My goal was quite different. I was there to gain a better understanding and insight into the complexities of development, especially the causes of poverty. I also hoped to gain some skill in how to address these problems.

I began to panic. I had made a mistake. I assumed it was too late to correct it. But as the irrelevance of what I heard set in, I decided I had to act. I boldly set forth to seek advice and guidance. I asked to meet and was granted a half hour with one of LSE's renowned development economist, Peter Bauer. I had already attended some of his classes. I was impressed by his convictions (truly pioneering at the time), even though I did not agree with all of them. He was a strong skeptic of the role of government intervention and foreign aid as means by which to eradicate poverty. He opposed central planning and believed only individuals could create their own path to prosperity. I did not think these positions were so black and white, but I did respect his courage to take up the cause for which he spoke.

Judging him to be both professional and fair, I decided to share with him my dilemma. His response was cold, factual and sound. He advised me firstly to be sure I was clear what I wanted to learn and why. Then it was a matter of matching that as closely as I could with what LSE had to offer, which was quite considerable. He advised me that I immediately approach what I considered other more relevant departments to see if they were willing to take me in.

I followed his advice and soon discovered a department called development administration. It was primarily established to provide graduate level students from developing countries with practical knowledge and skills in managing development. The courses had nothing to do with the grand themes of international relations. Rather they focused on the study of basic development economics, social development and efficient development administration and management. It was an integrated and inter-disciplinary program.

It was run by professors and lecturers across a wide range of departments. I was given an opportunity to sit in on a couple of the classes. I found an instant rapport with both the subject matter and the students already enrolled. These included students from Nigeria, Cyprus, Mexico, Iran, and another half dozen or more countries. I was the only Westerner in the program besides one other who also happened to be an American. I liked what I had found. I was particularly grateful for the special interests the professors showed for my experience in the Peace Corps. They seemed to understand and appreciate the perspective I had for how problems were seen by villagers. Convinced this was what I was looking for; I shifted over to the program. I never regretted the decision.

In the meantime, Sheila explored opportunities for herself. She wanted to involve herself in some kind of work or volunteerism that would build on her interests in children. Sheila had majored in psychology (mainly child psychology) and her natural tendencies (especially following her pre-school initiative in Peru) were to look for something along those lines. She worked at it steadily and eventually came up with a volunteer position at a local children's orphanage. She found the work very rewarding.

During the Christmas break at LSE, we made a visit to Moscow. The National Hotel on Red Square where we stayed was a step into the past. Its rococo architecture and atmosphere reminded me of what the life of the Russian elite of nineteenth century must have been like. Enormous lunches and dinners of cold fish and Russian Salad preceded huge helpings of steamed potatoes and roasted meats. Local Russians and foreign visitors mixed easily at each table delighting in boisterous Russian humor administered in broken and often outrageous English.

This contrasted with the maid supervisors. They policed each floor of the hotel. They kept a close eye on everything that took place. We found it both comical and annoying. But we gave it little thought until a certain event. A young professional looking fellow who sat at our dining table particularly delighted us with sophisticated talk and jokes. After a few days he invited Sheila and me up to his room to meet another friend. We accepted with pleasure. When we reached his floor, we found the maid inspector frowning at our unexpected appearance. And as we strolled toward his room, the inspector rose and strained to see which number we were entering. Once inside, we had a few drinks (excellent Scotch whiskey, which I've never liked). Soon the mood turned serious. Far different from what we had experienced at the dining table. Both men began to share their unhappiness for the Soviet system. They said they had a great admiration for anything from or about "the States" as they liked to refer to America. They complained about the constant surveillance. They confided how they could not pursue their business ambitions while the government controlled so much and made impossible demands.

We met them again at the dining tables where the mood again reverted to revelry and non political discussion. Not fully understanding the threat they felt, we decided one evening to pay them a surprise visit. Our sudden appearance at their door caused shock and undisguised anger. The conversation was stifled and short and we left in less than ten minutes. We never saw them again, nor at any of the dining tables. We assumed they had left the hotel entirely. We began to understand our naiveté and our stupidity. Of course it was too late.

We also visited the home of another gentleman who was known to one of my professors at LSE. He was an academic and very warm in welcoming us into his home. We talked freely. He shared his honest views about the shortcomings and the positive attributes of the Soviet Union. The conversation turned to a similar discussion of the pros and cons of the American system and lifestyle. He held a genuine admiration for America. But he was highly critical of our aggression in the on-going war in Vietnam. He put it all very diplomatically. He seemed to assume we would be too embarrassed to reply to his queries. We actually were not. But we were poorly informed about the issues. We were especially ignorant about anti-war viewpoints, naively influenced as we were by American propaganda. My own strong anti-war views took shape a couple of years later when we moved to New York. So at this stage I gave bland statements which awkwardly seemed to be defending US policy.

Our visit to Moscow was our first face to face encounter with communism. My main impression was of the enormous warmth of the Russian people regardless of their political environment. They were also well educated and bright. They had a certain down to earth honesty about them that reminded me of my own country. What I did not like was the unrelenting attempts of the communist system to control the lives and minds of its people. I found its greatest harm was in stifling the spirit of its people to be whoever they wished to be. Not that we Americans were totally free ourselves, encumbered as we were by our own brand of propaganda (more of which I will speak later). It was more a matter of the humiliating subservience demanded by the system. It showed in so many often petty ways that appeared to me to break the spirit of the people. I thought then and long after of whether communism was any different in this respect than fascism. I concluded it was not. They were basically the same. There were of course certain superficial differences in the rhetoric. But both carried the same lies and deceptions of working in the interest of the people while actually working against those interests to the benefit of the small elites who ran both systems. They were both systematic affronts to basic decencies of honoring the innate capacities and rights of people to use those capacities to the fullest.

Back in London, Sheila was four months pregnant. We had decided, with our volunteer work behind us and my final graduate studies nearly over, we were ready for a family. On April 18, 1967 our first daughter, Tanya Theresa, was born in Westminster hospital, not far from the Houses of Parliament. We rushed to the hospital just before midnight. The actual birth took place near dawn. Tanya was a healthy five pounds and five ounces. Sheila was back in our apartment within a couple of days.

My education at LSE continued uninterrupted. I began to see how far different it was from my days at Stanford. In many respects it was far more demanding. American higher education, at least through the master's degree, was highly structured. There were lots of reading lists and periodic exams by which one could constantly measure one's progress. The British system was different. It introduced the subject but did not lead anyone by the hand through the substance. It was more a self guided voyage. The challenge was to figure out what it all meant or at least what were the salient learnings or historic insights. For each course one had to quickly ascertain the main features of the topic to determine which were most worthy of more in-depth investigation and understanding. The process stimulated more questions that gave increasing insight into issues and problems but not necessarily easy or ready answers.

Besides the final exam, we had to research a topic of our own choosing. I chose to investigate *Agricultural Production and Other Essentials of Rural Development in Peru*. I did this under the supervision of our economics professor who was extremely demanding of factual accuracy and persuasive argument. The intellectual exercise was thankfully complemented by my own personal knowledge of the realities of poor villagers. This along with what my professor saw as my improving ability to make my case clearly and logically was both humbling and rewarding as an indication of what I hoped was some maturing on my part.

Most difficult for me was the fact that no examination was held until the end of the scholastic year. And in our case, the disciplines of our study (development economics, social development, political systems, and the management of development processes) completely intertwined so that what we would be questioned on could literally be anything. Our challenge was not to provide "correct" answers but to demonstrate sound analysis of any given situation and offer reasonable recommendations and a practical course of action.

My purpose in coming to LSE, to find answers to the causes of poverty and solutions to its alleviation, was not realized in the manner I expected. I began to understand more fully that development was not a simple phenomenon. There clearly was no one cause, and certainly no single answer or solution to poverty. Indeed, poverty had many origins and many contributing factors. Poverty continuously fluctuated and mutated depending on how elites manipulated their power and benefits at the expense of the poor. I came to better understand (or more accurately to believe and reaffirm) that poverty was purposeful, largely a consequence of greed and power. The instruments the elites used to manipulate and maintain it to secure their own extravagant well being were complex and often difficult to decipher. They spanned the gamut of political, economic and social life, and beyond that cultural and religious practice.

I slowly began to get a grip on the fact that development required an understanding and engagement with a very wide-ranging human dynamic. Poverty could not be overcome by any one technique or breakthrough. Every development context required its own unique tailor-made analysis and set of approaches. Development needed open minds and fresh ideas, innovation, creativity, flexibility to changing circumstances. It needed continuous attention and determination to overcome unending attempts to subvert it. Above all, I think I was beginning to understand, it needed an unrelenting examination of the role of power, both as the root of and the potential solution to poverty. It was something I would spend most of my years in development trying to comprehend and resolve. I assumed it would require risk taking and above all fierce human empathy and political courage and commitment.

I became further convinced that these were the elements of a worthy life's work. They were an exciting challenge to which one could hope to make a contribution. I concluded this was what I wanted to do with the rest of my life.

On June 10, 1967 we took our final exam gathered together in one classroom. An intensive three hours to answer three questions. They ranged across economic, social and political fields and a perplexing set of issues set in the context of the interaction between each of these disciplines. The practical realities I had known in Peru combined with the insights of my studies at LSE enabled me to broaden and extrapolate my answers to the wider context that these exam questions posed. I passed the course.

Chapter 6
New York

Maturing the Commitments
1967-1971

Courtesy of Ad Meskens

Internship

Sometime during the final couple of months of my study at LSE, I came across a bulletin board notice about a UN internship program in Geneva, Switzerland. It looked interesting and a great opportunity to learn about the UN from the inside. Definitely I was interested in the possibility of working for the UN. So I applied. After a month I received notice that I had been accepted to the two month program.

Sheila and I arrived in Geneva in mid-June 1967. We were taken directly to an apartment building in the Old City on Rue Toepffer, near the Russian Orthodox church. Our accommodation consisted of one bedroom and nothing more. We brought along a baby stroller for Tanya which folded down into a bed. That is where she slept for the two months. Our room had a marvelous view of Lake Geneva. From there we watched the hourly gush of the water jet fountain for which Geneva is famous. Since we had no cooking facilities, we tried out many small restaurants in the Old City. In those days they were still very reasonably priced.

The internship inspired me. We spent most of our days in the huge UN *Palais de Nations* complex across the lake. We learned about the organization and workings of the UN, along with some of its major historical events and accomplishments. Most exciting to me were the mock conference sessions that we acted out. Fellow interns honored me to serve as the chairman of the conference. I managed to steer the discussions and conclusions in a direction that seemed to please my colleagues. The experience further motivated me to pursue a career with the UN.

While in Geneva, I sought out contacts with a few UN agencies based there. I had a couple of interviews. The International Labour Organization (ILO) and its department of vocational training showed a particular interest in my background with the Peace Corps. Before I left Geneva, one Mr. Fauchon who headed that department offered me a starting position.

Career Launching

At the same time, a UN staff member who was leading our internship program also advised me about the United Nations Development Programme (UNDP) headquartered in New York. He strongly urged me to pass through New York to meet a few key senior officials of UNDP with whom he was kind enough to put me in touch.

As good fortune would have it, I met Paul Marc Henry. He was an Assistant Secretary General in charge of the programme division of UNDP. Paul Marc was known as "Mr. UNDP" with good reason. He was a driving force of knowledge, detail and commitment. He had worked for many years in French West Africa. He wanted to know about my experience in Peru and whether what I had done had made any difference. That went straight to the heart of the matter in terms of what I had asked myself so many times before. I told him that indigenous Peruvian society and culture had existed and survived many hundreds of years before I got there. I said that the continuation of what I had introduced (the famous chicken raising cooperative) would depend on whether the villagers involved felt it met their needs rather than mine. I confided that I was unable to give a definitive answer to that as only time would tell. But I let him know that I hoped the process of building trust and working together would be lasting and useful in other ways. I also volunteered my view that development was a rather long and complex undertaking even (or especially) at the level of a village. Change would come in small doses according to how much people took it on as their own and what support they had for it.

Whether he liked or agreed with these answers I could not discern. I had the sense that he was more interested in my personal attributes (whether I could work and get along in a multi-cultural setting) and in my honesty to reply to queries that he felt should have no self-serving or glorifying answers. But I also think my commitment to work in a village for two years impressed him (there were few Americans at that time with such experience). In any event, he announced on the spot that he would appoint me as a rural development project officer. It was an honor I could not at the time fully appreciate. As I later learned, he was not someone to take on people in any unconsidered manner. His confidence filled me with increasing pride and gratefulness as I gradually more fully understood what he had done for me.

UNDP in 1967 was still a very small organization. It had been created under what the UN General Assembly initially called the "Special Fund" for development. It had a total of 200 professional staff at the New York headquarters level. The entire organization was accommodated on one floor (the 3rd) of the Alcoa building located immediately north of the UN Secretariat on 49th Street and 1st Avenue. Assigned a small inner office with no windows and one US government-issued (or so it seemed) metal desk and chair, I settled into my new job.

On my first day my supervisor, an energetic Dutchman, handed me a file containing a project proposal just received from the UNDP Philippines' office for some type of rural development. He asked me to read and analyze it. He wanted me to make a case for either approval or rejection by the next morning. I worked on it all day and took it home that night. I knew nothing about the Philippines. I certainly had no idea what was needed or possible in the region that would be targeted under this proposal. The project was mostly about setting up rural village schools. So I fell back on my experiences in Peru. I contemplated whether the approach could possibly work in Manzanares. Was there enough commonality with the situation described in the Philippines? I made my comments as practical as possible: how would the villagers be involved; how could we make the curriculum and teacher training relevant to the real life needs of the students as future farmers; what resources would be needed, from the UN and from the villagers. I handed it in the next morning. I had no idea whether my supervisor would see eye to eye with my rather mundane assessment. As it turned out, he liked it quite a lot. He even took it around to other senior colleagues. It was a good start for me.

I felt an instant affinity and camaraderie with the team that made up the human resources division to which I was assigned. I felt I had landed into a world that knew and shared my values, aspirations, experiences, and life goals— all at the same time and in the same way. It was an exhilarating feeling. All those in the other sections and divisions of UNDP, the substantive units as well as the regional coordination offices, shared similar experiences and commitments. I began immediately to interact with most of them. Because we were all on one floor, I would usually see almost everyone in the organization every day as I moved around the halls from one meeting or consultation to the next.

I worked mostly with a group that had been mandated to come up with a clear strategy on the latest development fashion—"integrated rural development". I felt comfortable and confident about this task. It was in line with my Peace Corps experience. It was an approach to development based on the real multiple needs (and problems) of everyday life in a village. Rather than focusing on one sector (such as education in the Philippines project), the "integrated" approach demanded a simultaneous attention to health, education, agriculture, small enterprise, and whatever else was important to improving people's opportunities within a defined geographical area. There were two other ingredients. One was to figure out the right mechanism for coordinating all these diverse activities. This proved much more difficult than it seemed. The second was the need to involve the local people in these efforts. In those days we still termed it "community development", and we thought this was something we really knew how to do.

In terms of finding an effective coordination mechanism, we thought the answer lay in creating new institutions within a participating government such as a "regional development authority" that would dedicate itself exclusively to the tasks of coordination. We learned over time that this too often turned into a "top down" bureaucratic control system. It created more obstacles (and resentments at the local level) than any positive accomplishments.

In terms of peoples' participation, we thought their involvement could best be ensured if they were properly informed and invited to join the program. The problem here was that "the program" was usually already defined. The people were simply asked to support it. This did not cultivate any sense of "ownership' nor foster any "empowerment" which many years later became the hallmark (especially for me) of such efforts.

Our experimentation with these various approaches across many countries over my nearly five years at UNDP headquarters was an important learning process. Looking back, I hoped these efforts at the very least "did no harm" to the local people who became "involved" (though I suspect that for some, the expectations raised were largely unfulfilled). It was later clear to me that our good intentions did not lead to essential fundamental reforms. In particular, they did not address the "power relationships" between villagers and the elites of various kinds. Putting people "in charge" of their own destinies would require that. It was much later that I understood this and aspired to build change on that basis. But our work in the mid 1960s was an important stepping stone in that direction.

Paul Marc convened bi-monthly (sometimes more frequent) meetings of all the divisions / sections. The point was to go through the list of projects (500+) to assess progress and problems. The most exciting part of the work was when these reviews led to the conclusion that a "mission" to a country was needed to address the on-the-ground realities of any particular project I was handling. That usually happened every six months for me. The idea was to make a firsthand assessment of its feasibility or to evaluate its performance. In some cases it was to entirely formulate or reformulate a project.

My first mission was to Mexico. It began in one of Paul Marc's review meetings. I was called on to share the recent proposal received by our UNDP Mexico City office from the Government of Mexico. It proposed a regional development programme for a vast valley area surrounding and spreading out from the city of Guadalajara in the northern center of Mexico. The proposal had landed on my desk only a week earlier. I had just begun to analyze the approach. It was very centralized. It did not give much importance to the participation or direct benefit of the village people in the region. Its purpose was mainly to build the rural and agricultural infrastructure, a worthy goal no doubt. But I was concerned with what impact this was likely to have (or rather not have) on increasing the productivity of the local farmers.

Paul Marc immediately jumped on this apparent flaw in the strategy that I had brought to his attention. He always seemed to like and support my first instincts. He particularly liked my passion for whether and how any proposal would engage and benefit the poor. He immediately conveyed his outrage for something that seemed more likely to benefit elite large farmers. As far as he was concerned, there was only one way to investigate and hopefully reorient this approach. And that was for me to go there. I responded positively (more like ecstatically, though I tried to hide my internal reaction). I pointed out that there were a lot of technical, mostly agricultural and infrastructural issues, not to mention social and political complexities that would have to be addressed. He agreed and asked me to quickly organize a full-scale mission. It had to be launched within a few days. Thrilled and overwhelmed at the same time, I felt committed and ready to do whatever it took.

I knew that such missions were not easy to organize. The main challenge was finding well qualified mission members. Especially important was a strong and competent mission leader. Fortunately, my team colleagues helped me out. I was on the phone with a Portuguese regional development specialist who by chance was available. We also quickly identified other candidates (all Spanish speaking of course). Most were staff from other UN Agencies. I soon had some ten mission members lined up. By the end of the week we were ready to go.

The surprise and rapid unfolding of all of this put me under more stress than I realized. On the way to Mexico, I stopped over in Washington D.C. for discussions with the World Bank and the Inter-American Development Bank. Each had a potential interest to join the project. I was already feeling exhausted. My flight to Mexico City was scheduled for that same evening. After the bank meetings, I headed to the lobby of a nearby hotel. I sat quietly in a corner alone to collect my thoughts and relieve my fatigue. I woke with a start at about 8:00

pm. I had slept in the hotel lounge chair for nearly three hours. My flight was at 10:00 pm. I ran out the front door, hailed a cab and jumped in. Somehow we made it to Dulles Airport in a record 45 minutes. I caught my flight.

I checked into a small but comfortable hotel in the center of Mexico City. I fell asleep mid morning and awoke about 2:00 pm. I felt very warm and was sweating profusely. It was Saturday and I knew I had to be in top shape for discussions with the government early Monday morning. I needed help. My mind immediately flashed to my two old friends from LSE who had returned to Mexico and were working in the government and the private sector. I had brought their contacts with me and to my enormous relief found them both at home and answering my call. They rushed over to my hotel accompanied by their own personal physician. He diagnosed my condition as a viral infection and prescribed a course of 500 mg antibiotics. To my amazement by Sunday morning I was already feeling better. Monday morning found me early to breakfast to meet the other team members.

After the morning deliberations with the relevant ministries of the Federal Government of Mexico, we flew that same afternoon to Guadalajara. The next morning we headed straight to the offices of the Guadalajara regional development authority. It was a very impressive establishment. A semi-autonomous government body, we soon learned it had a great deal of power. Power to plan and implement development activities with substantial resources. It was headed by an imposing "General Manager", good looking, well dressed, charming and highly confident. He was as much as anything a strong political leader. He knew how to get his way.

Our team had detailed discussions with him and mainly with his various department heads before making a one week tour of the region ourselves. We met and spoke with business councils and farmers associations, and mayors of several municipalities. We visited small towns and a few communities. I was impressed with how well organized these bodies were in terms of clear development goals and agendas. I was even more impressed with their commitment to put their human and financial resources behind the task. But I was also struck with the poverty that was pervasive in the rural areas. I sensed an enormous gap between these villages and the impressive, dynamic and prosperous institution that was set up to coordinate their development.

As the facilitator of the mission, I produced the initial draft of the project document. I did my best to emphasize a peoples' participatory approach which was ultimately adopted.

Some months later, I undertook a similar but much smaller mission to develop an integrated regional development approach in the Nile Delta of Egypt. This time I had almost complete say in designing the project with the government counterparts. I made sure that the central focus was on the village people and the active role of their communities in planning and carrying out the project.

I was firmly committed to this "integrated" approach, and basically remain so today. I found it reflected most accurately the real life situation, difficulties and potentials of people and their institutions. I believed it would only be through the interaction of economic, social, political and administrative realities that any development challenge could be fully addressed and overcome. I remained confounded however by how to "empower" the poor to lead these efforts (indeed I did not yet think of it in those terms), but I made certain they were involved.

Different Vision

Over these formative years, I gradually became convinced that "people centered" and "integrated" approaches to development had relevance not only to "developing" countries but equally to the so-called "developed" ones. I began to conclude that there was a need and an opportunity for developed and developing countries to help each other by crossing their divide in both directions not just one. Specifically, I had in mind how my own country, the United States, could benefit from such an exchange. This was "radical" thinking at that time, and probably still is. What could a great power such as the United States have to learn or gain from such sharing and assistance from poor countries?

This was in fact the beginning of my personal view of the potential of a cross border world. It was a pretentious concept for such a very inexperienced development novice. But my gut kept telling me that everyone—rich and poor—had something to contribute to improving the life of others elsewhere. People faced similar problems around the world. Most all had wrestled in one way or another with trying to overcome such problems in their own communities. They each had found or were still trying to find their own paths to making life a little better. While there were frustrations and setbacks everywhere, there were plenty of examples of small breakthroughs and improvements. It seemed obvious to me that everyone would gain by sharing what they were facing and how they were dealing with it. The world would benefit from an equal extending of hands from all sides, rather than ideas and help moving in one direction only.

In my enthusiasm that I was really on to something, I decided to write up a project proposal for funding by UNDP. It was aimed primarily at an exchange of peoples from poor countries around the globe to work in poor communities in the US. The focus was on working in the ghetto communities of America.

I had taken a special interest in this problem. This was the era of the late 60s and early 70s when Vietnam overwhelmed all social issues. But it was also the era of the "war on poverty" in America. It was the era of the challenge to turn the civil rights movement into a meaningful better life for poor blacks. I thought there was no better opportunity for the UN to play a useful role. It would not be a role of traditional "technical assistance". It would be a role of "facilitating" people to come together across borders (physically, culturally and economically) to help each other out. It would be based on what worked regardless of the obvious differences that existed between them—to give space and opportunity to figure out how to do that. It would have also included visits by Americans to poor communities in the other participating countries. My Peace Corps experience was clearly at work, but turning it into a level playing field where all contributed equally was what I hoped I had learned correctly was our unique opportunity.

I packaged the concept. I sent it on up to the top management of UNDP. To my surprise, there was considerable interest. Fortunately there was an American at that level, Mark Cohen (Deputy Administrator for Programmes) whom I had come to know and respect. He seemed to see the potential of the proposal particularly well. He offered to take it to the very top—the Administrator of UNDP. When I was given the opportunity to meet with the Administrator, Paul Hoffman (also an American who had gained a high reputation before coming to UNDP as the administrator of the "Marshall Plan" in Europe), his reaction was similarly positive. But his encouraging response was also mixed with a clear sense of reality. While endorsing the concept, and praising my efforts, he confided that he believed it was a bit "ahead of its time". I was sure he meant this as a compliment, and I took it as such, but I braced myself for what I expected to follow—that he felt it was "politically" unworkable. Once it gained a certain profile in the media, he was sure it would attract the interest and probably the ire of certain US politicians who would immediately label it as UN interference. He was undoubtedly right. I was nevertheless deeply disappointed at the time. The important question that lingered for me long afterward was whether my vision could still have relevance and somehow eventually be implemented.

It took forty years for me to find an answer to that question. But find it I did. The answer came in the form of a different development approach from what I had in mind at the time. But it was an altogether similar vision. It came from Bangladesh, long considered one of the poorest countries in the world (Dr. Henry Kissinger infamously described Bangladesh in the early 1970s as the "basket case" of the world, a particularly ignorant statement I concluded when I came to work there some thirty-five years later). It was the approach of the Grameen Bank of Bangladesh, founded by Dr. Muhammad Yunus who won the Nobel Peace Prize (2006) for his work in microcredit with the poor. Dr. Yunus had shown that poor people, particularly poor women, were as responsible, indeed more responsible than many better off clients, in paying back their loans (averaging a 98% repayment rate) to start small businesses. What Dr. Yunus also showed was that this phenomenon was not unique to Bangladesh. He spread the approach to many other developing countries where it was seen to make an important contribution to development (whatever may have been its shortcomings that I learned about later).

What many did not expect, however, was that Dr. Yunus would take and apply the same approach to the United States of America. By 2009, Grameen America was established and lending to women, mainly immigrants trying to start a new life in New York City (just where I had hoped to initiate community activities with the help of experienced volunteers from developing countries). The loans averaged $1,625. That was sufficient to kick start small businesses by women in clothing sales, jewelry stores, flower shops and food stands.

In an interview in *Time* magazine (October 19, 2009), Dr. Yunus remarked: 'Today Grameen programs are everywhere. We even have a program in New York City, and it works beautifully. It's the same system as in the villages of Bangladesh.' It was more than a feeling of quiet pride that I took in this vindication (or so I saw it) of my original ideas (no matter how inexperienced I was in promoting them at the time). For me, what was important was the validation of human capacities and talents from poor countries to contribute meaningfully to a resolution of needs and problems in America. I am all the more convinced and confident there is need as well as enormous potential for a continuation of this kind of exchange on a far greater scale. To my mind, it is an opportunity for people to share across borders an innate common concern and deep sense of decency to come to the aid of each other on a basis of genuine equality and mutual benefit. Not an unimportant result.

Early Intentions

Before departing New York, which I will shortly explain, I decided to undertake a pilot experiment in bringing rich and poor together. At the time, I seriously thought I would stay on in New York and leave the UN to pursue this work. I came up with the idea of establishing a project called LINK. It was 1970. I wrote up the concept, and printed out promotional materials. I began to make contact and interact with two totally diverse universes.

On the one hand, I went into Harlem and began to network with organizations and individuals. I met with single mothers in the Harlem housing projects, witnessing the rather shockingly poor yet homey and warm environment which they struggled to create for their fatherless children. At the other extreme, I shared my ideas with a few wealthy business people, mostly fathers of a few American friends I came to know in the Westchester suburbs. My experiment was disappointingly brief as I soon decided to resume my UN work abroad. What I did learn in the short time I devoted to the effort was a surprisingly genuine interest on both sides to try something new. The women of Harlem could not initially understand what and why I was doing this, but after a while, began to see the possible benefits. Similarly, the business people thought this was a practical, down to earth business approach to a serious social divide, and were enthusiastic to get involved. The basic idea was to create through the business contacts a mentoring and training of the women in Harlem in skills that would qualify them for employment or a small business. We never got very far in identifying exactly what these opportunities would be. Nevertheless, looking back, my personal growth and insight gained enormously with the realization of the latent good will and eagerness that existed on both sides to work together across social, economic and cultural lines.

Innovation

One of the most exciting experiences of my time working at UNDP headquarters was my mission to India. Again, it was a small mission, consisting of myself and the team leader, Dr. Wilbur Schramm of Stanford University, a renowned academic in development communications. We were also joined by a staff member of UNESCO's communications department. The Indian government planned to use satellite communication to bring education to hundreds of thousands of villages across India and requested UNDP to join this effort to design such a programme.

It was 1970 and it was my first visit to India (indeed to Asia). I felt instantly awed by the quality of the people I met in the government. Meeting them attired in traditional dress gave me a sense of their confident self-identity. Their quickness of mind and wit impressed me. I assumed there was a lot of heavy "red tape" wrapped around it all, but that seemed insignificant in the face of such inspiring displays of decorum and intellect.

The Indians were way ahead of most developing countries in so many ways. Their empathy and priority for the well being of the village poor stood in sharp contrast to what I had witnessed elsewhere. The antecedents of this undoubtedly stemmed from the example Mahatma Gandhi had set for his country. Nevertheless, the truth was that India, for all its good intentions, still had hundreds of millions of poor. Indian government policy was committed to alleviating poverty, but the ways of doing that (with a lot of bureaucratic approaches even at local levels) often yielded small returns compared to the size of the problem. Regardless, among government policy makers and administrators, there was a clear sense of determination to rid India of this scourge, mixed with occasional flashes of innovation. The idea of using modern communication technology to bring knowledge and greater opportunity to the village poor was not the least of these.

We traveled to the city of Ahmadabad in Gujarat State. That was the home and office of one of India's leading scientist, Dr. Vikram Sarabhai, who headed the Indian Space Research Organization (ISRO). His vision of the use of science to reach humanity-yet-unreached was deeply inspiring to me. His home lay flat and unpretentious along a high ridge above the broad, dry river that passed through the city. We gratefully accepted his invitation to dinner. As with most Indian homes, it was simply furnished. But its spaciousness gave a sense of grandeur with a sweeping veranda overlooking the river. The buffet spread on that veranda introduced me to the exquisite tastes of India's vegetarian cuisine. Every conceivable vegetable prepared in an almost infinite variety of ways. Dr. Sarabhai's white "churidar" pajamas let in the cool evening breeze and enhanced his natural elegance as he strode gracefully forward to greet us. Spending the evening discussing the opportunities for transforming India's educational system through the miracles of technology was for me an extraordinary experience.

On our return to New York, Dr. Schramm and I presented our findings and the key elements of a satellite education programme to Paul Marc who found it fascinating and voiced his full support. As it turned out, the initiative took considerable time to mature, not least from the side of the Indian government which sought the views and consensus of a wide range of its bureaucracy. It was only after I had left UNDP headquarters that the project took on a more defined shape. A pilot experiment was conducted during 1975-1976, with technical assistance from NASA, named the Satellite Instructional Education Experiment (SITE). It was a notable effort to build bridges to and between India's poor, opening new channels of information and education to rural villagers on agriculture, family planning, and a wide range of development subjects.

The experiment eventually led to the launching by India in 2004 of the world's first satellite exclusively devoted to educational purposes *(EDUSAT)*. I was honored to have been a small part of that historic effort. From a purely personal standpoint, however, what was equally important was the initial introduction it provided me to a country and a culture that would eventually transform my life in innumerable ways. That is a story I will share in the upcoming chapter.

Elite Life

While my early UN career was playing out, Sheila and I settled into life in New York. We were enjoying it thoroughly. We sought out the excitement of the city and the peace and quiet of non-city life. We opted for Westchester County, the town of Scarsdale, and found a lovely New England double story three bedroom house on tree-lined Robin Hill Road and rented it for the amazing low prices of those times. On February 7th, 1971 our second daughter, Natasha Briana, was born. Sheila gave birth at Westchester Hospital in White Plains, New York, and all went well. Natasha was a healthy, cute and calm kid.

Just before Natasha's birth, we moved quite unexpectedly to a new home. We had some very close friends who lived in the city but decided to try country life. He was a contractor and he decided to build their dream home. It was located in Bedford, New York, another thirty to forty minutes commute north of Scarsdale. Bedford was an idyllic New England country village surrounded by large estate homes of four and five acres each. It was absolutely stunning to drive and walk through the back roads of this countryside. It felt like another era of early American rural life. As it turned out, my friend's wife did not like (more precisely, could not endure) that country life. For the sake of the marriage (so he confided in me) they decided to sell the house and move back to the city. Before putting it on the market, he mentioned to me their plans and asked if we were interested. We had not given it any thought but decided to have a look.

The property was on the edge of Bedford, not in a posh area but more something akin to a sub-division. The properties had more land than usually expected, and their house had two acres. You could not see the house from the road. Once you entered the property by the graveled driveway over a small mound, it came into full view. Really an unexpected delight. It had no affinity to the nearby homes. My friend had opted for a California modern design. It was constructed with redwood, natural gray stone, and lots of large glass windows looking out onto the natural forest setting and empty field at the back.

Anxious to return to the city and the life they knew, our friends offered the house at what it cost them. It turned out to be surprisingly inexpensive given the materials used and the architectural splendor achieved. We bought our first house.

Transition

Then, as time went on, I began to question the direction our life was taking. I was enormously honored to serve the United Nations. I was highly motivated by my position and responsibility to work on rural development. Yet I began to wonder how effective I was or could be in this role. I came to UNDP headquarters after two years living in a village. In Manzanares I grappled with development problems directly with the people. I knew it was unrealistic to think I could have a career in development working only at the village level. Such work, admirable as it may be, would unlikely have much impact beyond the village. But the distance I now felt from villages began to play on my mind. I questioned whether my personal goals in development could be satisfied working in such a remote manner. The opportunity to participate in and even lead UN missions to countries all over the world was no doubt special, a responsibility I could not have anticipated. But I began to see more clearly with each mission the layers that separated me from the hard issues and challenges. I felt a growing gap from the people who were crucial to finding solutions. Working from New York not only preempted me from stepping into a village (except on those occasional missions, most of which were spent in the capitals), but even from interacting with governments and development organizations on a regular basis.

I began to reach some clear cut conclusions. UN headquarters certainly had significant roles to play in global development—articulating and promoting broad policies and sharing development experiences between countries and across regions. It also had to ensure financial and administrative accountability of the UN system world-wide. But for me, the headquarters role pretty much ended there. Major development efforts had to be made closer to the people and their local institutions. I was convinced that UN work must be undertaken as directly in support of those people and institutions as possible.

While these thoughts about my job were crystallizing, I began to develop doubts and guilt about my personal life and life style. I had grown up in modest surroundings and by modest means. Later initial resources that my father and his family provided me gave me advantages early in my adult life. I did not use these to embellish my material life. I used my resources mainly to take advantage of special opportunities I might not otherwise have had (especially my Stanford education and my travels abroad).

But the purchase of our first home in Bedford took us into a new realm of living. Although very reasonably priced, even for those days, it was a luxury style I had never previously known. It felt out of sync with the rest of my life and especially my work. I started to worry we may be settling into a comfortable life, one that could become both boring and permanent. My inner values and goals were different and I instinctively felt the difference. I was not fixated on avoiding a good life or occasional luxury. But I wanted my life to be primarily driven by a strong sense of helping other people. More than comfort, I wanted my life to be stimulating, challenging, adventurous, full of rewarding experience, and beneficial to others.

I made a personal choice. I concluded I could best realize my inner drive by returning to live and work in other countries and cultures. From what I had already experienced in France, London, and especially Peru, I felt much more "on the front edge" of my life when immersed in a new cultural and physical setting. I knew that only through such a life drawn into other people's values and exposed to their hardships could I hope to learn of the problems they faced, the roots of those problems, and what it would take to overcome them.

Soon after returning to New York from India, I began to exchange messages with our UNDP Resident Representative in New Delhi, Dr. John MacDiarmid. I was following up with him what I had already indicated while there, namely that I would like to explore the possibility of a transfer out of New York to work and live in India. We had got along well during the mission, and he gave me a lot of support for such a move. Sheila and I did of course discuss this move. She was less enthusiastic since she was feeling well settled in our new home. She bravely began to shift her position in the face of my growing enthusiasm. At about this point, I received the timely and wonderful news that my transfer to the UNDP India office (New Delhi) had been approved. I was thrilled, and by this time, Sheila had become enthusiastic about the adventure that lay ahead for us.

My last six months in New York were exhausting for me. It was an accumulation of over four years of commute which once we moved to Bedford became a dreary three hour voyage back and forth each day. I was arriving home late in the evenings and rising to begin again early each morning. I was worn out and I felt it.

The prospects of our move to India changed all of that. Deep down I believe the anticipation of the change and excitement that this unusual land held out for me was indeed what I must always credit for the complete renewal of life and spirit that I then realized.

Chapter 7
India

Deep in My Soul
1971 – 1973

Night and Day on the streets of Calcutta

Earning a living as one can

Suvira meeting with Vikas Bhai, a Ghandian NGO, in the City of Varanasi

Beyond Clichés

Where to begin? India changed my life. It is a culture of such immense depth, expressed through such astonishing artistry and such simple wisdom. It is a culture that, more than any other I have experienced since, has continued to practice so many of its traditional values, beliefs, and modes of life. It is a culture of diversities and contrasts that go beyond its own clichés. It is a culture that constantly excites the mind and spirit. It is a country where rich and poor often live side by side; where they mix so vibrantly each day on its streets. It is a country of color, incredibly rich color. It is a country that respects individual freedom, but whose bureaucracy adeptly stifles economic initiative. It is a country where more than a third remains desperately poor. It is a country that shows great compassion for the poor, with social policies to match. It is a country that discriminates and brutalizes the poor in the name of "caste". It is a culture of haunting musical expression that for me reaches closer than any other to the spirit it seeks to discover and embrace. It is a country of families. Families whose binds are almost as inseparable and loving as they are, or can be, oppressive. It is a culture that values learning and contains enormous intellectual force. It is country that is modernizing rapidly through intellectually-inspired technology. It is a culture that values human warmth and lasting friendships. It is a people that inspire humanity everywhere, through their dignity and humility in a steadfast struggle to overcome adversity. It is the land of Mahatma Gandhi, both adored and long forgotten. I did not realize how powerful an influence India would have on my life until I came away.

Deepest Love

India is where I found Suvira, my deepest love, my life-long hero and my eternal inspiration. India is so deeply personal because of her and what she is. Her beliefs and principles so purely held and practiced day to day. I have changed in so many ways as a result, not realizing when and how, but feeling and knowing the profound difference. Something way inside that seeks truth, good and justice, especially justice. Something that was there but that only she could give me the confidence and courage to purposefully seek and pursue. India became more comprehensible because of her. I saw it more from the inside. Not that I understood it all, or even a significant part, but that I did understand some in ways not possible before. She brought me into touch with Indian people. I discovered their values and their commitments. It reinforced my realization and experience that cross-cultural communication and empathy was natural and easy for human beings if it was enabled to happen. These were for me insights to the profound potential and importance of "human decency" and "human bonding" as the basis for building world peace and prosperity.

India Disclosed

I was in India with the United Nations Development Programme as its Assistant Resident Representative. My passion was to work on rural development, close to people. I ended up handling a wide range of development projects; some very removed from people, at least those in the villages. I did not fully appreciate then how much my travels across this land gave me the opportunity to move about and experience the culture of India. I did not fully realize that this was the richest gift I would take away.

During my field visits, I worked with state, bloc and district government officials on a wide range of development ideas and initiatives. I became aware of how much more they had thought about grassroots development than I or even the UN. As I traveled through many of India's states, I appreciated the exquisite uniqueness of each. I relished the lush green serenity of rice fields and palms and the incessant crowing of black birds in South India. I relaxed on house boats facing the vast Himalayas of Kashmir. I witnessed for the first time total human deprivation on the streets of India's many overcrowded cities. I felt like a time traveler a thousand years removed at the Golden Temple of Amritsar as old Sikh warriors roamed the balustrades with lances so long they seemed mythical. I gave speeches at local Rotary Clubs. I drove across the endless dusty roads of Uttar Pradesh. I visited remote towns where immense populations moved on foot with the rhythm of a sea. I lunched at long tables in old colonial railway stations with local politicians in white caps and pajamas sitting cross-legged belching and hand washing in their water glasses. I talked with professors at the Indian Institute of Technology in the Punjab about the miracle of the "green revolution" then in progress. I never ceased to be amazed at the endless rows of motor garages fixing every form of vehicle and tractor with parts improvised as necessity required. I wondered how people toiling in long mountainous valleys of Himachal Pradesh could continue to survive so removed as they seemed to be from modern life. I was profoundly impressed by their resilience and unperturbed air. I felt pain in each major city I visited, knowing how many of the children living in make-shift cardboard huts and concrete pipes, as along Bombay's airport road, would die on those streets before they were five.

As I continued to move about India, I kept wondering how these people must feel and think about their lives. What were their concerns, their problems? Did they have aspirations beyond their daily grind? I wondered what dreams they held. What opportunities they sought if change ever made it possible. I wondered if their views had ever been sought. I wondered if they would participate in change if given a chance. I particularly wondered who would have the decency to make sure they were given a chance.

Two-Way Communications

About this same time, I met two young American men who had been living in New Delhi for a couple of years. They were there to learn and absorb the culture. They worked for no one. They lived simply. They had an interest in new technology, and had brought with them a video recorder and camera and some simple editing equipment. As we came to know each other better, we shared concerns about the apparent lack of people's real involvement in their own development. The idea began to emerge that technology could help break through some of these barriers. We conjectured that videotape held the potential of unlocking a stream of thinking and new insights of people into what they wanted and what changes could bring real benefits to them. We decided to put this to the test.

This was the start of a long journey that continued for me for many years. Our idea was to begin a process of interviewing village people about their lives and about their perceptions of development. We chose the State of Rajasthan in Western India for our work. Spending weekends there, and with the help of one of Suvira's Indian friends, Bunker Roy, who was experimenting with peoples' participation, we began to interview the people of Telonia village. What were the main difficulties they faced in their lives? What was the most important thing they would like to do to improve their lives? How in practical terms could they do this, and what did they need to accomplish it? What was their experience with government assistance in these matters, or other development agencies and programs in the area? What needed to be done differently, better, by whom, and what would it take? What were they willing to do or contribute?

The communication and outpouring of sentiments and views that followed was nearly unbelievable. It was an outpouring of frustration as well as hope and determination. There was a great deal of resentment, but also understanding. There was a lot of poking fun at each other and at Government. There were concrete ideas of what could and should be done. We began to spread out the dialogue beyond the village to the wider district and "Bloc" area. We interviewed government officials, extension agents and workers at all these levels. Much to our surprise, they were very open and honest. Admitting to the shortcomings of their programs and efforts, they also gave ideas of how things might be done better.

It was in playing back these video interviews at joint gatherings of villagers and government officials that the power of communications became strikingly clear. Both sides sat in amazement, initially in stunned silence, at what they were hearing. Then began roars of laughter for what they had said. An almost disbelief in the honesty and funniness both sides were hearing from the other. There was a lot of nodding of heads for some of the ideas put forward. There were a lot of doubting frowns in response to others. There was a thunderous applause when it was over. We felt we were onto something important.

Back in New Delhi, we decided to edit it all into a half hour program for presentation at an Indian Government and UN-sponsored symposium on the uses of media technology (again, satellite was the focus) in development. We had gathered in our field visits video takes of a rich sampling of Indian music performed by local artists. The one we chose for the opening sequence of the video presentation was extraordinary. To capture it, we sat down one early morning in the city of Ajmer, Rajasthan beside a blind woman who sang in the tradition of "Mirabhai". Her lilting, soulful and strong voice pierced the video images of the desert and its camels and people at work. It was a stirring preparation for what was to follow.

The audience of international and Indian experts and scholars sat in silence as the video revealed the voices of people. There was an obvious tension. Depictions of strong views between local people and government officials were unusual, even in this largest democracy. After the initial twenty minutes, a certain restlessness set in among some of the audience while others seemed spell-bound by the frankness and strengths of conviction so vividly depicted. The reaction was mixed. Some felt it was an unfair play on local frustrations, others that it was an extraordinary, or at least unusual, look into reality.

For my own part, the enormous power this type of communications potentially held was immensely exciting. Though not realizing it then, I would dedicate many years in attempting to release this power of peoples' voices. And although I was eventually disappointed in the "failure" of video to "take off" as an instrument of development for this purpose, I became increasingly convinced as the years rolled by that such communications (whatever the medium) was an absolute key to building understanding and cooperation among people in any common effort to improve their lives. Looking back, the currently rising power of social media seems to point in this direction, perhaps vindicating some of my early sense of this though with much still to be understood and realized.

Decencies of Youth

Alongside these events, there was another set of experiences I had in India. These equally affected my belief in the power of people to come together for their mutual good, particularly when it was based on a sense of commitment to make it happen. It is a remarkable story.

Through Suvira I came to know many young Indian men and women who had dedicated their lives to helping the poor. Suvira was working under the "Action for Development" program of the Food and Agricultural Organization (FAO) of the UN. Her job was to facilitate a network of non-governmental groups around India working in rural and urban areas. She had good organizing skills and a lot of tenacity. She traveled to all parts of the country to identify and pull together these otherwise dispersed and isolated individuals. Bringing them together to share what they were doing was a very empowering process. It enabled them to help each other find ways of overcoming the common problems and obstacles they faced. They were all highly committed.

Many of them were highly educated. It seemed incongruous that their PhDs and MAs in physics, law, and management could be applied in any meaningful way in the villages and slums where they had dedicated themselves to work and live. But what I knew from my Peru experience and what was confirmed, was that their backgrounds, combined with their deep sense of justice and sheer determination, provided them with exactly the analytical skills and confidence they needed to address the profound political challenges found in local communities and the institutions that were suppose to serve them. They were welcomed as brothers and sisters by the local residents.

They sought out and faced the toughest impediments to development. These were often issues of discrimination, prejudice, corruption, and violence. They revolved around the denial of land, and the absence of any meaningful social or economic opportunities among the people and their children. The young professionals displayed great courage in revealing and fighting these injustices. They did it not as heroes, but as people going about the ordinary business of the day. They sought no recognition or reward. Their guiding light was fair play. They lived with the people, a simple, often hard existence. They did not see it as sacrifice, but as their life's work and they were certain they would be there for the rest of their lives. Extraordinary (to them, ordinary) examples of decency and caring.

Saintly Example

During my two years in India, I bore a privileged witness to another example of caring and commitment, but not by the young. Somehow in going about my work with video, I met a man who had come to India from Morocco. He had come because of his concern for India's lepers. He had taken me to the leper colony on the outskirts of Delhi. It was a memorable experience. It was a large complex of old buildings surrounded by a wall. I had never up to that point seen a leper, let alone a leper colony. There was a semblance of everyday life as lepers sat and worked outdoors on a variety of small items to be sold. I began to see their sores. Fingers missing, noses half gone. Healthy young children running about, probably already knowing that one day they would likely be afflicted.

The families lived in a long line of rooms facing an open veranda. One particular family invited me into their home. I will never forget their sweetness and generosity as they prepared tea for me. I was stunned to learn she was a doctor who had contracted the disease. They were very cultured. We spoke of music and other joys some of which they were no longer able to experience. They were so grateful for my visit. I could see they were especially moved by the respect I had shown simply by coming.

Then one day several months later, my Moroccan friend came to my office and mentioned in passing that he would like me to meet a woman who would be visiting from Calcutta. He mentioned that she was also working with lepers. I had nearly forgotten the remark, when a few weeks later my secretary buzzed my line that the Moroccan gentleman had returned with a visitor and that they would like to see me. I asked that they should please come in. In those days of the early 1970s, she was well known in India, but not yet as a recipient of the Noble Peace Prize and as a living saint. Nevertheless, I was completely overwhelmed when Mother Teresa walked in and greeted me with a warm smile. My friend let me know that Prime Minister Madam Indira Gandhi and Mother Teresa would be meeting in the afternoon. He asked whether I would be free to join them. Astonished, I of course had no difficulty in affirming my availability. He also said that since there were no other meetings until then, he wanted to invite Mother Teresa and myself for lunch at his home. And so I spent most of one day with Mother Teresa. It is strange, I have often thought since, that I do not remember much of what we discussed. What I do remember was how easy I felt in her presence. How natural and totally unpretentious she was. How interested she was in me. How that almost transparent smile and warmth never left her face.

The meeting with Madam Gandhi took place on schedule that afternoon at her residence. Madam Gandhi was an elegant lady. Her sari, as with all saris, enhanced that elegance. The dark wood floor and furniture of her office and the coolness of the thick-walled premises lent an air of formality to the occasion. Once Mother Teresa began to chat and Madam Gandhi to reply, the meeting became more like the visit of close friends. The discussion was mostly about whether the prime minister could help in securing more land for the leper colony outside Delhi. There were assurances that all possible would be done though government regulations may cause some delay. It was a communication of two historic figures, made only slightly less dramatic by the occasional furtive glances Madame Gandhi cast my way, undoubtedly wondering what this young American had to do with all of this.

Ever since that day I have often thought about Mother Teresa. How she personified human decency and caring in its purest form. How her communication was so simply focused on others, never herself. How she always showed genuine interest in another person, whoever was before her and often in the most mundane way. Or the real concern she held for the situation or predicament of others, and how they must be helped. I have often thought that this selfless caring was the purest form of all religions and religious leaders, without the institutional trappings. I believe that the way she lived her decency, so simply and easily in everyday life, was inspiring precisely because it made it possible for each of us to see how we could achieve our own decency in our own simple and everyday ways of kindness to each other.

Cruel Streets

I continued my work and travels about India. One trip made a particularly deep impression on me. It was my first visit to Calcutta. The city had long fascinated me, conjuring up as it did masses of the poor swarming over one another to survive. The extraordinary thing was how true that turned out to be.

I checked into the Grand Hotel on Jawaharlal Nehru Road opposite "The Maidan" park that many referred to as the "lungs" of the city. I arrived mid afternoon, and after a quick shower, began to stroll the nearby streets. They were crowded and in constant motion. Every form of transport and mobility was taking place. Lean and diminished men, young and old, were trotting in front of rickshaws hand pulling those few who could afford their low charges. Those who could not had to get about on foot. Cattle roamed the streets freely. Small black and yellow "Ambassador" taxis dodged between them and around each other as they plied their way through the approaching darkness.

With that emerging darkness, I noticed the numbers of people began to swell. I soon realized that many were returning from their daily occupations as street vendors, day laborers, garbage collectors, toilet cleaners, tannery workers, and an unending variety of mostly unpleasant jobs and arduous tasks that those who could chose to avoid. What struck me most was how these masses began to settle into the night. The frenzied motions of the day began to yield to the slow rhythm of nighttime chores. The sidewalks filled to capacity leaving little space for anyone to cross over anyone else. People began to assemble in small bunches as the night wore on. I assumed these were families who had gathered back together for some relief and rest following a day of exhausting work in unrelenting heat (often hovering at 105 and more in the summer). Such relief was short lived, especially for the women, who began to cook rice and vegetables over small fires or primus stoves. As each group finished their meager meal, they began to unravel cloth on which they bedded down close to each other for the night. Soon the sidewalks were a carpet of wrapped bodies in deep slumber as I made my way back into the entrance of the hotel they had nearly blocked.

Before this sleep fell over the city, I began to notice young boys milling about separately from any families. Some seemed barely out of infancy; most were probably five to twelve years old. Some shared whatever food they had managed to scavenge during the day; others remained entirely on their own, looking very hungry.

One young boy, probably not more than six years old, caught my eye. He walked around in no particular direction. He held a thin rigid wire that extended down to a small dog. The wire wrapped around its head and muzzled its mouth. As the dog began to walk in one direction, the boy yanked it in another. When the dog began to move in that direction the boy jerked him violently again toward a different one. Their aimless rambling continued endlessly. With each pull of the wire, the dog—more precisely a puppy—yelped in pain as the metal cut into the sides of its mouth. The boy seemed unfazed by this, almost unaware. He wore an air of confidence about him, and I sensed he found pleasure in the dog's predicament, helplessness and pain.

The image haunted me for years. I had difficulty in understanding how such cruel behavior was possible at the hands of an otherwise, seemingly innocent and equally helpless boy. It was only as I began to see similar behavior in other young boys in my later journeys to other countries that I thought I had begun to understand the roots of their common behavior. In all cases, particularly under circumstances of extreme poverty and especially war, I found these abandoned youth sought to regain some sense of control over their own desperate lives by dominating and controlling the lives of others. Unfortunately this usually turned to more violent behavior as their alienation continued unabated. It explained for me the many inhuman atrocities I would witness over the ensuing years, which I would have otherwise found impossible to explain or believe.

In the face of these realities, I continued to reflect back on the life of Mother Teresa. I admired her not as a saint but as a human being not different from us except for the entirely caring way in which she lived and dedicated her life. I realized even then that not many people, certainly not I, were willing to devote an entire life to caring for others. She devoted herself to the dying, but I am certain if time permitted she would have wanted to devote herself to the young. More than her particular actions, she epitomized and demonstrated for me that caring could be lived as a core tenet of one's life to the degree and nature of one's own choosing. It reminded me of my growing conviction that practicing that same caring, in whatever form, as a core value of any society was every society's main challenge.

Social Commitments

Calcutta stirred my mind for the first time to these concerns. India in general revealed to me more than Peru the raw extremes of human life and the desperate conditions into which people fell, or more often, were born. India had many places where such desperation was common place. Over the years India had many responses to these conditions. They ranged from the traditional charity of temples and mosques which fed the poor each day. They included an unchanging commitment to alleviating poverty by the Communist Party in West Bengal (whose capital is Calcutta) in spite of a perennial lack of resources. They were contained in the broad sweeping efforts of rural village development of the Indian government amidst widespread corruption that inhibited results. They were certainly present in the dedication of the young professionals I had met who devoted their lives to living among and helping the poor. And these commitments persist even to the current day, including recent national reforms to make health insurance and services available to all the poor for the first time.

India has by no means rid itself of poverty. Yet poverty across India has declined significantly. I followed these trends carefully over the years, and while they were always controversial and challenged, the national poverty statistics recorded a drop from over 50% of the population while I was in India in the early 1970s, to nearly half that rate some three decades later.

I revisited Calcutta (changed to Kolkata by that time) nearly 35 years (in 2006) after my departure from India. It was a dramatically different city. No where could I find people living on the streets as in 1972. Nowhere did I find a rickshaw hand drawn by coolie-type runners. Poverty was certainly present. A third of the populations still lived in slums (many having shifted there from their homes on the streets). But their conditions seemed less grinding and desperate compared to the life of sheer survival I had witnessed before.

The new Calcutta had a vibrancy, economic dynamism and optimism. The serious economic decline Calcutta had experienced in the 1970s and even 1980s, due in no small measure to the political chaos that accompanied communist rule and the frequent strikes of a strong trade union movement, began to reverse itself from the early 1990s. India's national economic reforms had a dramatic impact on the city. It brought in new businesses including the establishment of the city as a hub of information technology. These changes were in large part the result of newly practiced free market philosophies and polices. Of course they did not benefit all of the poor (50% remained tied to informal trades of street vending and the like). But they clearly were having a positive impact.

There was no doubt in my mind that an equally crucial (perhaps more profound) factor contributing to the improvement of the lot of the poor was the long and consistent determination of the Indian government, and more broadly the Indian society, to fight and eliminate poverty. There have been many human failings and resource shortages that have impeded these efforts. Some of these are the consequence of a growing elite of very rich who have little empathy or time for such concerns. India is not free of greed and corrupt behavior, not only among politicians, but especially among centuries-old and powerful rural elites who have subjugated the poor through control of land and exploitation of an enforced caste system.

And yet I have seen and continued to observe that India as a nation remained dedicated to core values of caring and decency for the poor. Some of this has been driven by the democratic system that has blessed India since independence. Rural voters have gained enormous power in deciding elections and committing politicians to their cause.

Yet there is more to it than this. Since its independence, India made a moral choice and lived (not without great struggle and setbacks) by the values of that choice. That choice was social democracy—not in a narrow political sense but in the broader terms of a national character committed to decency toward others. It is a tenacious commitment to social justice. It is embedded in policies and programs dedicated to overcoming the worst of human conditions. In adopting the new capitalism, India managed to bridle it with these underlying and uncompromising social commitments to its people. They are the same social commitments that have faded and failed in so many other countries. In this light, India remains in my mind an inspiration, however imperfect, to the entire world.

With Fresh Eyes
1973 – 1979 – 2013

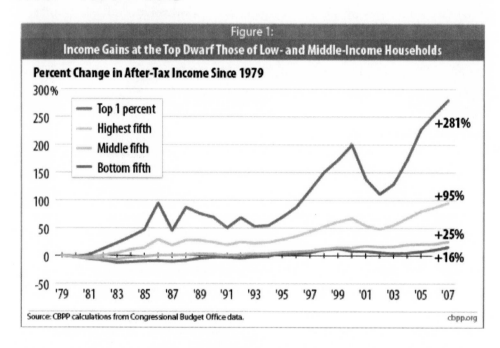

Figure 1:

Income Gains at the Top Dwarf Those of Low- and Middle-Income Households

Percent Change in After-Tax Income Since 1979

- Top 1 percent
- Highest fifth
- Middle fifth
- Bottom fifth

+281%
+95%
+25%
+16%

Source: CBPP calculations from Congressional Budget Office data.   cbpp.org

Income Gaps Between Very Rich and Everyone Else More Than Tripled In Last Three Decades,
New Data Show

By Arloc Sherman and Chad Stone
Center on Budget and Policy Priorities
June 25, 2010
"The gaps in after-tax income between the richest 1 percent of Americans
and the middle and poorest fifths of the country more than tripled between
1979 and 2007 (the period for which these data are available), according to
data the Congressional Budget Office (CBO) issued last week. Taken
together with prior research, the new data suggest greater income
concentration at the top of the income scale than at any time since 1928."…

Inside / Outside

America always loomed large in the background of my life. While working for the UN I remained outside the US for most of the next forty years, but I would regularly return to it (every one or two years) as a welcomed "home base". It was also my window on a rapidly changing society that I continuously compared to the life and values of the countries in which I was living. In fact, my absence turned into a benefit. The vision and understanding of one's own culture is sometimes clouded by closeness and familiarity. Coming home on leaves from my job abroad placed me in the position, as much as is ever possible, of the dispassionate observer. It gave me new insights and perspectives on the changes that were taking place. The opportunity and privilege to partake in the American experience as both an insider and an outsider was exceptional.

Most of these return visits were short, one or two months. But they provided a continuing and changing snapshot of the way America was evolving. Most important, they opened my eyes to major phenomena that were occurring in America common to those in other countries and cultures which I would never have expected or understood otherwise. These insights illuminated a set of common human conditions and challenges that I learned cut across all societies whether "developed" or "developing". They helped me to understand both the difficulty and the possibility for change on a global scale.

Bridging the Gap

Early in my sojourn, I decided to return to America for an extended period. It eventually spanned five years (1973-78). I decided to seek a leave of absence from the UN to explore and develop the work I had started in India on communications between people and their institutions. Since Suvira and I were starting a new life together that would unfortunately include going through what became a painful divorce, we thought our professional and personal interests could best be served by returning to America. We arrived in San Francisco in mid-1973. We had not much clue as to what and how we were going to pursue our professional life. But we knew we were going to do it together.

It was my first real experience, or rather grueling task, of finding a job. It was not a pleasant experience. We spent six months contacting and meeting a huge number of potential employers (or so we hoped). They were mostly universities, local government, and private social agencies, and we set out to convince them of the merit of our proposal. What we offered was to create for any of them a "bridge of communications" with the people they were trying to serve. The purpose was to enrich the relationship and build collaboration for action on whatever it was they were hoping to accomplish. We stirred a lot of interest among some very bright and creative people who saw the potential of our approach. But very few were prepared to put up the "venture capital" for such an experiment.

Fortune was eventually on our side. We managed to capture the imagination and interest of authorities at the University of California (San Francisco) Medical Center. Our proposal was quite simple. We would use video to build a bridge between the medical center "on the hill" and the surrounding most needy communities of San Francisco. The aim was to promote cooperation on a wide range of health issues. This fit well with a public perception at the time of a growing gap between large institutions such as UCSF and community people who correctly or not felt those institutions must be there to serve them as much as anybody else. There was no interaction between them, no communication, just a lot of stereotypes of an "uncaring" medical establishment on the one hand, and a "demanding but unfocused and unrealistic" community on the other. We proposed to take on this gap.

The Administrator of the UCSF Medical Center Hospital, Robert Durzon (who later worked for President Carter to manage medicare) was intrigued. He of course saw the "goodwill" image this could create for the university. He also held a genuine belief that preventative health care should reach all people regardless of economic status, race or religion.

There then began for us a long process of rapport building in the communities as well as among the diverse university staff. We soon learned the strengths and limitations of technology in these efforts. The video was superb at capturing the drama of ideas and emotions. But it could not replace what had to go before and after. One does not gain the trust and confidence of people through interviews alone. This has to be done through the old fashioned one-on-one approach that requires investment of considerable time and energy. Similarly, once the video interviews were completed and edited, even after they were shown back to motivate joint meetings, it was the follow up that counted most. It was a matter of organizing and turning ideas into action by working long hours side by side with people. There were no short cuts.

So that is what we did—long hours both days and evenings spent getting to know people, individually and in groups. We probed to know what was important to them. We sought to know their problems. After each interview, we spent time chatting and searching for ways in which those problems might be lessened if the knowledge and expertise of the university could be brought to bear.

On one occasion we talked to a middle-aged man in his home in the Sunset District. He explained in heart-rending language how his wife had suffered from his years of alcoholism and abuse. In spite of the anguish written deeply on her face, she in turn spoke quietly but firmly of the hope she held for any way to help him out of his addiction. Based on this trust to "open up" and share what we needed to understand, and many similar interviews and discussions, we were able to build the elements of an alcohol education program.

We spent long evenings with young homeless girls. They lived on the streets of the Haight Asbury neighborhood. They were clearly embittered by the memories of their past neglect, abuse and addiction to drugs. One young woman particularly impressed us. Dressed in an Indian blouse and a long flower-printed skirt popular at the time, she confided in us as we sat late one evening in her small, one room loft. Her biggest mistake she realized was in letting her former boyfriend talk her into ever more harmful drugs. Looking back, she felt she had no one else to turn to and very little knowledge of the danger ahead. Again, the drug education program we organized was created on the basis of real life experiences such as these, and ideas of what could work.

We heard of the quiet anxiety and loneliness of black senior citizens in the Fillmore District. None were ever sure if their social security checks would stretch to the end of the month or whether anybody cared. We built a senior health program based on those words. It aimed mostly at finding ways to alleviate their stress and fill their lives with a greater sense of companionship and caring.

We engaged and motivated dentists and hygienists of the university to address the need for preventive education across all age and economic groups. We based the dental education program on that goal.

It was a hard-won process of opening communications, building trust, and finding and working on common goals. It was all based on a growing respect for each other and a sense of equality in assuming roles and responsibilities. Presumably for these reasons, the programs, once started, kept going. Not that everything went smooth and easy. There were many examples of delays, frustrations and bickering, and certainly some share of failed initiatives that seem inevitably to accompany human cooperation. But after nearly five years, and as we prepared to return to our UN work, we felt that however imperfect it still was, we had learned and practiced a great deal about bringing people and institutions together. We understood the importance of letting them determine their common interests and to figure out how they could best work together.

Our work in San Francisco was immensely valuable to our renewed work with the UN. It provided us with a new understanding and confidence in how the challenges of bridging the divide between advantaged people and institutions and those who are far less privileged is similar whether in rich or poor countries. We learned that change is feasible (and critically needed) across all cultures if it is based on the same basic principles of respect, trust, and caring. Above all, we learned that the approach we took could only have been possible on the basis of the sense of decency that both the institution and the communities shared for providing those in need an opportunity to improve their conditions.

During our years in San Francisco, I undertook short term assignments with the UN in Ethiopia and Pakistan (see the next Chapter 9), and then we finally departed America in February 1979 to renew my UN service with an initial assignment to the South Pacific (see Chapter 10). This set in motion our regular return visits to America that revealed over time a strong commonality with wider global disparities.

Witnessing the Divide

Unbeknown to me at the time, the late 1970s and early 1980s was a crucial turning point in American socio-economic history. What I was seeing in the changing way of life on the surface of America was altogether puzzling and disturbing to me. I was unable at the time to identify these changes as manifestations of the more profound change that was occurring.

What I and Suvira saw, and what we pondered, discussed and shared between us for those thirty years, was a growing and deep class divide in America. We saw it clearly, much more clearly than our family or friends who seldom if ever commented on it. It did not occur to us immediately either as the changes took time to gain momentum and sink fully into our consciousness.

The divide was initially camouflaged by the recession of the early 1980s.

Our returns to the US in those years were to Oregon where Suvira's sister Sarojini, and husband Mahendra, had taken up residence, and where we eventually settled ourselves. Oregon like much of America was overwhelmed in the first half of the 80s with news of the economic downturn and serious levels of unemployment. These concerns in Oregon were focused primarily on the demise of the timber industry which had been a mainstay of its economy throughout much of its history, and the question of what would replace it.

While we were living in Fiji (1979-1981; see Chapter 10), Ronald Reagan was elected president of the United States. He took office in January 1981, was reelected and served through 1989. President Reagan has long since acquired a special place in the hearts of many Americans. Without a doubt he was unique in his ability to communicate and uplift Americans in a period of what some saw as an era of national despondency. Likewise, his accomplishments in bringing down the Soviet empire remain historic.

At the same time, his domestic policies changed the social fabric of America. It was a change that continued to have an impact over more than thirty years. They were policies that blatantly favored the rich. They were justified on the premise that such wealth would 'trickle down' to working people through greater employment. At the heart of these policies were significant tax cuts for the wealthy and a deregulation of business practices. Employment did in fact rise and inflation was substantially reduced, but this came at a heavy price. Both the federal budget and the national debt rose significantly, the latter quadrupling during his two terms. Equally disturbing in my mind was what Reagan did to crush labor unions in America. This resulted in the loss of what had always been a sacred American value—a decent living wage to support every family. And in this atmosphere, greed began to grip American business as never before. CEO salaries began to take off to new heights. A great divide was opening up in America.

To be completely fair, while Reagan initiated these changes, he was not alone in making them a permanent feature of American society. These policies continued basically in place and unchanged throughout these years to the present day through and with the support of both Republican and Democratic presidencies.

This was all in sharp contrast of course to the legacies of social caring, social security and public employment of Franklin Delano Roosevelt during the Great Depression of the 1930s and 40s. It stood in equally sharp contrast to the morally responsible policies of Lyndon Johnson in the 1960s. His passion ensured medical care for older Americans, equal civil rights for black Americans, and a "War on Poverty" that reduced poverty from 22% to 12% within a span of eight years.

I reflected over this period on how these fundamental shifts in social policies and moral principles were distorting the life that I had known growing up in America. They led to consequences that were disastrous for most working families. They have been nearly impossible to reverse. "Reaganism" embedded a new paradigm in America of government as the problem, which in that broader context, I boiled down to "look after yourself and let others take care of themselves". It was an ethos so powerful and accepted that even liberal Democrats failed their constituencies in not seriously attempting to turn these trends around. Clearly too many elites in power on all sides were benefiting too much to inspire and drive change.

The biggest problem this created, as I saw it unfold over those many years of visits, was not just the poverty per se. Rather it was the rise of great wealth among a few. The combination rapidly grew the divide.

After the depression, poverty rates fluctuated and reached peaks in the early 1980s and 1990s of about 15%, then gradually leveled out around 12.5%, rising again with the Great Recession of 2008-2009 to 15.1%. The deepest impact was in creating severe poverty among those living below half the poverty line (about $11,000), who constituted some 20.5 million in 2010 (6.7% of the population).

What these statistics did not show is how poverty became more institutionalized and hidden in America. This was partly the result of safety net programs of both state and federal governments (cash and non-cash assistance, including food stamps benefits (SNAP), refundable tax credits like earned income tax credit, unemployment insurance, etc.). These programs on the one hand reduced the numbers in poverty (according to the Center on Budget and Policy Priorities, poverty rates would be nearly double without them). But due to the erratic ways these programs were applied and managed, they made the poor dependent, unstable, and (for many) eventually poorer. They shifted people randomly into and out of poverty depending on current policies that took away assistance and then returned to provide it.

It was a welfare system that in effect played with poverty, and according to Peter Edelman's *So Rich, So Poor: Why It's So Hard to End Poverty in America*, led overtime to an actual "demise of welfare" (which let us not forget was a bi-partisan policy championed by Bill Clinton). But whatever positive results may have come from moving (some of) the poor out of welfare, there were and continue to be serious detrimental impacts on the lot of the poor today. A prime example is the impact this shift has had on poor children less than half of whom benefit from public assistance in the present day compared to those in the mid-1990s.

An article by the *Associated Press* dated November 3, 2009 ('Food Stamps Fact of Life for Half of U.S. Kids'), clearly showed the growing vulnerability of both children and adults: "Nearly half of all U.S. children and 90% of black youngsters will be on food stamps at some point during their childhood and the current recession could push those numbers even higher, researchers say. The estimate comes from an analysis of 30 years of national data, and it bolsters other recent evidence on the pervasiveness of youngsters at economic risk". Equally revealing, the article reported that "The analysis is in line with other recent research suggesting that more than 40 per cent of U.S. children will live in poverty by age 17 and that half will live at some point in a single-parent family. Also, other researchers have estimated that slightly more than half of adults will use food stamps at some point by age 65."

Slowly, however, I began to see that the real culprit, as Peter Edelman later pointed out, was that "we've been drowning in a flood of low-wage jobs for the last 40 years" during which wages stagnated (since 1973) for those working in the bottom half of the income spectrum. This was a result in no small part stemming from the lack of any enlightened policies over this period to provide relevant education and skill training truly geared to preparing people, young and adult, for jobs.

Sadly, I began to notice that despite these problems, politicians increasingly ignored the lot of the poor. They focused instead on helping the "middle class" without a word about the worsening situation of the overtly poor who clearly had no political clout or reasons why politicians needed to court them.

Nor did I notice any of these politicians seriously protesting the incredible concentration of wealth that was occurring in America over this same time period. All the more amazing since this increasing inequality was creating a rapidly declining standard of living for a much broader spectrum of Americans that went far beyond the poor.

I began to see an increasing focus on these problems by academics and researchers, though mostly coming only after the widening divide culminated in the Great Recession (2008-2009). The Center on Budget and Policy Priorities played a particularly active role, and with continuing research by Thomas Piketty and Emmanuel Saez, they laid bare with good analysis the trends over the past eighty years (going back to 1928). What they showed was that following the high peak of income disparities between rich and poor in the late 1920s, and the subsequent collapse of the economy into depression, incomes for all income groups began to rise fairly evenly, doubling across the board between the 1940s and 1970s. It was truly a period of shared prosperity (with the exception of course of the markedly lower incomes for American blacks, and the sharp wage discriminations against women).

The same research made clear this all began to change dramatically from the mid 1970s when income gains of the top earners significantly outpaced those of the rest. By 2007, the top 10% took 47% of all of America's income (with 21% going to the very top 1%). Even more astonishing, nearly three-quarters (73%) of the total wealth (all assets minus liabilities) in America was concentrated in the top 10% (35% for the 1% alone). Again, this was due in significant part to tax and economic policies that blatantly favored the rich. Moreover, the studies confirmed that these trends continued to exacerbate throughout all political administrations over this period. Specifically, 45% of total income gains went to the top 1% of earners during Clinton's administration, reaching a further high water mark of 65% under George W. Bush, and eventually an astonishing 93% (which amounted to a staggering $288 billion) under Barack Obama in 2010. All the result of policies firmly entrenched since the Reagan era and clearly perpetuated under Democratic administrations, whether purposefully or not, to enrich the rich.

The increasing divide has been particularly harsh on minorities who have struggled over these many years to pull themselves out of poverty and discrimination. This was highlighted during the aftermath of the Great Recession when in mid 2011, Hispanics and Blacks slipped back to the far end of the income spectrum. Hispanics lost 66% of their net worth (mostly the houses they had managed to buy and then had to foreclose) while Blacks lost 53% (having to sell whatever assets they had to keep heads above the financial water line).

The result of all of this is that the US has the dubious honor today of having the highest income inequality of all developed and wealthy countries.

Underclass

The most troubling part for me over time was as I have indicated to see the concept of poverty and the poor metamorphose into a new (but unrecognized) and much larger phenomenon I began to refer to as an 'underclass'. These working 'low income' people made up one-third of the US population (more than doubling the conventional poverty rate). We would meet them on our visits. We began to see they simply could not keep up with the American Dream that had long motivated them. They slipped into a state of declining opportunities whether in education, health care or secure employment. They became victims of the unregulated system, fell into debt and lost their homes.

We saw this ever more difficult struggle among our families and friends. It was a struggle to maintain respectability, dignity and a decent standard of living. No one talked about the problem initially, but we all knew it was taking its toll. For many, getting a fair compensation for their efforts was a constant challenge, facing as they did an increasing culture of short term, low wage, expendable "temp" employment with few if any benefits (justified under new management mantras of keeping one's business "mean and lean"). And of course an ever increasing outsourcing of services both at home and abroad. Pensions were no longer offered. Retirement depended on success in investing savings in increasingly volatile and risky markets. Health insurance was uncertain if one moved to another job, and unavailable to those (still nearly fifty million Americans) who could not afford the basic premiums and remained uninsured.

Some of these problems touched me personally. My sister Mary had moved to Hawaii and after some time began to suffer from a debilitating spinal arthritis. She was denied long term care insurance because of her "pre-existing condition". She resided in a costly assisted-living facility that rapidly pushed her into "destitution" which was required for her to qualify for a government-run facility. She ended up in a private home, government licensed and funded to provide care but which, unknown to me at the time, neglected her basic health needs to the point at which her body and mind deteriorated so rapidly she could no longer be treated. The next step was hospice care.

Anticipating her death, I flew to Hawaii to see her. In the hills behind Honolulu, I found her in good hospice care but in a nearly comatose state. She was in a permanent fetal position with knees nearly touching her breasts and literally no sign of life beyond her almost inaudible breath. I held her hand and talked to her of our childhood and of remembrances only she would know about. I told her how much I loved her and that I wished life had been kinder to her, that she was as sweet a person as I had ever known. Without a stir, a word, or change in demeanor, I could not believe my eyes when tears formed and rolled down her cheek one at a time. I believe she was so relieved and happy to have me with her in her dying moments that her whole being could not hold back a wish to express that to me. She died that night.

I only gradually began to fully understand what the shift in America was all about and how it was impacting the lives of people denied decent care like my sister. It became increasing clear to me, as harsh as it sounds, that the shift was purposefully set in motion to benefit the few without genuine concern for the rest. We were watching America decline before our eyes. It was sliding into a kind of nation not unknown to us. A nation in which elites dominated. A nation is which care for others had diminished. A nation in which the majority found it increasingly difficult to live (and die) decently.

Comparisons

It was a shock because I had been studying for a long time this phenomenon of inequality and disparity between rich and poor in every country in which I had worked. I never thought it was very relevant to my own country. To my family. I was wrong. The fact was that America had a greater gap between rich and poor than many of the countries in which I lived.

The tool for measuring this inequality, used by the UN in my own work, and by academics and professionals in the development field, called the "Gini Coefficient", is a rather esoteric terminology to describe a simple index for measuring the distribution of wealth in any society. The measurement ranges between zero and one. The former (0) indicates a country with very even (equitable) distribution of wealth. The latter (1) indicates that all wealth is concentrated in the hands of a few, meaning a very high degree of inequality in income distribution. Denmark and Sweden usually rank lowest (meaning quite equitable wealth distribution) with a coefficient just above .20 (even former Soviet sphere countries such as Hungary, the Czech Republic, Bulgaria and Romania are all below .30). Countries like Zimbabwe, Namibia, Lesotho, Guinea, and South Africa are at the other end of the spectrum, between .60 and .70. Before thinking to look at the data for the US, I assumed it would be somewhere near Sweden but not very much different. In fact, the US averages a coefficient of between .40 and .50. This is considerably higher than any Western European country, and places it on a par with countries such as Philippines, China, and Turkey.

The picture becomes more alarming if one looks at the ranking of states within the US (some estimations of this have been projected based on US census data): Alabama, Louisiana, Mississippi, Texas and (not so surprising given the side-by-side existence of great wealth and poverty) New York and Connecticut—all have coefficients (.470 and above) equivalent to Nepal, Mozambique, Madagascar, and Venezuela!

What was particularly disturbing in all of this for me is what it showed about the gradual diminishing state of the middle class in America. In fact, if the disparity trends continued in the US as they had been over the past three to four decades, it appeared possible that the "middle class" would indeed for all intents and purposes disappear to become replaced by what we again may more accurately term the "underclass" in which the working poor are increasingly prominent.

Nothing brought this decline of the middle class more vividly to my attention than a couple of articles I read in the *New York Times* at the height of the Great Recession.

Let me first share what was the background for me to the first article. It was an experience I had in 1983 when I took my daughter Natasha, then twelve, down to the river and the "burning Ghats" (where people were cremated in Hindu ceremony) in front of our home in the Kathmandu Valley (Nepal). As we trekked along that river bank, Natasha walking some paces ahead of me, I suddenly stopped in utter shock at seeing a face in the river mud staring back at me with eyes wide open. It was something not that unusual in Nepal (and neighboring India) where the very poor could not afford to cremate their dead. Instead they floated them down any river to their natural resting place. But to actually see this for myself, especially as I was not in the least expecting it on a riverfront over which I gazed each day, was very disturbing. I quickly recovered my composure and resumed my brisk walk. Natasha did not notice or inquire. I never told her about it.

The *New York Times* article (October 11, 2009) that brought this incident back to mind was entitled "Number of Unclaimed Bodies Increases as Families Can't Afford Burials." The lead paragraphs of the article summed up the story: "Coroners and medical examiners across the country are reporting spikes in the number of unclaimed bodies and indigent burials, with states, counties and private funeral homes having to foot the bill when families cannot. The increase comes as governments short of cash are cutting other social service programs, with some municipalities dipping into emergency and reserve funds to help cover the cost of burials or cremations." The next paragraph particularly unsettled me: "Oregon, for example, has seen a 50 per cent increase in the number of unclaimed bodies over the past few years, the majority left by families who say they cannot afford services."

So there it was. Proof perfect for me, if ever there were need for it, that America—and particularly my own state of Oregon—was on a downward spiral of human indignity that I never thought possible. Not only that, but it coincided with an overall decline of governments "cutting other social service programs". Moreover, this had been happening "over the past few years". Clearly this was not just a one-time recession-driven phenomenon.

The second *New York Times* article came less than a week later (October 17, 2009). It was actually an Op Ed piece by the columnist Bob Herbert entitled: "Pricing the Kids Out". It was about the New York Yankees new home. Herbert commented that "The game was played in the *new* Yankee Stadium, which is equipped with all the upscale accoutrements that are becoming essential in professional sports—enormous video screens to give you the real-life feel of watching the game on television, luxurious restaurants, luxury boxes, outlandish prices and so forth. You need a mortgage now to get season tickets. Someone recently told me that at the prices the Yankees were originally charging for the best seats in the house, it would have cost around $800,000 for season tickets for a family of four. A lot of those seats stayed empty earlier in the season, so prices were dropped enough so that you only had to be rich to afford them, not superrich... Maybe this is not the biggest issue facing the country, but I can't help feeling we're making a big mistake pricing these games out of the reach of today's boys and girls who are growing up in families of modest means."

So again it was crystal clear. Increasing numbers of Americans could no longer afford to bury their loved ones. At the very same time, America continued in the midst of our deepest recession ever to cater in ever escalating proportions to the whims and petty appetites of the rich at the expense of all the rest who were increasingly left out of "American life" as we once knew it.

Mind Sets

And all of this was happening, I was sure, in the context of real available solutions that could (and still can) reverse these desperately negative trends: e.g. changes in tax rates and credits to provide a fairer distribution of wealth, reestablishment of the role of unions and the benefits they bring to working people, increases in the minimum wage, universal health care, low cost loans for college education, public works, housing vouchers—all of these and many other policy options were available. And America was a country, contrary to the ones we were working in, that could afford to adopt at least some of these policies if its costly priorities for defense and tax breaks for the wealthy were reset. America had the possibility to place a decent life for all Americans as its highest priority. So, why hadn't it done so? And I also asked myself, if America did not choose to reverse these trends that were dividing our society, what hope was there that other poorer countries could bridge similar (often more entrenched) divides.

The basic problem I concluded was one of elite attitudes and mind sets— and I would add moral character—whether in America or elsewhere. In practically all cases some resources were available to start a process of change. What was holding back less resource-plentiful countries was the same attitude that held back America, an overriding belief of their elites that people must shift for themselves, just as those who prided themselves for making it into the elites had done to achieve their wealth (or at least those who had not benefited from their parents' trust funds).

Reagan had introduced more than tax cuts. He had introduced a new way of thinking—about oneself to the exclusion of others. That mind set was later vigorously perpetuated as I saw it by George W. Bush who cut the taxes of the rich even further by a resoundingly unbelievable $1.3 trillion with support of both Republican and Democratic politicians! The "greed is good" mantra of the 80s was very much alive and well as we moved into the 2000s. The total disregard for the lot of the rest of the people was for me astonishing.

Even more perplexing, as I watched all of this unfold, was the acceptance by the working poor of the basic premise that *they* would eventually benefit. Much of the exorbitant sums of money spent in American politics have gone largely into creating and maintaining this myth. And acceptance of this myth has prevented the poor and even the middle class from adopting a political stand against it. It has deprived them of an enormous political power they would otherwise have to demand greater equal opportunity and justice. It is this absence of power, and the possibility of still acquiring it, that I shall return to in the final chapter as we look at our options for future action.

Yet I gradually realized that these attitudes should not have been entirely unexpected. I became more convinced than ever that the concept of the

"American Dream" was created by elites to keep the masses tread milling incessantly in the hope of catching up to them (which they knew they never would) while they enjoyed the early (and perpetually exclusive) fruits of runaway materialism.

Antecedents

Over these thirty years, I began to reflect more and more on the background of these distorted values in America. They were indeed given new impetus in the modern economics and ethos, but surely the roots of these attitudes went far deeper into American history. In fact, they were blatantly evident from the earliest colonial times.

It would surprise and shock most Americans to learn that even the Pilgrims and early settlers such as in the Massachusetts Bay Colony resorted to violence to gain control of what they wanted from Native Americans. In spite of the fact that these same Native Americans had shared essential food and survival skills with these colonists, who would likely have perished otherwise, the latter turned against them and decimated their societies. It was a cultural practice that continued over more than 200 years until most Native Americans were either dead from disease or annihilated by killings.

The chief motivation of the early European Americans was greed for land they occupied by force. They used every conceivable ways and means to deceive, betray and continuously break treaties with Native Americans. These indigenous people lived in an entirely different value universe of equal reciprocity that could not under any circumstances contemplate the taking of the fundamental resources that defined their very existence and way of life.

But this is precisely what happened to most Native Americans—from the atrocities of the colonial period, to the eradication of American Natives across Southeastern America, to the rapid opening and expansion into the American West under an arrogant doctrine of "manifest destiny", to the active and aggressive presidential policies (under President James Polk 1845-49) to rid of the "Indian Problem"—systematically Native Americans were forced to surrender their home areas. Some fled to Canada as in the case of the *Nez Perce* tribe from my state of Oregon. Their leader Chief Joseph resisted demands to move his people to a distant reservation but eventually surrendered in 1877 to the pursuing US Army after a 1,500 mile harrowing trek into Canada and back.

For the most part, Native Americans did move, initially to "prayer towns" and eventually "reservations" where they stagnated. They continue to suffer lasting humiliation and deprivation even to this day, many caught in a vicious cycle of alcoholism and abuse.

No doubt, America's many achievements in pursuing basic democracy and "the rights of man" for its people remain admirable accomplishments of our society. But these have too often been pursued within an historical and cultural context of profound greed and indifference to human suffering. This inconvenient past has in my mind, without question contributed to the environment in which current day avariciousness of elites determined to maintain power and wealth at the expense of whomever else has flourished.

Values Imposed

Over these same times I also began to see another more global dimension to all of this. It was in terms of the influence these values were having on US foreign policy. Most disturbingly, it was these policies that were directly impacting the lives of poor people in a multitude of countries. I was puzzled by this for many years. I believed the United States of America was truly the beacon of hope and liberty around the world. But if it was, why was it consistently supporting dictatorships in other countries at the expense of the masses of poor people in those countries?

I had studied the phenomenon particularly in the case of Latin America during my masters program at Stanford. But I was more taken by what was unfolding before me. There was a long history of these practices. America had intervened in Central and South American politics for many decades. It had overthrown governments and replaced them with right-wing dictators who were favorable to American economic interests. This included, for example, bringing to power the Somoza regime in Nicaragua in the mid-1930s (following a US military invasion of the country as far back as 1912) based on fear of a revolutionary takeover. Somoza pillaged the country's assets to the detriment of an already desperately poor citizenry. He was overthrown by the Sandinistas only in 1979, and then only in spite of US support to keep him in power. A similar and parallel case was the long-standing US support for the Batista regime in Cuba before Castro overthrew it on January 1, 1959.

The latter case particularly caught my attention when I saw on television a replay in the early 1960s of an interview with Fidel Castro at his hideout in the Sierra Madre Mountains of Cuba in 1958. While Castro was being interviewed by an American reporter, I noticed that he was kneeling on the ground with a young man who looked very familiar to me. As the interview proceeded I realized to my enormous surprise that his companion was none other than an old grade school classmate of mine in 1954 at Sacred Heart Elementary School in Coronado. He was the son of a naval officer who had been reassigned from Coronado to the base at Guantanamo, Cuba. He did not say much in the interview, only that he had joined Castro to fight for the people. As I remembered him, he was a very quiet and thoughtful youngster in my eighth grade class. Hardly someone I would ever have expected to see fighting with Fidel Castro. He could not have been more than eighteen at the time. It raised in my mind a lot of questions about what had inspired him to do this. Most of the American media had portrayed Castro as anti-American. So I was doubly shocked, and impressed, to find my friend at his side. I later understood that it was a reflection of the immense resentment that Batista had instilled in the Cuban people. I understood that in spite of seeming American interests, Americans could rightfully side with Castro and the vast majority of Cubans as they fought for a cause they felt was right and just in overthrowing a ruthless dictator. On a visit that Suvira and I made to Cuba in 2012, we realized that in spite of the many profound economic flaws of Castro's own dictatorship and the hardships caused by an unrelenting US embargo over more than fifty years, the people of Cuba still steadfastly valued the rejection of so many years of US-sponsored suppression.

Similar American interventionist actions in support of dictatorships had a long and consistent history, increasingly justified on ideological grounds. This was enshrined in the post-war "Truman Doctrine" that condoned such interventions as central to fighting communism and supporting pro-capitalist governments opposed to any state control of the economy. Soon we were directly conspiring and acting to set up a plethora of dictatorial regimes across the globe to protect those interests. Among these were: support of the fascist dictator Trujillo in the Dominican Republic (1930-61); the overthrow in 1953 of the fledgling democracy of Iranian Prime Minister Mohammed Mossadegh whose policies were seen as a threat to American economic interests, and installation of the absolute monarch Reza Pahlavi as Shah of Iran; the overthrow of Patrice Lumumba in the Congo in 1960 and US support for his replacement who became one of Africa's most horrendous and long-lasting dictators,

Mobutu Sese Seko; even John F. Kennedy's effort to overthrow Castro through a bungled attempt to invade Cuba at the Bay of Pigs; support of the South Vietnamese dictatorial and corrupt regime of Ngo Dinh Diem during the late 1960s and early 1970s. The CIA role in overthrowing Chilean President Salvador Allende (1973) largely for his anti-American economic policies was followed by 17 years of the dictatorship and atrocities of General Augusto Pinochet. A series of Honduran military dictators instigated originally by the profit interests of America's United Fruit Company were more evidence of U.S interference motivated by economic self interests.

The open-arms welcome by President Ronald Reagan of Sgt. Samuel Doe, dictator of Liberia, on the steps of the White House in 1981, shortly after Doe had personally butchered President Tolbert and his entire cabinet was a particularly cynical and despicable political act as I saw it, knowing what I later personally observed of Doe's treachery. Similarly, I was shocked by US policies backing the South African "apartheid" regime, and in turn, its support of Kamuzu Banda's 30 year dictatorship in Malawi where I was to later reside and to know firsthand of his notorious brutality and the final demise of his regime in 1994. The financing of Saddam Hussein during his war with Iran throughout the 1980s; continuation of that support until fabrication of weapons of mass destruction led to the second Gulf War in 2003, epitomized for me the deep cynicism and utter inhumanity of US policies. The list goes on and on.

Again, this shameful history was primarily a consequence of narrow, selfish American economic interests and a determination to prevent the ascendency of communist regimes that would work against those interests. There was little American concern for promoting liberty or democracy or the rights and well being of the majority of the populations in these countries. Any attempts following the Vietnam war to reorient the "moral compass" of America's foreign policy or to refocus it on a "human rights" agenda under the Carter administration was soon stifled. The Reagan Presidency reverted to supporting right wing regimes (such as Marcos in the Philippines) and movements to eliminate left leaning governments (such as anti-Sandinista forces in Nicaragua that I have mentioned).

I dwelled on these foreign policy issues over the years for reasons beyond foreign policy. I began to see in them the same clear common roots of hyper greed and power playing that were simultaneously distorting internal US domestic policies. I began to see why and how these same domestic political mind sets that betrayed America's working class at home could be so easily geared to do the same to the poor overseas.

Decency Denied

In reflecting on these basically unchanging policies that persist to the present day, (again whether by Republican or Democratic administrations), I have searched deep into my soul with astonishment and shame to understand why the American people continue to support such self-centered values and acts at the expense and suffering of so many people at home and abroad.

Most disturbing in my mind is that these same attitudes have allowed other social policies and practices to take hold in America that go beyond concerns of economic fairness. For me, these policies and practices strike at the heart of who we are as a nation, as a society, in how they define our basic human values, our national character and integrity, and our sense of decency.

One example that stands out and greatly disturbs me is the incarceration of people. Not only is the justice system in America highly discriminatory in putting more than double the number of blacks in prison than whites, but in how anyone in prison can be treated with impunity. I refer here to the increasingly common practices of prison isolation, a blatant but accepted form of torture.

These practices came to a particular high pitch when 1,700 prisoners in California went on strike to protest so-called "supermax confinement" in 2011. In the *New York Times* of July 18, 2011, Colin Dayan laid bare the physical conditions endured in isolation facilities (referred to as "special management units"): 'There was no paint on the concrete walls. Although the corridors had skylights, the cells had no windows. Nothing inside could be moved or removed… Inmates had no human contact, except when handcuffed or chained to leave their cells; or during often brutal cell extractions. A small place for exercise, called the "dog pen" with cement floors and wall, so high they could see nothing but the sky, provided the only access to fresh air.' Shamefully, 'many of these prisoners have been sent to virtually total isolation and enforced idleness for no crime, not even for alleged infractions of prison regulations. Their isolation, which can last for decades, is often not explicitly disciplinary, and therefore not subject to court oversight. Their treatment is simply a matter of administrative convenience.'… 'The Supreme Court, over the last two decades, has whittled steadily away at the rights of inmates, surrendering to prison administrators virtually all control over what is done to those held in "administrative segregation". Since it is not defined as punishment for a crime, it does not fall under "cruel and unusual punishment" the reasoning goes.'

This represents to me an extreme form of inhuman behavior and values that should not be allowed in any society. The fact that it is condoned, however indirectly, by our highest court and carried out by a callous and inhumane system of mindless administrative "justice" is the strongest example of the same indecency that our political and foreign policy systems have allowed others to suffer in similar ways. It is a culture of indifference of an elite to the majority of the people, in which even the most egregious behavior is accepted by those in power to protect their interests and ensure their security as they see it, whatever the human cost to others.

What resonated in my mind each time I reflected on these matters over those thirty and more years were words that made a deep impression on me at age thirteen. It was while I listened to the Army – McCarthy Hearings on television in 1954 (my obsession with politics dates at least to then!). Having accused the Army of harboring Communist sympathizers, Senator Joseph McCarthy attacked the Army's chief counselor (a country-style lawyer named Joseph Welch) of having a Communist sympathizer in his own Boston law firm. Mr. Welch found the accusation and the behavior that lay behind it so offensive and reprehensible and so representative of McCarthy's values and tactics, which had caused such immense suffering to so many, that he replied by cutting to the core of the moral issue: "Have you no sense of decency, sir, at long last? Have you left no sense of decency"?

Unfortunately, as I gradually understood, there was a history of harsh reality to overcome. The US government had no credible track record (with some blessed exceptions such as civil rights and fleeting attempts to reduce poverty) of determined, steadfast and consistent policy reforms, domestic or international, that addressed the conditions of the underclass. Comparison of policies with other "developed" countries (mostly European) ranked the US the lowest mainly because the government did very little actively to sustain a reduction in poverty and due to the pervasive and growing gap between rich and poor. This in the face of the fact that new policies aimed at a fairer distribution of opportunity and wealth and a reduction of poverty were possible. But history has shown that change that threatens the establishment and its money in any country, in whatever significant or insignificant ways does not come easily. There are many reasons to despair.

I continued to reflect on all of these structural injustices in the US and in all countries in which I was living over what eventually became fifty some years. I could find few signs of fundamental change. Worse still, I could see little recognition or admission of the problem. Sadly, in America, as far as I could determine, a culture of denial and callousness imposed a firm grip.

1% v. 99%

So you can try to imagine my shock and tentative elation on 17 September 2011 when suddenly these very issues of ingrained inequality, injustice and a void of basic decency hit the headlines of the *New York Times* and all other media outlets. It was the birth of the "Occupy Wall Street" movement. And as I was on a UN assignment in New York at the time, it was taking place in my own front yard!

The greatest contribution of this movement for me as it continued to evolve was its instant shattering of denial (and ignorance) and the laying bare of the hard facts of what had been taking place in America for a very long time (again well documented by the Center on Budget and Policy Priorities in Washington). The catch phrase of the 99% (whose income rose over the period 1979 to 2007 a mere 25% for the middle quintile, about $11,200, and only 16% for the bottom quintile, a measly $2,400) versus the 1% (whose after tax income rose a staggering 281% over the same period, a total increase of an amazing $973,100) said it all. It was understood and viscerally felt by most Americans. Again as noted, it was the greatest income concentration at the top of the income scale than at any time since 1928. It was a true awakening. And it led to an increasingly deeper understanding of what the "gap" was all about.

What I particularly appreciated was how the movement laid bare not only the income and economic gap between rich and poor, but a much more profound cultural gap that was the ultimate consequence of the former. It created a cultural transformation in the way people lived which was entirely different at the two ends of the spectrum. At both ends, the transformation fed and built on itself and began to redefine who belonged to each and why. For the privileged, it was a classic case of class advantage in which the offspring of the rich reaped enormous benefits of a stimulating environment and educational opportunities, not to mention their leg up in early inherited wealth. They in turn provided the same advantages to their own children, and the cycle of a self-perpetuating elite continued to repeat itself. The lifestyle of the underclass also perpetuated itself as they were increasingly locked into their disadvantages at the opposite end of the spectrum.

This transformation was best and most timely (2012) set out in Charles Murray's book *Coming Apart*. None of it was positive by traditional values: single parent households became common (52% of the underclass did not marry compared to 83% of the privileged who did marry); a much higher percentage of the males in the underclass with no more than a high school diploma dropped out of the labor force (about 12%) while only 3% of the privileged with a college education dropped out; crime surged in the underclass neighborhoods while remaining basically flat in the privileged ones; and all during these social changes, the underclass became more secular (nearly 60%) than religious while ironically it was the privileged who clung more decisively to their religion (60%).

Exacerbating this cultural divide was the physical divide that accompanied it. When I grew up in Coronado, California from the mid 1940s through the mid 1960s, as I have already described, the middle class and the less privileged tended to live side by side, or if not, at least attended the same schools and churches and participated in the same events. There was a shared experience and a greater understanding and positive feeling for each other. Overtime in America, the middle class who evolved into the privileged drew away to more expensive and prestigious residencies (often gated), while the underclass moved down to less attractive and subserviced residential areas or were left to cope in their old but deteriorating neighborhoods. Along with this physical divide came the division in the quality of schools and education available in these respective neighborhoods. In many ways, this became the most egregious factor of their separateness as the children of the underclass were effectively pushed out of quality educational opportunity. And these changes were accompanied by the continuously stagnating wages of the underclass not unrelated to the suppression of the labor unions that could no long fight effectively for a living wage. And less income in turn meant that the underclass had less to feed their often malnourished children which from their early childhood affected the quality of their educational attainment. This spiraling cycle of under privilege fed on itself and further deepened the lot of the underclass.

And in the meantime, the rich used their power to throw up protections against or to preempt any possible threats, internal or external, to their wealth and lifestyle. This included support for extravagant military expenditures, and a resulting huge budget deficit (further exploded by those tax cuts for the rich), rather than fiscal policies aimed at rebalancing life opportunities for all citizens.

What I found was that the "Occupy" movement had effectively cornered the well off (though not all) into grudgingly admitting the facts of these phenomena. This was a critical achievement in that it began to break the myths held by both the privileged and the underclass that the latter could, whatever the problems they faced, always hope to move up. Buttressed by a fresh array of research studies taking place around the same time, this American myth of upper mobility was exposed. People of the underclass were no longer moving up (much less than those in European and other countries). The harsh realities of their existence which severely and systematically limited their opportunities, as confirmed by the emerging data, kept the underclass in its place.

Nevertheless, and not surprisingly, the elite began to assume a defensive and rationalizing position and to make a contrary case. For them, it was not the income gap that was at the root of this widening divide. Rather, it was a question of choice. A choice among the underclass to live the way they lived. It was a problem of their values and indeed their morals! (Charles Murray made this absurd case). The underclass was undisciplined and lazy. The solution was for them to emulate the hard work, moral character and religious fortitude of those who had proven their virtues by what they had achieved.

I had heard this argument so often before, in so many similarly divided countries and it truly nauseated me. My entire adult life experience had shown me that poor people are hard working and virtuous (often demonstrating more than the privileged few the values of decency and kindness despite the hardships of their circumstances). What was at the heart of the transformation of the underclass and its downward spiral was a system directly and purposefully stacked against them. It was a system created and managed by the privileged to protect and grow their wealth and power at the expense of others. Again the same old story. It was not racially based per se (though minorities usually suffered the brunt of the system in spite of the gains in rights they had achieved), but rather the crudest and crassest example of a systematic pushing and holding down of one class by another.

So I came to realize that however encouraging the "Occupy" movement has been, it faced an enormous challenge to overcome the arrogance, self deceit, and selfishness of the privileged.

Nothing more exemplified this state of affairs in America than the Presidential Election of 2012. I had followed the Republican Primary contest closely, astonished by the extreme viewpoints of the right that increasingly pushed their core economic and social agendas onto mainstream Republican values already favoring the rich. The result was a Republican Party that fell out of touch with that mainstream. A party that created an impression that the bottom half of the country was beyond redemption and that only the well off could save the nation. That impression deeply impacted the general election. It also stirred me personally. Joining the Obama campaign in east Akron, Ohio, I came up against the reality in stark terms. Walking the neighborhoods of East Akron with other Obama supporters to get out the vote, I was taken aback (in spite of my years of poverty work around the world) by what I saw in the decayed housing and the fortress mentality of these high crime areas. The previously shining "Tire Capital" of America had degenerated for many of its residents (as their jobs were shipped overseas) into a permanently unemployed or underemployed class. This contrasted with the immense and growing wealth of most of the companies that had abandoned them. The reaction to and result of this continuing sharp disparity, and the line that it finally drove people to draw in declaring enough was enough, is now part of our electoral history, but the challenge goes on.

The lesson of America for me over these fifty years was simple: bridging the divide in any society, at home or abroad, wealthy or not, requires a clear code of conduct and set of beliefs that all people are created equal, that they have a right to equal opportunity, that those opportunities must be fostered and supported by the wider society for the benefit of all. I concluded that we have a responsibility to unrelentingly pursue these goals in all countries, and certainly my own, as a matter of fundamental common human decency.

I also firmly believe that America rightfully remains a beacon of high hope and expectation for most of the world to continue the difficult struggle to attain these goals and to confirm what is possible—an enormous and worthy responsibility. A potential based on America's fundamental democratic values, to create, to inspire and to achieve fundamental change that is equally relevant to the rest of the world. I will address whether and how this could happen in the last chapter.

Chapter 9
Ethiopia and Pakistan

Rule of Elites
1974 & 1976

Ethiopian Villagers Speak Their Mind

Lyari Slum Karachi, Pakistan

While at the University of California in San Francisco, I undertook some consultancy work with UNICEF. I valued it as an opportunity to test some of our techniques and learnings from our work in America and their relevance to the realities of the "developing' world. The assignments were too brief to implement the full process of the approach. In any case our purpose was to design and pilot that process for later full-scale application in the two countries where I was sent. The experience provided further insights into the root social issues and the potentials for providing poor people an opportunity to work with those in power for their mutual benefit.

Dethronement

In the case of Ethiopia, my visit took place coincidentally at the time of an historic event. I arrived completely exhausted and checked into the Ras Hotel in the center of Addis Ababa. I went to bed in the late afternoon. Waking at 4:00 am (September 16, 1974), I drew the curtains to find the streets full of tanks, a rather unusual custom I thought. It was the very moment that the Emperor Haile Selassie was overthrown and taken from his kingly palace to his own dungeons from which he never returned.

Courageous Voices

The weeks of my visit that followed were a period of extreme euphoria over the liberation from dictatorship. Little was then imagined of the growing, in many ways worse, horror of repression and brutality of the regime to come. During this brief window, I worked with Ethiopian officials to introduce a new educational approach based on the voice and participation of people. Once again with video in hand, we traveled into the remote and rugged countryside, to test and demonstrate the approach. The outpouring of sentiment was remarkable. For a people so long suppressed, they seemed somehow very free. It was not a question of the emperor having been overthrown. Most people knew about that, but seemed less interested. What they were finding hard to believe was that people had come from far away (not me, but the Ethiopian colleagues from the Ministry of Education with whom I was working) to talk and listen to them about their lives. This was definitely unusual. No one had ever done that before.

It triggered an outburst of complaints about the fact that the government never did anything for them. But it also touched off an outpouring of their ideas as to what needed to be done. It was the voice of a very independent people, who in spite of whatever political repression at any particular moment of history, had always managed to survive even in great hardship and suffering. It was a people who knew better than anyone else ever could about their own lives and what would be needed to make them better. They were not shy in sharing that with us.

As I had done previously in India, we also captured the voices of the government officials working in these remote areas. Their frankness, presumably this time emboldened by the overthrow, was equally astonishing. Yes, government did not serve the people. Government was corrupt not only at the very top, but quite a way down the ladder. Money and resources for "development" were never seen at the local level.

This happened also to be the year of a catastrophic drought. We traveled into the region most seriously affected (Wollo). We saw people in the most desperate state, many near starvation. Along the journey there was a six hour stretch without towns or people. It was during our lunch time and we were hungry. There was no place to eat. We had brought along a little canned cheese and sliced bread. We asked our driver, Wurku, to stop along the long desolate road. We divided the cheese and bread with him and ate in silence. I thought then that it was one of the best meals of my life. I thought of how any small food could become an enormous blessing both to the palate and to the very survival of body and soul. I could only imagine how the people we saw longed for such a similar respite from their suffering. A respite few ever knew.

Surprisingly we found the people, even in their weakened state, no less ready to speak their minds. Inevitably of course it was with a greater sense of despair. But there was also a flame of hope that refused to die. There were ideas that made sense. If only they could be heard and taken seriously.

Betrayal

Returning to the capital after this round of visits, we edited the material. It was a powerful juxtaposition of views and emotions. Word rapidly spread of this "revolutionary film" that seemed to epitomize the new liberation. After a few showings to small groups, mostly within the ministry and the UN agencies, we were suddenly notified one day that there would be a viewing by some "senior officials". I had no idea what this meant. In any event, we showed up at the designated, somewhat smallish room, with equipment in hand. As we were in the process of connecting cables, the room gradually filled with some dozen young men in casual short sleeve shirts, many of whom greeted us in mildly American accents. We were asked to run the film. The room remained silent throughout the showing. At the end, one of the young men said that the film was an extraordinary testimony to the inhumanities of the emperor and his regime. Then they all suddenly stood up and left. It was some days later before we learned that the young spokesman was Mengistu Haile Mariam. "Mengistu", as he would become known throughout the world, had led the overthrow of the emperor. All of those who had accompanied him to our showing had partaken in the coup. We later learned many had received military training in the US which explained their accents. Mengistu soon after became head of the "Derg", the communist military Junta that ruled Ethiopia for 13 long and horrific years (1974 – 1987). He was responsible for the "Ethiopian Red Terror" (1977-78) that killed thousands of the opposition to the new regime, many former officials in the imperial government and even some leaders of the Ethiopian Orthodox church. It has even long been rumored that Mengistu personally smothered and killed Haile Selassie with a pillow.

We anticipated none of these events at the time of our work. We felt proud that we had contributed to inspiring in some small way a new generation of leadership. We were confident they were committed to democracy and the well-being of people. It was only after I left Ethiopia, more than two years into the new regime, that the terrible truth revealed itself. These self-styled liberators had become the new oppressors.

It was all a shocking lesson for me personally. Good intentions to "open up" communications between people can easily be abused and distorted for unexpected purposes. In this case, the new regime attempted to profile themselves as "champions of the people", while their later actions proved quite the contrary. Not only had former leaders suffered repressions and death, but the poor of Ethiopia never benefited from the new dictatorship. This was all the more evident when another catastrophic drought hit the country in 1984 and finally exposed the world (with help of the Michael Jackson and Lionel Richie's "We are the World" concert in January 1985) to the same immense almost biblical poverty of the people that Suvira and I witnessed in 1974.

Power to People

In any event, through this experience, I came to realize what now seems self-evident. It is not simply a matter of bringing people together that is important. It is doing this through a genuine process of empowering of those people to take charge of their own lives that is crucial. I became absolutely convinced that this process must never be directed by governments or any other institutions. They can be supportive, but never must they control. Rather it is the phenomenon of human-to-human communications and peoples' collaboration for self reliance (again, with government support but not control) that I later came to understand was our main goal. It is a process that can be facilitated, but must never be led except by people themselves.

Slum Alliance

In the case of Pakistan, where I worked in 1976, the experience was quite different though the approach was very similar. The city of Karachi was surrounded by a number of slums. The largest was Lyari which at the time had a population of some 500,000 inhabitants. The Karachi Municipal Corporation, or KMC, was a government created, semi-autonomous body in charge of providing services to this slum community. The World Bank and UNICEF were collaborating with the KMC to develop and implement a plan for upgrading the slum. This was an enormous undertaking. It would require the participation of the people. My job was to work within the KMC to facilitate this process.

There was very little experience within KMC for this work. They were managers and technicians focused on basic municipal water, sanitation, health and education, and housing services. The problem was that these services were totally inadequate, in part due to very limited resources. There was also a great deal of resentment within the slum over a perceived disinterest and ineptitude of government. The infusion of international assistance was aimed at improving the resource problem. But there was an early appreciation within KMC and its international partners that no amount of resources would fundamentally change the slum unless the people were involved.

The KMC assigned two young officers to the task (Rafi and Usman), and together we made a team to take up this challenge. The period of my involvement was a short few months. Our hope was that as a team we could develop and set in motion a concept and approach of "peoples' participation" that would continue.

Karachi was an extraordinary city. The slum was a vibrant place that exploded into action and color from the earliest hours of the morning until deep into each night. It was a constant swirl of motion that included huge trucks belching hideous exhaust, people (many people) on foot, camels pulling flatbed carts piled high with goods of all shapes and sizes. People were busy, very busy. In Lyari, unemployment had very little meaning. Most people survived by their wits. Almost everyone had some small trade or business. Their homes ranged from mud hovels to some rather splendid multi-storied houses. Of course most people lived in the hovels. The streets were very narrow lanes, sometimes impassable. Gutters lined most of those lanes and open sewage was common. Water was obtainable only at certain community points. Health dispensaries were located in most neighborhoods, but they lacked medicines and staff. Schools were overcrowded, teachers underpaid, and books simply not available.

People talked about all of these things. Their views were strong and extremely well articulated. Playing back their images at community meetings created an enormous response. There were cheers of approval and a new understanding of the limits and frustrations within the government, KMC in particular. There were commitments to work together, and ideas for immediate action. So a process had been defined and set in motion. It would be followed up with further UNICEF support in the months and years that ensued. But my contribution was done. It left me feeling a bit unfulfilled, even somewhat empty.

I began to sense an inadequacy, even a certain guilt about my role. I had come into this situation with ideas of bringing a new hope and ways of moving forward with people in the lead. But pulling out of the challenge after such a brief stay seemed, and still seems, not right. I began to feel a need to take up and stick with development work more decisively and more long term. After returning to San Francisco, Suvira and I were convinced that we needed to make our way back into the UN for this purpose. It took us another two years to accomplish this.

But in the meantime, and even after, Pakistan never left my mind for long. I began what became an extended and steadfast interest (indeed obsession) in Pakistan's continuing social, economic and political challenges. This interest reached a special relevance when in 1994 I was nominated by UNDP to be their

Resident Representative in the country. For reasons beyond the apparently positive view of my candidacy, circumstances suddenly changed and I was appointed instead to another Asian country. But it never curtailed my interest in Pakistan and how the country personified for me the enormous frustrations and opportunities for development of poor countries.

Feudal Realities

I gradually came to realize that Pakistan must be understood first and foremost as a feudal society. That feudalism was rooted primarily in the country's rural areas. By 2011, the country's population reached nearly 190,000,000. However, while considerable urbanization had taken place over these thirty years (Karachi alone had 13,000,000 residents) nearly 2/3 of the population remained rural. And poverty among the rural people grew significantly higher, approaching 30%. Much of this poverty emanated from the feudal class structure that continued to dominate rural areas and influenced national politics.

During our time in Pakistan (1976), Suvira and I managed to travel to the capital Islamabad, including the nearby Swat Valley, on to Peshawar on the western border with Afghanistan, and later to Lahore on the eastern border with India. Some of our travels were by car, and we were able to absorb the rural scene and talk with the local people. What stood out most for us was that Pakistani society in these rural areas was deeply divided between landed and landless. The landed class, known by various names including *Zamandars* (as well as *waderas, sardars,* and *khans*), owned vast agricultural acreage, none of which they worked themselves. These landlords were very limited in number, confined to an estimated 5,000 families. They constituted about 2% of the rural population. But they owned nearly 45% of the rural farmland (I later found the similarity of these statistics to current day income disparities in the US remarkable!).

As we drove across these vast expanses, we could see village people working their fields, growing wheat and other cereals. They owed their very existence to the landlords, and remained constantly in their debt. They were in a state of perpetual indentured servitude. They were expected to show an unwavering loyalty to their landed masters. This loyalty was equally anticipated in the political arena to which the privileged class increasingly aspired.

Over the years, this landed gentry accumulated more and more power and wealth. This manifested itself in the political offices they monopolized (into which their subjects voted them); in their effective control of the provincial and national assemblies; and in their many diversified economic interests such as textiles. In the meantime, and as we witnessed with growing repulsion from our vantage points outside the country, the villagers stayed mired in their poverty. There were no (or at least very few) increased opportunities for education, health, or employment outside their subsistent and serf-like lives.

During our stay, Prime Minister Zulfikar Ali Bhutto (1972-1977), made gestures of land reform to improve the lot of the poor, just as his predecessor Ayub Khan (1958-1969) had done. But the conservative landowners and the religious leaders combined forces to effectively undermine these efforts. Even the military, which had ruled Pakistan for nearly half of its existence, was co-opted into an elite nexus exemplified by corruption and greed. While poverty intermittently declined over the years I kept my watch, it always returned to similar or higher levels. Any serious efforts to secure the rights of the poor, and improve their lot, were repeatedly frustrated by political neglect or elite self interests. Democracy simply could not flourish in this atmosphere. People suffered in silence.

Recent developments in Pakistan, particularly the rise of the Taliban, have been viewed through the prism of "terrorism" and as a threat to Pakistan's national security. The greater reality as I have followed these developments is that they are but a further reflection and manifestation of feudal practices. The Taliban have in fact been able to play very successfully on the hatred and animosity of many of the poor for the ruling elite. They easily motivated and manipulated these people, especially the young, to join their ranks in a seeming revolt against such oppression.

Pakistan provided me with further early insights into the roots of class divide and the suppression of people. I was to learn later, however, that "feudal" societies were not alone in practicing these distorted values. Feudalism institutionalized such values, but they were equally to be found across a wide spectrum of democratic and undemocratic, wealthy and poor, countries. The common feature, once again, was a disregard for basic human decency.

Chapter 10

The South Pacific

Island Insights
1979 – 1981

Traditional Welcoming of Guests – Fiji

Resignation

I departed the UN from India on a "leave of absence" in quest of my own personal goals. At the time, I thought this my right and my responsibility to explore and find a new paradigm of development. Rather pretentious to say the least, but still well meaning. Suvira and I were serious about what we were trying to do, and both of us looked back on this period as a time in which we grew and learned a great deal. But the UN had already given me an unusual three years to find my path. When I asked for more, patience ran out. I had to choose. In the end, we decided to remain and finish our work at UCSF. Resigning from the UN was one of the most difficult decisions of my life. I could not be sure whether I would ever be able to return to this heart and soul of my life's passion for work in development.

Parental Dilemma

As our work at UCSF continued and then began to wind down, I faced a serious choice. I had enormous love for my two daughters, Tanya and Natasha. They were pre-teen children during our stay in San Francisco. We had them stay with us in our two bedroom apartment almost every weekend. In many ways, it was a marvelous time. A load of activity and great fun. Suvira and I would take them to the Golden Gate Park for bike rides and birthday parties. We would drive up to Sonoma in the Napa Valley for a ride on the miniature train and a picnic on the grounds of an old Victorian home. We made Nancy Drew mystery films with them on the streets of China Town, somewhat to the consternation of the local shop owners whose sales temporarily plummeted while their clientele delighted in our antics. We had a retinue of Mexican restaurants that we enjoyed, at one of which Suvira overdosed on chili sauce and passed out before the meal arrived. Tanya, Natasha and I hovered over her in our secluded leathered booth. We alternated between fear, panic, and shame that someone would notice, and utter hilarity when she came to a few moments later and the enchiladas arrived!

But I had to make a choice. It was a choice between continuing our life close to the girls but with what I saw as an uninspiring future, or one of leaving them behind so we could pursue what I thought would be a uniquely exciting and fulfilling life of work abroad. In the end, the joint custody I longed for became at least a partial reality on multiple occasions when the girls came to live with us and school in various countries.

Whatever I have done to help and guide my daughters through those years, including the best education and graduate degrees and experiences of other cultures, I continue to feel that I let them down. In many ways I believe it gave me a far greater understanding and empathy for the fate of so many people, always much poorer than I, who for whatever multitude of reasons had little choice in such matters and saw their own children drift behind and away. That was an important insight, but by no means ever compensated for my own sense of loss and a promise unkept to never leave my two daughters. It has been my deepest regret. To my everlasting and undeserved gratitude, both Tanya and Natasha matured into adults with an early wisdom of life's blessings, a healthy and complete void of arrogance, a heartwarming sense of humor, and a compassion and determination to pursue what they valued most. Not least they continued, I felt, to carry a love for me.

Blessed by Friendship

As I looked to my future, and began to contemplate a return to the UN, I learned that good friends can change your life. I had little or no appreciation of this until it happened to me.

As I began to express renewed interest in a UN career, I was not totally surprised to find the reception less welcoming. The UN had moved on without me. Others had taken my place. There were many more that now had the experience I uniquely had when I first joined. Maybe there was a certain feeling that I had turned my back on opportunities that could no longer be offered. It was entirely understandable.

Our life became tumultuous. Our work at the university was rapidly coming to an end, and we were "let go". Consultants were, it was explained to us, never supposed to be permanent. Perhaps doubt of our loyalties and long term commitment to the university came into question. We had fallen between the cracks. We were soon without a job or income. A period of growing anxiety, a twitch of panic, set in. We were coincidentally asked to leave our apartment as the owners had decided on a no-children policy (yes, even in San Francisco in those days!). We began to stay with friends and in a long list of temporary accommodation. Not a settled existence.

I flew to New York to try to rectify the past. I re-established contact with some of my former UN colleagues and met with new ones. Nothing materialized. I began to meet with other non-governmental international organizations working overseas. Nothing gelled. Because we were without income, I pursued my search on a low budget. I put myself up at the YMCA on the upper West Side. The rooms were low priced and for good reason. They were tiny. A single bed took up most of the room. A small window looked out on a gray brick wall of the adjoining building. The sun never entered the room. I had my evening meal in the "Y" cafeteria. Very basic American fare. I tried to strike up a conversation with some of the other residents. They were mostly unresponsive. None appeared indigent, but most gave me the impression they were living on the edge of poverty. I remember one man in particular. Probably in his 50s or early 60s, he sat glumly at the dining table, uttering not a word. Unexpectedly, we got up together to return to our rooms. As the elevator doors closed, he muttered more to himself than to me that nobody cared about people like us. His eyes never left the floor. He got off before me. I never saw him again.

Back in San Francisco, Suvira and I decided that if we were to have any chance of renewing our international work, we had to go after it every day based in New York. We packed up and drove across the country over six exhilarating days that included the friendliness of the South and a warm "ya'all come back now" every time we pulled out of a gas station.

Pounding the streets of Manhattan was a different story. Every door, whether in the UN or among the non-governmental organizations, led to disappointment. Old acquaintances and colleagues wanted to help, but all were caught up in the frantic pace of their working lives. None found time to make an extra effort for me. None except one.

After many weeks of growing despair, a genuine friend came to my aid. He and I had known each other since my earliest days at UN headquarters. He was a Dutchman, Joep Van Arendonk. From the day I met him back in 1967 when I started my UN career, I felt an unusual bond. It was something I had not previously known. We simply thought exactly alike. Our view of the world was absolutely common.

We were deeply convinced that any true and lasting improvement in peoples' lives had to be based on the will and actions of those very people. We felt equally strongly that people's opportunities also depended on the good will and values of their societies to care and help them reach their goals. We agreed that "developed" countries (whether the United States or Western Europe) were just as challenged by the need to assist their disadvantaged people as any "developing" country. We also believed that all of this depended on a moral foundation. We both adhered tenaciously to the moral principle that everyone must be concerned about those less fortunate than they. And that they must feel responsibility to help them in whatever way made sense. We had both grown up as Catholics. We would debate long hours whether those influences were what shaped our beliefs. We had both left our Catholicism behind, but we believed in the unique qualities, wisdoms and human goodness of great religious leaders. We sometimes vainly compared (quite outrageously) our clarity on social issues with what those spiritual leaders must have seen which others could not. We were soul brothers in the most profound way. I have never felt that way about anyone else except Suvira.

After some four years working together at the UN, we parted company in 1971. I went on to India and he moved on to a new UN agency (UNFPA) just created to deal with the problems of overpopulation. When I returned to New York those few years later, he was there. There was no need to convince him who I was or what I was committed to. He knew it all. He introduced me to his bosses. Joep was determined I should be brought into the organization. It was not just about my needs but what he thought the organization would gain. He spoke further to the leadership and convinced them I was a good choice.

It was a remarkable lesson for me. A lesson in the overwhelming importance of friendship based on deeply shared values. I was humbled to realize that I was so dependent on and graced by a belief in me—who I was and what I stood for, or at least hoped to work toward. I think Joep never realized even to this day how important he was to my life. The opportunities he opened up for me to work with so many people around the world were incalculable. His loyalty and devotion to me was a remarkable lesson in the power of deeply held affection and commitment to helping those who share your values.

Stretched Out

So, hired by the United Nations Fund for Population Activities (UNFPA), I was posted immediately to the South Pacific in 1979. Excited to be back "in development", Suvira and I took up residence in Suva, Fiji. As the UNFPA Coordinator, I was assigned to develop population programs all across the South

Pacific region. That would be more daunting than I first realized. The region consisted of seventeen countries, some (Nauru and Niue) as small as 5,000 people, all members of the UN, many having up to 400 islands each. Quite a territory!

Traveling around that territory over 30 million square miles was a challenging venture. Small planes over vast oceans defined much of what I spent my time doing. Contending with frequently rough weather especially in the hurricane season, I experienced more than one occasion when our landings did not go exactly to plan. One time, our approach to the airport of Tuvalu (a country of 7,000 people) in a heavy rainstorm aborted three times until on the final attempt the pilot came into the landing strip at a ¾ angle. Quite an unsettling experience as I watched it happen. It was only after touching down that I realized the strategy behind it—to land the plane on one wheel (in this case the left one), then spin it into the gale-force wind, letting the second wheel make contact only at the very moment the plane straightened itself out. Not likely a procedure written in the books. The pilots, mostly Australian, were uncanny.

Once on the ground, I instantly came across another kind of amazing behavior. One I would admire over and over as I continued my work in the South Pacific. The small aircrafts that transported us from island to island had to keep their services rudimentary including how they handled the baggage. After deboarding the plane, I always scurried to the rear loading dock just in time to catch my bag hurled out in no particular order. After catching mine, and as I began to carry it away, a gentleman in Tuvalu traditional skirt and shirt and sandals approached me and asked if he could help. I thanked him but said I could carry it myself if he would be so kind as to direct me to the nearest hotel. He still insisted and said he could easily balance the bag on the back of his bike while he accompanied me to the hotel. I saw that his goodwill was genuine and I found myself strolling and chatting amicably at his side. The hotel was a twenty minute walk and I was grateful for the assistance. Before entering to register, I shook the gentleman's hand and suggested that since I would be there for another couple of days we might have lunch. He said he would enjoy that. As I headed up the stairs, I turned back to ask how I could find him later. He said that would be easy as most people on the island knew him. So who should I tell them I am looking for? To which he replied 'just tell them you're looking for the prime minister'.

Yes, he was the prime minister, and we did have lunch. It was just my first experience with the incredible informality and singular absence of pretension that marked many, actually almost all, leaders I was privileged to meet across the Pacific. Ceremony was important, as I will later describe, but I learned quickly that Pacific Islanders are an amazingly open and friendly people who like to keep status out of the equation in relating with you. There were exceptions of course, depending on who they were relating with. I later observed (and will describe) in the case of Fiji how rough they could get if their status were threatened.

My time in the South Pacific was a constant juggle between the pressures of work and the need to create a good home environment. Suvira was preparing to have our child. My two daughters had come to spend the school year with us, their first of many experiences with international schools. It was a British international school and Tanya had some initial difficulty adjusting both to her classmates and to the teaching methods (quite demanding compared to US schools). As always she did well in the end. I was very preoccupied to make sure they were feeling "at home", but I was also on a whirlwind of "programming" for "population activity". It was quite stressful for me, running around the Pacific while thinking mostly about my absence from my kids.

I was working with government officials and a lot of NGOs. I had come with the idea of embedding "community development" and "peoples' participation" as the key ingredient of our programs. This we did. Yet somehow I felt it all a bit too removed from reality. I was not interacting much with the people themselves. I pressured myself to get as many 'country programmes' put together as possible—five was as far as I got in those two and a half years—but seldom did I come in contact with the local people whom I hoped would manage them.

On those few occasions when I did engage with the village people, I often encountered some unusual moments. In those days, we had a large number of UN "project managers" scattered around the Pacific, a trend which would soon die out as we moved to "national execution" (a strange term for getting the government to take charge of managing these projects). On a trip to Kiribati (which had just gained its independence from the UK in 1979 as the former "Gilbert Islands"), one of these experts with the International Labour Organisation (ILO) invited me to see his project the next morning. He suggested I might want to bring along my swim trunks. We set out in a motored craft that had the appearance to my inexperienced eye of a miniature tugboat. Heading out and across unlimited blue water, some two hours later he suddenly cut the motor and dropped anchor. Tying up whatever knots he did to secure the boat, he asked if I had brought those trunks. I said yes, but asked why. I could see a small island about a mile and a half in the distance. I figured he had in mind a quick dip before we proceeded there for the formalities. No, that's not what he had in mind. He said we would complete our journey by swimming the rest of the way! I thought myself a pretty good swimmer, but setting out over an unknown mile or more of water was not for me a particularly intelligent notion. He assured me it was no problem. We entered the water and began to swim. In fact, the water was not that deep. Maybe a bit under six feet or so. One could stand with extended toes and just keep the nose above the water line. Despite his reassuring words, I kept enduring the sting of salt water to peek at my lower environment, just to ease my mind that we were the lone inhabitants. After forty minutes of rather vigorous breast strokes we came rather thankfully ashore.

The reception we received by the local people surprised and delighted me. Men, women and children gathered on the shore greeting us in their local attire of long and mid-length skirts (worn by both the men and the women) and multi-colored blouses. Their rhythmic dances brought an instant reminder of those I had seen in Hawaii in far less natural settings.

There then took place an extraordinary day of discussion and planning for a "vocational training" program which these people would implement. Their enthusiasm was genuine. They appreciated the respect and responsibility we showed and gave them. Still, again it was "our" programme, already designed before we got there. There was no empowering of these people to come up with their own approach. Nevertheless, the program did eventually get implemented later with good (however limited) results.

The trip back to our tugboat was a lot easier. I discovered then why we had left it so far out to sea. We walked on sand almost all the way back to the boat as the waters had now receded. Tides in these areas pulled the waters out a very long way. Bringing the boat to shore would have meant spending the night, something I would have enjoyed, but that our busy schedule did not allow.

Other times, such as on my visit to the Mariana Islands, I would sit on the shore and watch fisherman stay out all night with petrol lamps to attract fish to their boats. They inevitably returned in the mornings with meager catches for local markets which brought little return for their labors. So, despite their seeming idyllic setting, most peoples of the Pacific lived in subsistence, many in poverty. On top of these economic stresses, people worried about their immediate environment. Without much scientific understanding or proof, people knew what they were seeing: a constant erosion of their lands by a sea whose levels continued to rise. Over time they understood the real possibility that these seas would submerge their homes and their way of life.

My responsibilities also included Papua New Guinea. Port Moresby, the capital, had become a hive of violence and crime, largely a result of the pressures of overpopulation on a poor and fragile economic base and social fabric. Young people had no jobs, little education, and seemingly no hope. How to reach out, involve and find employment for these young people was everyone's highest priority. We again came up with a rather conventional youth vocational training approach. It did over time impart practical skills, though not always relevant to the needs of the market. I knew that the problems of youth ran much deeper and wider, including a pervasive sense of alienation. We needed more time to engage the young to self-identify their problems and their own solutions.

As I traveled incessantly around the islands of the Pacific and witnessed the poverty and the threats to daily existence of many kinds, I also noted in many places a remarkable resilience and a spirit to face their adversities together. While people were poor, their social traditions and culture were rich in the practice of mutual caring and protection for each other. Caring not only for the elderly who were seldom if ever left alone, but for the young and the less fortunate, who were often taken in to provide protection and support. I felt strongly at the time that this spirit, if combined with the goodwill and resources of their governments and other countries, could provide the essential elements that would enable them eventually to overcome what seemed otherwise overwhelming odds.

Elites in Paradise

Back in Fiji, I was able to spend more time with the people and their leaders. I saw similar qualities of traditional resilience and determination, but I also bore witness, sometimes unknowingly, to more ominous clouds of change.

Each time I returned to Fiji, I looked for an opportunity to visit the villages. I gained a special appreciation for their traditional ways of meeting and working out their problems and assessing their needs. This usually took place around a *Kava* ceremony. Kava, or *Yaqona* as it was locally known, was made from the root of a pepper tree which young girls of the village pounded (or more traditionally chewed) into a pulp or fine powder and mixed with water. The ceremony was formerly performed only between chiefs of the villages, but had become a way of welcoming guests and initiating friendly discussions. The liquid was stirred in a hardwood—*Tanoa*—bowl which usually had a dozen or more short legs and a fine crafted appearance. The village chief would serve up the drink in a half coconut cup called a *bilo* to each visitor. As you took your sip, the chief would clap his cupped hands making a distinct popping sound and murmuring *"maca"* in a deep voice to signify that each participant had accepted the gift properly. The drink was more potent than its milky white look portrayed, causing a slight numbing sensation in the mouth and a calming effect on the body as the ceremony went on. I found it very relaxing. It was a way of interacting with the village leaders on their own terms. It was a form of traditional hospitality that had a way of breaking down mistrust or barriers of any kind almost instantly as it most certainly was intended to do. It helped to create harmony and good will. It facilitated our work to understand local priorities and what people were wanting and willing to work toward.

One of the reasons I was able to work in greater depth with Fijian leaders and people was the close relationship I had with the director of Fiji's family planning division of the ministry of health, Dr. Timoci Bavadra. Like many Fijian men, he was solidly built and self-assured, and I was taken personally by his confident manner, traditional style (he always wore the traditional male skirt and shirt), and his sincere concerns for people's well being. He and I worked well together. He took me to villages to meet chiefs and their people whom I would never have otherwise come to know and befriend.

While I did not realize it at the time, Dr. Bavadra was becoming politically active. I was not surprised when I learned about this after I had left Fiji (1981), given his strong views on peoples' needs. He had become particularly active in the Labor movement, and that movement led to a multi-ethnic party victory at the polls some years later (1987). The significance of all of this, and why I followed it so closely from distant countries to which I had subsequently moved, was because power playing among Fiji's elites (motivated by selfish interests and greed) began to change and redefine Fiji in stark and negative ways.

The roots of this problem are found in Fiji's history. It became a dependency of the British Crown in the late 1870s, and a few years later the British began to bring Indians as indentured labor to work its sugar plantations. This set the stage for what became a long, tense relationship between indigenous Fijians and these Indo-Fijians whose population continued to grow before and after Fiji gained its independence in 1970. By the time I was living and working in Fiji, the Indo-Fijians already constituted slightly more than half the population. With their size came a growing power at the ballot box, and indigenous Fijians felt threatened. Timoci Bavadra's unique role was in crossing over to join the Indo-Fijians, creating the multi-ethnic coalition that won the 1987 election, placing none other than Dr. Bavadra himself as its new prime minister.

What followed is a sad story of brutal and deadly ethnic politics and conflict that benefited none of the people of Fiji, caused an exodus of its most skilled labor force, and won the country a near pariah-status internationally.

Dr. Bavadra's labor-led coalition victory was short lived. A military coup overthrew the newly elected government (escorting Dr. Bavadra from the parliament in the most humiliating manner), all in the name of protecting the land and representative rights of the indigenous Fijians. Subsequent coups in 2000 (after another multi-ethnic coalition had won and was again overthrown) and in 2006 were carried out in spite of constitutional guarantees of rights and democratic representation for all. The real motivations behind the coups were clouded by narrow land and financial interests of the elites which had nothing to do with the lot of the common people. Unfortunately, it was and continues to remain for me another example of manipulation by elites for their own gains at the expense of developing opportunities for the overall population. I was to witness these same behaviors and practices over and over again as I continued my journeys to other lands, but I never expected it in Fiji.

Investing in People

My time in the Pacific was fascinating and exciting, but my visits to so many countries were too short and hurried. I did my best to put together programs with participatory principles. But there was just too little time to work side by side with people. Too little time spent in enabling them to manage their own development. I realized as never before that good intentions and ideals are never enough. Development is above all an investment in people. If the investment is to reap returns and rewards, sufficient time must be taken to work with and empower the people to do their own development. It's as simple as that.

Chapter 11

Nepal

People of Poverty
1981 – 1985

On the Road of Survival from a Young Age

We were ready to move on. We had developed a warm feeling for the people of the Pacific, and later missed their genuine cheer and casual friendliness. But something in what I was doing, and the rather academic work that Suvira became involved in at the University of the South Pacific, did not strike the right cord. We felt disengaged from the people, not totally, but just enough to question whether we were doing anything useful. The chemistry we wanted was not taking place.

The possibility of a reassignment to Nepal was a delightful piece of news. We made a brief trip to Kathmandu while living in India in the early 1970s and found its still medieval aura completely enchanting, at least to our romantic eyes. Most of the buildings were made of mud brick, but stood majestically as reminders of a deeply expressed culture and a fascinating history. As our assignment firmed up, we routed our "home leave" travel from Fiji through Kathmandu for a short visit before heading on to the US.

Among the People

Traveling from the Kathmandu airport to the hotel at night, we were mesmerized by the crowded low-lite streets and shops. As we began to live in the country, we felt an increasingly special rapport with the people, not least because of the affinity of their history and customs with India. But Nepalis were fiercely independent people. They had never been colonized. They were poor, even poorer than most in India. But their self-assurance and natural pride were striking. They bore no airs. They had a marvelous sense of humor, and a healthy self-effacement. They were straight in their relations though the intrigues of their kingly history were infamous, and their modern political intrigues equally so.

It was a country and people in transition. Opening to the world only in the 1950s, they still lived in the past. Yet commitment to change, some of it radical change, increasingly became a hallmark of a rapidly growing and educated youth. Social injustices were too glaring to be ignored in the face of little evidence of real change. Life was clearly deteriorating for most people in a country where more than 90% lived in remote mountainous areas. It was a country of immense physical beauty interspersed with persistent and wide spread pockets of pervasive poverty that refused to yield. It seemed to my still formative philosophy that the latent power of people was the only possible answer.

All of these impressions, images, and realities took shape over four years. A rich learning experience for me; one of the richest of my life. And the best part was that, probably really for the first time since Peru, I felt close to the people. There was no choice. If you worked in Nepal, you worked with people. As I learned over many years working in development, each country has its own unique "development culture". It has to do with the way in which those in government, in local groups, and international development workers such as myself, conducted themselves as they worked. In many countries, it is development by remote control. Grand ideas postulated and put forward in impressive documents. In Nepal, everything credible had to be based on your "field work". Everyone was constantly "in the field". To be in the field in Nepal meant to be on foot. Roads were extremely limited. You would drive to well known take off points, then it was a matter of walking. To visit one project site might often take four days getting there, or more, and four days back. These trips provided you time to build relations with the people.

Not just the people whose lives you were hoping could be improved. But with the people who were your colleagues in these efforts. The UN in Nepal, as everywhere, worked out of offices that were staffed mostly by well educated nationals of the country. The Nepalis in the office I headed—Lamaji, Adhikariji, Lajja, Dongol, and many more— became a special family to me. They represented a cross section of the society, coming from various parts of the country as well as caste groups. In Nepal, only a small minority of professional people came from Kathmandu. Most had their roots, their families and their homes in the rural villages. Nepal remained a country of village people, no matter how well educated or urbanized they were. They maintained a tremendous affinity and loyalty for these rural areas. They knew the life, the thinking, the ways, the problems, the possibilities in these rural areas. My privilege was to travel with these colleagues, from the office but also from the government ministries, continuously learning about all of these matters.

Witness to Deprivation

As we traveled, I would see every manner in which people lived from one end of the country to the other, be it the hot plains of the *terai* lowlands, or the most frigid regions of the high mountains. No matter how diverse the housing or clothing or food, the pervasive commonality among all Nepali people was their deep and abiding poverty. I would witness this time after time. It never failed to touch my heart.

Soon after arriving in Nepal, I made an early field trip to Dhankuta in the high hills of the Eastern Region of the country. We stayed the first night in a modest local hostel on the main street. Very spartan but clean. I fell asleep quickly after a busy day of travel and some interviews with local government officials. Around 1:00 in the morning, I woke to the sound of a crying child. I lay still for a couple of minutes trying to decide where exactly the sound was coming from. I concluded it was from the street just below my room. I opened the wooden-shuttered window and peered down. A baby about one year of age was sitting on the dirt road. It was clad in thin ragged garments and appeared to be shivering in the usual cold of the Nepali mountain night. It continued to cry unaware of my presence. I looked up and down the dimly lite street and could not see a soul. I told myself this was not possible.

The baby had the appearance of those I had seen in documentaries of the Second World War, particularly after the bombing of Hiroshima, when so many infants suffered and died alone. I woke my Nepali colleague, Lamaji, in the next room and told him what I was seeing. He said it was unusual but not entirely unknown for poor parents to leave their babies in the street at night in the hope that someone would take them in to care for them, or would provide them some food. He thought it best we should not disturb the tragedy unfolding but should wait to see what transpired. I returned to my room, and the child's cries continued but lessened over time. Soon I was in a half doze, and before long I was fully awake again, probably around 5:00 am. I opened the window to see the state of the child. It was no longer there. There was no one else in the street. I assumed (and deeply hoped) that someone had come to retrieve and care for it. It was many months into my first year in Nepal before the images of that child slowly subsided from my mind. But the memory haunts me to this day.

On another occasion, we were trekking to villages in the interior of Gorkha district in the Western Region. On our return we had come off of the mountain trails onto a rough road and began walking along it. Before too long, a large truck hauling timber came to a stop and the driver asked if we wanted a ride into town (where our vehicle was waiting). We gratefully accepted. On entering the cab of the truck, I immediately noticed a middle aged man sitting in the back compartment and beyond him the body of a young boy lying still on an improvised bed normally used by truck drivers for rests during long hauls. The young boy could not have been more than ten years old. The deep dark sockets of his eyes, against his unusually pale complexion convinced me he was near death. The lines on his face disclosed much hardship in his short life. He occasionally moaned almost inaudibly, and his weakened body stirred ever so slightly as the truck jostled back and forth down the mountain. His father told me that he had been ill for several months, but he did not know what it was. The traditional healer of the village had not made any difference. The father decided it was time to take his son to the health clinic in the regional center. He had not done so before because of the considerable distance and the expenses that he could not afford. He bore an air of resignation and ill-fate. It proved a premonition of his son's death which occurred shortly before we reached the town and the only clinic. We later visited the clinic to find it had neither a health worker on duty nor any medicines to offer. It was among the first of many times I would witness and understand the plight of poor people in Nepal. They could not rely on anyone for their survival or that of their loved ones, including the children many Nepali parents would have to bury in their own lifetime.

Sometimes we would travel together to the remote Far Western Region. On one occasion, after walking some distance, we came across local horses no higher than my elbows. The owner was going the same direction and proposed that we mount and ride to the next distant village. One of our government colleagues was taller than I, and the image of him wincing to hold his feet up off the ground for hours over rugged terrain still makes me smile.

But mostly we walked. Sometimes we were not sure how far it was to the next place we were going. We just kept walking until we got there. On more than one occasion, this found us groping along in the dark. I recall crawling down a mountain for several hours in the dark. We held on to each other as best we could until a small light appeared unconvincingly in the distance. Nevertheless that light guided us as though we were on a superhighway. We arrived in a remote town in the early morning hours. Inevitably, we were warmly received. Such hospitality always stood out all the more strikingly in contrast to the poverty of those offering it. It seemed it was because they were so poor that they were so kind. I think I have understood ever since that it was because poverty heightens the value of human relations and the ultimate importance of treating others decently that the poor are so humane. Nepalis were no different. But their genuine warmth in welcoming us into their humble dwellings was so consistent and sincere, it seemed unique.

Pervasive Monarchy

Nepal, as Pakistan, remains in many ways a feudal society, though with its own unique history and character. Centuries of rule by the king, and local vassals, embedded a deep and unbending allegiance to authority. And in fact, as I soon learned, the rule and power of the king was practically omnificent during my time in the country. Nepal had a long history of kings and ruling families, including that of the "Rana Dynasty" which held absolute power (with collusion of the British empire) through a policy of isolating the country for nearly one hundred years until some modicum of democracy was introduced in 1950. But the then King Mahendra threw out all political parties and systems and created the "panchayat" (council) system from village to national level. It was a mechanism and tool for ruling absolutely, based on the loyalty of local rural elites. When we arrived in 1981, his son King Birendra had recently held and managed to defeat a referendum between a continuation of this system and the introduction of multiparty democracy. And even when pressure for change continued to build and a multiparty system was finally adopted (1991) some years after we had left the country, the innate corruption of the old system prevented real reform and enabled an intrinsically "feudal" system to persist.

Maoists

It was about that same time that a new phenomenon began to emerge. It was a far more radical approach to reform than anyone heretofore dared to contemplate. It was the rise of the Maoist communist party of Nepal. To my amazement in watching these events from afar, this movement reflected almost exactly what had occurred in Peru a decade earlier. The model of Peru's "Shining Path" that had successfully stirred the isolated rural poor in areas where government forces were weak soon became a groundswell of resistance to centuries old oppression. This time, contrary to the fate of the revolutionary leaders in Peru whose movement died with their imprisonment, the Nepali radical leaders were triumphant even to the point that their famous guerilla leader, Prachanda, assumed the prime ministership in 2007. The story would not end there of course as the fundamental political instability of the country continued even up to today.

214

Rural Elites

It was certainly the same old story in which elites, royal or rural, greedy for power and wealth found every way and means for turning back the tides of change at the earliest opportunities.

So as I faced this history in my stay between 1981 and 1985, any notions of creating a truly democratic process of participation, decision making and empowerment of local people seemed, as I looked back on that period, naïve if not impossible. I was determined nevertheless to try.

My first undertaking was to revise our entire UNFPA population program to make it much more participatory. We did this, but we clearly fell short. We introduced ideas of local planning and decision making. But it was almost always done with and through the local elites. Never did we manage, I now feel, to engage the vast majority of the people. The elites, with whom we built very good relations, always managed to take care of and control these matters. That is not to say we were unable to introduce some important innovations. Our new cross-cutting "district focus" approach, by which we adopted and applied an "area based" integrated package of development activity, was a signal contribution to the concept of bringing power and resources to the local level. But the gap between those who ended up wielding that power and the rest of people remained very wide. The benefits of whatever development activity we supported, from the production of crafts to the growing of vegetables for greater income, somehow always seemed to accrue to the local elites first. My initial belief in the latent power of people to solve Nepal's problems and reap the results was not misplaced. It was just a truth whose time for applying it had not yet fully arrived.

Nature's Power

While striving to address these political and often insurmountable problems in Nepal, and the frustrations that accompany them, Nepal welled up in me an entirely different kind of passion to understand life and human relations. It was more spiritual than professional. It was not focused on religion, but rather on the unique and immense physical context of the country and the sheer power of nature which over time seemed to yield a different (or at least parallel) understanding of human existence. Toward the end of our sojourn in Nepal, we had one such experience that seemed to capture and personify all of them together.

Nepal is rightfully famous and proud to be home to the world's tallest mountains. No amount of written description or perfect photography can convey the beauty of those mountains and the people who reside on them. Our journey began at just over 9,000 feet where a small plane had negotiated one of the world's tiniest landing strips to bring us to Lukla. Over the next five days, we struggled with the help of Yaks carrying our goods (and our daughter!) in large wood-woven baskets, up and down those mountainsides. We slept by ice cold streams. We saw the white snow peaks break the vivid blue and pitch black of the sky. Peaks that seemed to go on without end. Women spinning their wool, and weaving their rugs. The joy was in reaching the summit of each ridge, and the mystery of starting down and back up again wondering what we would see next. But it was in taking the one most extraordinary step of our lives, when we saw nothing different until the very last moment when we stepped over the final ridge, that we realized how privileged we were to be there.

Spread out before us was the scene of a heaven hitherto unknown to us. The highest places in the world (Sagarmatha, Ama Dablam, Lhotse, Nuptse, Makalu, Chamlang, Pumori, and others) lined up in a circle of unlimited beauty, lay within our gaze. The stunning silhouette of Tangboche monastery and its infinite array of colored flags waving freely in the wind filled us with a sense of human peace and awe. We had traversed the poorest Sherpa villages to arrive here, and saw that the Tibetan monks were equally poor. We could not rationalize the uplifting spirit we felt by pretending that an absence of material things was its cause. Not in the presence of such blatant poverty. And yet we felt so inspired. The single cloud streaming out from the very tip of Sagarmatha (Mount Everest) at the break of dawn seemed to tell us we were witnessing all but the final revelation of earth's treasures.

Life's Needs?

How many times since then have I remembered that sight and that feeling? How many times have I asked what do we really need in life to make us feel fulfilled and happy, not just "developed"? How many times have I wondered since then if a simpler and more serene life was possible wherever else we may go? How often have I felt the guilt and humiliation of not following or at least exploring those feelings? How much do I still believe it is possible for all of us to discover a different way of life? One that eliminates poverty and satisfies, but does not satiate, our material needs. One that has the courage and humility to show our dependence on each other. One in which we find our truest happiness in human understanding, decency and caring. Warm human relations and a wonderment of nature. It seemed attainable. It seemed worthy of earnest pursuit.

Chapter 12
Kenya

Hopeless in the Slums
1985 – 1989

Kibera, Nairobi

Value of Life

Reassigned, we were already living in Nairobi for three months. I was on another field trip to get to know the country. This time to the western town of Kisumu on Lake Victoria. It was an arduous day of driving with the director of the national population council. We were both exhausted. After an early meal, I went to bed in our hotel on the shores of the lake. My room was on the fifth floor. Suddenly around two in the morning I jerked from my sleep and sat straight up in my bed. I had no idea why. I sat there for a few moments, not moving. Then I heard a low moaning coming from the open veranda, accompanied by what sounded like the splashing of water. Then nothing. After a few more minutes, I lay back down to try and return to sleep. Again the moaning and splashing. This time I pulled aside my mosquito net and stepped out onto the balcony. After another few moments, the same sounds returned, muffled but definite. I couldn't see a thing through the swaying palms below. I decided to go down the elevator to find out what was going on.

The low-lit lobby was empty. The clock on the wall said 2:15 am. Nothing to be seen or heard. I was about to return to the elevator when I decided to go out to the hotel patio to have a look. The long pool was calm except for a few ripples stirred by the breeze. Again I was returning to the lobby when I decided to have one last look at the far end of the pool.

My eyes strained in the dimness to make out what I thought was some form at the bottom of the pool. I stood there suspended. In a flash I realized. There was a dark body down there, presumably an African. I am not certain at all what went through my head in a matter of seconds. I was in my pajamas. I found myself taking off the top. I slipped over the edge of the pool and swam to the center. Thinking one last moment whether this was the wise thing to do, I doubled up and bolted toward the bottom. Eyes open, I could hardly make out a thing. But the dark shape of a body resting peacefully on the pool floor clarified as I approached. I could not decide exactly what I should be trying to do. My hand and arm thrust before me almost of their own doing. Then I felt my fingers wrapped around an arm. I gave a tug. Instantly I felt a response, a reflex reaction without purpose. I held on tight and began to swim to the surface, dragging the body with me. It was the body of a man of some size but the water did most of the lifting. I broke the water with an almost involuntary scream. I called out at the top of my voice for help. Nothing happened. I pulled the lifeless form to the side of the pool and began to push it over the top. It was surprisingly easy. There was not the least resistance. I rolled it over the edge. I took a quarter of a minute to catch my breath and my wits.

I then lifted myself out of the water and turned what was a stark naked African man onto his stomach. Pressing down on his back with all my strength, I strained to assure myself this was the best way to revive his life. After several attempts, water gushed from his mouth. A slight barely audible groan followed. By this time I saw several hotel balcony lights switch on. Yet no one emerged from their rooms. Then I noticed what appeared to be a flashlight searching from a distant area beyond the other end of the pool. It appeared to be a night guard. I called urgently for his assistance. He stood frozen in his tracks. After more pleading, he slowly came my way. On reaching me, he called out in shocked recognition the name of his friend who lay beside me. He told me it was his fellow guardsman. He had been drinking earlier in the evening. By this time, the body was beginning to move. The guardsman grabbed and lifted him up on to his shoulder. He muttered to me that his friend must have decided to take a swim not remembering he didn't know how. He dragged him away to the guardhouse. I returned to the lobby and my room. After some time, in spite of my bewilderment, I fell back asleep.

The next morning I awoke amazed by the whole episode. So many times have I thought about it since. I take no particular credit for what I did. I was there and I had little fear of water. And yet, I had clearly saved a human life. How had I come to be the one to do so? What did it mean? So many, many years later, as the events of 11 September 2001 unfolded, I heard a remark on television that to save one life is to save all humanity. Is that true? Again feeling no right to any commendation (and at the risk of appearing to solicit one), I am even more astonished that I had such a privilege. It was a personal revelation that took many years to understand. That is, if it is not too pretentious to think that I now do. The message for me seemed universal and simple, and no surprise. All of our life's actions should be guided by the value we hold for each other. To treat everyone as we would wish to be treated. I am proud of what I did even though I feel I cannot claim any attributes of heroism. I had done it without much thought, as a natural impulse, based on an unconscious wish that someone would do the same for me because it was the decent thing to do.

I have thought since that such actions are important not just at the moment of imminent death. Far more important—and difficult—is to show such compassion and an extended hand in the everyday life of people in need. We are all in such need, rich and poor, at one time or another, during our brief lives together. It is the willingness and readiness to respond to the needs of others that defines our common humanity. It reflects the best in human nature. But human nature has its selfish side. To step away from it to help others is not always so easy, caught up as we are in meeting so many of our own needs. But we have the potential. We can make acting decently toward one another based on a sense of equal human value the very foundation of our human relations and our society. Perhaps that more than anything can change the world.

Peoples' Dignity

Kenya helped me to further understand the full implications of this in the context of development work. That helping others out of poverty needs to be based on a sense of decency. But I also began to gain further insight that if decency is to change peoples' lives, it must be based on a true respect for people's innate dignity and capacity rather than a charitable impulse. To preserve that dignity and to realize the full potential of human capacities to find their own path to a better life, development needs to be done not for but with and by people. I was to conclude that my work in Kenya failed to appreciate this sufficiently. It was a lesson I was determined not to repeat.

I had come to Kenya at a time when it held the dubious reputation of having the highest population growth rate in the world (4.2%). Slums spread out around all the major cities. Poverty was increasing. Young people living in these circumstances had and felt no way out. They turned increasingly to crime. I witnessed the government beginning to recognize and to admit to the population problem—always the most important first step. But efforts to contain the growth were superficial in comparison to the problem.

The national population and development council went through the motions of promoting population education and family planning, but clear results were not evident. Many NGOs were at work, but there was very little cooperation between them and the government which held most of the donor money. The donors themselves spoke of no higher priority to Kenya's development than limiting population growth. But their support was fragmented and often duplicative and wasteful.

There began to take place a greater cooperation. Many were involved and responsible. We in the UNFPA played our role, increasingly a lead role. We advocated for an "integrated" approach to population. No longer were family planning education and birth control enough. The reasons adults had many children were multi-fold. They were often justified. Infant mortality was dropping, but parents still could not count on all the newborns living beyond their one to five year danger zone. They needed children to support the family economy. Women were tied to the home, and fell victims to the husband's demands and frequent abuse.

We began to open up and support new population activity aimed at increasing the life chances of the newborns and their mothers. We saw and supported the need for enabling those mothers to earn outside the home, and to have their daughters educated equally with the boys. We financed programs of skill training and credit provision for small entrepreneurs. We encouraged and facilitated the NPDC to bring a multitude of similar government-led efforts together through closer cooperation in their operations. We ourselves brought together the donor community. We held regular meetings to discuss plans, frustrations and the ever-evasive "coordination" so sorely needed. We proposed and funded a national conference of parliamentarians on population. Exposing politicians to the realities and dire results of the population explosion was a real "eye-opener" that went well beyond the previous platitudes of their understanding.

Somewhere in the middle of this process, I began to think it was just not concrete enough. We were attempting to influence national population strategies, policies and programs, but in reality we were not bringing these to the level of people. We were not impacting their lives in any direct, visible manner beyond routine health services that were the traditional pillars of population work.

Kibera

I tried to break out of this mold. I concentrated on my most immediate environment, the poor of Nairobi, and determined myself to better understand their real situation and needs. I came to realize that the most disturbing phenomenon was the ever growing problem of slums. Nairobi slums were already famous. Thousands of poor Kenyans from rural areas flooded every month into Nairobi's centers of urban squalor looking for jobs. Places such as Kawangware, Riruta, Mathare, and Kibera. The steady flow turned into a mass human movement and settlement increasingly defined by desperate poverty and crime. People struggled to survive. Few found jobs or ways of earning income above absolute poverty.

One of these slums—Kibera— was particularly extreme. It was the largest and most densely populated. At the time I was not sure how many lived there, nor did anyone else seem to have a precise idea (even today the estimates are between half a million and well over one million). But what was clear, as I observed the slum from a distance was that it was probably the densest concentration of humanity I had ever seen. I decided we should explore the possibility of working there.

I made contact with some local residents through NGOs who were already working in Kibera. My first up close visit was a shock. Viewing the area from afar was very different from walking through it on foot. Kibera had a unique topography marked by many gullies and steep embankments. Most of the slum had no roads. I found myself venturing along worn footpaths navigating rivulets of open sewage and mounds of rotting garbage. The housing did not deserve its name. Barely shacks, these temporary shelters were made of used wooden slates filled in with cardboard or plastic. Roofing consisted of whatever materials were available, from used corrugated tin to more plastic sheeting. Many of these shelters built over refuse piles collapsed in heavy rains. Entire densely crowded areas were frequently consumed by fires started by anyone's careless use of kerosene. In fact, the primitive physical conditions of Kibera were far worse than those I would later encounter (and still felt repelled by) in Liberia. Kibera was the worst possible example of African poverty. Something I had not seen since Calcutta.

Originally settled by Nubian soldiers from Sudan (who had been rewarded with land by the British government following their services to the crown in the First World War) Kenyans gradually moved into Kibera from all parts of the country. It became a polyglot of all tribal cultures of the country. Unfortunately, this eventually provided the context for tribal rivalry and frequent conflict. Kikuyu tribesmen of the central highlands came to dominate the administration of the area as loosely and ill-defined as it was. This led to corruption in the leasing of lands. It also led to resentment of other tribes and outbreaks of tribal violence often instigated by outside political figures. In this environment, the challenges of development and efforts to slow population growth were acutely daunting.

On my return visits, I entered individual households to speak face to face with residents. Even with all my previous exposure to poverty, it was always heartrending. On one occasion, I accepted an invitation of a middle-aged woman to sit down in her one-room hovel. It had three beds squeezed together, a table and two chairs, and a small open fire stove. She told me she had come to Kibera from Western Kenya. She was of the Luo tribe, along with her husband and five children who ranged in age from three to sixteen years. Her husband had started some local carpentry work, a skill he had learned from his father in his home village. He earned enough to feed his family. Then he died, a year before my visit, from some unknown illness. His wife and children fell immediately into destitution. Although they had no extended family to help them, they decided not to return to their home on the shores of Lake Victoria. Their hope was that the elder son could still find work in Nairobi. He did not. With their meager food supply running low, they did not know how much longer they could count on the hand outs of a local charity. There was no solution in sight. I left, and on a later visit found they had gone. No one knew where or what was their ultimate fate.

On another visit, I met a young man probably eighteen years old. He sat alone outside a dilapidated dwelling, staring in the distance. I came up to greet him. He turned in my direction and attempted a warm smile as I held out to shake his hand. His bearing betrayed his desperation. He had a brother and sister, both younger than he, and neither attended school. He had finished the first year of secondary school, and had acquired some basic electrical skills in a vocational program. But he never found work. His parents had both died two years earlier. He was solely responsible for his siblings. Worried about his younger brother's association with boys he knew were committing petty crimes in the area, he saw only calamity for all of them. He had no idea what to do.

I was deeply moved by all of this, as anyone would be. I decided to bring together many of the NGOs working in Kibera into a sharing workshop. It was a great success. We used colored cards pinned on a board. We clustered them into categories of ideas that flowed back and forth on what we could do to help the people of Kibera. We promised ourselves to work together but did not identify a specific joint initiative. Our goodwill did not turn into any immediate action.

I decided that cooperation would only come if we first established our own presence and credibility in Kibera. We did pick up on ideas coming from the workshop and consulted further with organizations already working there. One of these was the Don Bosco program (founded by the Salesian Society of Catholic Priests and Brothers in the nineteenth century it rapidly spread across many countries of Africa including Kenya where they had a vocational training school in Nairobi targeting street children). They were particularly active in Kibera. Training included a wide range of skills, from carpentry, welding, mechanics, plumbing, even tailoring. We collaborated with them and were especially pleased as young boys mastered practical skills. But finding them jobs or self employment opportunities was considerably more challenging; some did but most did not.

Their Way

As my time in Kenya began to wind down, and as I reflected on my work there from later assignments, I came to realize much more clearly that the immense problems of Kibera could not be resolved by our well-intentioned technical support. The problems of Kibera were in fact a microcosm of the broader fundamentally and institutionally entrenched problems of Kenya. Widespread corruption and ruling class greed quickly stifled (or at least severely limited) most local technical initiatives no matter how well designed and implemented. These initiatives simply did not address the core root problems that oppressed poor people.

Those core problems centered on the fact that people were powerless in the face of the overwhelming power of those who controlled their lives. The critical need, before any technical work could hope to be effective, was to address this power imbalance squarely. The need was to begin a process of empowering local people. To empower them about their rights and to build their confidence to define what needed to be done to improve their lives. To support their efforts to do it. The need was to work not with one segment of the community such as youth, but to work with the entire community. To put them in charge of their own development, with the financial and management skills to achieve it.

Instead our narrowly defined programs were imposed. They were not driven by the communities themselves who undoubtedly would have had entirely different priorities. Of course such a bottom up approach would need to be complemented by broader institutional changes to democratize Kenya's government to serve its people, at national and local levels. That would gradually emerge later as Kenya rewrote its Constitution and continued to democratize its political system. But our opportunity to contribute and to demonstrate a small model of what bottom up development in Kibera could achieve was missed.

I learned a lot in Kenya. I learned mostly from my shortsightedness. I learned that any effort to overcome oppression must confront its roots in a courageous, positive, politically astute and practical way. I learned more convincingly than ever that people were the solution. I learned through my mistakes that decent intentions and actions, however important they may seem, would only create more frustration if they were imposed on people. I learned that true and lasting change could only come about through a respect for and support of peoples' fundamental dignity, right and capability to create a better life their own way.

Chapter 13
Malawi

A Nation Reborn?
1991 – 1994

Hastings Kamuzu Banda

In Praise of the Life President

The Ambassadorial Team in our garden

The People Decide
Voting for Multi-Party Democracy

From Kenya I took up what turned into the "war assignment" in Liberia (1990) that I have already recounted. For Suvira, it was a period of constant and growing anxiety. Following her and Kavita's evacuation from Liberia and return to Oregon, she undertook some consultancy work mainly to West Africa. She learned of my initial return to Liberia with great consternation while on mission in The Gambia. She spent much of her time back in Oregon wondering how I was and whether I would make it out alive. For these reasons, once the emergency relief operations were up and running in Liberia, I rather happily accepted an offer to transfer. Although I could not know at the time, the new assignment to Malawi would be equally momentous to my life and offer opportunities to begin to practice some of what I had learned in Liberia, Kenya and other assignments.

Solace in the Trees

Malawi is a country of great beauty and exquisite people. Much of it lies on a high plateau, and its capital, Lilongwe, is like a paradise of temperate to tropical vegetation and endless rolling hills. Our home was among those hills, a modest government-provided bungalow with a huge garden—four acres! One of my first undertakings was to build (actually to supervise the building of) a very large tree house. It was more like a deck among the trees at the upper end of the garden. It had a serene view of innumerable trees and a small pond in the distance. I built the tree house partly under the pretext of giving my daughter a place to play, but really it was as much for me as anyone. A wonderful place of undisturbed quiet. I sought respite there in the evenings after work, and especially on weekends. On Friday nights Suvira and I took up a bowl of home-made hummus and flat bread, a bottle of rose wine, and just relaxed under the stars.

Kavita entered the British International School. She enjoyed our new home. It was single storied, with living, dining and two bedrooms and baths at one end, a large open patio in the middle, and what we ended up calling "the women's quarters" at the other end. The latter had two bedrooms and a bath, where Suvira kept her wardrobe and used it for daily dressing and washing. Whenever we had guests or family visiting, they stayed in these quarters, private and relaxed. Kavita also enjoyed getting back to horse riding. We enrolled her in riding lessons with a British lady who had set up a small but quaint riding arena and stables. And we all enjoyed our occasional six hour trips down to Lake Malawi, one of the deepest and most beautiful in Africa running almost the entire length of the country. It was wonderful for sail boating (on the same "hobycats" I had sailed in Fiji), though you had to make a special effort not to overturn or fall off. The lake was full of hippos submerged in the water except for thick noses and ever alert ears.

Crafty Dictatorship

Malawi was and is one of the poorest countries in Africa. Some 60% of the population lived in absolute poverty, probably more. The country, formerly known as Nyasaland, and its government, were dominated for nearly thirty years by a dictator, Dr. Hastings Kamuzu Banda. He had wrested the country from the British, first as prime minister when it was granted self-governing status in 1963, and then as president when it became independent in 1964.

Kamuzu Banda ruled with an iron hand. In 1971 he declared himself "President for Life". His rule was notoriously harsh. According to the living legend, he reputedly would have his enemies including disloyal ministers thrown into the Shire River which flowed out of Lake Malawi and into the Zambezi River. They were certain to be devoured along the way by crocodiles or bitten in half by hippopotami which inhabited these waters in great numbers.

Malawi was the arch-stereotype of an African disaster case ruled by a despot. And yet there were important differences from that stereotype. Whatever repression and suffering Banda's dictatorship had wrought on his people; he also brought about a great deal of discipline and efficiency. He commanded the blind loyalty of many whether out of respect or fear.

In the eyes of most Western countries and institutions, the government of Malawi assumed the role of a model for Africa. Malawi followed Western and international advice to the hilt. It adhered to the "structural adjustment" mandates that were vigorously promoted at that time in exchange for substantial international loans. The World Bank and International Monetary Fund took every opportunity to hold Malawi up as an example of fiscal and monetary responsibility. It was another case of imposed Western "capitalist" policies, complied to by a dictator who was ever-willing to prove his anti-communist and pro-capitalist credentials. It was in turn rewarded with generous financial support. That benefited mostly Kamuzu Banda and the elite around him at the expense of a never-improving entrenched poverty of the vast majority of the people.

Malawi was also a friend of South Africa, apartheid South Africa. Kamuza Banda had cleverly seen an opportunity to apply an "open dialogue" policy with the most ostracized country in Africa. Malawi was the sole African country to do so, and to reap all the benefits that such a maverick policy brought to the country's dictator from a most appreciative South African dictatorship. The entire new government infrastructure created in Lilongwe—office buildings, housing, a stupendous hill-top palace for the "Life President", and much more—was made possible only through South African financing and construction.

Lilongwe was an idyllic place, so well planned and laid out. I would hardly pass more than five or six cars on my ten minute ride to work each morning. The air was pure. The food and wine imported from South Africa and sold at highly subsidized prices, kept everyone at the top, including the international community, very comfortable indeed.

Prostrate for Indiana

Kamuzu Banda was a master diplomat. I learned this personally. He had the habit of welcoming all new diplomats to Malawi himself. Malawi gave the UN Resident Coordinator diplomatic status, and I was summoned to the palace on the outskirts of the southern commercial center of Blantyre to meet the Life President and to present my credentials. The long drive up to the palace was absolutely splendid. Lined with a canopy of jacaranda trees that turned a brilliant light purple in bloom, the road was surprisingly open with only one check point of indifferent guards before it wandered into the surrounding countryside. Local farmers and women carrying vegetables to market used the passage with a sense of community ownership rather than in awe of the palace's occupant residing high on the hill. There were no signs of security concerns. After all who was going to threaten a leader whom everyone knew had complete power and whom they were conditioned to revere?

I waited in a side room of the entrance foyer to the palace. I was soon joined by one of the government ministers who usually handled diplomatic visits. We were both ushered into a very large reception room with an enormous table on which lay a leopard's skin, head and all. Told I should stand when Kamuzu entered, I of course did so. What I was not prepared for was how the minister suddenly fell to the floor. For an instant I thought he had passed out. But as I saw he remained on his knees I realized it was a ritual demanded of him. He did not rise until the president seated himself at the head of the table, and then only after Kamuzu gave the appropriate signal.

Kamuzu spoke softly but with energy and curiosity. Informed that I was the new UNDP Resident Representative, he apparently did not know my nationality. His first utterance was to ask me where I was from. I replied the United States. He asked which state. I said California. He then said, 'Oh, I'm from Indiana.' I wasn't sure if he was kidding me or what, so I showed only a slight smile of recognition and appreciation. 'No', he said, 'I mean it; I lived in Indiana in my youth.' He then began a half hour story of how he had been taken by American missionaries for schooling in America. He first attended high school in Ohio, after which he received financial support from local benefactors to enter Indiana University, and later transferred to the University of Chicago from where he earned his bachelor's degree. With further philanthropic support, he attended Meharry Medical College in Tennessee. At the time he told me this, he was reputedly well over ninety years old, born in 1897 by some accounts, though no one knew for sure.

Kamuzu Banda later went on to earn another medical degree from the University of Edinburgh in Scotland so he could practice medicine in Britain. He practiced in London for some thirty years before returning, via Ghana, to Malawi in 1958, to head the Malawi congress party and gain independence for his country.

Well, in spite of my strong inclination to quietly despise this old man who I was sure had done and continued to do great injustice and harm to his own people, I was genuinely flattered that he took the time to share all of that with me, and with such delight. In spite of my diplomatic status, I was not a major ambassador (at least in my own mind), but that seemed to make very little difference to him. I wanted to assume it was his way of showing respect for the UN. By the end of the meeting, I was impressed in a grudging sort of way.

What happened next however brought me quickly back to reality. As the president rose to exit and extend his hand to bid me farewell, I noticed from the corner of my eye that his minister had resumed a full genuflection. As Kamuzu strode across the room, the minister followed him to the door some fifty feet away, this time entirely on his knees, culminating his respects with a full bow of his head to the floor as the door closed. I stood there in utter disbelief. Somehow I managed to retain a wise diplomatic silence. It occurred to me then that this was going to be a very unique and challenging assignment. I had no idea how prescient those thoughts were.

Reality Denied

So what was I going to do in Malawi? I had come from a life-changing experience in Liberia, but the practical relevance of that to what was going on in Malawi took time to sink in. I concentrated on what my conventional "development mindset" told me was most logical and important—to refocus the UN program on an eradication of poverty. A new cycle of programing was just beginning within UNDP, undertaken afresh as it was every five years. Amazingly, in spite of the obvious, the priority for the government and even the international community was not on "poverty". It was considered politically incorrect terminology. Very few seemed willing to classify a country with such an impressive macro-economic track record, and World Bank attributions to prove it, in the category of "one of the poorest countries in the world" as it certainly was. But the reality seemed just too glaring and flagrant to me to be tucked away under some other labels.

I was encouraged in this thinking by UN colleagues of other agencies, and by my own national staff. So our new program was focused on poverty alleviation, and we labeled it as such, though we did take every opportunity to highlight the more acceptable "human development" terminology as the best means to achieve it. This of course included my usual ingredients of "decentralization" and "peoples' participation". We absorbed ourselves in designing a program on this basis and getting it off to New York headquarters for review and approval of resources.

Winds of Change

About this same time, some six months into my assignment, I and others in the international community unexpectedly began to see signs of internal dissent within Malawi. Something unimaginable back in the brief time since I arrived. It would easily have been ignored, and certainly squashed, except this time it was coming from the churches. No less than a "Bishops' Letter" had been formulated and articulated to what were still dumb-founded but receptive congregations. It was a letter which questioned, indeed protested, the political and economic repression of the people, and called for change. It sparked and energized almost overnight a groundswell of opposition to the past and present. It was a demand for reform.

Malawi had never known such a spontaneous movement. Malawi under Banda held strong to its pro-Western reputation, and was rewarded with friendship and support not least from the United States. America's long-standing policy during the cold war of catering to dictatorships throughout Africa, so long as they rejected soviet influence and any notions of communism, found in Malawi the paragon of what it hoped other African countries would become. It clearly made no difference in what way and how Kamuzu Banda ruled his own people with blatant oppression. What counted almost exclusively was that America could maintain at least a "balance of power" with the soviets, here and all over Africa.

Unconditional Adulation

Without doubt Malawi was a police state. People were expected to conform to a retinue of daily rules and regulations. At the time of our arrival, these rules included a strict puritanical code against women wearing any clothing that revealed their legs above the knees, or men wearing hair below their collars. Unbelievably, we found ourselves conforming even before our arrival when I had my own long trademark locks shorn above the ears to the bewilderment of friends and foes alike. Suvira stocked up on a supply of ankle length skirts, not easy to find at that time in US department stores. The sycophants behind the throne, ever anxious to prove their loyalty to the Life President, used "youth brigades" to monitor and enforce these rules, even among foreigners.

More startling still were the efforts to create and maintain a "cult of personality" for the Life President among the populace. Every private and public establishment and business was expected to display prominently a photograph of the president. Most importantly, any public appearance of the president had to be accompanied by a show of adulation and great fanfare.

Suvira and I attended many celebrations in the national stadium, as did all of the diplomatic corps, to mark the day of independence or any other anniversary significant to Kamuzu's dictatorship. These were extraordinary events. The stadium always filled to capacity, maybe 50,000 people, including everyone in the government at top and bottom levels. Royal trumpets announced Kamuzu Banda's entrance into the stadium along with flashing lights atop a seemingly endless procession of limousines and military vehicles. Most important in the vanguard was an assembly of hundreds of women dressed in traditional attire printed with Kamuzu's image on every garment. The women were always in a joyous mood. They sang jubilant praises of the president and danced with a slow and sensual rhythm that can only be seen in Africa. The entire entourage would make two complete rounds of the stadium floor before stopping in front of the presidential boxes just below our diplomatic seats.

Then began an almost ceaseless number of speeches by government officials, all in the utmost praise of the Life President. These events culminated in the keenly anticipated words of wisdom of the president. He would stand at the podium accentuating every point he wished to highlight with a dramatic swish of his traditional fly whisk made of long animal hairs. To the Malawians, this clearly conveyed his supreme status and ultimate power. During these occasions we and other members of the diplomatic corps exchanged frequent glances of astonishment, but were no less impressed with the precision and discipline by which everything took place. The absolute apogee of these ceremonies was when Kamuzu descended from his royal vantage point to join the women in a last round of dancing before he reentered his open vehicle and exited the stadium waving in recognition of the rightful respects bestowed upon him by all.

On some such occasions, these outdoor events were followed by dinner at the presidental palace attended by high government officials and again the diplomatic corps. These were equally extraordinary experiences for Suvira and me. The dining room itself was utterly impressive, like a convention hall with a capacity for more than 500 guests and filled with white upholstered chairs and long flower-covered tables meticulously adorned with fine china, silver place settings and crystal glassware, every seat occupied.

Every guest had a clear view of a high stage at one end of the room. It was from this elevated point that the evening's celebrations were orchestrated, literally. A military officer of considerable rank entered on to the stage shortly after everyone was seated. On his initial signal, which he gave by blowing a large whistle and waving his right hand, scores of waiters carrying trays of sumptuous food high above their heads, entered the room from different directions each conveying their victuals up to a precise and predetermined point. When each had reached that point in unison, another blow of the whistle signaled the next command for them to change directions and march again with absolute precision and synchronization to their designated tables. It was like watching military drills in an enclosed parade ground. Its purpose was not lost on the guests. We all marveled at the discipline by which it was performed and the strong hand of the supreme leader who had made it happen.

Behind the Throne

Kamuzu's power and oppression was reinforced by a small elite who wielded great influence and increasing power of their own behind the throne. First among these in terms of conformity to strict conventions was Kamuzu's "official hostess", Mama Kadzamira, who was his former nurse turned informal wife. Besides her reputed role in advising Kamuzu on political intrigue, Mama Kadzamira took special interest to ensure that rules were followed. One example of this occurred a few months after we had arrived. Just at that time a song entitled "Cecilia" had shot to the top of the international pop charts (made famous by Simon and Garfunkel in America). It so happened that Mama Kadzamira's first name was Cecilia. She apparently took the lyrics of this song—which many in Malawi began to sing—personally:

Cecilia you're breaking my heart
You're shaking my confidence daily
Oh, Cecilia, I'm down on my knees
I'm begging you please to come home…
Making love in the afternoon
With Cecilia up in my bedroom
(Making love)
I got up to wash my face
When I came back to bed
Someone's taken my place…

The song was quickly outlawed on Mama Kadzamira's orders. No one dared to play or sing it (except at a few diplomatic parties behind closed doors!).

Much more ominous were the political maneuverings and repression orchestrated by one John Tembo. He more than anyone else ruled the roost in Kamuzu's name. Everyone knew it and feared him accordingly. It was John Tembo with whom we would have to deal as Malawi began to transform, as transform it did.

Facilitating History

It was in early 1992 that the "Bishops Letter" was read to congregations throughout Malawi. The fact that by this time, the soviet union was well in decline with its influence rapidly diminishing not least in Africa, the period did not work in favor of the regime. There was a sudden "born again" enthusiasm for democracy among the western representatives in Africa. They conveniently cast aside references to their past history of siding with and supporting the oppressors as an unfortunate chapter of historic "real politik". They became overnight crusaders for the future of democracy in Africa. I do not condemn those diplomat who did this, they were right in leading this change in policy, however long overdue. They were brave to stay just a step or two out in front of this trend. Many of them became my closest friends.

The UN had been a neutral player in all of this history. Carefully avoiding political issues, our job was to promote and support development whatever the context. But change was in the wind. Not least it began to affect the UN. This included its development agenda. Some time not long before I had arrived in Malawi, the UN and UNDP in particular, began to stand up for "good governance". We were gradually realizing that a focus on economics and social services per se was not enough. There was an equally, if not more important and urgent need to reform the way governments related to and served (or mostly did not serve) their own people. They must become more representative institutions based on fair play, justice and human rights. And they must be guided by the will and active participation of the people.

These were high sounding words and they appealed to me. They struck a resonant chord from my Liberian experience. They began to ring more clearly in my head. It was increasingly logical to me that countries could never begin to realize development in a political vacuum. In fact, development had to be based first and foremost on a democratic process that truly empowered people to take charge of their own development; and at the same time committed their governments to work in their best interests.

It was at this time that the events described above began to unfold in Malawi. I wondered what it all meant and how we should react. I knew that the UN could never, nor never should, enforce political change in any country. But I perceived that we could now more openly advocate for such change. I saw, as had already some of my colleagues in other African countries, that we could play an important role not through power, but through our neutrality and commitment to our principles.

Still not sure what this meant in reality, however, I began to meet with the ambassadors of the donor countries, one on one, and eventually as a group. These ambassadors were now the strongest advocates of the new politics of representative democratic governance as a prerequisite of development aid. They had responded with immediate enthusiasm to the Bishops Letter. They wanted to do whatever possible to encourage democratic change. What I could offer was a neutral UN facilitation for exchanging their views among themselves, and sharing their positions with the government in power and the opposition forces. It became a new dynamic role for UNDP.

It was welcomed by all the parties to the dialogue and drama unfolding. It had nothing directly to do with my development role per se, but as became increasingly clear to me, it would make all the difference to whether development would ever take place. In this way, the meetings of ambassadors that I chaired weekly in my rather modest office, created a unique forum for promoting (and pressuring for) change.

The occasional messages which I was asked by the ambassadors to transmit to the government were taken very seriously. I was enthusiastic and proud of the role I was playing. I was also relatively new to such high stake political deliberations. My early naiveté became blatantly clear (mainly to myself) when early in the process of serving as the middleman, I was unexpectedly approached by the then minister of health who held considerable political clout within John Tembo's cabinet. He requested me to convey a message, not to the ambassadors, but to the opposition parties who were then meeting in the southern commercial town of Blantyre. It was at the time these parties were building pressure for a multi-party democracy to replace the one-party rule. The message was not all that important (having to do with some procedural matters relevant to this issue) but I felt honored to facilitate dialogue and jumped at the opportunity.

I phoned ahead to the coordinator of the opposition party meeting. He welcomed my visit. I traveled the six hours down to Blantyre the next morning.

Before sharing the message with the full meeting, I met with two party leaders. I immediately sensed some tension. They were puzzled to know why the government was conveying a message through me rather than directly. I explained that the minister had informed me he felt I was especially well versed in the details of the issues, particularly as some were linked to the concerns of the ambassadors. He felt I could explain them most clearly.

But I immediately began to understand my folly. As I had not yet conferred on the matter with the ambassadors, I could not speak on their behalf. I certainly did not want to be seen as speaking on behalf of the government. I went into instant "crisis management" mode, aimed at hopefully extricating myself from this embarrassing and potentially damaging political blunder. Fortunately, the two party leaders were well known to me and we were on friendly terms. I confided that I did not want my actions to be misinterpreted, and that I should probably take the opportunity instead to brief the meeting on issues recently raised by the ambassadors regarding multi-party democracy. These were issues that I knew would find favor among the opposition parties. So this I did, and none (except the two party leaders and me) were the wiser.

On my return to Lilongwe, I drove directly to the US embassy and asked to see the Ambassador, Michael Pistor. He and I—along with a few other ambassadors (British, German, EU, etc.)—had a close working relationship and I felt I could confide in him and the others in turn. I explained everything that had happened. He appreciated this and advised that we should best keep the matter to ourselves, which we did. Nothing ever came of the incident. But I learned a lot from that experience—in terms of never repeating it, but also in terms of the importance of building trusting relations on every side with those who could help me out in such moments.

As the ambassadors continued to meet in my office every Friday morning, they gradually reached a consensus that their most effective influence would come in backing the call of the opposition parties for a "referendum" on multi-party v. one party political systems. The donors phrased it in terms of representative democracy. There had been an immediate and strong resistance by the government to this proposal, especially by John Tembo. He saw it as a blatant donor-supported ploy to oust the government. He insisted that reforms could well take place within the existing system. The ambassadors held firm to their position, saying it was the best means for letting the people decide which form of government they wanted.

I was by this time receiving excellent advice and support not only from the electoral affairs office of the UN secretariat in New York, but also from the UN centre for human rights in Geneva. With their backing, I put forward to the ambassadors the idea of bringing in a neutral and respected international figure to discuss these matters with the Government. They liked the idea. We identified a highly respected African legal scholar who was then heading the international centre for jurisprudence in Geneva. His visit proved a turning point.

The key session with Mr. Tembo and several of his ministers began around nine in the evening and lasted well past midnight. The arguments from their side were strong and unrelenting. The present political system would bring reforms without any need for itself to be reformed. Mr. Tembo would not accept any of the experiences or purported successes put forward by our respected scholar and administrator. I had offered a few remarks and points from my side, referring to the more recent indications of Malawi's readiness to make change peacefully. These arguments fell on deaf ears and were summarily ignored. A certain despondency set in with my eminent colleague and myself. We were witnessing what was clearly a total stonewalling that became more strident from the ministers' side as the night wore on. The meeting ended without agreement.

We drove back to the hotel mostly in silence, certain our efforts had failed. The next morning we returned to Lilongwe. That same night, I went to bed early, exhausted from the tensions and apparent defeat of our efforts. I slept poorly, and was contemplating the unpleasant task ahead to explain to the ambassadors the next morning what had transpired. Suddenly at about 2:30 am the phone rang by Suvira's side. She answered and told me it was Mr. Tembo. I could hardly believe that. I took the receiver certain she had been mistaken. Mr. Tembo spoke in a low voice. He had considered our discussion very carefully. He felt that the government's position was right, but for the good of the country, he would agree to the referendum. That was all, except to express thanks for the role of the UN.

I was astonished. I later analyzed these events more carefully. I came to the conclusion that Mr. Tembo had probably entered our meeting already certain that a referendum must take place, given the pressure of the opposition and of the donors. He wanted his ministers to hear the argument, and to release their steam, realizing that they would feel loyal to him and would never give in. This set the stage for him to then acquiesce without any of them having shown disloyalty, thereby retaining their unconditional loyalty and support. In any case, it makes no real difference. The important point is that despotism had bent to the winds of change, and it would never straighten again. The UN had played a pivotal, albeit low-keyed, role in facilitating that change. And it was that change which would give democracy, and eventually development—or so I hoped—a chance.

The referendum took place on June 14, 1993. The vote was overwhelmingly in favor of a multi-party system. The UN electoral unit had assumed responsibility for the electoral process, including training of the election officials and workers, preparation of ballot papers and boxes, and setting up of the polling stations. They did a superb job. With their support and that of the donors, we also managed to bring in a large contingent of international monitors, over 200.

Suvira and I signed up as official "UN monitors". We rose at 3:00 am, and were at our designated village by 4:30. At first we thought our headlights were deceiving us through the heavy mist that morning. But as we drew closer, we realized it was true. The lines of villagers already waiting to vote extended far into the darkness on the other side. A pent-up thirty years was about to burst. Later we drove to other villages in the area, and the story repeated itself. I took photos to convince myself of what I was seeing. Many women and men stood in garments torn and faded by their poverty. Yet their weathered and worn faces reflected a new hope and determination. Over 90% of those eligible voted that day. The news passed quickly around the world.

The next night we celebrated. I had invited all UN monitors, the government ministers and officials, leaders of the opposition, the diplomatic corps, and the UN family for an evening in our garden. Everyone mixed in a spirit of camaraderie. Jokes between old, sometimes bitter, foes warmed the night. The drama of history in the making reached a climax when several of our portable radios turned on simultaneously at the designated hour to hear Kamuzu Banda declare the results. There was no gloating, but the atmosphere of having "overcome" was poignantly clear among most Malawians who had gathered under those magnificent African skies. The diplomats were ever diplomatic, but clearly elated.

The festive decorum broke later in the evening when the Finnish ambassador joined others for drinks but leaned back just too far in his chair atop that famous tree house of mine. He rather undiplomatically fell backwards a dozen feet into the dark bushes on the far side. My initial panic eased as we pulled him safely out of the thick bush that thankfully cushioned his fall. I walked him up to our house where he accepted my offer to lie on our bed. Soon and with a slight air of bravado he rejoined us for further drinks, this time "below deck"! It was an evening I shall long remember.

Following the referendum, change moved rapidly forward. A presidential council was formed and by late 1993 they had abolished the life presidency. The next logical step was to organize elections for a new government. Once again, the UN played a central role. We brought in an expert on party and voting systems. A vigorous Yorkshireman and former member of the British Parliament filled that job exceedingly well.

It was also clear that any new government would need a new constitution by which to govern. The UN centre for human rights provided a resident advisor, and a model constitution embedding all possible principles of democracy and human rights was finely honed by a body of Malawian legal and political sages. The crowning achievement of the UN contribution was in supporting a debate on the draft constitution by a three day special session of parliament broadcast to the entire nation. Completely unprecedented, it was a signal event for the ten million Malawians listening to words and pronouncements shaping their future. It was followed by further discussions with those people in their districts. The resulting document was eventually approved as a "peoples' constitution" in 1994.

The national election for public offices was held on May 17, 1994 and resulted in a resounding defeat of the long-ruling Malawi congress party and a victory for the United Democratic Front (UDF) and their coalition ally the Alliance for Democracy. A popular new president, Bakili Muluzi, leader of the UDF, ushered in a new team of Ministers drawn largely from the leadership of the opposition. I knew all of them personally, and it was a special period for me to witness so closely their rise to power. They made very clear their appreciation for the role the UN had played in helping to open the window of freedom they now enjoyed.

Malawi convinced me more than anything before that people working together, around shared values of decency and democracy, both within their country and across international and cultural lines, could achieve a better life for all. A pretentious thought, but one that seemed now well founded in the hard evidence of what had transpired. I was particularly impressed by the special chemistry of the diplomatic and international team that so spontaneously rose to play an historic supporting role. The key had been creating open communication, firstly among that team, and later with the local leaders and people. A common purpose had been identified, and all had found respect, tolerance and eventually appreciation, for the roles that each could play in achieving that purpose. Humanity's common quest for justice had prevailed, at least for this historic moment.

Imperfections of Success

Was this a perfect ending? Was the argument for the overriding strength of human caring and cooperation now irrefutable? Could this be the example, from what is to some an obscure land in Southern Africa, which we were looking for to serve as our model in a newly troubled world? The answer, as it turned out in my mind, was one of yes and no.

Real and important change did occur. A country, more importantly a society, opened up. Parameters of equality and rights were set in place. The foundations of freedom and opportunity were established. This was no small achievement. One that we would undoubtedly welcome to see in other countries today.

But was it enough? Decidedly not in my view. The changes were important, but they were also limited and in some ways artificial. The truth of this struck me deeply when toward the end of my stay in Malawi, I made a field visit to a village not far from the capital, but worlds away. We had the usual discussion with the village elders about the priorities of the village. We also visited a one room primary school, unusual for such a small village. We were then taken by the village chief to a nearby field where a man and his son were turning the soil for planting. The man was very old. He was lean and his hair completely white. He was starkly handsome. The very moment we encountered his deep set eyes stared unrelentingly into mine. It seemed they were determined to penetrate and understand my soul and to make certain I understood his. His eyes seemed to ask why I had never bothered to come before. Why had I come now. His erect posture and deeply etched face bore an air of wisdom and an inner knowing pride and self respect. Yet he also exuded hopelessness. I sensed it was not so much for himself, but for his family and his community. Without saying so, he told me they had been forgotten in their poverty over so many generations it no longer mattered. As I departed, his steadfast composure and understanding of my limitations, unknown even to me, conveyed a simple message. I would never return, though my home was only an hour away, and neither he nor his children nor theirs would ever know a better life. They were permanently isolated and alone in their poverty. Nothing would change that.

What I slowly began to understand more clearly is that changing systems of governance, as we had claimed to have done in Malawi, could only improve peoples' lives if those changes were accompanied by changes in values that are then practiced. The question was whether those values had changed. Was the new leadership truly committed to realizing a better life for the people?

I departed Malawi elated with what I considered many achievements realized in so brief a time. Not long after, however, I learned that peoples' lives were not much better. In fact many were worse off. Some of the new leadership fell into the very same corruption of the past. Undoubtedly, of course, the resources required to transform political change into practical social and economic opportunity were still sorely limited. My growing concern was that the "will" to effect change may also have been deceptively missing.

I concluded that whatever caused such disappointment and failure in the light of so much seeming success and change, cannot blind us to our need to find better ways to sustain our efforts to realize a better life for people. Clearly a lot more needs to be done beyond the initial euphoria of change. The hard work of creating opportunities only just begins a process. Without the initial change, nothing can follow, but without building and converting that change into a new day to day way of living, nothing meaningful for people is achieved in the end.

So the challenge and the answers to how to bring about a better life for people remained still unclear for me in the case of Malawi. I am convinced nevertheless that Malawi bears the seeds of a new wisdom. I am convinced that humanity pulling together through a commitment to decency for others, across whatever barriers, can eventually overcome and realize a better life for all in the long run. Based on the experiences and continuing progress realized in Malawi and other countries, our generation's greatest opportunity is to show how.

Chapter 14

Thailand

Power of Alliances
1994 – 1999

Akha Village
Courtesy of Sputnikcccp

Upended Plans

What an exciting prospect—our next posting would be to Pakistan. Our previous brief assignment in Karachi and our travels about the country in the mid-70s made us yearn for a return to this place of physical majesty and deep culture. A country already of more than 125 million people in 1994, many of them lived in dire poverty. As I had spent my entire career working on the issues of poverty, mostly in what the UN referred to as "least developed countries", I was hopeful this experience would have relevance in Pakistan. I was certain I would bring a great deal of enthusiasm to the job. My candidacy had gone through all the steps of the UN approval process. We had already set a tentative date for our departure from Malawi. But at the last minute, not uncommon in the complex and ever changing world of the UN and the countries it serves, it was eventually decided that my services would be better applied to a very different challenge.

Figuring Out Opportunity

I could not then imagine an assignment more suitable and challenging to my experience and interests than Pakistan. To my good fortune, however, the leadership of UNDP assigned me through what I can only describe as wise clairvoyance to what over time became one of the most rewarding experiences of my life—Thailand. At the particular moment, however, I was not sure what I could possibly do in a "medium income" country which was in the midst of an "Asian Miracle".

I first visited Thailand in 1970. Still a rural country, I remembered profuse green rice fields as I drove from the airport into Bangkok. There was then a marked American presence in Bangkok. Many US military took their leave there between bombing missions over Vietnam from Thai bases. Later in the early 1980s we visited the country from Nepal for our own rest and relaxation. But nothing prepared us for the Bangkok we entered in November 1994. Completely transformed; overwhelming traffic; truly unrecognizable. Unending new construction and buildings made us lose all our bearings. Thailand was in a boom. It was certainly not an "LDC" country. So what would I be doing? What could I offer? I was not a degreed economist, so delving into macro-economic fine tuning did not seem an option.

Thailand had long been a regional hub of UN operations in the Asia Pacific. Our office had the largest portfolio of Asian "regional projects", mostly dealing with regional transport, infrastructure, communications and the like. My title in fact was UNDP Regional Representative, and I was expected to take over and move forward the management of this regional portfolio.

But what about Thailand itself? We had a program there, quite an interesting one. Largely focused on education at community level and rural/urban income generation, it was to my liking. But I still could not figure out what we should be doing in Thailand. How could we make any difference in this already economically advanced country? Was there a special opportunity to make some difference; and if so, what was it?

Collapse

These initial questions were the beginning of a very long journey. Again, I was to learn and gain far more than I could ever contribute to the country. My education took place through the generosity and wisdom of the Thai people. Thai colleagues in and out of government, and within my office, were the source of my new insights. It was a new generation of development thinking and practice. It enabled me to transcend the notions of least developed and advanced countries. It impressed upon me as never before an understanding of the universal needs and opportunities common to all societies, rich and poor.

Thailand epitomized the "new poverty" of the world. It was potentially as severe and possibly more disruptive than the "old". Thailand was and remains at the very forefront of the great divide that is occurring with frightening speed around the globe.

Of course the macro-economist could point to Thailand as a model country. It had done everything right. Thailand had found an important niche in a robust global market. It catered to the needs of that market, from textiles to computer assembly. Its exports were impressive. Thailand became an investment magnet for the "Asian Miracle". Thailand's business elite prospered. Consumption began to take place in extravagant ways. There was a proliferation of shopping malls that never stopped selling. There was a new addiction to building offices, apartments, and always more shopping malls. The addiction was fed by an ample supply of capital, mostly foreign capital. It was an unending orgy of speculative investment. Not an investment in productivity, but in quick returns.

In the meantime, the average Thai seemed to be getting nowhere. And they were not. They flooded into the major cities, especially Bangkok, to escape the hidden poverty of the countryside. They wanted a share of the boom, or at least a good wage. They got neither. They inhabited pockets of poverty throughout the city, in back neighborhoods well disguised from tourist eyes, and in the surrounding megapolis. They led a grinding existence. Up at 4:00 am or earlier to reach their places of work. They lived not in the new high rises, but at the ground level where the "new pollution" was at its most extreme. Their spouses often remained in the countryside, or at least their parents and other less adventurous family. The lot of these "left behind" villagers was not much better, in some ways worse. Even the pollution began to seep into their rural towns from the proliferating modes of transport of every kind. The exquisite beauty of their land was blighted by "strip development" extending out from Bangkok and other major cities as endless ribbons of pollution and shabby construction. Their traditional economy rapidly eroded. Agricultural productivity accounted for alarmingly less and less of the Gross National Product. Rural people became increasingly trapped, as did their kin in the cities. There were no obvious alternatives for either. The imposed new ways of life had taken a depressing grip on their hopes and aspirations.

In July 1997 I saw it all come crashing down. It was not difficult to predict. Very few did. Overnight, the speculators pulled the plug. The government desperately attempted to save the situation. They shored up the currency. In the process they lost nearly $25 billion in reserves. Construction stopped overnight. Many of the middle class lost their jobs. Investors in the stock market lost their money. The world reacted with growing anxiety. The international financial institutions stepped in to provide their usual plethora of bail out loans conditioned on "reforms".

Then the soul searching began. Thais started to self-analyze. Yes, they had taken the fast track. They failed to invest in the long run sustainability of their development. They failed to invest in long term infrastructure and production systems.

Far more seriously, they failed to invest in people. Contrary to other countries in the region such as South Korea and Taiwan, or even China for that matter, Thailand did not make the same significant investments in education of the majority of their citizenry. Thai skill levels remained very low. This benefited the short run returns of the investors as the wages of laborers stagnated and profits skyrocketed. But when the bubble burst, there was little solid human resource on which to restart the engine.

Slowly the economy began to respond to the palliatives of international assistance. But it was an assortment of not very fundamental economic and financial reforms. Little was done to address urgent institutional reforms on how corporations governed themselves. Government continued to turn a blind eye. The likelihood of a replay of the crash could easily be predicted. It was not clear who cared.

Shared Vision

What was I doing throughout all of this? Early in my assignment in Thailand, I had raised the question of what was being done to address poverty. The surprising answer I received from many quarters was that poverty was not an issue—and that sounded familiar! Many cited recent statistics that confirmed a steady decline in poverty over the past thirty years. Current estimates were around 15% of the population. That was low, even for a middle-income country. I was hard pressed to refute the arguments.

At the same time, I was hearing a lot of talk, especially from the non-governmental side, about a growing gap between rich and poor. I started meeting with many of them. They were clear about the existence of significant poverty in the country. It was mainly a question of how the term was defined. In the traditional use of the word, extreme poverty (narrowly measured by World Bank standards of income and food intake) was evident mostly in the Northeast Region, known as Isan. But widespread poverty was defined by the people in many other ways beyond the conventional criteria. For the poor, in both urban and rural areas, their poverty was real. It consisted of both a perceived and an actual lack of opportunity to get ahead. The poor felt frozen in time. It was a matter of low education, limited knowledge and skills, and the lack of access to resources, including land and credit. Their income might be above the poverty line, but their purchasing power steadily declined. They reflected and obsessed on their situation compared to their surroundings. They saw so many others in the city able to educate their children, buy consumer goods, and become rich. Their poverty was embedded in a deep frustration over this growing divide.

During this same period, I became increasingly struck by the fact that Thailand had unique advantages that I had not seen in any other country. Whatever the faults and shortcomings of the economy, there was no doubt that

Thailand had a very robust business community. Thailand also had an extremely vibrant and active non-governmental movement with which I was now in close contact and the government of Thailand was comparatively efficient and increasingly concerned about the social and economic situation of its people. Thailand was an emerging democracy. Following many coups and military takeovers, Thailand's military was shocked into a new reality during riots in 1992. Blood in the streets signaled that a clear choice had to be made. It was a choice between spiraling into chaos or moving toward real democracy. The choice made was democracy. While not perfect, all governments were now elected by the people, albeit with a lingering vote-buying habit. Overall government had to be more accountable.

This was an unusual mix of advantages. I wondered if it could be brought together as a force for lasting change. Had Thailand reached a point where a stronger democracy and eventually opportunities for a better life for all Thai people were possible? Even I was intimidated by the potential naiveté and false idealism of such thinking. Yet as I discussed these points with others, I found a far deeper understanding and commitment than I would ever have thought possible. There was a "shared vision" for these ideals among many Thais in and out of government, including some in the business community. Was it possible to coalesce these ideals and to work on some common plan of action? Could the UN and other international partners join or at least support the effort?

Bangkok Delights

While contemplating the plus and minus of these opportunities, Suvira and I settled into an extremely bustling and electric urban lifestyle. Initially that was not easy. We had lived in mostly small rurally oriented countries and settings. Suva, Monrovia, Lilongwe, and even Nairobi and New Delhi, all had a soft feeling and manageable logistics about them. Bangkok was completely different. We lived in Sukhumvit, the heart of tourism, entertainment, business and high rise apartments. Getting to and from work was a matter of knowing which roads were going which way at which hours and when to take them. Knowledge of this was of no value when the monsoons flooded the city. That happened regularly. On one such occasion when I needed to attend a formal evening diplomatic event across town and decided to risk the flood then rising, I and my experienced UN driver (Khun Sarakum, a delightful man full of dry humor about the impossibilities of living and driving in Bangkok that kept me amused everyday for five years) soon found ourselves stuck in bumper to bumper traffic with water reaching up to our door. After an excruciating five hour wait, I decided to chance an escape. Rolling up my tuxedo pants, I set out across the city on foot. Wading through two to three feet of water all the way, I actually arrived home some two hours later. What I didn't realize until colleagues with whom I shared the tale later told me was that such adventures are highly ill advised given the not infrequent presence of open manholes beneath those waters into which one could easily slide and disappear!

The Royal Sports Club of Bangkok was our salvation from such urban chaos and excitement. Every Saturday and Sunday I would head there around 11:00 am for a long swim in the most beautiful Olympic size swimming pool I have ever known, set in an arena of swaying palms, lounge chairs, and a steady supply of Thai chicken kebabs and peanut sauce. Suvira and I returned in the evenings for drinks and nuts with sliced chilies in the American style bar, followed in the dining room by a course of Tom Yum soup, spicy prawn cocktails, and tapioca pudding, all accompanied by a three-piece violin, piano and saxophone orchestra playing melodies of the 50s and 60s. Yes, a world of old fashioned privilege that we seemed to feel less guilty about as our five years stretched out and Bangkok's congestion (before the rapid transit trains were completed) grew nearly impossible.

Most wonderful of all, however, were the occasional lunches and dinners I enjoyed with UNDP staff sitting out over the Chao Phraya river (especially as sun set and night enveloped a constant flow of Thai long-tail boats—Ruea Hang Yao—propelled by truck engines carrying all manner of urbanites home from work), always in small obscure inexpensive restaurants serving the best Thai food in the world.

Alliance for Action

Finding my way forward in what to do in Thailand was beginning to take shape. It was the Thais who led the way. None of the change that followed would have been realized had it not been for the Thai people who got behind and led it.

First and foremost among these, in the context of the UN effort to support a coalition for change was the Thai staff in our UNDP office. I understood early on that my own role in such a complex social and cultural setting as

Thailand must be peripheral. Only the Thai people, who spoke the language, understood the profound complexities of the culture and the politics, and who knew each other and how to build trust and partnership between themselves, could make things work for real change.

I was immensely privileged to have Thai staff with these attributes. Staff who were completely dedicated to what we hoped to do. Khun Net and Khun Nipa were particularly instrumental in our early attempts to identify a clear purpose and focus around which to organize our role. That focus would be poverty, so much denied and neglected up to then. But our unique contribution would be in building a coalition of national and international partners around that goal.

Khun Nipa began to take me around to meet a wide network of development activists she knew well in the government, non-government and business communities. Khun Net had her own network, and while there was inevitably some overlap, we managed to canvass and feel the pulse of a very broad spectrum of Thai leadership in all these communities.

The process took quite some time. It included meetings with Khun Anand Panyarachun. He was the highly respected former prime minister of Thailand (1991-1992) who had introduced several economic and political reforms in his brief hold on office, including the drafting of a "peoples' constitution" that was adopted in 1997. Khun Anand, as he was known by everyone, immediately related to the ideas we had to share. He convened an initial meeting of leading NGO activists to discuss the possibilities of partnership.

We also met with Dr. Prawese Wasi a prominent doctor of medicine and winner of the Ramon Magsaysay Award, the famous Asian award for government service. Dr. Prawese was chairperson of the Local Development Foundation, an NGO dedicated to the role of civil society in development. All NGOs looked upon Dr. Prawese as the most senior and respected leader of the NGO community. He eventually played a leading role in our partnership. Soft spoken, kind and considerate, and exceptionally insightful in how best to organize and manage a government and NGO alliance not dominated by either, he was invaluable to creating what became a social movement.

Another prominent NGO leader was Khun Paiboon Wattanasiritham then president of the Thailand Rural Reconstruction Movement (TRRM) and later (1997-2000) director general of the Government Savings Bank. Khun Piaboon was especially adamant that community development should be undertaken only on the basis of supporting genuine "self reliance" of communities. He insisted that we must never create dependence on outside patronage from any side, national or international. We also consulted Khun Mechai Viravaidya, the famous "Khun Mechai" of family planning campaigns of the 1960s (who blew up condoms and floated them on the streets of Bangkok to break down taboos and barriers and start Thailand down a road of responsible family planning before most other countries of South East Asia were even aware of the urgent need). Khun Mechai headed the Population and Community Development Association (PDA). He was particularly strong on the need for practical economic and income generating activities and incentives for Thai communities.

In parallel with our efforts to engage NGO leaders, we also identified "change activists" (as we saw them) within the government. The main government intermediary organization for UNDP on government policies was the National Economic and Social Development Board (NESDB). We were fortunate that at the time the secretary general of the NESDB was Dr. Sippanond Ketudat. Dr. Sippanond was himself in the process of exploring new approaches to development. It would involve a greater voice and participation of people in development. He was open and enthusiastic about building an active partnership to incorporate these ideas in the latest Eighth National Development Plan (1997-2001). This was a giant breakthrough. Under his leadership it became the first national plan drafted with the participation of a wide range of non-governmental and business partners. It emphasized "human development" and local control of resources for self reliant communities. In this way, we found ourselves in complete sync with the national planning process and priority on grassroots development. Our commitment became one of reinforcing this movement by further strengthening the bond between government, the non-governmental community, and their links with business leaders. Specifically, we focused our energies on turning these ideals into action.

Our approach was clear. We would center our efforts on peoples' participation beyond planning, to implement small scale bottom up development projects in poor villages in selected areas throughout the country.

We called it THAI-UNCAP (Thailand – United Nations Collaborative Action Plan). And it was all possible because of the trust and confidence built between NGOs and government and our own UN community. We were doubly privileged to have as the chairman of THAI-UNCAP Dr. Sumet Tantivejtkul. Dr. Sumet was the director of the King's Royal Projects, a position of enormous prestige, managed directly under the King. It funded some 2000 mostly community based projects all across Thailand. Dr. Sumet had the conviction of his words. Development must come up from the people. He helped us to build the coalition and was instrumental on bringing into the movement (as we began to call it) two successive prime ministers. In the earliest stage of the partnership (1995-1996), the then prime minister (General) Chavalit Yongchaiyudh personally officiated at the inaugural ceremonies for THAI-UNCAP in "Government House". Attended by the entire corps of senior officials of the Thai Government, the UN agencies representatives, the participating NGO leadership, and the diplomatic corps, it was an historic gathering of diplomatic & development circles. From 1997-1999, the subsequent prime minister, Chuan Lek Pai, actively and enthusiastically supported the initiative. He not only helped to secure substantial additional government funding, but visited many field sites where we began to support small community driven projects.

Again, this was all possible due in large part to the leadership taken by our Thai staff. Khun Net was particularly effective in building bridges between organizations and government that did not previously exist, at least not for supporting work at community level. She was highly respected by both the NGO and government leaders, and as a consequence, able to take initiatives that more easily brought all sides together.

We were also fortunate to bring onto our team Khun Parichat. She was well known in both government and particularly NGO circles. She teamed up exceedingly well with Khun Net in building and consolidating the partnership. Khun Parichat had an especially friendly and pleasant personality, seeing the humor in our challenges, and sharing a particularly infectious laugh when things looked impossible. For my overachiever personality, this was a much needed salve that aided me to keep our ambitions in proper perspective.

We eventually developed a government/UN "umbrella project" to support the THAI-UNCAP initiatives in five pilot provinces across the country. We retained a respected development manager to launch and monitor the community based activities focused mostly on income earning community enterprises.

An independent feature report on Thai-Uncap was published in the *Pattaya Mail* newspaper at the end of 2000 (Vol. VIII, No. 49, 8 December 2000), some eighteen months after I had left the country. The following excerpts give some insight as to how it was seen by Thais:

Thailand: Matrix for a development partnership
Story and photos by Peter Cummins

There are a number of excellent examples of "Partners in Development" in Thailand. Initially proposed by the United Nations Development Programme (UNDP) just over three years ago, the Thai Government and UNDP established the Thai-United Nations Collaborative Action Plan, known since the accord was signed on 11 September 1997 simply as "Thai-UNCAP". So successful has this been, in fact, that even in the far reaches of the field where the projects are operating, the Thai beneficiaries (partners, actually) – even without any knowledge of English – can all pronounce Thai-UNCAP and always with that famous Thai smile!...

Thai-UNCAP established people-centred pilot projects in five areas of Thailand, so selected because they represented the poorer regions of the Kingdom and had a broad geographical scope: north, east, south, west and central Thailand, namely: Payao, Mahasarakham, Petchburi, Pattani and Yannawa...

It is amazing that a country like Thailand has been the matrix for such a bold scheme. Up until the Eighth Development Plan, Thailand was, to a certain extent, still emerging as a virtually feudalistic state. 'Development' was imposed from above onto a relatively docile people who rarely, if ever, questioned the 'top down' concept. On the contrary, in fact, often the people waited to be told what to do...

Thai-UNCAP has changed that to such an extent that the Ninth Development Plan, now being prepared, is promoting the alleviation of poverty, economic recovery, sustainable development and good governance as four areas of focus...

The momentum gained from three years of Thai-UNCAP will be continued under the Thai Pattana Foundation, which will continue the funding of the joint secretariat team, formerly supported by UNDP.

Faith in the People

As the "Asian Financial Crisis" began to hit the rural areas (from 1998), this "empowerment" approach began to build more steam. The government adopted the approach as a way of addressing the crisis, not the macro-level issues but rather the micro-level problems, those that touched people who had lost their jobs and were looking for some practical way to make ends meet. The government put hundreds of millions of Bhat into the programme, a "stimulus package" for the poor. The results were positive for many of them, creating as it did some minimal source of income in hard times. Not everyone saw the benefits of course, as the impact of the financial crisis was deep and widespread. Yet the spirit and actions to bring more equal opportunities to a wider spectrum of people was adopted and resoundly valued. That spirit continues, and has contributed to other post-crisis initiatives such as the famous "one tambon, one product" approach of later governments (notably Prime Minister Thaksin Shinawatra, 2001-2006) aimed at enabling each sub-district to specialize and concentrate on making a product identified exclusively with them.

In Thailand my personal growth and understanding took on totally new dimensions. I learned that showing respect and complete faith in peoples' capacities to lead their own lives in combination with minimal encouragement and support from their government and other partners (such as ourselves) had the effect of lighting a fire. It was as though people had discovered a new-found freedom, not political, but of the human spirit.

When I first arrived in Thailand, as I have recounted, I tried to envisage its future. Initially I could only see a future of poor people immersed in an environment of wealth and material consumption of which they could not partake. It was an increasingly class divided society not unlike that I was witnessing in America. It posed in many ways as critical a challenge as the pervasive poverty of India, at least in the sense of suffocating human hope. The vision of THAI-UNCAP made I believe a significant contribution to addressing these problems squarely, opening up an entirely new perspective and approach. It was one of both self-reliance and partnership based on principles of fairness and decency. It was based on an achievable goal of building a good life for the majority of Thais. It was a broad social commitment that empowered and enabled them to do it themselves.

Chapter 15
Kosovo

Struggling Back to Better
1999 – 2000

Kosovo Women Assert New Power and Roles

I was now on the threshold of retirement from the UN. An assignment to Kosovo was entirely unexpected. In the immediate aftermath of a sudden and tragic conflict, the UN was asked to assume responsibility for the governance of Kosovo. Within that broad mandate, I was appointed to coordinate an early "development response" in an environment almost entirely focused on post-war "humanitarian relief". By total coincidence, Suvira accepted an assignment as Chief Technical Adviser and head of UNIFEM in Kosovo, and we headed to this conflict zone together.

Background to Hatred

We had some vague ideas of the special challenge to be faced in working with two ethnic groups with a long history of animosity and conflict. We did not appreciate the full dimensions of that challenge until we began to understand the depth of hatred that had kept them at violent odds over centuries. A quick study of that history before arriving there was important to explaining what we were up against.

Kosovo was a region that shifted back and forth over more than a thousand years between, on the one hand, European Christian rule (initially as part of the Bulgarian Empire from the ninth to thirteenth centuries and later as part of the Serbian Empire from the thirteenth to the fifteenth centuries) and, on the other, the dominance of the Islamic Ottoman Empire. The Ottomans defeated the Serbs (in current day Kosovo) in a famous battle of 1455. They ruled over this territory for most of the following 500 years. During this time, Serbian Christians on the one hand, and mainly Albanian Muslims on the other, alternatively gained local control of the area. Each in turn expelled the other or migrated out under various circumstances usually involving force. Subsequently, during the Balkan Wars (starting in 1912), Kosovo again came under Serbian rule as part of the Serbian kingdom, and in post World War II, Kosovo eventually gained autonomy and self-rule within Marshall Tito's Yugoslavia. The animosities between Serbs and Albanians continued throughout this history, each group gaining and losing the upper hand depending on their political strengths at any one time.

From the late 1980s, Kosovo's status gradually diminished under the Serbian government, including control over education and language. Discrimination against Albanians denied them employment opportunities. Eventually a deep resentment triggered guerrilla separatist fighting by the Kosovo Liberation Army from 1996. A harsh crack down by the Serbian Government initiating its infamous "ethnic cleansing" program resulted in the displacement of over half a million Albanian Kosovars. NATO forces began bombing Serbian forces which led to a full-scale war from March to June 1999. A NATO-backed Kosovo Force (KFOR) then occupied Kosovo and turned over the reins of governance to the United Nations Mission in Kosovo (UNMIK).

Suvira and I arrived in Pristina, the capital of Kosovo, the following month (July 1999). In those initial weeks of our stay, I had flashbacks to Liberia. We were in Europe to be sure, but the aftermath of atrocities, and the continuing tensions and uncertainties were all too similar to those I had experienced in Africa.

Our house perched itself on a small hill outside the center of Pristina with panoramic views of the entire city. Bursts of automatic gunfire and periodic explosions marked each night. Suvira and I stood at our open bedroom window most of those nights. KFOR helicopters plied the night skies shining long intense light beams into every corner of the city. They circled incessantly in all directions. They hovered in one spot whenever they identified live skirmishes between Albanians and Serbs below. In spite of their efforts most nights lit up with the glow of burning houses.

In fact, it was the indiscriminate burning of houses (even in broad daylight) that gave us our earliest first-hand understanding of the intensity of the ethnic hatred. On our second day in Pristina, we entered a house we were considering to rent. On exiting some fifteen minutes later, we found the house next door burning. It belonged to a Serb. A small crowd gathered quickly to watch. No one lifted a finger to put out the flames. No one informed the police. If they eventually turned up, they did nothing. Such reprisals and senseless violent acts defined those early weeks.

Mafia Tactics

Our driver was neither Serb nor Albanian. He belonged to an entirely separate ethnic minority called Gorani. In the seventeenth century they converted from Christianity to Islam while retaining many of their Christian traditions and holidays. They were treated with disdain by the Albanians. During our house hunting, our driver invited us to his uncle's small restaurant along one of the side streets of Pristina. We enjoyed his hospitality of kebabs and flat bread. But when our driver met us the next morning, we sensed something was wrong. He informed us his uncle's restaurant had been burnt to the ground. A new mafia had taken control in the city. They threatened anyone starting up a business. Either you sold out to them at ridiculously low prices, or your property was burned. There was no choice in between. He drove us by the place. His uncle had nothing left and would have to return to his village. There was little if anything to look forward to there. The devastation in those rural areas was far greater than initially thought. Much of the housing was destroyed in many regions. In certain pockets the destruction was total.

UN Governance

I had my introduction to this wide spread destruction when I visited the still inaccessible communities by helicopter in the company of Bernard Kouchner, the UN Special Representative to Kosovo. We witnessed for the first time the immense trauma left behind by months of killing, kidnapping of kin, and raping of women.

Bernard Kouchner was one of the original founders of Medicins Sans Frontiers (MSF). Later, following his assignment in Kosovo, he served as the French minister of health and then minister of foreign affairs. I first met Bernard in Liberia. He courageously accompanied Liberian refugees who had sought safety in Ghana to return to their homeland by boat. A very dilapidated merchant ship brought them across those open waters crammed with traumatized and ailing refugees. I met the ship and Bernard at the port in Monrovia and expressed my readiness to assist. Though we had no opportunity to work directly together at that time, I remained highly respectful of his commitment to similar work in the ten years that followed.

Now we found ourselves the first to witness the full devastation of post-war Kosovo. In each location our helicopter landed, extremely distressed people came out to meet us. Completely bewildered by our arrival, they had not had contact, let alone assistance, from anyone up to that point. Some were attending to their own wounds inflicted in the cross fighting. They shared vivid stories of family members lost or dead. Many tearfully conveyed a sense of complete isolation and abandonment. Food was their most urgent need and housing a main preoccupation in anticipation of the approaching winter. I wondered quietly to myself at the time how realistic was my assignment to initiate early "development" in the face of such devastation.

By sheer necessity, the UN had to place the highest priority on maintaining security and providing humanitarian assistance to the population. And those efforts were an extraordinary example of the much unheralded but critical support of the UN to populations in crisis across many countries. In this case, the UN Administration had in effect become the government of the province. And UN personnel worked tirelessly to deliver what people needed most urgently, food and temporary shelter. While there was continuous criticism of inefficiencies, in the end the most urgent needs were met. Even the beginnings of a governing system were set in place including local elections. Significant accomplishments under the circumstances. Again, I struggled to envisage my role.

Empowering Women

In the meantime, we unexpectedly welcomed my daughter Natasha to Kosovo. She had applied and was selected for an assignment as a UN volunteer. She ended up working in the southern city of Prizren, without doubt Kosovo's most beautiful city adorned by a multitude of ancient turreted Mosques that climbed its hills and silhouetted its evening skies.

Emotions ran high in Prizren. While it had escaped much of the fighting, nearby towns suffered some of the worst atrocities of the war. Working out of the UN Regional Administration office, Natasha confronted some of the harsh realities of the war's aftermath. Serbian women complained bitterly of mistreatment, worsening discrimination, and perceived neglect by the UN. Caught in the middle of one such outburst, Natasha narrowly escaped women literally tearing at her hair and averted injury as she ran and found safety in a UN vehicle. It was a brutal awakening for her to the intensity of ethnic passions. It did not deter her from later working with these same women, and she went on afterwards to serve similarly in Somalia.

As head of UNIFEM, Suvira searched more broadly for ways to bring Serbian and Albanian women together across the region. Meeting initially with each group separately to address their immediate need for rehabilitation from so much recent trauma, the dialogue gradually shifted to the practical urgencies of their lives, especially how to support their families. They welcomed opportunities to assume new roles not previously open to women. The concept of women's economic empowerment began to gain credibility. Training them as "tractor drivers" was definitely an unorthodox but impressionable starting point. Women started to take charge of restarting agriculture in the pilot areas of the program that emerged.

Suvira and her team turned to the far more challenging task of how women could become politically empowered. It was a matter not only of preparing women for roles in the new government. The biggest challenge was in getting Albanian and Serbian women to come together to discuss and train for these roles. Suvira spent many hours, often late into the night, convincing them of their unique historic opportunity. Despite considerable distrust and ill feelings, the women gradually agreed. That had never been done before in their long history. The post crisis urgency seemed to encourage new thinking and new possibilities. The UN administrators began to appoint women to positions in the new civil administration and governing system.

These women (including Suvira) showed great courage in working across previously forbidden lines and in a context of real physical danger. Their efforts were rewarded by their growing confidence and activism to lobby their cause and assume their new roles.

Later, Ibrahim Rugova, who had long fought for Kosovo's independence and became President of Kosovo in 2002, honored Suvira for what she had demonstrated was possible in bringing people across assumed insurmountable barriers for their common good and that of Kosovo.

Home Life Challenges

Meantime, home life for Suvira and me was a constant challenge. The house we rented (actually the upper two floors of a Kosovar family home) had a good European finish and look inside, with wooden floors and comfortable furnishings. Our main problem was water and heat. That was a problem for everyone living in Pristina. The war had knocked out the electrical grid. The repair work (under UN contract) was excruciatingly and inexplicably slow, and a favorite topic of conversation. We had no central heating and the nights were very cold. We ignored this problem by wearing lots of warm clothing and jackets around the house. What was a problem—or at least a major personal discomfort—was every morning taking a shower in icy cold water. We soon got into the technique of compensating for this by routinely heating large pots of water on our kitchen gas stove early every morning. We carried them upstairs in buckets which we mixed with the cold tap water. Unfortunately we still had to contend with the freezing temperature of the bathroom itself. We stood in the tub and poured the warmer water over ourselves. I always saved half the bucket for the very end, luxuriating in one last gush of warmth over my head. I immediately rushed to the bedroom and jumped into my clothes before that warmth wore off.

One early morning (Suvira and I always rose about 4:00 am, having acquired the habit in Nepal where everyone gets up early), I came down the stairs from our bedroom. As I reached the living room I noticed a pile of bananas lying on the floor. I was confused. But as I was more focused on making our first pot of tea, I figured one of us must have dropped them the evening before. As I came back out of the kitchen, I noticed the front door was half opened. That startled me. I looked around and found nothing more out of place. I rushed up to tell Suvira something strange was going on. She was taking her shower. As I called to her I glanced into the extra bedroom which we were using as a small office. To my further shock the computer, printer and all related equipment and discs were gone. I rushed into our bedroom to see if anything else was missing. To my horror both our watches we kept at our bedsides were gone, as was my wallet and Suvira's purse.

We could not believe such a thing could happen without us knowing it. Suvira and I slept lightly and usually woke at the smallest disturbance. It was clear that thieves had entered our bedroom and taken these items resting right next to our heads.

We got dressed and headed immediately to the UN police headquarters in the center of Pristina. They asked us to file a police report and give them a verbal account. By way of what seemed a routine response, we learned that crime had increased exponentially ever since the war ended. Small mafias increasingly crossed the border from neighboring countries. There was an alarming rise in crime, not only robberies, but trafficking in women. The police advised that the criminals may have put us into a deep sleep with chloroform-soaked clothes over our faces. We found this hard to believe. They assured us it was a technique being used. How these criminals entered our house (which had its own entrance that we locked religiously every time we returned home) was another mystery. There was no sign of a break in. The landlord, on hearing what had happened became extremely agitated. He thought he might be accused of plotting the robbery. He called for a thorough police investigation on the premises. But that turned up nothing.

It was an unpleasant experience. It took us quite some time to replace the missing items including my credit cards. It was an entirely unanticipated event that in hindsight we should have understood was increasingly possible. From that point onward, we took extra precautions, including keeping an eye out for strangers who might be scouting the house for further attempts. Fortunately it never happened again.

While we began to feel settled once again in our Pristina home, we felt a trip out of Kosovo would refresh us for the work ahead. With this in mind, we planned to meet up with Kavita then studying at LSE in London, and to go for a brief Christmas holiday in Egypt together. Traveling by UN transport across the Kosovo border into Macedonia, we planned to catch a flight to London at the Skoje airport. To our surprise, though we arrived early, the small airport was packed with a mob of people trying to depart for the holidays to distant families across Europe. We could hardly make our way to the check-in counter through thick nauseating smoke as some 5000 or more passengers incessantly relit their cigarettes trying to ease their nerves. To everyone's frustration, all flights were not only irregular and changing, but many were cancelled. After some two or three hours trying unsuccessfully to find a new flight, we determined we would never leave Skopje by air.

Upon exiting the airport, we learned that taxis were taking people, at premium prices to Greece, where reliable flights were reputedly available to various points in Europe. Though not knowing for sure the reliability of the taxis to get us to the international airport at Thessaloniki, or the availability of flights once we were there, we decided to take our chances facing as we did the alternative of cancelling our trip. It was already becoming dark as we entered the taxi and the driver sped off into the approaching night. We traveled in silence to the Greek border not entirely comfortable with a driver completely unknown to us who spoke no English. Suvira and I whispered to each other to reassure ourselves that all would be fine. When we reached what was a rather isolated border crossing, the driver pulled up to the guard house and showed his papers. There then began an animated and increasingly heated exchange between the driver and the guard which went on several minutes. Finally the driver appeared to relent and agree to the guard's demand. What happened then was something we never anticipated. The driver took out from his inner coat pocket a large size hand gun and turned it over to the guard.

We eventually completed our trip across northern Greece and arrived in Thessaloniki at 2:00 am, at which time the driver, who unknown to us was following local taxis practices in carrying a loaded weapon, showed every kindness in helping us locate a decent hotel. Boarding the flight the next afternoon, we concluded that our determination not to give up on reaching Kavita and eventually an inspiring visit to Luxor was the right decision.

Cutting a Path

By the time we returned to Pristina, some six months into our stay, my own work was well underway. It was a much bigger challenge than I had counted on. In 1999, the UN system, even at the global level, was barely beginning to recognize the critical importance of "early recovery". Few guidelines, procedures, tools or separate financial resources essential to such efforts had been contemplated or provided. But UN leaders had already seen this shortcoming in other crises and were determined this time to do something about it. They knew that a failure to initiate a restart of development in the crisis stage had often caused enormous frustration and delays in peoples' overriding desire to return to a normal life. Too often post crises reverted to further crises. There was determination that Kosovo would not be another failed opportunity to sustain peace. The commitment was to fill this gap by initiating early development work in the immediate aftermath of war. Not only was this critical for practical reasons of longer term prosperity, but equally to raise the morale and determination of the people to overcome their crisis.

Leadership of both the UN Secretariat and the UNDP together decided it would take a dedicated effort to bring about this shift. They assigned the task to the UN Development Group (UNDG) which was responsible for joint UN system approaches, particularly among the main UN funding agencies (UNDP, UNFPA, UNICEF, WFP and WHO). I was appointed as UN Special Delegate to lead the effort for UNDG, and was initially assigned to Brussels to work with the European Commission and the World Bank to develop a coordinated approach. It soon was clear that doing so from such a distance was unworkable. So it was not a surprise that I very soon found myself on a UN plane that took both Suvira and me from Rome to Pristina.

I was determined to keep the work as simple and practical as possible. There was some skepticism among UN agencies about this supposed need to jump headlong into development. They were preoccupied with the urgent needs of food and shelter, whether people would fall victims to disease, whether they would be able to replace the tens of thousands of livestock lost, and how they would be able to plant crops after the winter. These priorities, along with restarting schools and health services, gave the emergency work its overriding importance. I felt that whatever we did to get longer term development initiated, it had to be easily understood and considered achievable within current realities if I were to gain the confidence and support of the UN agencies.

In close consultation with UN colleagues in both New York and Pristina, I developed guidelines for the work under the rubric of a "human development strategy". The strategy adopted an "integrated approach" familiar to the UN agencies and certainly to me. It looked at both the social needs of the people (long-term health care and education) as well as potential economic opportunities (emphasis on micro and small enterprise). An empowerment of local government and people to manage these activities, from "the bottom up", underpinned the strategy.

The key was in assisting the UN agencies to find their own role in the strategy amidst the pressures of the emergency. In the process, the Agencies began to identify "development" activities they had already initiated within their emergency work (e.g. developing school curriculum and restarting primary education; reopening of health clinics; providing inputs and equipment to farmers). This began to build a broader consensus and a certain shared "ownership" for an "early development" agenda.

In parallel, it was equally (if not more) important to find support for the human development approach among the Kosovars themselves. As it turned out, the Kosovars were the first to recognize the need and significance of an early focus on development. Kosovar people were weary of the war and its aftermath and all the incessant political maneuvering. They wanted to get back to a routine, hopefully "building back better" the life they had known.

I found many allies for a "development focus" among these Kosovars. Since there was no Kosovo government, I interacted and worked mainly with non-governmental Kosovars. The leadership came largely from the academic community. Having suffered ten years of what they considered an "apartheid" regime dominated by the Serbs, all were committed to a more democratic and prosperous Kosovo. In fact, they had survived those years by falling back on their own resources and their own wits. They created their own "development" system, including parallel systems of education and health. I soon concluded, based on their deeper understanding of their past, that it would be this same spirit of self-reliance and determination that would define the new Kosovo.

It was a vision of democratization and decentralization and a renewed sense of values based on decency in helping one another. It was an exciting prospect, worthy of their every effort. But the question was how it was going to be accomplished. The province had not even emerged from its humanitarian crisis. Even its very political future was still in doubt.

We came to the conclusion that the only way was to demonstrate what could be done in a few local areas. This would provide a foundation on which to build the approach more broadly for the future. For this purpose, and as my year assignment was winding to a close, I invited an outside UN Team to work with local "municipalities" to take charge of detailed planning and to develop their own course of action from organizing skill training to arranging market outlets for new products. Tying early recovery and development to these still reemerging local institutions (municipalities) meant it would take time to mature. But after so many years of suppression, helping to lay the local foundations of a new democracy seemed a critically important step.

Bridging the Divide

In Kosovo, in spite of the terrible experiences it endured, ultimately people were willing to move beyond (though never forgetting) the past. What they wanted was a chance to start over within a just environment. I came away more convinced than ever that instilling a sense of fairness and decency at the core of a new governing system was the most effective way of overcoming a dark past and initiating a development path out of crisis.

Chapter 16

Bangladesh

Indigenous Dignity
2002 – 2007

*Rich Tribal
Cultures*

*Medical Care
for the First
Time*

*UN service boats
reach the Interior
Villages*

Roots of Atrocity

'It's much worse than we thought. 400 homes burnt to the ground. Three tribals killed. Nine women raped.' I listened to those words from my office in Dhaka, Bangladesh, transmitted from our field team in Rangamati, the regional center of the Chittagong Hill Tracts (CHT). UNDP had set up its operations there to help restore peace and promote development after nearly twenty-five years of civil war. The world knew nothing of that long conflict. This "incident" was just another in a long line of atrocities. But it was the first major outbreak of violence since the signing of a peace accord in 1997 between the government of Bangladesh and the indigenous peoples' political movement known as the PCJSS (Parbatya Chattagram Jana Sanghati Samati, or United People's Party of the Chittagong Hill Tracts).

Again more reports came in from our team. With each one, my spirits fell. My confidence in what I thought we had achieved so far began to wane: 'Tribal leaders tell us the army helped the Bengali settlers attack and commit these crimes. Already hundreds of locals have fled into the bush. Men, women and children, without food or shelter. It's now nearly a week. They're suffering badly. The government is doing nothing. It seems they're not even going to investigate what happened.'

I had worked in the CHT already one year when the attacks occurred. I was shocked. Given the long history of tension and ethnic hatred, I should have expected it. I did not.

Seizing Opportunity

Accompanying Suvira on a new assignment, I arrived in Bangladesh in April 2002. Hired by the International Labour Organization (ILO) of the UN, Suvira was going to take up another technical advisor role, this time to put together a project to train women in rural villages with skills to start small businesses or other livelihoods. We managed to settle quickly into our life in Dhaka. Pleased with our new modest but pleasant apartment in the Baridhara residential area, we enjoyed overlooking well kept homes surrounded by swaying palms under a perpetually hot sun. Actually we lived in Dhaka some months the previous year (2001). That time Suvira had taken up a short term consultancy with UNDP to evaluate a project supporting socially disadvantaged women (specifically, sex workers). UNDP thought she had done a great job and suggested she apply for the longer term ILO position. So here we were returning to Dhaka in 2002.

I did not go to Bangladesh to work. At least not for the UN. I wanted to volunteer my time or join a local non-governmental organization working with the poor. I spent some time in the hospice facility of the Sisters of Charity, established by Mother Teresa. To be sure it was a moving experience for me. Witnessing the caring of the dying and the serene compassion of the nuns, I shall just never forget it. At the same time, I met several other NGOs, and took up a part time assignment with CARE to help develop a new grass roots strategy to their work.

Over one particular weekend, I relaxed on our newly acquired bamboo furniture with soft white cushions. I usually treated myself every Friday morning (weekends were observed on Friday and Saturday in Bangladesh) to a big slice of blue cheese purchased regularly from the Government "bonded warehouse". Savoring that cheese while reading my weekly *Economist* proved particularly relaxing.

That precise Friday, the phone rang and the UNDP Resident Representative (for whom I had done an assignment the previous year), asked if we could meet. He wanted to share an idea. Naturally I was curious. We met that afternoon. From that point onward, Jorgen Lissner and I became close colleagues, professional soul mates so to speak, and good friends. Jorgen was special. Not just another international bureaucrat carrying out UN development mandates (though he held those skills superbly as well), Jorgen worked from a sense of deep commitment. From his gut. With an unusual readiness to take risks. He valued the opportunity in his work to represent and shape the UN role in Bangladesh. He knew it would make a difference only if he found a special way in which to do it. He had a sense for "seizing opportunities." He began telling me about the Chittagong Hill Tracts and its unique and turbulent history.

I soon found myself unexpectedly and deeply involved in figuring out how we might help to stabilize and develop the region and alleviate the chronic poverty of its people. I began to study that history of the CHT and the violence of its past which continued into the present. It was the beginning of my struggle to comprehend a perplexing dichotomy: just how did an ethnic minority become so cut off and alienated by an otherwise exceptionally decent Bengali people?

Reviewing the History

I learned my history of the CHT mainly from its people, especially those who became my colleagues. Let me share with you some of that history. It is important.

I learned that the CHT existed for hundreds of years. It was the homeland of so-called tribal peoples (more appropriately referred to as *Paharis*—meaning hill people—or *Jummas*—meaning those who practice shifting agriculture) most of whom were Buddhists. I soon discovered that their history and cultural lineage was not well recorded. But I was told they migrated originally from South East Asia. Probably mostly from Myanmar (Burma) and possibly even Vietnam. There were many ethnic groups among them. The *Chakmas* were always the largest. They and the *Marmas* and the *Mongs* each had their own kings. Smaller groups such as the *Tripura, Chak, Mru, Lushai, Khumi*, and others—twelve in total—were mostly poorer and politically weaker (though never less proud of who they were). History had protected these people of the Hill Tracts. Considered an autonomous indigenous— "excluded"—area in the wider context of India, even under the *Mughals* (direct descendants of Genghis Khan whose Muslim dynasty ruled India most of the sixteenth through the eighteenth centuries), and under the subsequent British rule (to which the region was annexed in 1860), it meant that the indigenous people were the only ones who could legally reside there.

Troubles began when the British divided India at its independence and created the Islamic state of Pakistan. Despite the fact that at that time (1947) the CHT population was 98% non-Muslim, the British decided (against the will and protests of many leaders in both India and the CHT) that the CHT must be part of the new Pakistan. The area soon lost its special autonomous status.

As I came to know the tribal population and colleagues better, I learned of later injustices from their perspective. Of particular note was a decision in 1958 by the then Pakistani head of state, Muhammad Ayub Khan. He authorized the building of a dam completed in 1962 (with USAID funding) in the heart of the CHT's most fertile valley. Almost overnight the resulting Kaptai Lake submerged 40% of all arable lands and displaced some 100,000 people, more than half of whom fled to Tripura State in India. To add insult to suffering, the royal residence of the Chakma King forever vanished under the rising waters.

270

What happened next was a turn of events which I had personally witnessed previously to some extent. Back in 1971, as I have already recounted, I had just arrived in New Delhi to start my assignment as UNDP Assistant Resident Representative in India. A couple of months later, Sheila and I, while shopping one weekend in the Connaught Circus market area in the heart of the city, suddenly saw a stream of jets blazing low across the city's sky. They were Pakistani jets, soon chased by two Indian migs. The war for Bangladesh (formerly East Pakistan) independence from West Pakistan was underway. We never expected to see Pakistani jets over Delhi. It was both unprecedented and frightening. We quickly scrambled to shelter under the broad arcades of the market.

For several nights, an imposed curfew across all of New Delhi restricted our movements. All residents dutifully turned off house lights and drew curtains throughout the city. That included ours in the Panshila Park colony. It was our first exposure to an arena of actual war. During the ensuing battles inside East Pakistan, West Pakistani troops raped and killed thousands of innocent Bengali women. India entered the conflict on the side of the oppressed Bengali people. They fought side by side valiantly. The outcome is history. Bangladesh was born.

My education about the newly found country now resumed as I began to reside there those thirty years later. Unfortunately for the CHT, the new proud country of Bangladesh outright rejected their demand for autonomy. It was soon after that that the CHT leaders created the PCJSS movement, headed by Manobendra Narayan Larma. They set up an armed wing known as the "Shanti Bahini" (Peace Warriors). Their aim—to protect their cultural identity and secure the autonomy they sought. Skirmishes, attacks and counter-attacks soon spread between the Shanti Bahini and the Bangladesh armed forces.

What I came to understand then was that in the early 1980s, the government of Bangladesh made an even more fateful decision that led directly to a quarter century of civil war. Authorized by Sheik Mujibur Rahman, "Father of the Country", the government applied a "settler policy" in the CHT. This was a disastrous step that created immense animosity and hardship between the tribal people, the government, and the settlers.

The Bengali leaders just did not trust the tribal people as they assumed they still intended to break away. The settler policy eventually brought nearly half a million Bengali (non-tribal) settlers into the CHT (mostly poor farmers and slum dwellers trucked there by the government and promised land and support if they came). I soon realized this was what humiliated and antagonized the indigenous people most. It led rapidly to a dramatic demographic shift that diminished the dominant indigenous presence in the region within a few years to less than half the total inhabitants.

Fighting intensified. Abuses grew worse. War ensued.

To understand the impact on the local people, I knew I had to absorb the details of this history. My colleagues recounted that history as if they had been there. It was readily admitted that atrocities occurred on both sides. Yet overall they insisted that history had clearly come down most harshly in condemning the armed forces and the Bengali settlers. They told me the first of many reported massacres occurred in 1980 at the Kaukhali Bazaar of Kalampati. Hundreds of *Jumma* people, responding to a call by the army to gather and deliberate over the reconstruction of a Buddhist temple that had been burnt to the ground, suddenly found themselves encircled. They were shot and killed. The retelling of these and a dozen more massacres targeting villagers and students during the 1980s and 1990s, made clear that in most of these incidents the security forces and Bengali settlers collaborated in the killings. Beyond these, there were other attacks that went largely unrecorded. By indigenous accounts, the most disturbing part was the disproportionate ferocity of these joint army-settler reprisals and the blatant deception and slaughter of hundreds and possibly thousands of their people.

Following this more than two-decade long travesty of events (and soon after the signing of the peace accord in 1997), the tribal leaders had an internal falling out that threatened their unity and prospects for realizing justice. Calling themselves the "United Peoples Democratic Front" (UPDF), a tribal splinter group broke away from the PCJSS. They believed the CHT had been "sold out" by their leaders and that Paharis would never retrieve their lands or realize any justice. This soon created a distinct impression that the tribal leadership was unstable and weakened. The rough tactics that the UPDF adopted further exacerbated this impression.

These tactics included "toll taking" (hijacking) of vehicles plying the roads of the CHT to earn income. More serious were the occasional kidnappings for ransom. When I first started working in the CHT the main storyline I heard from the international donors was about an incident two years earlier (2000) when two Danish and one British enginers were abducted while traveling along a road they were assisting to rebuild. Donors immediately panicked. Donor aid to the CHT, already minimal, suddenly shut off. Even in 2002, the ambassadors who had experienced the event (and had unsuccessfully tried to mediate a release of the abducted) described it to me in highly emotional terms. They apparently felt responsible as the kidnapping dragged out over a month and the captives were made to trek through the hot jungles from one makeshift camp to another to avoid army search parties. In the end, the three foreigners were freed. UPDF denied involvement. The army claimed credit for the "rescue". The confused public generally believed a ransom had been paid from the donor side.

So it was in this state of uncertainty and general lack of confidence, even a year into my work, that I was informed, as Director of UNDP's Chittagong Hill Tracts Development Facility (CHTDF), of the attack on the nine villages in Mahalchari. Though consistent with history, the attack was unexpected and disturbing coming as it did after nearly six years of relative calm following the signing of the peace accord under which the Shanti Bahini relinquished their arms (possibly half a million). I was deeply concerned to understand why such blatant widespread violence had suddenly re-erupted.

Core Values

As I have already shared, I was especially unsettled by the attack because of the overall positive impression I had by that time acquired about the exceptional qualities of the Bengali people.

Anyone fortunate enough to live in Bangladesh as I was doing knows that it shatters all the negative myths and stereotypes often held about it. It is a marvelous country. And it is mostly due to its people, their way of life and their values.

The London School of Economics carried out a global survey in 2000 (to be found on the internet) to understand what constituted "happiness" around the globe, and to determine who were the happiest people in the world. To most everyone's amazement, Bangladesh ranked number one! That result compared to the United States ranking of 46th. The study showed that money and wealth were not the keys to happiness. Positive human relations were. Growing purchasing power of countries did not lead automatically to happier or better quality lives for their citizens. Bangladeshis were happier largely because of the value their culture placed on close personal human relationships. Compared to many rich countries, Bangladeshis suffered much less from the emotional poverty caused by the drive and competition to consume. Their happiness stemmed largely from their strong family life and circle of friends.

I had seen some of these same values practiced in other countries. India for example ranked 5th in the survey. I also always noted and appreciated, as I have shared with you, the kindness and resilient happiness (certainly humor) of the poor all over the world in spite of their poverty and hardships. But Bangladesh did feel special to me, and I experienced their values in very personal ways especially among those with whom I began to work.

On the team we eventually put together, the Bengali colleagues came to mean a great deal to me. One was my assistant, Clifford Rodrigues, known to everyone as Keith. I had an early special affinity for Keith. What I quickly valued and appreciated about Keith was his sincerity and loyalty in helping me through each day. He was genuinely concerned about what I was doing and who I was. He was always very courteous, but more than that, he conveyed warmth that told me he cared. He never wavered in his kindness and generous heart. Another colleague I cherished was Dr. Niaz Ahmed Khan. Niaz played a difficult role as a senior but minority member of what was otherwise mostly an indigenous professional team. Niaz came into my office several times each day. He always showed me a lot of respect based I thought on his own dignity and appreciation of others he felt were special to his values. That meant a lot more to me as time went on and I came to see how he lived those values himself in so many innumerable ways of kindness, humor and caring. And then there was Malik who took care of our financial accounts. He worked quietly and diligently, but always displayed a sense of concern and caring for all his colleagues whether Bengali or tribal. So in my own way I was soon seeing how Bangladeshis placed exceptional importance on how they interacted with and treated others whom they came to know. Not that Bangladeshis made a religion of these values. I suspect many did not even realize how strongly they held and practiced them. All the more reason those values were so impressive to me. They defined a way of life. I could not say that Bangladesh was a perfect model of a "caring society" (whether such a model yet exists is of course open to debate). But within each of their circles of family, friends, and colleagues, the values and practices of caring were steadfastly honored.

But I simply could not square all of this with what I was seeing in the CHT. The overall prejudicial attitudes and behavior of the Bengali people toward the indigenous people, along with severe government policies that clearly worked against the interests and status of those people, continued to confound me.

The Indigenous Team

What I did realize early in my work, whatever may have been the challenges of inter-ethnic strife, was that the key to improving the life of the indigenous people would be in enabling them to do it themselves. And to do this, I knew it was critical that we bring on board a team of indigenous professionals to lead the effort.

The first was Prasenjit Chakma. Prasenjit was young, well educated (MBA from Michigan State) and development experienced, having worked for the World Food Programme in the Hill Tracts for some years. Beyond his professionalism and friendly manner, he had a deep first-hand knowledge Hill Tracts history and politics. It was Prasenjit, and later his colleagues, who educated me about the hill people and their many hardships. He made sure I knew about the long struggle their leaders had endured to gain autonomy. He made me privy to so many insights of both suffering and courage few foreigners would ever know or be able to appreciate.

Before the search continued for other indigenous professionals, I was particularly fortunate to bring on to the team a young Finnish woman, Heli Uusikyla. Heli did her PhD research in Bangladesh on women's issues and had also worked for the WFP in the CHT. Heli was very Nordic, completely open and honest. That was refreshing. Heli and I came to understand while never speaking about it, that we shared an abhorrence of oppression anywhere by anybody. With her natural Scandinavian sense of what was right and decent, she forever bolstered my instinct to promote the basic rights and opportunities of the people of the Hill Tracts even when I was not sure how we would do it.

Heli, Prasenjit and I vigorously set about finding other tribal professionals to join our team. But hiring a major contingent of young *Jumma* professionals was no small feat. We did it against a pervasive image about the CHT people as "backward" and "incapable" of managing their own affairs (despite their proven adroitness in successfully fighting the national Army for nearly a quarter century!). Many Bengali settlers and Bangladeshis outside the region held firm to these prejudices and openly ridiculed our efforts to bring tribal people on board to run our program.

Heli, Prasenjit and I ignored these stereotypes and plunged ahead with our recruitments. We gave a lot of importance to finding those who had worked at the grassroots across the Hill Tracts. There were many eager to join. They had worked for small local NGOs, were paid very little, but had gained invaluable skills in how to organize and support communities. They were extremely proud and highly motivated to be part of the United Nations. Besides the core who worked out of our main Rangamati Field Office, we assigned many more to our two 'District Offices' (Khagrachari and Bandarban Districts). The majority however went out to the villages as UN volunteer "Community Facilitators". They were joined in increasing numbers by the local NGO workers we contracted.

Back in Dhaka, in the UNDP country office, we knew we needed to build up our team there as well. We did just that. We called them the "Gang of Four". Prasenjit was the original member. His affability, smartness, management skills and energy commanded enormous respect and influence with the others. Biplab Chakma was the youngest. Singularly determined and committed to turning our program into a village reality, we eventually appointed Biplab as manager of our village project financing window (the "QIF" that I will describe in detail below). He knew every village and villager receiving the funds. Over the long run he ensured the integrity and accountability of our delicate operation which was critical to building confidence and trust in what we were doing. The oldest member of the "Gang" was Professor Predanendu Chakma. An academic, he was also well known and trusted by the tribal leaders. His seniority and rapport regularly helped us to reopen channels of communication with that leadership each time we needed to repair some misunderstanding.

And then there was Nishan Chakma. Nishan personified in every way possible our deepest passions for the work. Especially the cause of justice that he (and we) felt it enabled us to fight for. Nishan grew up in the CHT as an orphan. He knew and felt the suffering of the *Jumma* people in a special way. He was completely committed to equality of opportunity for those who had never known it. He was strikingly proud of the indigenous culture. He led our efforts to raise the profile and respect for that culture. It motivated every aspect of our work. Nishan more than anyone crafted the step by step systematic approach to our work of "community empowerment" that I will describe below. He had an inner fire in all that he did.

Initially, the "Gang of Four" did their work out of one room in our Dhaka Office. The atmosphere was chaotic. Phones, laptops, heated discussions, all carried on and buzzed incessantly at the same time. In the midst of all this, a lot of ideas got thrown back and forth—like fish to the highest bidder. Hence they named their intimate workplace "The Fish Market". The "Gang of Four" traveled extensively in the Hill Tracts. They negotiated over many months our role and position in the CHT. They built the trust and earned the acceptance we gained among the political leadership.

Sheer Enjoyment!

The CHT team we assembled and the work they did over the five years I was privileged to be among them became a model of people-empowered development. But before sharing that story with you, I want to first share what the CHT meant to me on a personal level.

The CHT is a place of exquisite beauty in its physical setting and its people. It was an unending emotional fulfillment for me every time I entered it. There was so much to take away into my future.

I was introduced to the Hill Tracts by Prasenjit. We made an initial visit soon after we began our work together. Flying from Dhaka to Chittagong, we jumped into our UN Land Cruiser for the three hour journey up into the hills. I was to make that same trip innumerable times over the next five years. Never did it cease to take my breath away. Still in the lowlands, we traversed carpets of rich green humid rice fields before ascending into cooler forests and a final summiting of the pass that rewarded us a magnificent full view of the long valley and pristine lake of the CHT.

Prasenjit invited me to his home on a solitary point overlooking the lake. We ate tiny curried shrimps fresh from those waters under the night stars. He introduced me to the rice wine of the Hill Tracts, as strong and smooth as any Russian Vodka. He brought me to what became our favorite retreat in the Hill Tracts. Located on its own small island in Kaptai Lake, Peda Ting Ting (meaning "belly full") restaurant and bungalows was like a micro paradise in the Pacific Islands. With its large bamboo and thatched roof and construction extending magically out over the water, it served a marvelous tribal dish called bamboo chicken made with spices grown only in the Hill Tracts.

Later I frequently joined colleagues as we journeyed in our speed boats to distant villages. Each time was a completely different experience. Following the rains, the lake filled to the brim. On calm sunny days, we glided over mirrored waters. I usually dipped and dragged my hand in the water just to feel and marvel at its coolness. Just to remind me of the realness of what I was witnessing. I watched the passing boats, more like double-decker ferries, overloaded with logs and varieties of produce, especially huge mountains of green bananas. It all seemed more than enough to sink these boats and passengers. Of course it never did, as skilled pilots steered these giant crafts confidently over many years to provide villagers from the far and wide reaches of the lake with their main mode of transport out of their isolation to the markets so vital to their survival. I also always noted with special interest the ethnic mix of the passengers, a rich blend of both indigenous and Bengali people. This reflected a common pattern in some areas around the lake where villages were either ethnically mixed or established one next to the other. It certainly reflected the everyday tolerance and positive spirit of diverse people living side by side in the mutual tasks of providing for their families rather than concentrating on their differences.

Further up the lake, at the far northern end, the shore line swelled with dense forests of reeds in bloom. Their top white tassels blew gently in the wind. An unending array of birdlife inhabited those reeds and surrounding waters.

But there was nothing more exhilarating for me than villagers welcoming us into their home communities. This happened often, usually when we were introducing outsiders (government or donors) to the program. Our boats crisscrossed the back waters, sometimes for miles. Eventually we pulled ashore below a village. Inevitably, the village turned out in force to greet us. From the shore to the village square, young children lined the steep pathway dressed in their colorful attire, handing out bouquets of flowers as we ascended. We sat on the ground shaded by trees and delighted by a generous array of fruits and fresh coconut drinks. Village youth inevitably swirled colorfully into an open area to perform traditional dances accompanied by musicians bearing their homemade instruments. Such lilting and haunting melodies and rhythmic and humorous choreography I had never before seen. Gazing out beyond the dancers to the distant lake and a setting sun, I frequently wondered whether such exquisite artistry would ever go beyond my privileged eyes to further enrich the country in which it took place. Beyond the professional enrichment of my years in the Hill Tracts, what I will cherish most is having lived in a world and among a people so refined and uplifting to my spirits.

Community Empowerment

Returning to our work at hand during these years, what drove all of us was an early shared conviction that whatever else we might do, our first priority must be to build our program from the people up. We knew instinctively that if we were to have any credibility with those villagers, and eventually with their leaders, government, and even donors, communities must be at the heart of our program, running it and benefiting from it directly.

We called it "Community Empowerment". A powerful formula, it focused on early visible results for people realized through their own efforts. We wanted them to be in charge. We wanted them to demonstrate that they could achieve whatever they set out to do. It reflected our working philosophy and unwavering belief in the enormous potential of poor people in the Hill Tracts to develop themselves.

In this way, our team enabled the poor to demonstrate their own innate capacities. Their initial task as they saw it was simple: reach the villagers, build trust with their leaders, and facilitate the communities to act in ways that would benefit themselves directly.

It was the step-by-step process starting with a self-identification of their problems. In each village they sat under a tree with large sheaths of brown paper and mapped out what they had, compared to what they wanted and needed. They were encouraged to begin with what they were already good at. They determined from their local knowledge what might work best to earn income or improve social conditions (especially their health and education). Each village decided what should be their number one priority. How they would make it happen their way. It was their decision. They alone would be responsible for the results.

Our team knew, however, that enabling poor people to identify and work together on their priorities would not necessarily guarantee those results. Coming as they did from among these people they knew all too well their resource limitations. The hard truth was the CHT villagers were extremely poor. What they needed most—labor and material and financing—were simply not available beyond their own capacities for hard work. They knew that money was particularly lacking, at least not enough to enable people to kick start their local economies. However, they also recognized the danger in providing "hand outs" (cash to get things done) as it could easily create a welfare mentality and dependence. Yet they recognized the hard reality, that people cut off for so long from the economic mainstream, living as much on a barter system as on market forces, faced great difficulties, maybe impossibilities, to overcome the desperate odds against them.

Together we came up with an answer. We called it the "Quick Impact Fund".

It was by no means a new idea. Such funds have been used by the UN in emergency settings when people lost everything and needed start up funding to get their lives back on track. In the modern day parlance, it was a "stimulus" package. We thought the situation in the CHT required it. We were convinced it needed to be applied on a substantial scale to have significant impact.

Nishan drafted the Community Empowerment Guidelines that set out twenty-four steps everyone on the front lines of our program would uniformly follow. It included early steps to identify and select the villagers' priority projects, and the process of funding, implementing and monitoring them. Each village would receive up to the equivalent of $6,000. That was a lot of money in the Hill Tracts, but based on past experience, it proved to be an optimal sum to undertake meaningful projects. The difference this time was that no one was going to tell the villagers how to use it. They would decide that themselves.

Soon a wide array of small projects sprang up all across the Hill Tracts. These ranged from cattle raising, to fish farming, to setting up a small school with a volunteer teacher, to purchasing battery-operated solar panels for night lighting in the village—and many more. We began in a few villages. Word of the program spread—rapidly! Others wanted to join. Soon we had hundreds of villages in the program. Each did what they thought best with their money. By the time I left the project in 2007, there were over 2,000 villages participating, and by 2012 there were closer to 4,000.

Building Trust

While all of this positive work (as we saw it) was going on, every day tested us from falling off our political tight rope. We realized quickly that nothing significant could be accomplished if it was not based on *trust*. We knew it had to be earned. Earned on all sides. That would not be easy.

Our first challenge was to gain the confidence and trust of the government. Even though as the UN we had a trusting relationship with the government on most all matters of development, the CHT was a special situation as the government had been a party to the conflict. They were understandably concerned about our intentions, given their still delicate relationship with the CHT leaders. Despite our efforts to assure them of our utmost neutrality and our development focus, they remained concerned about whether we would maintain a fair balance in providing opportunities to both indigenous and

Bengali people in the Hill Tracts. As time went on, they expressed particular concern with our "affirmative action" approach to hiring mainly indigenous professionals.

Eventually serious demonstrations by Bengali settlers erupted over these issues. This included animated road side protests. They were ever alert to find out when we planned to bring donors, particularly ambassadors, into the CHT. Many times our convoy of UN vehicles entered district towns to encounter long lines of Bengali settlers holding placards and banners. They accused us of excluding them from our program. We were not immediately sure how to respond but felt ourselves on the defensive.

What struck (and touched) us most was the poverty of the settlers. Men, women and children, all shabbily dressed. Their faces betrayed a life of unrelenting hardship. Clearly their protests had some validity. Settlers had been cheated. Not by the tribals, not by the UN, but by the government policies that brought them there. They ended up among the most ill treated victims of these policies. The land promised to them on arrival never materialized for most. Deprived of farming, they had to adapt to new ways of livelihood—such as fishing—for which they were unaccustomed and untrained. Many had to work as day laborers to survive. Worst, most of them ended up in "settler camps" set up by the government for their protection near Army posts. Becoming entirely dependent on government food hand outs, they stagnated there year after year. They had no prospects for a decent life. Betrayed and belittled, they had no one to turn to.

We knew from the beginning of our program this was going to be a serious problem. There was clearly a need to help these settlers. Yet this flew in the face of the political position of the tribal leaders: the settlers must leave the Hill Tracts! This created enormous frustration on the part of the tribal leaders. It was in this context that we were caught—between the settler's humanitarian and development needs and the fiercely determined political position of the indigenous leadership.

As a result, Jorgen and I spent a lot of time traveling from one end of the CHT to the other. We hoped to convince the Bengali leaders of our plans and we urged them to let us begin with the urgent needs of the *Jumma* people, and gradually open more opportunities for inclusion of Bengalis as the atmosphere for cooperation improved. It was a hard sell. Our sincerity managed to calm things down, though barely. We had earned more time, but that time was fast running out.

Setback

Unexpectedly our biggest shock came at the hands of the tribal leaders. We had spent an extraordinary amount of time explaining our approach, seeking their advice, and adjusting our project design to reflect their views. A matter of gaining their *trust*, we gave it our highest priority.

But not everything was what it seemed.

The most respected and honored of the indigenous leaders was Jyotirindra Bodhipriyo Larma, known as Shantu Larma. He was the brother and successor of the original founder of the PCJSS, Manobendra Narayan Larma. Shantu Larma remains for me one of the most impressive and endearing political leaders I have ever known or observed. It was he who led the insurgency in the bush over more than two decades. It was he who held up the morale and confidence of his forces and those of the village people against overwhelming odds. It was Shantu Larma who continued to display unwavering courage, condemning at every opportunity the government of Bangladesh for its failure to honor the peace accord.

A slightly built man, almost frail in appearance, it all belied his inner steel. He always reminded me physically of Ho Chi Ming, without the beard, though I never dared to make the comparison. He was mild mannered and polite. At the same time, and often without notice, he could be brutally frank. He held his beliefs and convictions unrelentingly. Above all, he was totally committed to the preservation of the indigenous culture against the "rising tide of an islamisation of the CHT" as he called it, and the rights of the people to live with dignity and respect. We were immensely proud to call Shantu Larma our friend. We saw him as the bright light shining in a new direction out of the darkness of a slowly emerging CHT.

We were about to inaugurate our new field office in Rangamati. Without hesitation we knew and decided that Shantu Larma had to be our guest of honor. We felt excited of what we had accomplished in a relative short time (about one year). We wanted to invite a big gathering to join in our celebration. The invitations went out to over 500. They included the local village headmen, our NGO partners, the army, Bengali leaders, Government officials from Dhaka, and the major donor ambassadors. It was our "coming out" event and we wanted to do it right.

Little did we realize how premature and naïve our ambitions were.

Shantu Larma came early, before the crowds gathered on our office compound. In contrast to the festive atmosphere we had created under colorful tents, Shantu Larma appeared unusually quiet and contemplative. We sat down in the entrance hall of our offices waiting for the ceremonies to begin. Shantu Larma invited me to sit next to him on the rattan sofa. Surrounded by large photos on all the walls that I and others had taken of *Jumma* life in the CHT, the atmosphere reflected a respect and pride for the CHT people we were all trying to serve. Quite unexpectedly Shantu Larma leaned over and took my hand. He shared with me in a soft tone, not to take personally what he was about to say. I had no idea what he meant. I knew it could not be good. Stunned and speechless, I tried not to show it. Absent of any way to share my anxiety with Jorgen, we soon all rose and headed out to the stage beneath the bright banners commemorating the occasion. The turnout was more than we dared anticipate. The Deputy Minister of the CHT Affairs, Moni Swapan Dewan, offered his welcoming remarks, followed by similar greetings from the District Chairman and myself.

Shantu Larma then rose and took the podium for the keynote address. The exact wording of his spontaneous remarks was not recorded. But the tone and message remained with us for a very long time. He straight away launched into a sharp criticism of UNDP's initiative. He made it clear that we could not understand all that the CHT people had endured. He blamed the government and its army for the inhumane and continuing poverty. He spoke of their arrogance in not honoring the peace accord. He insisted the UNDP program would ultimately not work in the interest of the indigenous people. Instead it would bend toward pleasing the government and the settlers. It would contribute to a permanence of a terrible legacy of conflict, suffering, resentment and a profound humiliation.

The guests fell totally silent. Anxiety filled all our faces. Shantu Larma trusted us. He was our friend. He spent many hours meeting and confiding in us. And we in him. He knew intimately of our work in the villages. Villages that had never been reached, let alone supported with development activity. Why were we suddenly the enemy? More than offended, we were deeply wounded.

Clearly a watershed moment for us, and certainly for me. In that forty-five minute speech, we came to recognize what we had failed to see in our ambitions to make an early mark for ourselves. So much began to flash through our minds then and later. Human relations are profoundly complex. People hold their experiences, their traumas, and their feelings in their hearts. In many ways it defines them. But this was not always fully evident or understood, especially the deep emotions attached to these feelings. To understand this required a careful building of trust to bring out what was crucially important to each other. But that in turn required a common understanding of what that trust must be based on. For Shantu Larma, that trust had to be based on mutual respect and commitment as he defined it and as he judged it. It was the same kind of trust he demanded from the government of Bangladesh. A respect for the cultural preservation and the rights of the people of the CHT. A deep commitment to the achievement of these. Shantu Larma seemed to be telling us we had not yet earned this kind of trust.

Above all, Shantu Larma wanted to be sure the people of the CHT could trust us not to betray these goals. He questioned whether we really understood what that meant and what it would take. It was one thing to understand the history of the CHT, even that told to us by the Hill people themselves. It was quite another to actually live through that trauma. It was an experience that had burned itself indelibly into the peoples' souls. It demanded a liberation that went far beyond development. Yes, Shantu Larma and the people were grateful we had come to work alongside them to achieve a better life. But that would inevitably be a long journey and a difficult struggle if it were ever to succeed. And it would never succeed unless it was based on a certainty of trust that in the process the identity and the rights of the people would never be compromised or negotiated away. Above all, that trust had to be demonstrated through actions rather than words (not least through an honoring of the peace accord). Were we aware of that? Were we aware that we had to prove our loyalty to these fundamental goals? Did we understand it was a test we had not yet passed, at least not in Shantu Larma's eyes? And did we have what it would take to help build that kind of trust between the government and the CHT people? Did we know that it would take a lot more time than the one year we were celebrating?

Reflecting on what I understood were these reasons Shantu Larma had for castigating us as he did, I felt there may be much broader lessons for me. In whatever role I might hope to assume in facilitating people to come together to build a decent life for all, it was an immense and profound responsibility. It would require me, or anyone who aspired to such a role, to fathom far more than the superficial technicalities of development work. It required me, under whatever circumstances, to practice enormous empathy, humility, and patience to be sure there was a true understanding and honoring of what was critically important to gain trust before moving on in search of solutions.

Cooperation Withdrawn

Following the speech, Shantu Larma called for a boycott of our work. Jorgen and I hurried over to his office the next morning. We wanted to know why the sudden change of heart. What went wrong? He greeted us calmly and self-assured about what he had said. He was not impressed by a defense of our good intentions. Within days, word went out to all the local NGO partners key to our work in the villages. Cooperation must stop. Our operations ground to a halt. Clearly distrust, real or perceived, had exacted a high price. To rebuild and deepen that trust, we would have to do a lot of things differently.

At the same time, we wondered whether there might be other factors at play. We had to be realistic. It would not be unreasonable to imagine that the political leaders of the CHT also saw an opportunity to further build their image as defenders of their people's interests and rights. Whatever their convictions, we realized we needed to remain carefully tuned to how they sought to gain their political profile.

We concluded that while we had to become more sensitive to their worldview and expectations, we also had to preserve our UN principles and continue to adhere to a neutral and balanced approach in the CHT, a balance we had already seen would not be easy to achieve. Gradually we began to regain some of our position, due mostly to the personal good relations our team rebuilt with the CHT leadership over this period. Full trust would take longer. What an acceptable "balanced" approach would look like was still unclear. But at least we were back in the villages.

Spanning the Villages

We had a vision. It was a broad vision of opportunity for youth and for others, particularly focused on the poor. We worked to make that vision not ours but one that all people would embrace. We began to shape and formulate with partners and people of the CHT, including the villagers and the youth, a broad multi-purpose program for development. The core remained the bottom up "community empowerment and QIF" approach for supporting small village projects. Beyond that, however, we knew there was a lot more that could and needed to be done.

Not everything could be solved by working in villages. There were certain cross-cutting big needs that went beyond village capacities to meet. These included non-existent health services in remote areas. High infant and maternal mortality. Life expectancy considerably below the national average. Education unavailable or of poor quality. Schools closed or badly run because teachers did not want to go to interior locations. Education methods based on rote memory with little interest or scope to stimulate children's minds. Youth dropping out in high numbers, unable to find jobs. An overall malaise with little hope for a better life.

We began to address these broader needs that cut across all villages:

We established three *mobile health teams* which each made a circuit visit of selected villages once a week. These teams each consisted of a doctor (both indigenous and Bengali), a nurse, a lab technician, a health educator, and assistants. It was the beginning of basic services to remote villages that had never known health care before. Only pregnant women with birthing complications were previously taken to district hospitals. Many did not survive. Now more than 5,000 patients regularly attended our weekly mobile clinics.

I monitored those sites (we called them "nodes") on the designated service days. I was amazed. Often 500 or more villagers and their children waited from dawn. They came in from very remote areas. They wore traditional dress of their tribal group. Many wore brightly colored thickly wrapped head dresses. I vividly recall one woman's brilliant pink turban that created an incredibly striking contrast with her otherwise entirely black attire, matched only by the dignified way in which she bore herself and watched over her children.

Systematically screened and checked, each patient's health status and problems were identified. Parent's gratitude spread across their faces as doctors or nurses administered first-ever injections and dispensed malaria pills. They seemed both awed and unsure whether these services would really continue. They did.

To save a lot more lives we trained village women as basic health workers to return and provide services in their villages. Imagine these illiterate, poor women deftly acquiring and practicing medical skills that did save those lives. These new found capacities, especially to test and treat malaria (the biggest killer in the CHT) amazed everyone including the health workers themselves. They and the mobile teams were a veritable revolution in health care in the CHT. Some 2 years after I left the CHT, the mobile program alone served some 250,000 patients. An extraordinary accomplishment by dedicated local professionals and competent villagers.

We also turned to addressing the absence or low *quality of education*. Our newly recruited teammate, Abhilash Tripura, took the lead in organizing a joint UN and government technical mission to formulate a project for 'community-managed schools". Knowing his people as he did, Abhilash based the approach on a belief in the capability of villagers (not outside administrators) to guide what kind and quality of education best suited their remote areas. That would include a training of teachers to teach in local tribal languages, and development of a new curriculum much more relevant to their rural lives. Construction of new community schools spread throughout the Hill Tracts. Abhilash was particularly well suited to designing these initiatives, given his own educational achievements (a master's degree in economics from Australia) mixed with an acute understanding of the educational needs of minority tribes from among whom he belonged.

Economic opportunities became another cross-cutting program, this time facilitated by Prasenjit. The focus was on youth. The aim was clear and simple— to enable them to make money. It was a "market-driven" approach, identifying products that were sure to sell in local markets. Training youth in the needed skills and services. On several occasions I joined the team to meet and lobby the mainly Bengali business community in the port city of Chittagong. These were well to do and pragmatic entrepreneurs who welcomed the prospects of contracting out agricultural production and services to the CHT people so long as it turned a profit. They also saw the potential of employing more indigenous workers in their industrial parks in Chittagong port where tribal workers already had a reputation as hard working and reliable laborers. In these ways, the program laid the foundation for bridging the divide between the hill people and the urban business community to the benefit of everyone.

The *role of local government* became another focus. The question was how were we going to sustain all of the initiatives we were setting in motion? We knew our project must eventually fade away and someone local would have to take over the responsibilities. That had to be local government. In the CHT, these were called Hill District Councils, one for each of the three districts. Every time we visited one of these districts, we sat down for hours with the district council chairman and his or her team to go over progress and problems of each program. They chaired what were often heated meetings of the project's district development committees to decide on constantly changing priorities and operational details. We committed ourselves to eventually handing over responsibility for these programs to them including the QIF. It was a push for decentralization of authority and resources, something the central government had shown little enthusiasm for not only in the Hills but all across Bangladesh. We began to train the district councils staff in management, technical skills and outreach to communities. It was an ambitious goal and we understood nothing could be done overnight. But we were convinced that sustaining opportunities for the poor could best be realized through a partnership of people and their local government. We were convinced it was a model of reform for the entire country.

From Under the Veil

Let me divert for a few moments to share with you another model of empowerment that was taking place on the other side of Bangladesh. It was Suvira's work within the Government Ministry of Manpower and Labour aimed at enabling poor Bangladeshi village women to engage in economic activities outside their homes. It was as equally challenging an undertaking as to what we were attempting in the CHT, and while the lessons were different they were equally rich.

Suvira's biggest initial challenge was sitting in the middle of a bureaucratic ministry with the purpose of bringing change. Even the physical setting was a reality check. The ministry buildings were old and run down. The elevators often out of order. Suvira immediately struck a warm and reciprocated rapport with all of the general support staff of the ministry, from drivers to clerks to cleaners. Dressed in her colorful *churidar* and with a broad smile and an energetic step, she soon became a welcomed breath of fresh air as she bounced up the ministry stairs each morning to her modest fifth floor office. Tea bearers prided themselves in bringing her morning tea. Women sweepers, taken aback by her open greetings and inquiries of their families, rewarded her with special attention.

Building relations with the officialdom of the ministry was quite a different challenge. Governments everywhere have heavy bureaucracies. The problem is not so much the red tape they create. Much more challenging is overcoming the disincentives in place that discourage innovation and risk taking. Most people working in government want to get something done. They tend to come not from the elites of society but from the middle and even working tiers who know the life and difficulties of the average citizen. They usually have a good deal of empathy for them. The problem is that they fear to do anything for those people unless they are certain it is blessed by those above them. There is a constant apprehension that one false move and they'll be thrown out of their jobs.

Suvira worked in the middle of such an environment. Her task was to assist the government to develop and manage a project that was potentially revolutionary to the lives of poor women. It had the possibility of opening up new opportunities for employment. That would not be easy for a number of reasons, especially cultural reasons.

Suvira's work was first and foremost a cultural challenge. The rural women of Bangladesh were 95% Muslims. They worked hard in the rice fields to ensure enough food for the family. But their economic life periodically switched to busy domestic chores. When agricultural activity was slow, they stayed in the home attending to those family needs. The social norms and attitudes of the men discouraged women to pursue economic activities in the public space (contrary to the indigenous women of the Hill Tracts who were the main traders in the markets).

Suvira had to face that difficult reality. Within these traditional attitudes and ways of life, how could you possibly hope to get women working and earning outside the home? It was not simply a matter of coming up with practical income earning activities for women, though that would be difficult enough. It was much more a matter of how to deal with these cultural norms, stereotypes, mind sets, and practices that seemed to say that change was impossible.

The technical approach that Suvira applied was called "Community-Based Training (CBT) for Economic Empowerment." The basic idea was to bring training (for women) to the community, rather than asking them to come to the training. So the first challenge was in getting the government vocational training institutes reoriented to training outside their centers. It was a matter of how to get the government trainers going out to these communities when they never thought that was possible or culturally acceptable. It was also a matter of determining what goods or services women should be trained for in which there was a sure market. And it was a matter of consulting the village women (and their husbands!) about these ideas to see whether there was any scope to begin something. In short, it required a gradual but steady process of building trust and a willingness to innovate outside cultural norms. Would the government and the villagers be willing to do this?

The village women showed surprising enthusiasm. They wanted to do these things. They knew the benefits. They knew that more income would help their children get a better education, better health care, and eventually better incomes as adults. The men were less enthusiastic. But some of them seemed willing to give it a try if it would really lead to more income. The trainers in the vocational training institutions, who were closer to the people, were also open and supportive. The main resistance came from the central ministry where officials were much more cautious and reticent about getting a strong cultural reaction especially from the men.

Suvira came home every night over several months to spill out her frustrations with me. The government officials were not opposing the initiative but active support was slow in coming. The enthusiasm of the vocational centers had to be constantly reinforced with further visits so work could begin in a few pilot areas.

Suvira and the team contracted an NGO to conduct market surveys in those areas, to identify viable products that would likely sell. Women were trained in specific products and services for which there was a market, training lasting on average three months for each skill area. They also learned simple skills of how to run a small business. They did remarkably well. They demonstrated capacities that no one (least of all themselves) ever expected.

Soon these women were setting up shops and small enterprises. Their businesses started to thrive. Communities and the male leaders were stunned. Husbands on the other hand were happy, even proud as the money came in. The range of businesses was equally remarkable. They were way outside the scope of what anyone dared to foresee.

One group of women was trained in rickshaw repairs. Rickshaws almost define Bangladesh. They are everywhere. They clog the streets of Dhaka and its 15 million population. They saturate the byways of all provincial towns and villages. They create congestion. They also provide the only form of transport most middleclass and poorer Bangladeshis can afford. They are in constant demand. Any breakdown can put a rickshaw driver out of work for several days. It's a loss of income he cannot afford. Getting a broken rickshaw repaired is always a matter of great urgency. But to have a rickshaw repaired by a woman was unheard of. In Bangladesh, only men were mechanics. So the whole notion of training women to become mechanics was literally preposterous. Nevertheless, in spite of the skepticism and warnings of the men officials, the training was done.

The outstanding performance of the women in mastering mechanical skills was the first shock. Then, once trained, the women quickly took their skills to the market place. They collected enough funds among themselves and from each of their families to rent a store front in the public market place. The project provided them a basic set of tools and equipment (essential support, just as the Quick Impact Fund was crucial to undertaking small projects in the CHT). The women soon had a steady and growing stream of customers. These customers were rickshaw drivers or the rickshaw owners of these three-wheel vehicles. The women soon earned a strong reputation. They improved their turnaround time, getting the bikes back on the street quickly and taking in more. They earned a respectable income. No one ever thought that was possible.

Other women trained in other skills. All was based on market surveys that pinpointed likely good returns on investment. These included production of metal boxes for bus travel, simple machines to sort harvest grains, electrical repairs, vaccination of chickens and other small animals. The opportunities seemed limitless.

It was an incredible demonstration of the possibilities of cultural change. It was a critically important lesson in the need and feasibility of overcoming seeming cultural barriers to bring people together—in this case women (and indirectly their husbands) and the government, to achieve a common practical benefit.

It was a confirmation of the enormous potential of human beings, women and men, and the supporting institutions, to coalesce around common commitments to achieve remarkable things. It was an affirmation that poor women have enormous latent capacities, talent and power to change their lives. It was a clear demonstration of their readiness to do so. A confirmation that such opportunity once offered is most always seized by the poor and turned into benefits for themselves and their families. It was proof that governments, both central and local, can and will commit to policies and programs based on simple values of decency and equal opportunity for the poor. It was a model of unlimited possibilities for the poor founded on both a moral and a practical approach.

Paths to Commitment

Back in the CHT, our challenge turned increasingly to how to gain the financial support it would take to spread our work on a much larger scale. We soon recognized that the most effective way to achieve this was by bringing potential investors to ground level, to see what we were actually doing and achieving.

Probably the most memorable occasion was when we brought more than a dozen ambassadors to see our work in a remote part of the CHT. Our plan was to show them the humanitarian operations we had organized in response to the Mahalchari attacks. We also wanted them to see our community empowerment activities and to understand the difficult challenges of balancing our overall development efforts between tribals and settlers.

Every ambassador was in an excited mood as we glided across the Kaptai Lake in the largest vessel from our new fleet of UN speed boats and cruisers. Eventually we reached the mouth of the Mahalchari River. According to our plan, it would take three hours to transport the ambassadors and their box lunches up that river to our relief sites. All had gone according to plan. That is until we reached the mouth of the river. There we encountered an unexpected drop in the water level. The level of the Kaptai Lake depended on the volume of rains that fell in the winter months, and the amount of water released through its dam every spring. We knew that the water was dropping in this season, but we had scouted carefully days before the visit to make certain we could still navigate those waters.

Nandit Roy was in charge of this operation. I liked to refer to Nandit as "Central Command". He was one of our most senior staff with special (almost military) expertise in managing all of our logistics. He had unusual diplomatic skills as well based on a terrific sense of humor (from which I benefited throughout my time in the CHT as he ribbed and kept me sane and humble with his sharp wit and perspective on whatever we were doing). I knew I could always count on Nandit to think through and organize things to a tee. He had done so this time. But what we had not counted on was the sudden shallowness of the river itself. That was never a problem before.

Still the ambassadors transferred themselves cheerfully on our instructions to smaller boats for the trip up the river. Everyone remained in an upbeat and adventurous mood. And everything went smoothly for the first mile or so. Then word came over our walkie-talkies that the lead boat had hit a sand bar. Soon the other nine boats, accompanied by army patrol craft, also ground to a halt in the same area. The only way to get over the bar was to empty the boats. So we sent each ambassador to the bank of the river to wait further instruction.

High spirits prevailed as they began to trek along the bank. What a grand sight. Twelve ambassadors in single file braving the midday heat and cracking jokes about reporting their movements back to their capitals the next day— assuming they survived the next few hours! Eventually our boats caught up to them. Everyone reembarked. We again cruised upstream. Again we hit a new set of sand bars, again the Ambassadors disembarked, this time was a little less sense of humor. Nothing was made better by the fact that the packed sandwiches had all gone sour in the sun and everyone was famished.

This time, the army commander accompanying us ordered one of his lieutenants to do whatever it took to keep us moving. The lieutenant immediately jumped overboard with full uniform and arms and proceeded to personally pull us by a long rope over the bar. Quite a remarkable demonstration of unquestioning loyalty to orders I thought.

By the time we reached the Mahalchari villages rather exhausted some six hours into our journey, the ambassadors quickly reenergized to focus on the desperate conditions of the nine villages burnt to the ground. They needed little convincing that the area was remote and urgently in need of assistance. That evening's discussions gave us a chance to share the difficulties we faced in supplying food and shelter to the tribal victims while addressing the needs of nearby settlers who claimed to have been victims themselves.

It was another example of building trust, this time with the international community. We continued to learn there was no substitute for taking the personal time and effort to build that trust. By showing them our own commitment to the work, sharing frankly our problems, and hearing their reactions, we established a relationship that became a partnership of support for the CHT. A partnership based on a common social commitment. A commitment that in this case eventually resulted, for both relief and development, in $160 million of support.

Reflecting back on this and similar visits, and to our increasing partnership with the CHT leaders and with the government, I grew ever more convinced of how critical it was to build such broad partnerships. Partnerships forged not in theory or aspiration, but partnerships built around real achievements on the ground that inspired confidence to join and support what looked doable. I saw a clear new reality: the readiness of the poor to come together and work for their common good made most feasible and sustainable when backed up by a strong coalition to support their efforts. A coalition that would not change the CHT overnight, but one that would raise the spirits, resources and determination of poor villagers to restore their lives and build their future in their own way. For me it was confirmation of the power of a compact between rich and poor.

Co-Opting Tradition

There was a whole other dimension to our work in the CHT. It was the royal traditions of the CHT. They provided us with another way to reach and work with the poor. And for me it was an extraordinary experience.

As far back as the twelfth century, the Chakma kings had battled with the Arakan peoples in regions of current day Myanmar. As a result of these conflicts, the Chakma kings migrated to and established their rule in the Chittagong belt. From there they entered into treaties with the Mughal nawabs of India in the eighteenth century, preserving their autonomy. Under the British administration, similar autonomy was maintained under royal Circles of the Chakma, the Bomang and the Marma kings. These royal systems had a common structure and hierarchy involving *headmen (*area wide leaders*)* and *karbaris* (village leaders). In the case of the Chakmas, homage was paid to their King through an annual ceremony of symbolic taxation in which each headman and karbari made a small offering to confirm their loyalty.

Our work in the Hill Tracts depended to a considerable extent on winning the trust and support of this "traditional system". The key was in building trust with each of these *rajas*, a title conferred by the British in honor of this royal tradition.

Our greatest good fortune was in working with the Chakma raja, Devasish Roy. Well educated and progressive, he was a lawyer trained in the law at the Royal Courts of London. He inherited the throne from his father who had hoped CHT would join Pakistan (as it did) during partition, and who opted to immigrate to Pakistan when Bangladesh won its independence. Unlike many of the kings before him, Raja Devasish actively engaged in defending the rights of his people, not only the Chakmas, but all people of the CHT. He took on these issues with frequent success in the Bangladesh courts, whether on disputes over land rights or human rights abuses or other transgressions. He traveled regularly throughout the Hill Tracts, often on foot to the remotest villages, to lend his personal moral support and to promote small development activity. Raja Devasish was a natural ally to our efforts. He was a key to our broader partnership and the potential of social change. We valued his advice and support at every turn.

In 2003 Raja Devasish invited us to attend a traditional, long neglected ceremony—the Investiture of the raja's son as heir to the throne. I will never forget this ceremony. All headmen and karbaris from across the hills walked over steep terrain for many days to arrive at his residence and pledge their loyalty. Dressed in long traditional garments, they filed in slow procession to the twin thrones where the raja and his son, dressed in rich silken garments and royal gold headwear, sat waiting. The young boys of the extended royal family sat in quiet observation resplendent in brocaded vests and pantaloons. Suvira, Jorgen and I sat in rapture at this scene from a magical and distant past, honored to be a part of a living history in the CHT.

Of course, these royal traditions also represented deep feudal practices. The headmen and karbaris were not elected. They were historically appointed by their kings. Their loyalty was to the king. And they were also useful to the interests of whatever the prevailing governing power, be it British or a current government. They had two main official duties: to overview law and order, and to administer land titles and disputes. They were well respected by the villagers and carried considerable influence in community affairs. For the most part they appeared to take the interests of the people seriously. The problem was that they had no mandate beyond their limited administrative roles. Whatever interest some of them may have taken in improving the lot of the people, it was severely constrained by the fact that they had very little if any resources to do their jobs. And equally important, they were neither educated nor trained for such responsibilities.

In the second year of our program, we convened a meeting of headmen and karbaris in the Bandarban District. Over 400 attended. What an extraordinary event, culturally and developmentally. They came in their traditional and elegant dress including tall tightly wrapped turbans. And their king, the raja of the Bomong Circle, Aung Shwe Prue Chowdhury, honored them and us as the guest of honor at the opening and closing ceremonies

Knowing Aung Shwe Prue Chowdhury was to step back into nearly a century of CHT history. He was ninety-five years old. We visited him every time we came to Bandarban. He was remarkably full of life and humor. He had seen so much over those years. On one occasion, he shared with us events (in the early 1900s) surrounding the death of a British high administrator who paid a visit to his father the then Bomong king. The British administrator had a passion for hunting tigers and the king obliged by arranging elephants to carry the hunting party into the jungle. By some unexpected misfortune, the visitor fell from the elephant which immediately crushed him to death in front of the raja. The drama was in hearing the raja tell the tale like it occurred yesterday. I felt myself truly witness to a part of history that had otherwise slipped into oblivion.

Our convention of headmen and karbaris focused on the practical opportunities for local village development. Our purpose was to have them exchange their own thinking on new ways of working, to recognize for themselves the potentials of a new era. An era in which they hopefully could have much more positive impact on the lives of their people. To take on roles not only as administrative leaders but more as "facilitators of development". Their surprisingly enthusiastic response inspired us to plan for systematic training of local leaders in modern development and facilitation techniques throughout the Hill Tracts.

The *Bomong* raja joined us again at the closing ceremony. He honored us with a keynote speech. He encouraged the traditional leaders to think and practice differently, along the lines we had shared. We were elated by his support. Following these closing remarks, he turned to thank me. In so doing, and to my utter surprise, he announced to the headmen and karbaris that they should be especially honored by my presence. He then let them know that I was the director of the *United Nations of America*! Stupefied, I sat silent, entirely immobile in fact. I didn't know quite whether or how to react. So I never did. I just tried (with considerable difficulty) to imagine how such an introduction would be received and appreciated in the distant chamber of the UN General Assembly!

The importance of our partnership with the Chakma and Bomong raja's could not be underestimated. It was a lesson in the significance of engaging respectfully with local leadership as crucial to gaining the trust of local people. It was equally crucial to embedding social commitments into the cultural fabric and values of the people.

Engaging the Army

Another challenge of our work was in building relations with the army.

Partnering up with the army initially seemed incongruous and even risky. Over time it proved to be very wise. The army dominated the CHT for decades, certainly during their counter-insurgency operations, but also following the signing of the peace accord. Their interest was to discourage or if needed to suppress any further insurgency. It was also to continue their protection of the Bengali settlers though that was never officially affirmed. They patrolled the Hill Tracts from an astonishing 500 camps, an exceedingly sore sticking point with the CHT leaders. These troops were supposed to have withdrawn to just six major camps under the accord agreements. They never did.

At a certain point in our efforts to expand our program, we began to receive reports from our sub-office staff that army personnel were visiting them seeking details and data about our activities. Particularly interested to know how our funds were distributed and used, we also learned they were concerned that some of these funds were being diverted to the purchase of arms for insurgent or general harassment purposes. The tribal leadership got word of this and was outraged, as was the CHT public when these concerns leaked into the local press.

Generally we felt the army was not completely at ease with our presence in the Hill Tracts. They remained unclear about our intentions. They shared the Government's concern that we may show bias toward the tribals at the exclusion of the settlers. Jorgen and I grew increasingly concerned about this obvious lack of trust. We decided we had to address it more directly.

Seeking out any kind of consultation possible with the highest level, namely the chief of staff of the Bangladesh Army, we were surprised when an early meeting was suddenly arranged. We were equally impressed by the warm cordiality and hospitality we received. The talks were frank and sincere. Their declared intentions to build harmony and peace across ethnic lines impressed us despite the background of conflict we knew from the indigenous side. We did our best to assure them that our resources could never possibly be diverted to unintended or violent purposes, given the tight management and monitoring of the QIF. As these consultations continued over many months, the generals always remained cordial. And in keeping with our intended "balanced" approach, we always made sure that the tribal leaders knew of these meetings, though we did not divulge the details.

Working carefully and delicately between historical antagonists was one of the greatest challenges of our mission in the CHT. It enabled and rewarded me with a far better understanding of the importance of earning a reputation for neutrality and fairness in bringing former enemies together to find common ground. Over time, the tribal leaders seemed to appreciate these initiatives, especially signs that the military was interested in closer contacts. These did not fully materialize during my time in the CHT, but I hoped that an important foundation had been laid.

Conflicting Values

This interaction with the Army brought back to my mind the questions and concerns I had raised when I first started my work in the CHT. How could the people and government of Bangladesh, including the army, have treated the people of the CHT in the harsh manner and ways those people conveyed over and over to us. As I have shared, it was in my mind out of character with the overall good will of the Bengali people and their historic values. I continuously searched for answers.

I searched for those answers in Bengal history. That history was largely one of struggle for political and cultural autonomy, not unlike that of the CHT in which I was working. Even after Islam entered Bengal in the twelfth century and the people eventually fell under Islamic Mughal rule from India (Delhi), Bengal sultans persisted and won considerable autonomy that enabled Bengali culture, identity and literature to thrive. Subsequent periods of Mughal and foreign rule saw a loss of autonomy, but the spirit and determination of Bengali cultural freedom persisted. Bengali culture continued to flourish. When Britain partitioned India, East Bengal became part of Pakistan. But as we have seen the people of East Bengal never easily accepted that union. Their rebellion stemmed largely from a deep seated resentment and resistance to efforts by West Pakistan to impose their culture and Urdu language. A "language movement" by the then East Pakistan, and innumerable other tensions, eventually led to a liberation movement and then war. The nation of Bangladesh emerged proudly from this war of independence led by its own "freedom fighters" (*Muktibahini*) and timely support from India in December 1971, that I have previously described.

But the relevance and irony of this history is that it did not result in a new spirit of respect and harmony for minority cultures such as the CHT, within the newly found state. In spite of the similarity of aspirations of the CHT for the same respect and recognition of cultural heritage and identity that the Bengali people had fought so hard to achieve for themselves, the Bangladesh government quickly denied the same to the Hill Tracts people.

Not long after independence, the country's first prime minister, Sheikh Mujibur Rahman, visited the Hill Tracts in 1973 and declared that from that time onward there were to be no tribal groupings in Bangladesh—'everyone is a Bengali!" You can imagine the impact of this declaration on the CHT people and leaders. It could be seen no other way than as a blatant threat to their long standing desire for cultural, religious and language freedom.

To its credit, and as I have indicated above, the Awami League government (1996-2001) of Sheikh Hasina reached agreement with the indigenous political leaders and signed the peace accord in 1997. But while this accord provided some administrative autonomy (establishing a Regional Council and three Hill District Councils in the CHT), it fell considerably short in protecting the cultural identity of the people. And many provisions of the Accord, including the return of lands and support to refugees who came back to the CHT from India, were never honored by Sheikh Hasina or later by Khaleda Zia.

Further political turmoil toward the end of my stay in Bangladesh (in 2006 and 2007) paralyzed the country until elections in 2009. Unfortunately in the meantime, the cultural and developmental priorities of the Hill Tracts remained frozen in time.

The affects of this unrelenting national political stalemate and the continuous suppression of CHT aspirations were profound. The CHT fell off the national political radar. No concessions or compromises were offered that would be instrumental to implementing the peace accord. The frustration of a continued "betrayal" of the agreement, including a growing resistance to it by the Bengali leaders in the CHT, embittered the indigenous politicians, particularly Shantu Larma. The people languished in overall poverty despite the progress we were making in some of the villages.

Understanding the Contradictions

So again, I asked myself why this unrelenting lack of good will for the people of the CHT? I did so not with the intent or purpose of condemning the Bengali people who I had already established in my own mind as otherwise basically, possibly exceptionally, caring and generous.

I began to conclude that Bangladesh was no different than other countries, including my own. All societies, I concluded, share conflicting values and principles by which they live. In the case of America, acceptance of slavery and the subsequent profound discrimination of the Jim Crow laws that relegated black people to a continuing despicable status took nearly 200 years to overcome, or rather to amend. The civil rights laws that emerged, clarified and inhibited future injustices, but they did not necessarily change the attitudes of many of the American people. And a similar continuing prejudice against Native Americans is a story I have already shared. Should I expect any more rapid transformation of attitudes by the Bengali people in their views of the CHT?

There were other examples of extreme prejudice against indigenous peoples that came to my mind. As part of our program in the CHT, we organized study tours to other countries that experienced civil strife and efforts to bring peace and development. In July 2006, I accompanied a mixed group of those working with our project, Bangladesh political leaders, parliamentarians, civil servants and CHT leaders and NGOs, to visit two countries: Guatemala and Canada. What we learned was that Guatemala had undergone thirty-six years of civil war (1960-1996). A war that had its roots 500 years earlier when the Spanish conquerors subjugated the indigenous Mayan people, took away all their lands, and committed them to forced labor. The small ruling elite of Spanish descendents continued over centuries to oppress these people who made up 85% of the population. Efforts by the indigenous people to gain their rights were ruthlessly suppressed during the ensuing civil war, when many had to flee into the mountains and remained there for some eleven years, constantly hunted down (even shot and killed by roaming helicopters) until more than an estimated 200,000 were dead.

In Canada, we met with the leaders of First Nation tribes who recounted the past and current injustices, including the forced separation and removal of their children to distant schools meant to socialize them into white society, where they were often abused. The First Nation leaders continued to protest the refusal of the Canadian government to honor past treaties and rights to their lands.

In spite of these horrendous stories of injustice and abuse, neither Guatemala nor Canada has resolved many of the core issues that their poor ethnic minorities have endured. In fact, as in the case of Guatemala, these minorities continue to be subject to overt often violent discrimination including rampant rape and killing of indigenous women. The problem in both cases and in many similar cases around the globe was, as I saw it, one of basic attitudes and values that place priority on protecting the privileges of elites against the glaring rights and needs of the less privileged.

These stories raised deep and dark doubts in my mind as to whether decency is possible when poor, ethnically different people are at the mercy of ruling elites. When such elites, and the governments and political frameworks they control, set aside values of human decency in their relations with minorities, they seem to eliminate the only possibilities for a serious effort to eradicate discrimination and poverty.

In the CHT, what I began to understand was that binding people together across historical ethnic and religious chasms of suspicion, distrust, hatred, oppression and violence is exceptionally difficult. It was and remained so in Kosovo, in America, in Guatemala, and so many other countries. It was no less difficult between Bengalis and the people of the CHT.

Society's Soul

To have any chance of truly overcoming such divides, something must exist beyond incremental efforts. Political will and commitment is critically important as are legislative initiatives. But political will and legislative measures alone cannot sustain change unless they are rooted in basic values that demand the change. What is more fundamental is that a society honors the values at their core equally among all people within that society. It is a matter of people remaining true to the core decency at the soul of whom they are. It is their responsibility to put decency into practice whenever and wherever needed, especially in the face of discrimination and poverty.

The story of the Chittagong Hill Tracts is the story of similar innumerable struggles around the globe to honor and to practice decency. It requires conviction, courage and commitment to those values. It all comes down to treating people as you would want them to treat you.

Chapter 17
South Sudan

Brief Encounter — Potential Lessons
2008

Poor and isolated

Courtesy of Naoko Anzai

302

Suvira and I returned to the US from Bangladesh in May 2007. At this point I had lived abroad since 1960 a total of thirty-two years, and had been employed and/or associated with the UN for more than forty years. Suvira had a similarly extensive experience of living internationally. We felt it was time to enjoy the natural beauties and outdoor life of Oregon. We settled into our home in Lake Oswego for the first time. My two daughters, Tanya and Natasha, had both moved in 2006 from Oregon to Arizona to pursue job opportunities (Tanya serving military families through USAA as a certified financial planner; and Natasha coordinating health education programs of the Mayo Clinic in Phoenix).

Our youngest, Kavita, was entering her second year of a second masters program, this time at the Bren School of Environmental Management and Sciences at the University of California Santa Barbara. She was already applying for jobs and we liked the fact that her search included Portland, Oregon. And that is where she settled from 2009 with her new British husband, Alex Head who she knew from her days in London and Bristol. She made us enormously proud as she pursued with passion a career in environmental conservation with American Rivers, then the Climate Trust, and later as sustainability coordinator for the City of Portland. Beyond that, her healthy lack of self-importance along with an inner fire for the ideals of social justice further endeared her to me.

Oregon was for us an exquisite place of pristine forests, rivers and lakes, and we did our best to take full advantage. Otherwise, besides writing this book, our interest was to keep abreast of the development field, and if we were needed, to do what we could to contribute on a short assignment basis. That opportunity arose for me first in South Sudan.

Years of War

In February 2008, the UNDP's Bureau of Crisis Prevention and Recovery (BCPR) requested me to go to the Sudan to develop a "Recovery Strategy" for Southern Sudan.

Sudan had undergone twenty years of civil war between the predominantly Islamic Arabic North and the mostly Christian (mainly Catholic) South. As I continued to write my book, most people, certainly in the US, thought of the Darfur Region of Western Sudan when they heard of the conflict in Sudan. Many knew that some 200,000 people had been killed in that regional conflict.

What the world had not paid as close attention to is the fact that another far more devastating war had previously taken place in Southern Sudan. That war originated in 1955 and continued up to 1972 with a decade long break before restarting for another two decades from 1983 to 2005. What most of the world also did not realize, or has already long forgotten, was that the fatalities (mostly civilian) of the second stage conflict (1983-2005) were ten times those of Darfur. Some 2 million deaths resulted, along with a displacement of some 4 million people from their homes, including probably half a million who sought refuge in neighboring countries, and possibly another 200,000 women and children taken north into slavery.

The roots of these conflicts were many. But from my quick study of the history, it was quite apparent that they were largely due to the same kind of oppression by elites imposing their will over poor people mostly from a different religion. This was practiced literally for thousands of years as the elite powers along the Nile regularly fought the people of the interior. When Sudan came under Anglo-Egyptian rule in 1899, effectively run as a British colony, it was cleverly administered as two separate entities—North and South. Under pressure from the Arab North, Britain eventually agreed in 1946 to unite these entities. The people of the South saw this as a first step, followed by the attainment of Sudan's independence (1956), as a movement to create an Arab domination of the South, including the imposition of Sharia law. It was against this seemingly inevitable progression toward Islamic rule that the leaders in the South fought the first war. The interim peace (1972-1983) was threatened when the then President Gaafar Nimiery initiated an Islamisation campaign including intentions to transform all of Sudan into a Muslim Arab State.

True to its policies in other regions of the world, the US government provided substantial military support to the central Sudan Government, mostly as a measure to counter Soviet influence in the Horn of Africa. The Sudan People's Liberation Army (SPLA) in the South was founded and led in 1983 by John Garang, to fight for independence. In the North, the brief return of a civilian central government under Sadiq al-Madhi ended in 1989 with a coup by Col. Omar Hassan al-Bashir who has remained in power to the time that I completed this book. He again promoted Sharia law across the country.

In March 2008, the International Criminal Court—ICC—issued an arrest warrant for President al-Bashir on charges of war crimes and crimes against humanity stemming from the conflict in Darfur, the first sitting head of state ever indicted by the ICC. Continued resistance to these perceived islamisation efforts as well as the importance of substantial oil reserves in the South, prolonged the fighting until January 2005 when a Comprehensive Peace Agreement was signed granting autonomy to the South for six years until a referendum was eventually held in the South in 2011, resulting in a vote in favor of secession.

Once again, it was another historic example of people suffering under and fighting against the oppression of elites who were bent on imposing their religion and culture and controlling others resources. The same story I had seen in so many other countries in which I had worked before Sudan.

Vision for Hope

My role was to assist in creating some practical platform for "early recovery" and development in the newly autonomous South Sudan still recovering in 2008 from the trauma of war and the continuing exigencies of emergency relief. Specifically, I was to help formulate a Strategic Framework for the newly created Sudan Recovery Fund for Southern Sudan (SRF-SS).

For and by Whom?

I arrived in Juba, the capital of Southern Sudan, in late February 2008. The field of "early recovery" had come a long way since my efforts to help establish a similar approach in Kosovo nine years earlier. Thanks largely to the leadership of UNDP's Bureau for Crisis Prevention and Recovery; the recovery field had become much more focused, systematized, and confident. It managed to make its case globally for urgent attention to recovery and early development work soon after a crisis occurred. What had not been settled however was whether this work would have its own separate source of funding, or whether it should be financed either through the on-going relief operations or alternatively supported as part of long-term development under multi-donor trust funds set up for that purpose. Once again, BCPR was pro-active to make the case for a separate fund as the only way of ensuring committed and predictable resources specifically for recovery. It decided to make Southern Sudan one of the first pilot cases for such a Recovery Fund. That SRF-SS was in fact formulated by my colleague Jorgen Lissner just a month or so earlier. It had already been approved by the Donor Consultative Group. There was one condition to donor support however: that the fund had to be based on a clear and practical "Recovery Strategy".

In preparing for this task to formulate such a strategy, the question that kept coming into my mind was: recovery for, of and by whom? It was an important question I felt since any new source of funding could easily be hijacked by a variety of eager development actors at the expense of those in most need, namely the people who had suffered from the conflict and who lived mainly in the rural villages. As it turned out, both the Government of Southern Sudan (GoSS) and the UN were equally determined to see these funds benefitting these very people. But this commitment did not necessarily answer the crucial question of "by whom" would the recovery be done. In my view that still needed to be made clear.

The Government was keen to bring visible "peace dividends" to the people in the form of basic services (health, education, water, sanitation, etc.). Their main priority was to build up their own capacities under the new Fund to provide such services. I very much agreed with this and made it a central part of the recovery strategy including the strengthening of local (state and county) governments to gradually take over these responsibilities.

Equally important, however, was to enable village communities to play a direct role in shaping and implementing this recovery. It was important for two reasons: to provide the people an opportunity to own the recovery by deciding what it would include; and secondly, to ensure the sustainability of the recovery efforts based on the self interest and commitment of these communities to see results for themselves and to continue pursuing these efforts. It was the now familiar "peoples' empowerment" approach that I and others had been working on over so many years which we felt was critical to post-crisis recovery and longer-term development.

Remote Perspectives

But I saw it as just too naïve to assume that such a bottom-up approach to recovery would be adopted given the enormous pressures to get things done quickly through top-down services.

I wanted to put my concerns to the test with local leaders and people in remote areas. Seated on a UN plane to the northern town of Aweil in the State of Northern Bahr El Ghazal, and as the flight gained altitude, the vastness and emptiness of what I saw below mesmerized me.

Geographically the largest country in Africa, not much smaller than India, and a quarter the size of the entire United States, the Sudan that spread beneath me made a deep impression on my sense of what would be possible. As far as I could see, Southern Sudan consisted primarily of interminable bush and dry savannah. Roads were few and far between. None were paved. Even more difficult to discern were the villages and houses of the people. Looking down, I was hard pressed to make out where were the villages. Made of mud with straw roofing that turned a dull grey as it dried in the hot sun, I eventually spotted the occasional clumps of such houses that constitute the villages of Southern Sudan. The question I kept asking myself as the flight sped forward was how people could survive in such isolation. Even more difficult to imagine was how development could be organized within such a logistical vacuum.

We landed in Aweil. This State capital, though of modest size and infrastructure, was of course more physically endowed than the surrounding rural areas. Besides conferring with our UN colleagues posted in the area, I asked to meet separately with three main groups: state and county officials and department heads; non-governmental groups working in the villages; and the villagers themselves.

Among these groups there was clear consensus: early development activity must be based on the closest consultation and active participation and decision making of the local officials and the local people. I was not surprised. I have always found that the more you engage with the local leaders and people, the more you hear their demand for a decisive role. I shared with them the possibility of a local (small grants) fund to finance their activities. Again not surprisingly this was embraced enthusiastically.

Based on further interaction with UN agencies and donors in Juba, I spelled out an integrated recovery strategy that would use the SRF-SS to support both top-down quick government service delivery and a parallel "bottom up" recovery process that enabled communities to undertake small projects supported by strengthened departments of local government. The SRF-SS has been operating on this basis for a few years as of this writing, including a small grants fund that empowered the participating communities to define and realize their own small-scale recovery. The challenges of remoteness and isolation of the villages remained daunting of course.

Collapse v. Reform

As hopeful as we were for our efforts, however, the broader context of Sudan did not portend well for realizing real early recovery. There were continuing genuine doubts and anxieties about whether a lasting peace with the North could be secured. Local outbreaks of conflict continued to occur with increasing frequency. In fact, the newly won independence of South Sudan has, far from inhibiting this violence, exacerbated it.

What chance under these circumstances does South Sudan have to realize sustainable development and peace? Are the efforts of "recovery" sufficient to give the people enough hope and encouragement to pursue their local development, and will it be enough to stabilize the rural areas and avoid the restart of war? In reality, South Sudan for all its newness remains at risk of becoming a "collapsing state". Its problems are so deep and embedded in animosities, especially from and with its northern neighbor that it seems unrealistic to expect any relatively small scale empowerment and recovery process such as ours could have significant impact.

What does this mean for the future of South Sudan and the many other increasing numbers of failing states? What are the prospects that international interventions along the continuum of relief, recovery and development will make a real difference? What are the prospects that these States, in spite of their fragility, can turn such situations to the positive, overcome their seeming collapse, and renew their societies along with their longing for a decent life.

These are fundamental and difficult questions that no amount of "tinkering at the edges" of recovery or development will resolve. There is an unprecedented urgency to find real solutions that go beyond immediate efforts, as important as these may be. Ultimately there is a need to address the potential for core fundamental reforms in both North and South Sudan. Reforms relevant to basic values of decency and justice and peace. Reforms that would strengthen democracy by empowering people to play a more direct role in determining how best to achieve a more equitable, better life for all. This is the challenge of the twenty-first century, in the Sudans and across so many rich and poor countries alike, and we will consider it further in our closing chapter.

Chapter 18
Vietnam

Excluded from the Struggle
2008-2009

Working from the commune up

Getting Started

In late 2008, Suvira was approached by the ILO to take up an assignment in Vietnam to develop a "Community-Based Training (CBT) for Economic Empowerment" program. It was the same approach Suvira had applied in Bangladesh, and for which she produced a CBT Manual that was used by the ILO worldwide. Though not knowing what I would do if I joined Suvira, I knew it was an opportunity for both of us to immerse ourselves in this incredibly rich culture and to engage in its development challenges.

We arrived in Hanoi in November 2008 for what became a half year sojourn. Suvira immediately engaged in the task at hand, working with the government and NGOs to design and initiate the programme in Ha Tinh province on the east central coast of the country. Within a few months the programme was launched and early training led to the successful development of a number of new small enterprises in the pilot communes.

We chose to live in an apartment hotel in the center of Hanoi. It was built atop the famous "Hanoi Hilton" prison where Senator John McCain involuntarily resided for five years. The place was uniquely well located especially for me as I could move about on foot to many of the main commercial and cultural areas of the city. I began to learn much more about the history of the country.

Results of Arrogance

Vietnam was a country of so much rich history, culture, leadership and deep values and integrity that were core to achieving its freedom. I found it spell binding. During my initial weeks, I reread several accounts of the country's incessant struggles. Learning how the Vietnamese people had managed to overcome (in the year 938 a.d.) nearly a millennium of Chinese military and cultural dominance, the country's tenacity amazed me. Equally impressive was the unrelenting determination and ultimate success of the Vietnamese in eventually throwing off (in 1954) a century-long history of French colonization, abuse and atrocity.

But what most influenced and compelled my interest was my personal obsession with Vietnam's war with America. The Vietnamese refered to it as the "American War." For me, it was the absolute depth of American moral decline and shame. It was a travesty of immense proportions, reflective of an elite arrogance and deception bent on a compulsive almost inexplicable self-destruction.

I am convinced that few Americans really know even to this day the origins, the evolution, and the many ironies of our "Vietnam War" (also known as the Second Indochina War). The war's antecedents were shaped immediately following the end of World War II. The Japanese were quickly rooted out of the country by China in the North and by Britain in the South. The French attempted to hold a firm grip on the vestiges of their former colony. With enormous historical significance and irony, Ho Chi Ming declared Vietnam's independence from the French with a reference to America's own struggle and inspiration for freedom: *'We hold the truth that all men are created equal, that they are endowed by their Creator with certain unalienable rights, among them life, liberty and the pursuit of happiness. This immortal statement is extracted from the Declaration of Independence of the United States of America in 1776. These are undeniable truths.'*

But Ho Chi Ming's pleas for American recognition of the newly created Democratic Republic of Vietnam and prevention of a restoration of French colonial rule were repeatedly turned down by President Harry Truman. Between 1950 and 1954, the US provided 80% of all war supplies used by the French to defeat the Viet Minh liberation forces (a policy continued by President Dwight Eisenhower to preempt the "Domino Theory" fall of South East Asian countries to communism). Nevertheless, Vietnamese courage and resolve doomed the French who were resoundly defeated at Dien Bien Phu in 1954 and thrown out of the country.

Based on a continued, almost unimaginable misreading of Vietnamese history following the French defeat, the US government aligned itself with the dictatorship of Ngo Dinh Diem of South Vietnam for nearly ten years. Then in another striking irony, Diem was assassinated in late 1964 under an American-supported military coup. President John F. Kennedy introduced what became a plethora of military advisers (more than 16,000) during these years. That commitment seemed miniscule compared to a subsequent commitment of more than half a million US troops by Lyndon Johnson. A mindless and prolonged bombing of North Vietnam and neighboring Laos and Cambodia (through which ran the supply line known as the Ho Chi Ming trail) ensued. At the end of the war, with the withdrawal of US forces from Saigon in 1975 by President Richard Nixon, the enormous human toll of the conflict gradually became clearer. Most Americans remained focused on the travesty of 58,000 American lives lost. The far greater toll was on the Vietnamese side—possibly in the range of three to four million civilian deaths inflicted by all sides in both South and North Vietnam—ultimately a result and responsibility of American foreign policy.

The "Vietnam War" was a consequence of fear and arrogance. The blame rests squarely with the political elite of America. They became fixated with "anti communism" during and after the era of "McCarthyism". It was a fear and arrogance based less on the reality of a world communist takeover. It was more the ignorance of supposedly intelligent and educated men who never bothered to understand other cultures, their history and their fierce nationalism and determination to be independent. This from leaders of a country who fought for these same goals in their own history. It was a classic case of an abuse of power. An abuse of both American and Vietnamese people to achieve elite political interests that in the end proved totally false. The American and Vietnamese people paid the price.

In my view and understanding, it was the American people who ultimately needed to assume responsibility for ensuring that this dark history would never repeat itself. Discouragingly however the same elite aggressive foreign policies that led us into Vietnam have continued to lead us into a steady stream of similar American foreign policy blunders and wars, particularly in Iraq and Afghanistan. It appears that unless America is ready and willing to rethink and redefine its own fundamental values of how we treat ourselves and others, it is doomed to continue on this self-destructive path. Again, we will explore the possibility of such core reform in our final chapter.

Pragmatic Admiration

It was in this historical context of both blunder and success (for the independence of Vietnam) that I felt uniquely privileged to be in Vietnam with the possibility of working among its people. To my amazement, I found in the process that many (certainly not all) Vietnamese held America and Americans in high esteem. While difficult for me to understand, I gradually attributed it to a number of reasons: it is easier for the victor to show forgiveness and magnanimity toward the defeated (as America did towards the Germans and Japanese following World War II). There was always an underlying respect and admiration for America and its ideals, as I have already referenced by Ho Chi Minh's emulation of America's declaration of independence as a basis for Vietnam's own. It was also a pragmatic acceptance of current day realities in which America, for whatever its continuing mistakes, retained a leadership in technological and economic realms that were important to Vietnam's hopes for a better life.

Left Behind

My own eventual emersion into Vietnam's development proved equally educational and rewarding. Having spent my initial weeks networking with a wide range of international and national development organizations, I became much more aware and understanding of the special development issues and challenges of the country. In the process, I came to realize that the "ethnic minorities" of the country had been left behind. This was a major issue and challenge for Vietnam, much more than in most other countries in which I had worked. Ethnic minorities constituted approximately 15% of the population, of whom nearly 2/3 lived in poverty, thereby constituting about 40% of all those living in poverty in Vietnam. I thought this inequity to be a glaring enigma in a country with such high principles for the well being of its people. It became a matter of national pride (mixed with a deep prejudice that I will address) to eliminate such a problem. As my recent experience in Bangladesh seemed particularly relevant, I decided to focus on this issue.

Of all the hundreds of organizations working in development, I soon found the one most committed to the problems and issues of ethnic minorities was OXFAM. At a certain point early in my stay, I made a presentation to them of my Bangladesh work. This sparked considerable interest. I soon found myself contracted to undertake a review and reformulation of their largest ethnic minority program. It was located in Nghe An province in the hills of central western Vietnam bordering Laos. It happened to be the original home of Ho Chi Minh. OXFAM had been working there nearly twenty years. It was an impressive program carried out in close partnership with the local district government. It supported a mix of development activity ranging from food security to agricultural production to housing. It achieved some impressive results.

Top Down

But when I made a field visit to the area, I discovered that most of the work was driven by the district government. Very little of what had taken place emanated from the communities. It was a major flaw, as I saw it, severely limiting real results for the village people and jeopardizing the sustainability of the program.

OXFAM staff were already aware of these shortcomings. We began to design an alternative approach. It was far more "bottom up" and community driven. Basically it introduced a decentralization of responsibility and authority from the district government further down to the communes. The latter were the lowest rung of the government administrative system above the village. They had responsibility for development but very few resources and capacity. Our vision was one of empowering the villages, through capacity training to manage their own development (introducing a Quick Impact Fund as we had done in Bangladesh). Simultaneously we would strengthen the communes to work with and support the villages in their self-defined small local development projects.

But the story I want to share is less about the details of introducing these innovation and more about why such innovations were necessary in the first place.

Vietnam is a country in which international development professionals dream to work. As noted, Vietnam is a country that has, over hundreds of years of struggle, imbued its national goals, policies and frameworks with the principles of equality and justice for its people. These plans and policies reflect international principles and standards by which the UN and other international bodies conduct their work. They embed a strong commitment to the eradication of poverty, including for the ethnic minorities. The dichotomy (and disappointment) that I soon found myself facing was that these grand principles and values were not as well practiced in Vietnam as they were preached.

Vietnam is a new model of development. In many ways, I saw it as a proxy for China. In both countries, development over the past 20 years was rapid and immensely impressive. It was achieved with the principle of human decency at its core. What both countries did in reducing poverty is historically remarkable (China moving nearly 700 million out of poverty between 1981 and 2008, in the process reducing extreme poverty from 84% to 13% over the same period, and reducing overall poverty from 33% in 1990 to 10% in 2007; and meanwhile Vietnam reduced its poverty from 61% in 1993 to 37% in 1998 and a very impressive 12.5% by 2008). Both countries achieved these goals with increasing openness. They did it with great efficiency. But they also did it on the basis of substantial control of decision making and implementation.

Vietnam's main poverty reduction programs are highly centralized initiatives of the State. Most development programs in Vietnam were known by the number they are assigned and the major ones for alleviating poverty of ethnic minorities were: "Decree 135"—mostly focused on improving infrastructure, and "Decree 30A"—focused on alleviating poverty in the sixty-one poorest districts. These programs were primarily focused on developing the roads and on construction of public facilities. But they also included some excellent extension and technical support services of the State to improve, for example, agricultural production and small industry. In all of these cases, it is the State which is primarily determining the priorities and carrying out the tasks. In other words, Vietnam is very competent in carrying out top-down development.

Absence of Faith

What I did not find in Vietnam was a belief and trust in the people, at least not the ethnic minorities. There was no driving principle that minority people must contribute to and drive their own development. There was no obvious faith in the capacity of minorities to be equal partners with the State in realizing their life goals. This was evident in the OXFAM program in the way the district government decided what programs were needed in the villages and how the villagers should participate.

The development programs of the government benefitted the ethnic people, no doubt, but in a limited way. There was no sense these programs were theirs. They participated, but seldom did they take their own initiatives. Seldom did they decide what was best for them and what they thought could work.

Development in Vietnam, and as far as I can see in China as well, will under these command and control systems confront limits to what they can achieve. To be certain, both countries adopted "free market" philosophies and practices (in Vietnam these were started in the late 1980s, known as "doi moi" reforms). These have gone a long way in enabling the people in business (small and large, farm and off-farm) to realize impressive economic returns. But even in these private sector achievements, there are already signs of severe constraints on creativity and innovation, not least from State impediments put in place on the free flow of information. Equally worrying in my mind is the "dependency" created by a paternalistic State in presuming to manage and carry out development for the poor, in this case the ethnic minorities, in a non-sustainable manner.

Blind Prejudice

The lessons of Vietnam were clear for me. Having lofty national principles and goals is critically important to encouraging and motivating those still left behind. But when those in power (however impressive their past achievements in gaining independence and reducing much of the poverty) apply these principles and goals in a manner that contradicts the values of respect and decency, the people excluded from power (in this case the ethnic minorities) remain in grave risk of never knowing a better and decent life. Such compromises in social values are as relevant (and detrimental) to rapidly developing (Vietnam and China) and advanced countries (US) as they are to the poorest of nations.

This realization again brought me back to the fundamental importance of establishing respect, trust and decency among and toward all people as a basis for truly equitable societies. As I saw it in Vietnam, respect and decency were lost as a result of elite attitudes that minority people were incapable of taking charge of their own lives and their own development. It was the same blind prejudice against indigenous peoples that I had seen in other countries. And unfortunately, these attitudes were not limited to the governing elite. They were pervasive throughout the country among most *Khin* people whose ethnicity constituted 85% of the total population. They simply looked down on the minority groups as incapable of undertaking their own development or entrepreneurial pursuits. Such prejudice definitely suppressed opportunities for these minorities. Such discrimination continued to keep them disadvantaged and unable to improve their future. As I saw it, these were issues of societal values more than about the socio-economic opportunities they pre-empted.

There is a great need to address these challenges of advancing-yet-controlled societies (and any others which are governed by powerful elites and powerful majorities) whenever they are prepared to compromise their otherwise exemplary social values to deny minorities their equal rights to a decent life. Again, the need for fundamental social reforms to address these unjust gaps between the powerful and the powerless is further explored in the final chapter.

Chapter 19
Yemen

We Are One
2009 – 2011

Always a
Warm Spirit

Traditional Values Define
Everyday Life

A Majestic History and Culture

Mysterious Encounter

Barely 4:30 in the morning. We were walking briskly down a dimly lit Hadda Street. As we turned the corner into a side street, we passed him by without looking up, just as we had done for the past couple of weeks. At 7,000 feet, the sharp cool air of the Sana'a desert refreshed us. Ramadan, the annual period of fasting in Yemen and throughout the Arab world, approached its end. Ramadan changed the way people lived. Day turned into night and night into day. Whenever I woke at 2:00 or 3:00 am in the morning, I heard young neighborhood boys playing soccer in the streets. Things started to quiet down around 4:00 am. Shortly after that and a first cup of tea, Suvira and I took our hour-long morning walk.

Perplexed, we shared with the manager of our hotel apartment our growing concern. Any young man who stood on the same street corner every morning staring at us was certainly unusual. He often held up a cell phone. We had the feeling he was watching us for some reason and maybe taking photos. That was strange indeed. We always felt totally safe in Sana'a, whether early morning or late evening. Most foreigners living in the city never ventured on foot on the streets especially at such an hour. We had no such compunctions. In fact we felt close to the people we regularly encountered on these walks. But this young man was different.

The hotel manager eventually asked his night staff to watch the movements of this man from a window high in the flat building. They found he emerged from a nearby shop around 3:45 am each morning, stood on the corner until we arrived, lingered there a few minutes until we had gone further down the road, and then left. This raised our suspicions even further. That was an unexpected reaction on our part. Yemen had gained a reputation as a terrorist stronghold, something we considered quite ridiculous. We always found Yemenis exceedingly polite and friendly including those we passed in the night or early morning. So why did we have doubts this time?

At a certain point, the manager shared his concern and felt we should take no chances. He was going to ask a friend of his who was in the police force to investigate what was going on.

The next morning we again started down Hadda Street. This time we saw through the darkness a couple of tribal chiefs in full turban and traditional dress huddled and conversing. It was not unusual to see local men out in the early morning. Most were returning from prayers at the local mosque. We felt these two were different. We quickly figured out they must be undercover police watching our movements. Indeed they were. As we continued down the side street, we eventually turned around to see what, if anything was happening. Much to our surprise, in fact shock, we saw silhouetted in the distant dark morning what appeared to be a rough scuffle of the two policemen with the young man we were suspecting. This was not what we anticipated. We never confided to our UN security colleagues that we routinely took morning walks. We feared they may insist we stop the routine. So no one was the wiser. But any incident with the police was bound to stir up a mess for us. Beyond that, we thought that any police involvement would be simply to question the young man about his daily activity. We never imagined they would forcibly arrest him.

We remained transfixed some two blocks distance from the scuffling. We couldn't be sure what was going on. We decided to double back for a closer look. We went around the block and came back along a side street. On reaching Hadda Street again, we turned down toward the corner where all of this was taking place. To our surprise, it was all quiet. There was another young man now sitting on the same corner. Suddenly another police van with a caged rear compartment quickly joined up behind us. It stopped just as we were turning the corner. Three policemen jumped out. Grabbing the young man and another who was by then passing by, they pushed them firmly into the caged compartment. The vehicle sped off into the early morning shadows.

Naturally we were upset. What had we caused? Why had we agreed to involve the police? Was there a possibility that some grave injustice was about to occur to the three young men taken away? Were we responsible? That same afternoon, we sought out the manager to question why the police had taken such drastic actions. Unfortunately he was not in and would not come until the following day.

The next morning we ventured out on our same routine. There was no sign of anyone on the corner, nor any sign of the police. The streets were empty. But as we turned the corner, we noticed a van parked across the street with its motor running and a driver with cell phone in hand. The driver appeared to be looking at us in the darkness. He suddenly drove the vehicle down the road in the opposite direction from which we were walking. We thought his actions a bit unusual. We continued our walk and brushed it off as sheer coincidence. A few moments later the lights of an approaching car came up behind us. Taken aback to discover it was the same van, we moved over to the far side of the street.

The vehicle passed by slowly. Then unexpectedly the vehicle turned around. It came back in our direction. Straight at us. We did not panic. But it was certainly whatever one calls panic just before it happens.

Every morning on these walks, we passed by a huge compound that took up a full block. It was a large stone house; you might even call it a small palace, with an interior courtyard and garden. The entrance gate was always guarded by two or three day and night uniformed guards. We became rather friendly with all of them. We always greeted each other. As the van drove back toward us, headlights blinding our vision, we found ourselves just in front of these gates. On impulse, we ran immediately to the guard house and hammered on the door. Two guards emerged quite surprised by our state of anxiety. We literally pulled them out onto the street just as the van stopped in front of us. We quickly explained to the guards in abbreviated English what had happened. They began to interrogate the driver who had by then stepped out of the vehicle. He protested his complete innocence. He was not following us. He was simply warming up the vehicle. This was not convincing. The questioning continued without any admission of wrong doing. At a certain point when the questions and answers were leading nowhere, we pulled away and returned to our flat.

That evening we found the manager in his office. We shared with him what had happened to the three young men two nights before. We expressed our surprise and concern with these events. He told us this was not unusual. Police always preferred to take any possible suspects to police facilities for thorough questioning. We insisted that apprehending and incarcerating people without clear evidence of wrong doing, no matter what suspicions there were, could easily result in a grave injustice. We did not wish to cause that. We asked him to request the police to release the three men immediately. He said he could not be sure they would be willing but he would try.

The next day he informed us that in fact the interrogation had turned up no plausible reasons or evidence that the original young man was stalking us or had any untoward motives. In fact he declared that he was simply calling his girlfriend each morning as that was the only time they could speak. The other two men seemed to have no knowledge or interest in our movements. All three were released that day.

The incident of the van driver was more difficult to understand or explain. We later assumed he may have been a relative of one of those taken away. Possibly he was angry with what he assumed we had done to precipitate their incarceration. We did not ask anyone to follow up or question him.

We never saw any of the men again. Nor was any similar incident repeated.

The entire affair was surreal. While indeed it fitted closely the stereotype of Yemen as a land of terrorist, it ran counter to all of our experience and feelings of trust, respect and affection for Yemenis. It was a peculiar set of circumstances that managed to create a momentary doubt. It was a doubt that we did not want to accept. Our reactions to the incident may have been understandable in the climate of what was becoming a heightened sense of insecurity in Sana'a even among Yemenis. Its main impact on us was to reinforce our overall sense of how free and at home we felt in Yemen among what we saw as exceptionally friendly and humane people.

And we continued to move about freely on the streets among them at all hours experiencing that friendliness and their keen sense of humor. On one occasion, actually over several days, we encountered on our early morning walks a young man who could never seem to get his car started in the lingering chill of the darkness. I ended up joining him each morning to push the car half way down the block whereupon on the half-run he jumped in to start the engine and shouted back to me each time what I assumed were a litany of morning blessings.

On other occasions, during our daily late afternoon walks, Suvira, famous for her high-speed pace, frequently left me some thirty paces behind. Old men sitting on the curbside not accustomed to such scenes watched in apparent amazement as she zipped by and I inevitably followed in a seeming struggle to keep up. Each time as I passed them, they greeted me with a knowing smile and a thumbs up, murmuring what I was sure were words of sympathy and merriment at my profound predicament. On that same daily route, Suvira on another occasion, scurrying as usual with hair streaming freely behind, passed two women. As they saw her go by, one of them pulled out her mobile phone camera from under her veiled attire. With a soft but uncontrolled giggle and murmur to her friend, she captured Suvira's swift and unveiled movements as though anticipating she may never see such carefree abandon again.

It is this story of these people, their everyday kindness, their profound culture and values, their keen sense of humor, and above all their struggle to free themselves of a long political oppression and an unjustified image of who they are, that I want to share with you.

Islam Introduced

On November 22, 2009, I was at 36,000 feet, almost in a slumber on the last leg of a long journey from Portland to Sana'a. The gentleman next to me asked in a whisper whether this was my first visit to Yemen. I had seen him in the airport waiting area before we boarded the connecting flight in Frankfurt. I assumed he was another of what were many Yemeni Diasporas visiting home briefly before returning again to their life abroad. I had no idea where he lived that life. He was slight of build, short, unassuming, wore an unpretentious suit and a pair of spectacles with fine dark grey rims that matched his hair. I replied that yes it was my first trip to the country. He ventured that 'you will like it'. I asked him where he was coming from and learned that he lived in Brooklyn, New York. He owned a small import/export business.

After we finished our evening meal, we both reclined our seats to relax. I decided to inquire how he found life in the United States. He informed me it was fine. He had accustomed to it though he was grateful to be living with his son and family. I rather boldly asked whether he felt any repercussions from the aftermath of 9/11. He paused briefly before answering. He shared that he had not felt any animosity, neither in his neighborhood nor in his business contacts. He knew other Arabs however who had not been so fortunate. They had been subject to some ridicule and felt less comfortable and welcomed than before the incident.

Without prompting, he volunteered his thoughts and feelings on the relations of Americans and the Arab world, more specifically Islam. He confided a disappointment in the many stereotypes and misunderstandings of most Americans about his religion. When I asked precisely what he meant, he shared his regret about the general perception he felt Americans held of most Muslims—that they were fanatics and extremists determined to impose their religion on others by violent means. He believed that Americans did not understand the religion of Islam, neither its origins nor its fundamental beliefs and convictions. He strongly condemned the actions of the few extremists who created this negative image of his culture and religion. He wanted more than anything that the real values and practices of Muslims who lived side by side with other cultures for so many centuries should be understood and appreciated.

When I asked him what those values were, he replied without hesitation.

They were a belief in the fundamental importance of treating all people equally and with respect. He assured me that throughout Islamic history, in spite of the many occasions in which violence had been used to both defend and spread the religion, these were miniscule in comparison to what attracted more than one billion to join the religion. Muslims felt a genuine sense of equality for each other he assured me. There was a common bond, a commitment and a daily practice of decency and peace among all Muslims.

Resplendent Heritage

Suvira had preceded me to Sana'a by two weeks. She had taken on a consultancy for UNDP as a conflict prevention adviser on gender. When I arrived she was living in a hotel located on a hill overlooking the city. We used it as our base while I began the search for a more permanent residence.

My initial travels through the city were exhilarating. Yemen is located at the far southern end of the Arabian Peninsula. Its only adjacent neighbors are Saudi Arabia and Oman. I was not sure how much this location influenced the preservation of Yemen's traditional culture and way of life. I assumed it was quite a lot. I arrived at the end of Ramadan (a year before the incident on Hadda Street I described) and its month-long period of fasting followed by Eid, a time of celebration as everyone breaks the fast for another year.

As I commuted daily in search of accommodation in the city and the residential suburb of Hadda where most foreigners lived, I traversed the main livestock market near the Old City of Sana'a. Vibrant colors and unending motion described it best. Hundreds, maybe thousands of herdsmen, clustered in small circles bargaining for the best price. All the herdsmen were attired in traditional dress—variations of a loose-fitting white cotton garment cinched at the middle by a broad colorful belt that holstered the *jambbiyah*, a dagger of substantial size. It symbolized the attainment of manhood and there was a traditional readiness to use it if needed. A fact well understood by everyone.

The herdsmen's attire was further accentuated by a western-style suit coat, and most prominently, a multi-colored turban. Seeing a thousand and more of these herdsmen jockeying vigorously to win each potential sale was like revisiting what one assumed was a common scene in an ancient Arabian past.

On some occasions, I entered and passed through the "Old City". The architecture was stunning. Houses were hundreds, some reputedly more than a thousand years old, made of local mud bricks with each window and door decorated ornately in white alabaster trim. Among these were a number of multi-storied "Tower Houses". They reached as high as eight to ten floors; they were a feat unequalled in the ancient world in which they were constructed. This architectural splendor was further embellished by towering minarets of numerous mosques that defined the urban landscape. Narrow lanes and alleys wound their way through an unorganized and random pattern of structures. By mid morning women in full *burqa*, men in traditional dress, and young children in a perpetual state of erratic motion swarmed in all directions.

Later in our stay, Suvira and I wandered these byways into the multitude of *souks*. Each specialized in a particular product from spices to old Jewish silver jewelry to modern plastic toys and kitchen utensils. We always stopped by one of many favorite local bakeries. These were no larger than the other innumerable small shops. Inside, each conveyed a dark warm frenzied world of young and old men. Each shuffled into red hot brick ovens coarse wheat and corn paddies the size of quarter plates. Long wooden flat poles quickly extracted delicious ready-to-eat steaming flat bread (known as military bread since it has long been the stable for the lower ranks of the armed services).

Sana'a is the oldest city in the world. It was reputedly founded by Noah's eldest son, Shem. The kingdom of Saba (ruled at one period according to mythology by the famous Queen of Sheba) dates from 1,000 B.C. It centered in Marib in the central eastern region of present day Yemen based on a thriving agriculture irrigated by a dam of unparalleled engineering accomplishment. Rival kingdoms in the eastern and southern areas were based on cultivation and overland exportation of frankincense, myrrh, and spices to the Mediterranean. The Romans invaded but failed to conquer the Sabean kingdom in 25 B.C. Soon after, the entire region of southwestern Arabia was united under the kingdom of Himyar which controlled the Red Sea and the coasts of the Gulf of Aden up to the sixth century A.D.

Islam came to Yemen during the life of the Prophet Mohammed in 630 A.D. Yemeni tribes were active participants in the Muslim conquests of the seventh and eighth centuries. Yemen thereby became an integral part of the Arab empire (under Rushidun, Ummayad, and Abbasid dynasties). It became part of one of the largest land empires in history—stretching from Spain to China and to the south as in Sudan in Africa.

As I reflected on this history, I recalled my conversation with my Yemini fellow passenger on the flight to Sana'a. I thought about what he had shared with me concerning the roots and precepts of Islam. Studying this further, I learned that Islam was a response to a deviation from traditional Arab codes of conduct that demanded decency and compassionate behavior toward others. The growing greed and avarice that Mohammed witnessed in his home town of Mecca as it prospered from flourishing trade provided a timely and relevant backdrop to the words of the Quran which he shared with his followers. The message was clear and simple: the need to return to respect, decency, compassion, equality, and social concern and justice for all human beings. In parallel to this was a need to lay aside false pride, elitism and selfishness, and to build a new common community (*ummah*) based on compassion and a fair distribution of wealth.

Perhaps even more impressive than his clear rendering of these simple truths was the Prophets declaration that they were not new but rather reaffirmations of the same truths that had been shared by all great religious leaders throughout all history. It was an expression of a primordial faith that cut across all of human spiritual striving and belief. It was a common message and call for human decency and justice. It was all based on a belief in one God, Allah, who would be respected with ultimate reverence through a life guided by such principles.

Number One

As I educated myself about these basic ideas of Islam, Suvira and I were astonished to suddenly find Yemen at the center of headlines around the world. It was Christmas Day 2009.

Umar Farouk Abdulmutallab was a twenty-three year-old University College of London student originally from Nigeria who attempted to blow up a Delta Airlines Detroit-bound plane with explosives sewn into his undergarments. The bomb failed to explode, but the incident created a huge reaction in America and around the globe. It revealed the vulnerability of aircraft to this type of threat. What was disturbing was the fact that the bomber had been trained for this mission in Yemen. He had lived a month with an American-born imam, Anwar Awlaki, who had returned to his ancestral home in Yemen in 2002 (and was killed by a US drone aircraft in 2011). He reportedly arranged for members of Al Qaeda to train Abdulmutallab.

Yemen was already suffering from a notorious reputation as a country that harbored Al Qaeda. Ever since AQ operatives blew a hole in the US naval ship, SS Cole, in 2000 killing 16 American servicemen that reputation stuck. The Detroit incident seemed to confirm that Yemen was the new center of Al Qaeda beyond Afghanistan. Some American politicians demanded that Yemen be made the prime new target of the "war on terror".

Family, friends and colleagues in the US were emailing Suvira and me non-stop, fearing for our lives. The general perception in America was that Yemen was rampant with Al Qaeda members who were out to kill any American they could in Yemen or in America. Yemen is a country of some twenty-three million people. According to the CIA reports at the time of this Detroit incident, the total number of Al Qaeda in Yemen was believed not to exceed 200 to 300 members. But despite these facts, the image of Yemen seemed severely, perhaps irreparably, damaged.

The UN and most embassies in Yemen applied new security precautions to which Suvira and I adhered for the most part. But in everyday reality, Suvira and I were not intimidated by any of these exaggerated images. We had the advantage of having seen similar incidents and reactions, actually far worse, in other countries where we had lived. We knew well the manufactured "hype" of the international press on these matters.

What steadied us and kept us to our basically normal, routine way of living were the people of Yemen. We continued to move around Sana'a at will, settling into our apartment, shopping our food and household items in the local markets, and attending meetings at various locations around the city. There was hardly ever a time I did not flag down and enter a local taxi when the turbaned driver would ask me in broken English 'where you from?' When I replied America, his face inevitably broke into a warm broad smile. Each time he then gave me an exuberant thumbs up. He uttered a couple other words he knew like 'very good!' or 'best!'

One evening Suvira and I were joining some of her office colleagues at a local restaurant. The taxi driver was having a hard time finding the place. We ask him to pull over to the curb of busy Hadda Street, so we could inquire with a group of young men who were standing about chatting at the curbside. We asked whether they could point us in the right direction. One of them spoke good English. On seeing that we seemed still not clear from his instruction, he bid his friends farewell and jumped into the taxi. He took us to our destination. He told us on exiting that he always admired America and what it meant to the world. He hoped one day to go there.

A month later I decided to get a routine medical checkup and went as recommended to the University of Science and Technology Hospital in Sanaa. I received the most courteous and helpful service, mostly by young female receptionists and nurses who were all under the veil. When I went for an X-ray and ultra sound scan, the medical doctor asked where I was from. I told him America and he stopped his procedure. He told me that he had studied briefly in Chicago. He liked Americans very much. He hoped one day to return.

Even in our residential neighborhood, where Suvira and I took those early morning walks I have already described, we would always encounter in the darkness of the hour men and young boys returning from prayers at the local mosque who had come to know us. They would invariably greet us with either the traditional *Salaam Alaikum* or a simple 'Welcome!' in English, even when we had been there already some months. And as we traveled throughout Yemen, the response to our nationality was without fail warm and positive. It included the group of men already eating in an outdoor restaurant by the sea in Aden who insisted that we join them for lunch. A similar feeling of goodwill came from a gathering of imams in Seyoun (Hadramout Governorate)—the ancestral home of Osama Bin Laden—who told Suvira that they wanted to see her share her ideas for women's economic opportunity on their local radio program which they hoped one day would become their own version of *CNN*! In this same valley area, in the town of Seyoun, I sat for a couple of hours in a local tea shop as scores of local men (mostly farmers from nearby villages) warmly greeted me and murmured their approval as the shop owner kept repeating (rather embarrassingly for me): 'America—Number One'!

Open Hearts

I share these details to make what for me is a salient and universal point: that most (nearly all) people around the world, Yemenis certainly included, are decent people. They have nothing but goodwill and respect for others they meet, especially those from other lands, and in my case, from America. Of course, a small minority (almost imperceptible in numbers) have evil intentions. The abuse of their own religions to carry out dastardly deeds has unfortunately enabled some of those who feel threatened to create the impression that all people of that religion (Islam) or nationality (Yemeni) are out to do the same.

Due to the interest of a few (mostly those in power) to create an atmosphere of fear, people are continuously being driven and kept apart. These elites (which as I have already noted several times exist in both rich and poor nations alike) thrive (for selfish reasons of greed and power) on creating a sense of dependency on them to assure the public safety. They are satisfied only as long as we cooperate in taking the fear seriously and keeping up our mutual guard.

Living in Yemen enlightened me considerably to the importance of tearing down the many unwarranted and untruthful images that continued to create unjustified animosity between people. I was struck with the significance of this as I faced the reality of open hearts and minds in Yemen. As I continued to learn more about the fundamental principles and root lessons of Islam, I also became convinced that in spite of the vile images of Islam held among many Western countries and people, it was really an ideology and lifestyle rooted in the same basic concepts, beliefs and behaviors as those core to Christian, Jewish and other religions.

Common Threads

At the same time, I was acutely aware how all religions have been distorted and misused throughout history. So while I knew that Islam was no exception, I also knew it certainly had no monopoly on such abuses.

I was particularly reminded of those examples of abuse that stand out most vividly in our Western European history. Indeed, in my readings I was motivated to revisit some of these in more detail. One of the most glaring of course was the Spanish Inquisition. It was a process of intimidation and killings that took place within the Catholic Church targeting Muslims and Jews. The Muslims, also known in Europe as *Moors* and *Moriscos*, had invaded (in 711 A.D.) and taken control of much of Spain for more than 500 years. They were eventually expelled (in the fifteenth century), but not all. There began a series of pogroms to exterminate those who remained in the country. In 1478, the Spanish monarch established Tribunals (officially known as the Tribunal of the Holy Office of the Inquisition) to enforce adherence to the Catholic dogma by those Muslims and Jews who had converted to Catholicism but were suspected of disloyalty. The inquisition lasted some 300 years. It made frequent use of torture (including the "invention" of a technique known as *toca*, which America much later insidiously adopted as "water boarding"). It executed thousands of often faithful Catholics (total numbers are not confirmed but range from a few thousand to nearly 150,000). It forced out from their homeland many innocents who could take with them only what they wore on their backs. All of this despite the fundamental precept of the teaching of Christ—that we must do unto others as we would have them do unto us!

And of course Islam has its own history to tell. Mohammad, who had begun to preach and convert from as early as 612 A.D., was not accepted by the wealthy elite of Mecca (who did not like his message that wealth would not gain them entry into heaven). He decided to accept an invitation of local tribes from Medina (known then as Yathrib) to migrate and live among them as one community sworn to protect each other. His enemies in Mecca sought to destroy this new community. They inflicted a severe defeat on them in the Battle of Uhud (in 625 A.D.). Muhammad inspired his people and troops to retaliate (in 627 A.D.) and won decisively in the Battle of the Trench. This proved a turning point in early Islamic history, leading to a confederacy of all tribes of Arabia. In the process, however, many of the allies of Mecca (including some Jewish tribes) were killed.

Muhammad died in 632 A.D. Soon after, many tribes across Arabia began to turn against the new religion, reverting to their former beliefs. Muhammad's immediate successor (known as *Caliphs*) was Abu Bakr, who began an intense suppression of these wayward and disloyal tribes across the entire Arabian Peninsula. Known as the War of Apostasy, it was a violent reaction to what was seen as a profound threat to Islamic unity. Once this adherence to Islam had been enforced in the homelands, Abu Bakr and the other immediate successors of Mohammad (Umar, Uthman, and Ali), known as the *Rashidun Caliphate* (632 – 661 A.D.), initiated an Islamic global war of conquest. It was an historically remarkable, indeed unprecedented, conquest of a huge empire achieved within an almost incredibly brief period of less than thirty years. It was followed by further successor Caliphates (notably the Umayyards—705 to 750 A.D; and the Abbasids—750 to 935 A.D.), which continued the expansion of Islam.

None of this was accomplished without immense loss of life. Among these, the losses resulting from the Islamic expansion into the Indian Sub-Continent (mainly territories of present day Pakistan—especially Sindh and Baluchistan) remains a matter of considerable historical controversy in terms of the extent of the loss of life. But whether from violent conflict, repression or by disease and famine, the impact on the people was severe.

It should be clear that these realities of religious history (and many others that could be cited) are unfortunately common to all institutionalized religious experience. No religious beliefs should or can be labeled as more abused in this respect than any other.

The question is what meaning does this unsavory history and current reality have as a reflection of whether the vast majority of those who practice these religions are violent. For me the meaning is very limited. Certainly there is clear warning from such history that universal religious precepts are always vulnerable and at constant risk of being used by a few for purposes of overpowering and controlling the majority. And such distortions are bound to continue in one form or another.

What is far more meaningful for me, however, as a barometer of peoples' fundamental beliefs, is how they act and treat each other in their daily lives. This is a matter of coming to know what is in their hearts. Some (few) religious leaders and zealots are always there on all sides to preach and practice hatred. What is far more revealing of the great majority of people, however, is how they live their religion in quiet everyday ways.

This is what I tried to focus on in my attempts to understand Islam.

What I have understood is that Islam is lived through human relations. Here, I refer not only to how Suvira and I have been treated, but to what I observed in how Yemeni people treated each other. Beyond the occasional difficulties that challenge all human relationships, Yemenis are rich in ways in which they show affection, caring and friendship for one another. Many of these are rooted in ancient Arab culture which passed down through millennia the codes of conduct and human interactions that are based on decency toward each other. It is expressed as I have seen through the goodness of open hearts. A genuine warmth and caring for one another. It is expressed in the embrace and kiss of men each time they meet. It is expressed in the salutations that always wish that "peace be upon you". It is expressed in the generosity of never sitting alone to eat unless one has offered the same sustenance to others present. It is expressed in the profound yearning for companionship in all realms of life and times of the day or season. It is expressed through the simple courtesies, respect, and goodwill that people show each other in innumerable ways throughout every day. It is expressed in the deep love of parents and children for each other, through the unfailing loyalty of friends, and in the deepest feeling of loss for those departed.

All of this to say (once again) that in terms of basic human values, Islam shares a core fundamental commonality with all other religions. It is to say that those who practice Islam based on this core are as decent as those who practice these same values taught in all those other religions.

Fallible Behaviors

In reaching these conclusions based on the simple observations I made of human interaction in Islamic life and culture, I do not mean to say that Islam is free of current day practices and behaviors that are disturbing. As in all human experience, these faults reside side-by-side with the overriding inspirations for decency and good.

Among the most unsettling of these practices for me were those related to the status of women that I observed in Yemen. Yemen is one of the few Islamic countries (Saudi Arabia being another) in which all women of every social and economic rank are expected to cover their bodies and faces completely under black robes and veils at all times in public. I tried to understand the background and history of this practice. I was not very successful. Nowhere in the Quran is this practice cited as a requirement (though modesty of dress is). When and why this practice was introduced is not clear or at least agreed, even among Islamic scholars. Some Yemen men informed me that it originated during times in which a significant number of women were held as concubines or slaves. The veiling of virtuous women was a way of ensuring their separate identity. A more common and apparently accepted view held today is that this is the most effective way of protecting women, both their physical security and their personal virtues, against the covetousness and lust of men. There are in fact many women who hold these views as strongly as men.

My own reaction to all of this was one of complete dismay. Before coming to Yemen and seeing the extreme of this practice, I always condemned it as a profound infringement of women's basic human rights. I held these views quite separate from the fact that Suvira spent much of her career promoting equal opportunity and status for women. I hold my views because I see this practice as a degradation and denial of the simple principle that all people are created equal. I also recognize these practices as a stifling of half the potential human capacities and talents of a society so crucial to its development.

Of course, the veiling of women is not the only form of discrimination against women in Yemen, though it is certainly the most visible and iconic. It takes many other forms (often legalized and institutionalized, but also practiced as custom in spite of constitutional guarantees) that seriously limit or preempt the equal rights of women in terms of ownership of land and property, inheritance, divorce, equal treatment in the courts, etc.

331

And of course there are practices that are equally contemptible in other religions, not least my own religion by birth, Catholicism. One of the most egregious of these, and of current day prevalence and concern as I write these pages, is the chronic practice of child abuse and molestation by many Catholic priests. This has been particularly exposed in America and more recently Ireland and other European countries, but I am certain it is not uncommon in many other Catholic prevalent countries. It is a complex issue, one which has at least some of its roots I believe in the repression of human interaction and feelings between the sexes. In the case of Catholicism, it is the prohibition of priests to marry. In the case of Islamic culture, or indeed that of Hindu and other religious cultures, the strict separation of men from women often leads to a ready abuse of women who are perceived to behave too independently or freely outside of marriage. These unnatural and unwarranted barriers create enormous frustrations that lead to dominance and disrespect of others.

I want to be clear about my own recognition of the imperfections that exist and are practiced in all religions along with all of the good they foster. In this context, I do not want to be misunderstood as a blind defender or apologist for Islam, Catholicism, or any other religion. They are all equally fallible. Indeed, if I be truthful, I should let it be known that I basically criticize all institutionalized religions. Although I was raised as a devout practicing Catholic in line with my mother's beliefs and my early parochial school education, I began to question these beliefs early on, especially during my time at Stanford. It was for me mostly an issue of respecting two principles I came to hold deeply: that no one should be subject to an unquestioning control of their personal beliefs, values and behaviors by anyone else (we are all responsible and capable of determining and living these ourselves); and, that one's relationship with God (in whom I believe) should (and can) be expressed and lived personally and directly with God, independent of intermediaries and rituals, by fulfilling the simplest of human values of acting decently toward others.

What I do admire and value in institutionalized religions is the way in which they were founded, promoted and maintained on the same set of core precepts. This was the contribution of great spiritual leaders, from Jesus, to Muhammad, to Buddha, and many others. It is what we have inherited as our common ground of decency. It is within our power to live this decency to the fullest.

Basis for Joining Together

There is a purpose I have in sharing all of this with you. That purpose is to clear the air about who we really are. That purpose is to recognize the common core that we share around which our "coming together" becomes possible. That purpose is to enable us to move ourselves beyond our stereotypes about the beliefs of others. That purpose is to rid ourselves of our arrogance that associates despicable behavior of a few with an entire country, culture, religion and people. It is a freeing of our minds and our spirits to see the innate goodness in the people of Yemen, and indeed people across the world, and their common desire for decency and peace. It is a call for all people to join together within each of our immediate contexts and across our borders, around these core values we hold in common, to bring down the false barriers that have kept us apart far too long. I am convinced that these true perceptions of each other will provide, indeed are providing, the foundation for fundamental social reforms based on our renewed commitment to our common human decency.

It was this fresh understanding of the universality of core beliefs and values that I gained in my early days in Yemen, which set the stage in an unplanned and unexpected way for my work in the country.

Precursors of the Awakening

While my initial six months in Yemen was spent getting to know the country, the culture, and the religion, at the same time I was keen to be more directly engaged in the work of development as I had always been in my past.

Although I did not know it immediately, I was living in literally historic times. There was a growing and disturbing awareness among Yemenis that there was something fundamentally wrong with life in Yemen. It was an awareness born out of centuries of authoritarian rule and a state of almost continuous repression. The Yemeni people were sensing the culmination of one calamity after another in their lives and in the political life of the country. They were rapidly approaching a breaking point. It manifested through outbreaks of political rebellion and fighting in both the North and the South of the country.

Yet, novice as I was to this unfolding drama, it seemed to me early on in my stay that there was something far more fundamental at play. While many of the international and bilateral aid organizations in the country were focused on the lack of Government basic services for people (and the need to strengthen them) as the root of the problem, I sensed a demand from the people that was far more basic. I began to analyze the social, economic and political context as revealing a fundamental alienation of the people that was not going to be resolved by superficial responses. I was sensing that as important as improving health and education and roads and jobs were to the Yemeni people, there was a deeper aspiration that was in their minds and their hearts. While not pretending to know definitely or certainly, I was increasingly convinced that the people of Yemen were seeking a freedom and power they had never before realized. And while I had no idea at the time, it was the first sign of the "Arab Spring" that was about to explode across the Arab world in February 2011.

All of the extremes of a deteriorating human and political condition were unfolding before my eyes in Yemen. Some of this was purely physical. Yemen had a serious shortage of ground water, and Sana'a, its capital, was expected to become the first capital to run out of water and be compelled within fifteen or twenty years to shift to an entirely new location. Yemen was also running out of oil. Never gifted with the enormous resources that one found in Saudi Arabia, oil nevertheless provided most of the financial resources that enabled the government to provide at least minimal services (such as health and education) to its people. In reality, however, even these limited resources were never managed primarily for the benefit of the people.

The reality was that these oil proceeds were used instead to construct what became one of the most flagrant and successful "patronage systems" in the Arab region and indeed the world. It was a system by which the president of the country, Ali Abdullah Saleh, maintained a tight rule for over thirty years. It was a clever, cynical and corrupt system whereby the president bought the loyalty of most of the tribal leaders of the country.

Yemen had always been a tribal society. Tribal leaders, or sheiks, had throughout Yemen's history assumed the lead role in protecting the rights and the needs of the people (at least as they saw them), speaking and fighting for them in any interactions with or demands made on the government. Saleh turned this tradition on its head. By paying a monthly substantial income to each of these sheiks in return for their loyalty to his power position, Saleh separated the traditional leaders from their people. Many of the sheiks were able as a result to buy or construct second homes and offices in Sana'a, visiting their rural home areas only occasionally. They enjoyed the relative high comforts of their new urban lives. Saleh came to believe that he had won their undying allegiance as indeed he had. The villages from which these sheiks originated fell increasingly into neglect, neither receiving government services (which were inadequate at best) nor the voice or help of their leaders who shamefully in some cases even took advantage of the weakened state of their constituents to demand financial payments from them.

In addition to this deterioration of the traditional systems, there was a continuous fracturing of the social and political landscape. Yemen had a long history of struggles for power: to control areas of the country by elites, military authority and foreign colonizers; to maintain separate states as well as to unify the country; and to resolve a continuous tension between traditional and modern systems of governance.

After centuries of rule by a Shiite Zaidi Imamate in Northern Yemen (in parallel with British colonial rule in much of Southern Yemen) revolutionary forces overthrew the royal succession in 1962 and formed the Yemen Arab Republic (YAR) in the North. In the South, after protracted fighting, the National Liberation Front (NLF) forced the British out in 1967, and established an independent Southern Yemen eventually named the People's Democratic Republic of Yemen (PDRY) ruled by the Yemeni Socialist Party (YSP). After continuous power struggles within and between these blocks, including outbreaks of war in 1972 and 1979, the leader of the YAR (the current President of Yemen, Ali Abdullah Saleh) and the leader of the PDRY (Ali Salim Al-Baidh) agreed on a draft unity constitution. The two Yemens became the Republic of Yemen (ROY) in May 1990.

There was to be a period of transition to complete the unification of the two divergent political and economic systems, with the understanding that the best of both systems would be incorporated. A presidential council and unified Parliament were established around three major parties (GPC, YSP and Islaah— the latter made up of various tribal and religious groups). Nevertheless, dissension among Southern politicians over perceived discrimination against the South led to a break up, the establishment of the Democratic Republic of Yemen in the South, and eventually to a civil war in 1994. The North crushed the rebellion and the attempted secession by July of that year. Since 1994, President Ali Abdallah Saleh was elected and reelected (1999 and 2006) and managed to maintain his political power for more than thirty years.

This recent history created a façade of democratic change and participation which denied the reality of one party rule and a corrupt system of governance that perpetuated itself based on the paid loyalty of a disintegrating tribal system I have described. It led to enormous frustration and increasing violence.

Since 2004, Shiite rebels known as "Houthi", based in the northern governorate of Sa'ada bordering Saudi Arabia, engaged six successive times with government forces, the last and most serious starting in August 2009 just before our arrival in the country. This rebellion was in part a response to what the rebels saw as a betrayal of the 1990 unification agreement in which many grievances about unequal treatment, underdevelopment, and deprivation of basic needs were at the core. The rebellion shifted increasingly toward an ideological battle that demanded greater recognition of the Houthi's religious differences from those of the mainstream mostly Sunni majority, with demands for "autonomy" or even secession. The conflict had a serious impact on the local population. Some 300,000 were displaced within Sa'adah and to neighboring governorates. A tenuous ceasefire did not hold and the Houthis eventually took control of the governorate in the wake of the Arab Spring.

In the South, a southern secessionist movement known as "Al-Hirak" (meaning mobility) posed the greatest threat to Yemen's stability. Ever since the suppression of the South's 1994 attempt to secede, and the perception in the South that they were treated unequally, with less opportunities for employment, a loss of regional identify, and a looting of their natural resources (oil), the South became increasingly disillusioned about unification. Again, as with the Houthis in the North, they moved increasingly from a position calling for more "autonomy" to one demanding secession. Although the movement did not break into all out war as in the North, the extent of the rebellion was more widespread and sharply focused on secession. The response of the central government was far from conciliatory. The government's resort to a harsh and violent suppression of demonstrations and protests exacerbated the situation. Only a lack of clear united leadership within the southern movement (including a division of those pressing for autonomy and those demanding secession) enabled the government to "divide and rule" and maintain control of the region.

Beyond these regional conflicts was the increasing threat of disruption and sporadic attacks on mostly government and military facilities by members of the Al-Qaeda in the Arabian Peninsula (AQAP). It was a threat that particularly preoccupied the Western countries, especially the United States, who believed as I have noted that the global center of Al-Qaeda planning and tactics was rapidly shifting to Yemen from places such as Afghanistan. These fears were supported by the attempted airline bombing in December 2009 that I have mentioned, and a subsequent failed attempt to ship explosives in printer cartridges to Jewish centers in the US. The reality, as seen by most Yemenis and by ourselves at the time, was that Al-Qaeda was a minor threat compared to the regional uprisings. Nevertheless, the potential for strengthening AQ's influence and ability to create havoc was evident in the increasingly volatile environment of Yemen.

Seeking Prevention

Once again, I have a purpose in sharing these historic details with you. For it was within my understanding of this background that I found myself unexpectedly presented with an opportunity to address these problems in the context of an international community in Yemen that was keen to prevent further conflict and the prospects of a "failed State".

I was approached by Mercy Corps, a non-governmental relief and development organization that happened to be headquartered in Portland, Oregon, to serve as their interim country representative in Yemen. I assumed this position with considerable enthusiasm and honor as it enabled me to delve far more deeply into the issues of conflict prevention and what role Mercy Corps might play. In the brief period of holding this position, I benefited from discussions and insights of a wide range of government and international actors and on this basis drafted a strategy for action. But it was only after I took on a subsequent role with UNDP as conflict prevention and early recovery coordinator that I began to mature my thoughts and ideas as to what was really happening in Yemen and what hopefully the UN could do about it.

I saw in Yemen what I had seen in so many other countries in which I had worked. An entrenched elite suppressing its people, except for a small entourage who were grossly favored at the expense of everyone else. After only a couple of months in the country, my gut told me already that resentment simmered just beneath the surface of the society. It was something very deeply felt, beyond the usual grievances that were festering. I felt I knew what it was. I believed I knew why this time it could explode as never before. It was a profound sense among the people of a blatant disrespect for them. It was the crude treatment and disregard for them that time had already proven was never intended to end.

My sense of this grew as my direct interaction with Yemenis expanded during these days. I was surprised and taken aback by their boldness. Before coming to Yemen I assumed dissent was not tolerated. Indeed, it was not. But people were incensed. Whether the taxi drivers I met each day on my way to work, or the many professional Yemenis in international agencies, and even some at the middle level of government, all were clear about the injustices taking place and all were insistent that it must end.

I was convinced these frustrations could not be answered by addressing the surface of what was taking place. No attempt to improve government services would distract people from their deep seated belief that government was corrupt and not working in their interests. If anything could be done to prevent a further deterioration of the already wide gap between the people and the elite, it had to address the way the existing governing system worked. Any support for this had to be done with considerable delicacy. Advocating too strongly and too forcefully for change, particularly in any manner that exposed and sharply criticized the existing system, was doomed to failure no matter who and how many may agree. A non-confrontational approach working to change the system from within would offer the best chance for success.

Since my days in Malawi, "good governance" had become even more legitimized as an approach within the UN. So long as it was cast in non-confrontational language and programs ("enhancing local governance" or "administrative reforms"), it was not seen as previously as an attempt to impose outside "Western values." But there was nevertheless considerable sensitivity to these initiatives if the situation involved any existing conflict between the elite and dissident elements within the society. This was clearly the case in Yemen. Even the mention of conflict and its prevention were unwelcomed.

Social Cohesion

The approach we adopted instead we called "social cohesion". It was a rather ambiguous wording that nevertheless conveyed the core purpose of what we were after: *bringing together in a common effort of positive change people and institutions that might otherwise confront each other and turn to violence.* The idea was quite simple: address the core resentment of the people in how they were treated by government and replace it with an entirely new approach of government to support peoples' direct role and decision making in their development. It was a simple matter of putting local villagers in charge of what they could best do for themselves to change their lives for the better.

In parallel, we saw the importance of linking this "peoples' empowerment" process with a new way of governing locally. We firmly believed there was an opportunity and critical role for the government to reform itself in the way it governed, starting at the local level and hopefully working its way up to the top. Poor people could do a lot for themselves if given the opportunity. But dire poverty held a firm grip. Government and its resources could make a significant difference if its energies and resources were focused on working with and supporting what the people wanted to do.

The answer lay in building a "partnership" of the people and their government. And into this mix, we added some "stimulus" to get the engine of this partnership started by establishing a "community development fund" that would finance small projects defined and carried out locally.

It was a formula which held enormous promise. It addressed the underlying alienation and animosity and offered practical steps to change the power structure and to vitalize the dormant local opportunities. It was a genuine people-centered and bottom-up approach. If tested and shown to be effective on a small scale, as we intended, and then taken to a much wider national scale, such a local partnership approach combined with broader institutional and economic reforms could make a huge contribution to building democracy.

Change from the Streets

Of course such a challenge would require time to get on its feet, to demonstrate its effectiveness, to build widespread credibility, to garner substantial resources and to position itself at the center of a new Yemen. In truth, the effort moved barely beyond the documents we had written. While plans and resources were coming into place to activate its goals and aspirations, events overtook the hopes raised.

Frustration had grown far too intense to allow the patience for such a process. The overturn of governments in Tunisia and Egypt were taking place at the very time our plans were crystallizing. They set in place a new model of change. A model that did not countenance delay. It was a call from the streets and from the villages for immediate action. It was real and it was powerful. It was from the people.

History has confirmed over and over that people will contain their suffering and indignity only to a certain point. Eventually, in different ways and by different means, the demand for decency becomes overwhelming. This proved true in Yemen.

Building It In

Yet it is also true that the demand for decency is seldom sustained by public outrage alone. It needs a strong and sturdy vehicle to carry it forward, to sustain it. Creating a society based on core values of decency is a very long and difficult journey. But while human beings have failed to perfect any sure ways of protecting human decency at the core of their societies, I do believe that people-driven and people-centered democracy, however imperfectly practiced, comes as close as we have been able to create an environment in which decency can flourish at that core.

Establishing democratic institutions and practices alone do not guarantee the "rule of decency" in any society. Decency has to be grounded in the fundamental attitudes, values and interactions of a people—as we eventually understood in Bangladesh. Decency embodies universal rights and justice coveted and shared by all human beings. Democratic institutions bring these values into a system of governing which can just as easily lose them if they are not constantly promoted, protected and practiced. That is because these values inevitably come up against the counter values of greed and injustice practiced by elites. So democracy based on decency is never easily achieved or sustained. It takes constant and concerted effort to build it in and to keep it there.

It is for these reasons I believe the transformation of power in any society to incorporate the rights and roles of all people, rich and poor, to play an equal part in determining the future of their society is essential to building a people-centered democracy critical to rooting decency in that democracy. Truly engaging the people of Yemen in the process of democracy based on fair and just treatment of each other will over time be the real test of their revolution. So there remains an urgent need to follow the "Arab Spring" in Yemen and elsewhere with the hard work of building decency into their emerging democracies. Indeed, building decency into how we govern and how we live has the power to unite all of us. Truly we are one in how we cherish and realize this ideal.

Chapter 20
Visions For Action

The Coming Together and Power of Rich and Poor

Envisioning the Future

So what have we learned from the journey we have now taken together? The picture is clearly a mixed one. We have witnessed impressive efforts to bring change to a world sharply divided between rich and poor. We have seen results, mostly locally achieved, including changes in peoples' greater access to opportunities, albeit usually on a limited scale. If we step back from our journey, we are encouraged to have seen many courageous people and some enlightened leaders persistent in their pursuit of more just societies. Yet overall, we may conclude that what has long divided the powerful and the powerless remains deeply entrenched.

What should we conclude? That fundamental change in our societies is unattainable, that greed and power is overwhelming and that beyond token changes we can expect very little from our efforts to create a more just world?

I have concluded that this need not be the case. That in fact there is much that we have learned to lead us to believe that people are capable of realizing elemental change. That we have an historic opportunity to rise above what may have been our greatest impediment, our limited vision of what is possible. We have underestimated ourselves. We have lost faith in (or never fully understood?) our intrinsic values and strengths and what we are still capable of if we bring these now into play. The fact that so much has not worked only should alert us that we need to change our course. That we need to explore other paths untried.

I want to share a vision of what is still possible, a vision that will require us to think and act differently, a vision that is undoubtedly unexpected but that I am convinced holds enormous promise for changing our world.

Decency: Definitions and Models

Let me begin with our core values. Again, based on our journey, I propose that decency stands out (even if too often in its absence) as a unique and powerful force for good. I have shared with you all manners in which decency is frustrated by human failings. Our challenge in this early stage of our twenty-first century is whether and how we can overcome these failings sufficiently to enable decency to realize a more just world. I am sure that we can, but I am equally convinced that we can do so only by joining together with common purpose and practical action.

I want to share for your consideration, a course of action that is based on the principles and commitments to decency that we foreshadowed as we began our journey together and that I hope we deepened and enriched along the way.

Let me begin by retracing what I trust we have learned about the basic forces working for and against decency. Let me first try to define decency itself. Then let us consider whether decency can be "tapped and organized" for the betterment of those most in need.

Decency is defined in the *Oxford dictionary* as "correct and tasteful standards of behavior as generally accepted". True, as far as it goes. The *Encarta dictionary* refers to it as "behavior or an attitude that conforms to the commonly accepted standards of what is right and respectable". *Wiktionary* defines decency as the "quality of being decent" and in turn defines "decent" as being "kind". That seems closer, but it still does not convey the full dimensions and power of what I believe it means. The online *Merriam Webster* dictionary goes further. It defines decency as "the quality or state of being decent", and again defines decent as "marked by moral integrity, kindness and goodwill". It lists as synonyms: "good, ethical, honest, just, moral, right-minded, straight, true, upright and virtuous". This is much closer to what I have in mind.

Decency is one of those fundamental human qualities that are not as easily defined as much as they are readily understood when seen and experienced, and mostly when felt in the heart. I believe that at the core of its power to change our lives, decency is an elemental human yearning, indeed an innate moral anchor, to treat each other as we would want to be treated, no matter how often we fail to do so. I also believe decency is underpinned by a common and deep sense of justice and fair play. All simple rules to live by. And I believe it is one that is equally possible across the broad spectrum of the poor and the powerful.

It was a poor custodian of the Manzanares town hall, Don Pedro, who reminded me in the face of my own cultural transgressions of the importance of adhering to a simple code of respect and decency toward others. It was an old farmer in a poor village outside of Lilongwe, whose deep set eyes stared back at me as I departed, who without a word reminded me that someone ought to have the decency to help his people fight their poverty instead of just visiting them to see what it looked like. It was a poor man on the streets of Sana'a who in returning my lost money, reminded me of the importance of honesty and decency even in disregard of his own desperate needs. It was a man of high position at the University of California who felt compelled that a powerful institution must reach out and serve the less advantaged. It was the Indian and

Chinese political leadership and bureaucracy, whatever their shortcomings, which placed and pursued a reduction of poverty as the highest priority of their country.

The Challenge

But if decency exists within everyone why has the world indeed become so divided—between the rich and the poor, between the powerful and the powerless, between the elite and the rest? Why have we too often been unable or unwilling to adhere to standards of decent behavior and equality of opportunity for all so that many more can enjoy a decent life? Why instead are people so consistently suppressed by the same small privileged elites that we have seen across all societies in our journey? Must we still conclude that with few exceptions, once the material benefits of greed, wealth and power are ingrained, they are seldom relinquished or shared, almost always to the detriment of everyone else?

I have shared many examples of this selfishness. It is unlikely we will ever fully understand the origins of these behaviors. Nor probably can we expect to rid of them. In recognizing these failings, humility must ever temper our search for decency. Yet we are still able to go beyond these human disappointments to commit ourselves to better the life of those left behind. It is a matter of not allowing an unattainable perfection to become the worst enemy of our noblest spirit.

What we can ask, and what we need to work toward, is how we can realistically begin step by step to break through the cycle of selfishness and the human distress it causes. However well we may hope eventually to perfect our human condition, our main responsibility in the meantime is to purposefully and actively improve it as best we can. In effect, we need to soldier through our imperfections to points along a path of change in which we strike a continually better balanced and more just life in our society. A balance in which decency towards others opens the door of opportunity for those so far deprived of it. Many of the experiences we have seen from diverse countries and cultures should encourage us that once basic decency opens opportunity, people do respond positively and actively to realize its benefits. Moreover, we should also see that elites are no less immune to the power of decency once we find ways to engage them, and certainly once they see it in their own self interest.

Just to be clear, this is not about creating utopia. I am not holding up decency as a path for achieving the impossible. We are all complex beings, and so are our societies. We are full of contradictions and imperfections. Nowhere was this better and earlier imprinted on my mind than the example of my parents. They were among the most decent people I have ever known. Yet they were incapable of expressing anything other than disdain for each other. They created a world of misery for themselves and for my sister and me. At the same time, they separately filled us with immense love and caring. They showed us the importance of doing the same for others. And certainly in my own case, whenever I reflect back on my efforts to live by decency, I am constantly reminded, as I suppose many of us are, of so many disappointments and shortfalls in honoring those expectations.

I have seen so much of these same contradictions across every society. I have shared with you the highest respect I hold for the social values of the people across many countries juxtaposed against their inexplicable treatment of minorities. I am reminded of the great social advances in opportunity, racial equality, and justice realized in America contrasted with the outright misery created by many of its domestic and foreign policies that continue to support greed and the well being of a few. But in spite of these failures, and this seemingly inevitable mix of good and evil, I believe the role and possibilities of decency are undiminished.

Our Options

But how do we bring decency into play? How do we bring about the change and the better balance we are looking for? How do we demonstrate its power to alter the way we live? How do we move beyond our ideals and high pronouncements to meaningful deeds that transform our lives and our world?

There are some options:

Drift

Our first option is the one we seem to have already resigned ourselves to: let the evolutionary process take its course to the point where the privileged finally begin to see that their advantages can and do work against them. Assuming they recognize this before some form of violence erupts, it becomes in their own narrow self interest to correct the imbalance by moving toward the more balanced approach—a more level playing field that provides the under-advantaged with more opportunity. There is some hope this process is taking place. A hope that even without a specific plan of action, our drift is creating greater awareness and scrutiny of injustices in our societies and a growing concern to do something about it.

However, whether and how long it will take for such a process to culminate in greater opportunity and ultimate justice is unclear. Or whether it will instead regress, as the privileged find new clever ways to retain their power and advantage without significant reforms favoring the powerless. These remain open and worrying questions. Certainly for those who continue to suffer under the current divide, it does not appear to be a satisfying option.

Non-Violent Activism

Another option is non-violent activism. History is a powerful witness to the successes of this approach, albeit with perhaps less frequency than we might have hoped.

Mahatma Gandhi

Probably, the most inspiring example of recent times was Mahatma Gandhi's campaign to end British Rule. It was a long arduous battle by a master who came by his skills through an unrelenting determination to test the practical achievability of his core convictions. Those convictions embraced his quest for the truth (*satya*) of human existence by which I understood he sought the purest meaning, purpose, and practice of life. A concept that included all the essentials of human goodness, among them: decency, compassion, caring, courage and sacrifice, equality, and justice. It was his life-long striving to achieve these manifestations of truth that Gandhi turned into a movement of an "adherence to truth" (*satyagraha*). That truth went far beyond the goal of achieving the independence of India. And this is why Gandhi is for me a hero in a tiny pantheon (none holding that position by reason of their perfection) that includes Abraham Lincoln, FDR, Martin Luther King, Nelson Mandela, and just a few others. It was a truth by which he sought an inner freedom of people from their poverty, their caste, their gender biases, their religious prejudices, and the denial of their basic inalienable rights.

Whatever he was able to realize in these pursuits, he did so on the basis of practical techniques of non-violent resistance and civil disobedience. Gandhi took a quarter of a century (1890-1915) in a far distant South Africa to hone his understanding and to test his theories and techniques, sometimes with brutal physical consequences to himself, before he applied them in his own country. On his return to India, he began to organize peasants, farmers and urban laborers to protest unfair land taxes and marketing practices. He headed nation-wide campaigns to end poverty and to fight for equal rights for women. His methods of "non-cooperation" included as part of his crusade for the independence of India, his famous "Salt March" in which tens of thousands of rural and urban people, rich and poor, journeyed with him on foot over many weeks and hundreds of miles to collect salt rather than pay an unjust tax to the British for it.

But it was always a difficult and long struggle. Jailing and prolonged imprisonments were inevitable and even purposefully sought and endured (the kind of sacrifice he considered essential to bringing social change).

In my mind Gandhi's greatness was also due to his human fallibilities. What surprised and impressed me was that Gandhi was able to achieve so much in spite of his many failings, mistakes and misjudgments. The inconsistency, for example, of his non-violent beliefs to his support for recruiting Indian soldiers to fight in World War I. The fact that Gandhi achieved his ends only through painful disappointments. His theme of transcending long implanted human barriers and his efforts to bring people together for the common good—for which I admire him most—often failed. His deep commitment to overcoming caste and the eradication of "untouchability", and his attempt to cross the divide between Hindus and Muslims, were examples of his moral rectitude but equally his political naiveté that led to historic setbacks. This was no better exemplified than in his greatest disappointment, against which he fought so long and unsuccessfully—the failure to prevent the partition and separation of Hindu India and Muslim Pakistan.

It is these failings and disappointments that I believe give hope to the rest of us with so much less fortitude in our convictions. His greatest commitment in spite of all the adversities was his steadfast belief and faith in the power of peaceful change. A belief in the power of staying on the right side of human goodness in demanding that very goodness from others. It was the respect and demand for human decency that gave Gandhi's non-violent resistance its power, a power uniquely able to overcome the indignities and violence of those in power.

Gandhi's non-violent principles and practices remain in many respects and up to this day the most successful model of peaceful resistance in the cause of social justice. And beyond these causes, Gandhi's historic importance in my view is in having demonstrated the holistic possibility of transforming society through moral force. Demonstrating the vision, courage and conviction it would take under any circumstances to overcome power and injustice. Not through temporary measures but on the basis of human decency practiced in the hearts and minds of people through their respect and caring for each other. It is these core moral principles and transformational goals that have and continue to inspire others to seek and pursue changes of immense human significance through non-violence.

Martin Luther King

One such disciple and practitioner of non-violent activism was Martin Luther King, Jr. He admired Gandhi enormously, perhaps mainly for his political acumen and methods—'Christ gave us the goals and Mahatma Gandhi the tactics.' With the help of the Quaker organization American Friends Service Committee, King visited India in 1959 to learn more directly of the life and political philosophy of Gandhi, concluding at the end of the visit that 'I am more convinced than ever before that the method of nonviolent resistance is the most potent weapon available to oppressed people in their struggle for justice and human dignity.' King's gigantic mark on American history and indirectly on the cause of social justice around the world was in leading (since the mid 1950s until his assassination in 1968) America's non-violent civil rights movement that ended legal segregation and the infamous Jim Crow laws of the South for African Americans. The impact of his actions and achievements extended to the enactment of the Civil Rights Act of 1964 desegregating all public accommodations and outlawing discrimination in public facilities.

None of this was achieved by chance or by accident. It was the result of systematic and unrelenting application of non-violent philosophy, tactics, and power. It consisted of planned, strategized and organized non-violent methods of marches, rallies, speeches, boycotts, sit-ins, and the peaceful confrontation and public protest of authorities' enforcement of discriminatory practices. It was classic Gandhian activism. And it was highly effective.

From its earliest stages, it was also pragmatic and politically astute. The initiating tactic was the Montgomery Bus Boycott of 1955. It grew out of a strong and long held disgust over the expectation and practice of "negroes" yielding their seats to whites, finding their own seats at the back of a bus if available. The challenge was how to contest this issue in the public arena in a dramatic, non-violent, and effective way.

The story is well known to most Americans. But little known is the fact that Rosa Parks, who the media cast as a middle-aged spinster too tired to give up her seat, was trained in non-violent activism and did what she did with premeditation and clear purpose. Her peaceful non-cooperation and subsequent arrest provided the perfect circumstance that enabled a ready response by the local NAACP chapter, which immediately appointed a prepared Martin Luther King to assume leadership of a year-long boycott of the bus system by all African Americans in Montgomery. The result was an unprecedented retreat of the city council and elimination of the law segregating public transport. Similarly, a decade later and this time with national impact, an organized civil rights march in Selma, Alabama, aroused national outrage to police brutality, creating wide public support that led to the Voting Rights Act of 1965.

But once again these successes did not come easily. They required enormous courage and fortitude. They were purposefully carried out in spite of the known risks of violent backlash, police brutality and imprisonment. It was not for the faint of heart. During the Montgomery Boycott, African Americans were regularly attacked, as were the homes of Dr. King and the local NAACP leader, E.D. Nixon. Later, African American students conducting lunch counter "sit ins" (which successfully ended segregation at lunch counters across much of the South) were both verbally and physically abused. Dogs, tear gas and police nightsticks battered demonstrators in Birmingham, Alabama, and hospitalized many during the subsequent "Bloody Sunday" march crossing the bridge in Selma. These violent responses gave the movement a worldwide profile it probably would never have achieved. But none of this would have been achieved without the remarkable courage of those who led and followed the movement.

Yet what impressed me most about Martin Luther King Jr. was not just his courage and leadership in advancing civil rights reform. What impressed me most, as I had admired most about Gandhi, was his vision and commitment to broad fundamental reform of society that went beyond specific injustices to a much wider concern about the values by which society lives. He saw discriminatory practice resulting not only in racial segregation but equally in the spread of poverty and in the placing of African Americans disproportionately in harm's way during the Vietnam War. His campaigns focused increasingly on these broader injustices which he saw impacting not only blacks but other poor Americans. He despised these injustices for the increasingly callous values they reflected in American society.

I have enormous respect for non-violent activism. Enormous admiration for what Gandhi and Martin Luther King were able to achieve through the tactics of such activism. The continuing relevance and importance of these methods impressed me personally in April 2012. It was at a time shortly after my return to Portland from a UN assignment in New York where I took the opportunity to visit the "Occupy Wall Street" camp in Zuccotti Park in Lower Manhattan. Back in Portland, I volunteered to host a neighborhood 99% spring training (later shifted to another venue due to a shortage of trainers) aimed at revitalizing the occupy movement and to further protest the unjust practices of the 1% elite who continued to "work the system" (financially and politically) solely to their benefit. Through this training, I discovered a deep and passionate commitment of America's young and old alike to the ideals and the practices of non-violence. I learned that many in America have renewed their belief in non-violent direct action as the only realistic path to fundamental social change. It gave me reason to reflect on how these same tactics have been successfully applied in other countries, as for example across Eastern Europe to dismantle communism, and across the Middle East of the Arab Spring to bring down dictatorship. It led me to understand that non-violence remains highly relevant to the twenty-first century.

Third Alternative: Coming Together of Rich and Poor

But beyond these above two options of "drift" and inaction, and of "non-violent activism", I believe there is a third alternative. It is an alternative that can benefit from both of the previous options, but that can also create a new path to change. It is not meant to replace the continued importance of direct non-violent action. In fact it retains non-violence at its core. But it applies a very different approach and tactics.

This alternative is based on the assumption that the *drift* option has already served an important purpose. It has brought us to a threshold of disgust and intolerance for our increasingly divided societies. It has enabled us to go beyond this increased awareness to a new commitment to do something about it. Similarly, the contributions and achievements of non-violent activism are clear.

The third alternative is based, however, on the assumption that non-violent activism uses, and certainly is perceived to use, mainly confrontational tactics to raise awareness and motivate action. While these remain critically important tools of change, the third alternative proposes that they do not preempt other tactics

The purpose and dynamic of this third alternative is simple: *to bring people across what divides them and to empower them to work together within an all-inclusive movement for fundamental change*. A movement that probably in many instances *for the first time* enables this *crossing over* between powerless and powerful, rich and poor, to engage on *common ground*. Its aim is to:

- activate local opportunities for those most in need
- catalyze profound society-wide reforms
- institutionalize peoples' democracy

Activating the Third Alternative

There is no one set way to introduce and implement this alternative approach. It will depend on each unique situation. But there are certain broad guidelines and measures that may prove useful in initiating this approach.

The overall process is simple:

- It begins with bringing rich and poor together in their local communities.
- It organizes people to initiate local, small, achievable actions that improve lives.
- It builds on this experience to pursue deeper reforms across the wider society
- Ultimately it empowers rich and poor to reform political systems to work for the common good

The process is pursued at two levels: it works locally to create dialogue, build confidence, and demonstrate local action and results; and on this basis and in parallel, it initiates, organizes, activates and institutionalizes people-driven social reforms. Let us identify some of the specific steps that could be undertaken at each of these levels of implementation of the Third Alternative, depending and adjusting in every case on each unique context:

Level One: Working Local

The Third Alternative is a people-driven and bottom up process of change:

Bringing Rich and Poor Together

The first order of business is to initiate contact and communication between rich and poor in or across local communities. The purpose is to enable them, usually for the first time, to get to know each other. It is a chance to explore their respective as well as their common interests and needs. It is an opportunity to discuss the values they hold in common about coming together and helping each other. It is an opportunity to examine whether there are reasons and possibilities for them to work together for their separate and their mutual benefit. It is an opportunity to identify what they could do together and why they should do it. It is an opportunity to do what heretofore appeared unlikely if not impossible.

This initial opening of relations between rich and poor is critically important. Perceptions of each other are too often based on misconceptions and negative stereotypes (and if some of these are true, they should not be reasons to keep them apart). While cultural differences between them are sometimes real, they are also often exaggerated. They blind out common interests and beliefs, present or potential. There is a lot of the "common ground" that is never entered. Opportunities never realized.

Face-to-face communications and understanding between rich and poor at this early stage will enable positive insights and empathy toward each other to take hold. It will begin to build a culture of respect and decency toward each other on the basis of which positive action is possible.

Facilitating the Cross Over

Coming together of rich and poor is unlikely to be spontaneous or easy. It will require someone to facilitate it. Who will do this? What we are likely to need is a corps of local facilitators to assist the crossing over to take place and to keep it on track to achieve results. There are many examples we have seen in our journey that demonstrate a willingness of self-motivated individuals to take on these roles. There are community people who already have some vision of social change. It is a matter of first sharing the vision of rich and poor coming together with an open-minded core on both sides despite any skepticism they may hold in common about such an approach. So once the idea of a peoples' movement of rich and poor is raised, some are likely to step forward to commit themselves to help make it happen. Beyond them, there will certainly be a need to bring others into these roles. This can be promoted and organized either by experienced local organizations keen to be a part of such a movement, or by an umbrella organization such as a "managed reform facility" that I will later describe, or a combination of both.

Either way, the core task will be to recruit and train up the corps of facilitators, both those with some experience and those without. It is a matter of imparting practical skills in how to cross over and how to sustain the efforts. A matter of sharing quite simple techniques and building the confidence to use them; techniques and skills we have already seen on our journey:

showing respect
projecting a clear purpose and pleasant manner
building trust
initiating contact and dialogue
practicing humility, patience and empathy
empowering all sides equally and jointly
organizing for joint action

"On the job" training can take place separately on each side of the dividing line as well as across the line. In this way it can work toward an early piloting of crossing over between rich and poor, sharing and learning from each other.

Organizing Action

The challenge of initiating a peoples' movement of rich and poor does not end of course with their commitment to common goals and good intentions. Crossing over must lead to action, and that requires sound organization.

There is a range of organizing models that each local community or area can choose from: linking up with an experienced existing community organization; starting up a new voluntary organization or group; retaining within either of these models a paid dedicated manager and core staff or advisers; and other models. Much will depend on the resources and time available in each local community, and the support they receive from outside it.

The uniqueness and importance of any local initiative will be that it was done by crossing the divide between rich and poor, getting something practical started, and achieving some definite results.

Starting small and building up on success will usually work best. There is no need for rich and poor to agree on everything. Better to find one or two issues they both are concerned about. Identifying and focusing sharply on one common local need and a set of actions to address it raises the chances for early success. Gradually agreeing on other issues and taking on other small and achievable projects to open more opportunities can follow.

In this process, it is critical that neither side is overwhelmed or made dependent on the other, or conversely that only one is benefitting. The initial risk here is on the side of the poor. While the process of working together should instill a confidence among the poor to forge a continuing partnership with the advantaged, that partnership should never replace the ultimate responsibility of the poor to make sure new opportunities work for themselves, to take charge of their own destinies. At the same time, the rich need to be sure that what they are doing is not misunderstood by themselves or others as charity. This will not be sustainable. They need to define either some self-interest in the joint effort, or otherwise some common good that they believe will enrich their community.

As these locally organized efforts of rich and poor begin to spread and show results, they will gain increased public profile and credibility as a united power base that will attract others to their cause. And on this basis, rich and poor will establish a power platform for broader and more fundamental reform across the entire society. Let us now turn to this latter challenge.

Level Two: Society-Wide Reform

Beyond "Working Local", there is a need simultaneously for a peoples' movement of rich and poor to work together on a broader front of social reform.

Local small initiatives and projects that open greater opportunities for a few are important, but they are simply not enough. In the end, change will be most meaningful and lasting in any society only if it leads to core fundamental reforms that truly transform what ails the heart of any society.

Traditional political systems have failed to achieve these reforms. Too many of these systems, even the most seemingly democratic, are corrupted for the purpose of protecting and sustaining privilege. There remain far too many loopholes, weaknesses and distortions in democracy as practiced that preempt and exclude decency, equal opportunity, and justice. Coming together of rich and poor at local level for their common good will provide new models for local action and change, but they alone are unlikely to change the overriding bias of the political systems that work mainly in the interest of the privileged.

In this sense, democracy itself is in dire need of reform. A reform of democracy based on principles of decency that truly work in the interest of its entire people not just a few.

How realistic is this?

Lessons from the Past

What have we seen and learned about social reforms and models of democracy based on decency from the country experiences I have shared with you on our journey? The lessons are highly varied to be sure, but there is a wide range of experience, including much that has fallen short, that gives us insights into what challenges lie ahead:

In **America**, there has been a sudden and impressive advance in recognizing the problem of a growing social divide. The "Occupy" movement helped bring about a new awareness otherwise shockingly hidden in self-deception for so many years. It influenced the language and issues of political debate including a call for basic fairness and decency. But it fell short in actually organizing and gaining a new power to activate reform.

The case of **Liberia** seems the most extreme example of an utter failure to reform society before it was too late. In that case, the divide between the elite Americo-Liberians and the indigenous people was not only wide, it was never crossed in spite of what may have been a strong potential to do so. Americo-Liberians were well educated and sophisticated and were quite capable of seeing what was coming after so many years of their self-imposed domination. Yet there was no reaching out to initiate dialogue and understanding. There was no thought of coming together to embed principles of decency and spread opportunities on this basis. Life was too good on their side and there was seemingly no compelling reason to risk a sharing of this least it result in less of the privilege they enjoyed. They did not recognize, or chose to ignore, the enormous frustration and anger of the majority. What may have been avoidable became inevitable; an explosion of the discriminated, the poor, and the oppressed. The ultimate irony was that the eventual path of change was not undertaken in the interest of freeing the people, but to further suppress them. It was a deceit and a betrayal led by an Americo-Liberian (Charles Taylor) who sought personal gain, control and power, nothing else. It is the best example of how a society can be fundamentally damaged if enlightened people-driven democratic reform is not undertaken before the threshold of crisis is crossed.

Similar was the case of **Kosovo**. Literally centuries of religious and culturally based hatred and discrimination kept people apart in the absence of any tolerant and progressive leadership to cross these barriers. It was a failure to lay a solid foundation for people-centered governance committed to equality and justice. Outside efforts to negotiate and pressure for change were futile. Selfish interests prevailed. War was inevitable.

Malawi was a more hopeful model. Again, there was no systematic approach to change. It came about unexpectedly through a public communication about injustices from church leaders. There was no attempt to engage the people to lead a movement for change. But there was a political response, led by lawyers and other professionals, resulting in new political leaders and parties to press for change. The process was peaceful. It gained the confidence and the support of the international community. It led to political change that resulted in the ousting of dictatorship and the establishment of democratic institutions. Development for the people improved as for example through the adoption of universal free primary education. But the base for fundamental reform was not strong. People were never encouraged or enabled to come together across the divide of deep poverty and power. Instead, power was retained by a new elite and corruption inevitably returned. Poverty increased. The divide remained. The opportunity for people to determine and change their own lives never materialized.

Thailand's reform process was impressive. By no means a full success, it brought peoples' grievances out into the public arena. It directly addressed the divide between rural poor and urban elites. It gradually built up a broad participation in a locally based national movement of development action for increasing peoples' economic opportunities. It organized peoples' political demands for greater people-centered democracy. It led to a generally peaceful change in government leadership considered far more sympathetic and favorable to the interests of the poor and disenfranchised. But while it did all of this, it did not realize a truly broad-based consensus for reforming its democracy. It achieved its results mainly through political parties and confrontational tactics, some violent, rather than through a full and open coming together and consensus of rich and poor. The achievements remain impressive, but whether deep rooted sustainable social reform will result is yet to be seen.

Bangladesh was personally the most rewarding attempt I associated with to precipitate fundamental reform. It dramatically opened up a presumed incompetence of the poor and revealed their enormous capacity at least on a small scale to develop themselves. It organized a strong network of village people whose achievements brought them confidence to pressure political leaders and government to support their efforts. It precipitated the engagement of entrepreneurs and won the financial support of the international community to continue these efforts. But it did not lead to core governance reforms. It did not honor the peace accord that would empower the people. It did not stop the blatant discrimination. It did not prevent continuing violence. It did not bring reform based on a crossing over and consensus, even minimal, of those politically and culturally entrenched on each side.

What we have seen in the case of **Yemen, Egypt and other countries of the Arab Spring**, the people mobilized spontaneously in a state of crisis to press for deep political and social change. It was a reaction to years of oppression. It was a sudden and unplanned rebellion. It was greatly facilitated by social media that enabled a rapid and pervasive spread of its message of reform based on fair play and decency. But it was also devoid of many of the preparatory steps, including a failure to organize local action, critical to laying a foundation for lasting reform. The ultimate impact and sustainability of these uprisings is still to be determined.

What we have observed is that while some of these diverse attempts to bring about social reform made impressive gains, few if any pursued their goals on the basis of fundamental governance reform to establish a more direct peoples' democracy.

The Unexpected Power of Rich and Poor

What we have learned is that social change seldom occurs in the absence of the power to make it happen. So while bringing rich and poor together is essential, the critical difference will be in enabling them to transform their unity into a new kind of power—a power of rich and poor committed to the common good. This is something few of us have heretofore thought possible, or have dared to imagine. It is truly an unexpected power. In effect, it is a bottom up commitment of both poor and rich to creating a people-driven democracy.

So our vision is one of creating a peoples' democracy far different from the kind of democracy that most societies practice today. It is about building a peaceful, democratic revolution that has enormous potential to achieve results for people so far unattainable.

But let me again address the overriding question about the reality of rich and poor joining such a movement. The conviction of this is based on two fundamental premises. The first is that as I have already noted decency resides in all of us, no matter how seldom we are perceived by others to practice it for the good of all. It has taken me fifty and more years, in the face of so much I have seen to the contrary, to be convinced of this but convinced I am. Decency runs deep throughout all of humanity whatever the transgressions of some who betray it.

The "rich" we are talking about are spread across a very broad membership. It certainly is not limited to the exceedingly greedy, power-obsessed elites that we have commonly witnessed in our journey. In the context we have in mind, the rich are better understood as "advantaged", having realized opportunities that have given them social and economic gains over those left behind. Many are often well educated. They are found across many lines of work and society, in enterprise, professions, public service, technical fields, small business, landed farmers, teachers, local leaders, and many more. They are powerful in their many competencies critical to change. They are capable of great empathy for those not as fortunate. And they include of course the corporate wealthy and politically and institutionally powerful. Among them there is more often than we have given credit a strong ethical core, a sense of moral principles and a latent untapped sense of social responsibility.

While not all will respond immediately to a call to meet with the poor, there are many of good will who when faced with a credible possibility of such an unforeseen partnership will join. A key to their willingness will undoubtedly be influenced by how they are approached, which in turn depends on the skills of those facilitating the process to convey genuine respect, a clear sense of purpose, and a solid understanding of what is likely to tap their interests and motivations.

Similarly, on the side of the "poor", images of their helplessness, their lack of capacities, and their basic unwillingness to respond to opportunities, all are long disproven by my own experiences and those of many others. In approaching the poor with the same respect and positive views of their potentially immense contributions, the possibility to bring them together with the rich is far greater than we have ever dreamed possible.

So how do we get there?

Empowering a Peoples' Movement

The aim is not to change existing political structures per se, though this may be an eventual consequence. The aim is to build the power of people, rich and poor together, as an added force within our political systems, to influence and change what our political systems do.

I am reminded of how the meaning and practice of "development work" in which I engaged over many years changed directions dramatically. It changed out of necessity. There was a growing recognition among many including myself that micro improvements in peoples' lives through increased skills, productivity, incomes, and other interventions, did not go to the heart of why people remained poor. The real problem was quite different. The root problem was the lack of power. The power of people to influence and control their own lives. The power to join together among themselves and with others to determine what should be done to improve their lives. The power to be at the center of doing whatever needed to be done. The power to set society's priorities, to allocate resources, and to act. It was less a matter of whether to continue to pursue traditional "development" and more a matter of recognizing the need to underpin this with a "new governance" of, for and by the people.

These lessons from development are equally applicable to our broader goal of achieving societal reforms by empowering rich and poor to play a direct role in realizing these ends.

Some will question whether this approach can be effective without first achieving political power inside the existing political systems. The fact is that this approach will create a profound new power base of rich and poor, almost certainly for the first time, that will begin to counterbalance those in power. Such power of people from all walks of life working together is enormous, even as the process takes time to build up. History has shown us this. Great social change has most often come about in this fashion, with people united around core concerns deeply held. Such was the case in Gandhi's fight for the freedom of India and Martin Luther King's era of civil rights. Such will be the case in our times and societies if we are united in what we must no longer allow to divide us. If we understand this power, if we are unwavering in our commitment and our patience and astuteness to use it for change, our political institutions will honor and respond (no matter how much they may initially resist and delay) to this new unprecedented force of rich and poor.

Managing Reform

I am convinced from past experience that none of the above is likely to happen or to succeed unless there is a dedicated management of such a peoples' movement. The human factor remains too critical to the difficult process of reform to leave the effort to chance. A purposefully organized and structured "managed reform facility" (or by whatever title one chooses to use) can best ensure the sustained human communications, interactions, negotiations, compromises, and follow up support required. The managed facility or organization could be positioned at national and/or regional centers depending on what makes sense in each situation.

However, there are some general principles that seem important to maintaining the integrity of a managed facility:

The facility should be built and constituted over time as an alliance of the local citizen initiatives (started up at the "Working Local" level) that it is representing and not as an independent body detached from local experiences, competencies, and commitments.

Those managing the facility and reform process should in large part rotate and come up from and return to their local movements, thereby generating fresh perspectives and commitments and avoiding a "bureaucratizing" of the movement.

Financing should not come from any political parties or interest groups, and to the greatest extent, should emanate from public support. Support from government would be acceptable if untied and transparently channeled preferably through a dedicated fund established for this purpose.

Any such umbrella body should assume responsibility to facilitate the following actions:

Support to Local Initiatives:

The facility will introduce the concept of a local peoples' movement and support local initiatives to bring rich and poor together, especially to motivate local people to get involved, to provide training to local facilitators in 'cross over' techniques and follow up, and to provide financial and other support to the local organizations as appropriate.

Advocacy:

The main task in this regard is to share what has been achieved at the local level and to advocate on this basis for the opportunity of a wider reform process. The work of advocacy is to gain the awareness and support of the general public, but also to take on the challenge of changing attitudes and behaviors of those in power, bringing them into the effort as partners, winning them over as allies and champions.

Establishing an "Advocacy Group" for the movement, consisting of rich and poor who have worked successfully at local level, may often be a practical starting point for achieving initial outreach to the public and the power systems.

Experimentation:

The call to reform democracy is not new. There is a long history and a more recent active interest in exploring new and "more democratic" systems and practices. A "managed reform facility" should take on the role of reviewing and learning from these past experiments, promoting and initiating those that appear

361

to have a place in building a movement of rich and poor and an eventual peoples' democracy.

This could include an examination and promotion of experiments in more "direct democracy" that break through the monopoly of "representative democracy" by empowering rich and poor to have a more direct role in deciding on social reforms. This may include further experimentation with voting on change through "referenda" with initiatives organized and carefully vetted directly by them. It could also include a close scrutiny of the role of social media (e.g. Facebook, Twitter, etc.) to find their most effective use as "tools" of change.

And importantly, the managed reform facility could test and introduce new institutional entities (e.g. public advisory councils, citizen boards, shared-culture groups, community action organizations as above, and peoples' reform coalitions as below) into political processes to formalize the direct roles, responsibilities and authority of rich and poor in a peoples' democracy.

Peoples' Coalitions of Rich and Poor to Initiate Reform:

A further major task of a managed reform organization will be to build and support coalitions of rich and poor that focus on the actual implementation of reforms across a broad spectrum of reform issues.

The process will be to build a hierarchy of these coalitions, starting at the level of local communities, and linking these to regional and national coalitions as appropriate to each circumstance. A managed reform facility will assume an active role in organizing and coordinating these efforts at and between all levels.

Coalitions of rich and poor can promote specific reforms with the public and with the political systems (at any and all levels) through work on and support of relevant policies, legislation, regulations, executive orders, programs, or other appropriate measures. Sample coalitions may include:

Governance Coalitions: Rich and poor working together to introduce and institutionalize people-centered democratic institutional innovations (as referred to above), and to address disparities between rich and poor through reform of relevant public and tax policies.

Business and Workers' Coalitions: To forge positive working relations of corporations and the working poor on issues of workers rights, job training, mentoring, decent living wages, small business support, and joint ownership and management of enterprises.

Anti-Poverty Coalitions: To focus rich and poor squarely on the dire needs of those below the poverty line, as a national priority.

Women's Coalitions: Rich and poor women coming together to initiate reforms that promote gender equality of opportunity, and the empowerment of women in political and economic spheres.

Youth Coalitions: A regular coming together of disadvantaged and well-educated youth to set common goals and to acquire practical knowledge and skills that enhance income earning.

Church Coalitions: To ecumenically engage churches and religious institutions in which rich and poor can work together based on the proven power of churches to create a sense of community committed to the good of all.

Education & School Coalitions: Partnering of school systems to bring children of rich and poor backgrounds together to inspire their own approaches for helping each other achieve educational and lifelong goals.

Health Care Coalitions: Rich and poor working together to effectively implement affordable, reliable and quality health care for all.

The resulting impact of any and all of the reforms emanating from these coalitions will begin to root new values and practices of a peoples' democracy into and across the entire social fabric.

Piloting and End Goals

Putting people-driven democracy of rich and poor into practice through such coalitions and other collaborative measures is in fact already taking place in limited ways in many countries. While few have done this in the comprehensive manner we are suggesting, there are increasing numbers of pilot initiatives applying key building blocks of grassroots democracy:

363

Organizing for Action: this was initiated following Barack Obama's reelection in 2012 in order to organize and empower community action in support of the legislative and political agenda of the Obama administration. It was established as a non-profit group working through a national umbrella and fifty State organizations. It is engaging community people from all walks of life around issues of immigration, climate change, gun control, education, jobs, and many more. Its eventual effectiveness is still to be seen, but it has already created considerable grassroots activism. The main flaw in the approach, compared to what we have in mind, is that it is heavily affiliated with one political party (Democrats), is driven by the top down agenda of that party, and excludes an open and broad membership from across the local society.

Oregon Public Engagement in Health Care: my home state of Oregon has been a leader in empowering communities to drive health care reform. A *We Can do Better* (formerly *Archimedes)* movement with a small core staff has facilitated the education, coming together and advocacy role of communities to provide local perspectives and assert influence on health legislative reforms. In parallel, Oregon health care systems have been decentralized around fifteen local area-based Coordinated Care Organizations (CCOs) each of which are advised by Community Advisory Councils (CACs) whose members span all social and economic segments of society. This has resulted in considerable out-of-the-mainstream, people-driven innovation and successes in new health care approaches based on local insights and knowledge.

Private Sector and Community Collaboration: Development organizations working across a wide range of countries are turning increasingly to cooperation with both local and international businesses focused on improving opportunities for poor communities while also benefiting business market growth. Examples include an initiative of Coca Cola and the UNDP called "Every Drop Matters" (EDM) which has 62 projects working across countries of the Commonwealth of Independent States, the Arab States, and Asia. It concentrates on how the private sector can support communities develop new ways to protect and replenish local water resources. It provides initial funding to pilot solutions, and works through equal partnerships of community steering committees, private sector and government to take these solutions to a wider scale. Another example is Oxfam's partnership with Unilever in Tanzania and Azerbaijan to pilot the sourcing of dehydrated vegetables from smallholder farmers. These initiatives in effect bring about partnerships of rich and poor facilitated by dedicated organizations managing the reform process in line with our vision.

The above examples, and many others that can be cited, each demonstrate important elements of a potential peoples' democracy, but they all fall considerable short of the ideal we are aiming for.

Our vision and end goal is to go beyond piecemeal reforms to activate an eventual fully functioning peoples' democracy. A democracy that provides a direct voice and an institutional role of rich and poor to bring about reforms aimed at the common good. The power of people to assert their will in shaping their destinies.

Such fundamental reform will not come easily or quickly. It will need to build up over time, from the work of grassroots initiatives, to the work of thematic coalitions, to the effectiveness of the supporting facilities, and to the success of newly introduced institutions evolving out of continuous experimentation and refinement.

It will depend largely on committed leadership and people to get behind the effort at all these levels. It will depend on achieving incrementally solid results that gain increasing credibility for change and reform.

The ideas I have shared in this book are meant to set out a general vision and initial course of action. But it will be the genius of the people who engage in the process that will determine over time how the reforms will be tailored, innovated, implemented, and ultimately successful in founding and running a peoples' democracy.

Global Contexts of Implementation

The space for a peoples' democracy is widening in many countries. Whether in full fledged democracies, or in those on the threshold of democracy, or even those still under authoritarian rule, change is possible. Change carefully managed on the basis of crossing over between powerful and powerless is increasingly possible in many cases. In varying situations, if done with sufficient political acumen, step by step measures are often acceptable and effective in bringing fundamental change.

What I think I have learned is that pragmatism must be the guiding principle. There is need to tailor the approach of people-driven reform to what is possible in each case and in each time period. The path to reform is built as much on incremental as on revolutionary change.

In the Western world, the scope for reform appears much wider and usually is, though achievement of reform is often surprisingly as difficult as in less democratic settings. Nevertheless the openness of these societies enables broad experimentation of the kind foreseen. It is in these contexts that a robust reform process (of whatever kind) will usually be countenanced (while also resisted), and often encouraged and supported. In these countries, such as the US, those in Europe, and Australia, there is an enormous (indeed historic) opportunity to pro-actively test peoples' democratic reforms across a wide landscape.

In the case of less democratic settings, again pragmatism is the key. There is no reason to rule out a dedicated approach of the kind envisaged for so-called advanced democracies. We have already seen in our journey many examples in unexpected places—Liberia, Malawi, Yemen, Kosovo, Nepal, Bangladesh—of an eventual interaction between the powerless and the powerful, leading to initial changes on which further change can build.

Granted there are many countries in which incremental change is a hard case to make. One thinks for example of a few intransigent countries across north Asia, the Middle East, and several despotisms across Africa and other regions. On the other hand, many countries that not long ago seemed equally intransigent have realized remarkable change, China and Myanmar being prime examples. Of course much of this change was controlled by those in power. Nevertheless, an increasingly enhanced voice of the people played a significant role.

All of this is to say that the potential for a peoples' democracy is feasible in many unexpected settings, to varying degrees and as a foundation for more ambitious efforts later. If pursued in each case through careful trust building, crossing over, and non-confrontational management of reform, much may be achieved that over time transforms society into a peoples' democracy working for the good of all.

Decency at the Core

For all of the enthusiasm we may have to see a partnership of rich and poor joining together for people-driven democratic reform, whether in democratic or non-democratic settings, we must continually remind ourselves that it will make little difference unless it is founded and maintained on the values of decency. A united commitment of rich and poor to those values is the most promising way to embed them into a people-driven democracy. Protecting and honoring these values, to make sure they never slip away, is their unending task and their historic opportunity.

Epilogue

A Way Of Life

As I reflect back over the twelve years I have taken to write this book, I am amazed at what I have learned from my journey and astonished at the simplicity of it all.

What I have learned is that what is most important in life and to our human relations is really very basic. It comes down to treating each other decently. Everything else springs from that.

We have chosen throughout our human history to ignore this simple truth. We have opted to complicate our lives and our relations. We have done this out of greed and arrogance, and our never ending and never fulfilling quest to secure our selfishness.

Our cultural, social, economic, political and moral values and systems have evolved out of these attitudes. As a result, they became fixated and obsessed with gratifying the false needs of those powerful enough to acquire them at the expense and the harm of others.

We lost sight of who we are at our core, individually and across all our societies. We failed ourselves in recognizing how we can achieve our greatest human fulfillment through our value for each other.

The potential is still there: an enormous promise that we can activate a new power of rich and poor to return to our core and to work for the good of all. We can transform our way of life. We can create and live in a better world.

CPSIA information can be obtained at www.ICGtesting.com
Printed in the USA
BVOW03s1111040514

352515BV00004B/9/P